Lumbee Indians in the Jim Crow South

FIRST PEOPLES
New Directions in Indigenous Studies

Lumbee Indians in the Jim Crow South

RACE, IDENTITY, AND THE MAKING OF A NATION

Malinda Maynor Lowery

University of North Carolina Press   Chapel Hill

PUBLICATION OF THIS BOOK WAS MADE POSSIBLE, IN PART, BY GENEROUS
GRANTS FROM THE UNIVERSITY RESEARCH COUNCIL AT UNC–CHAPEL HILL,
THE CENTER FOR THE STUDY OF THE AMERICAN SOUTH, AND THE ANDREW W.
MELLON FOUNDATION.

Designed by Courtney Leigh Baker and set in Whitman with Trixie display by Rebecca Evans.
Manufactured in the United States of America. The paper in this book meets the guidelines for
permanence and durability of the Committee on Production Guidelines for Book Longevity of
the Council on Library Resources. The University of North Carolina Press has been a member
of the Green Press Initiative since 2003.

Library of Congress Cataloging-in-Publication Data
Lowery, Malinda Maynor.
Lumbee Indians in the Jim Crow South: race, identity, and the making of a nation /
Malinda Maynor Lowery.
p. cm. Includes bibliographical references and index.
ISBN 978-0-8078-3368-1 (cloth: alk. paper)—ISBN 978-0-8078-7111-9 (pbk.: alk. paper)
1. Lumbee Indians—North Carolina—Robeson County. 2. Robeson County (N.C.)—Race
relations—History—20th century. 3. Group identity—North Carolina—Robeson County.
[1. Indians of North America—North Carolina—Robeson County.] I. Title.
E99.C91L69 2010
305.897′30756332—dc22   2009039434

cloth   14 13 12 11 10   5 4 3 2 1
paper   14 13 12 11 10   5 4 3 2 1

To Lydia Louise

Contents

Figures, Tables, Maps, and Genealogy Charts

Telling Our Own Stories

This story unfolds in low-lying swamps of lazy, rippling black water. The swamps have names like Deep Branch, Burnt Swamp, and Turkey Branch. Fingers of water from the swamps drain into a river, which is known as Drowning Creek, the Lumber River, or, simply, the Lumbee. The river follows its own path to the ocean, flowing through lands now known as North Carolina and South Carolina; these waters have nurtured a People in a place that became known as the South and the United States—names that came later, after the identity that marked the People as Indians.

Today they are known as Lumbee Indians, and some are known as Tuscarora,[1] though in the past 130 years, the People have also been called Croatan, Cherokee, and Siouan. Each name, past and present, was the result of strategic choices about how to represent Indian identity and gain affirmation of it. But all belong to land around the Lumber River and the town of Pembroke in Robeson County, North Carolina. How those identities took shape over time and in this place is the subject of this book.

Questions of identity influence the documentary record on which historians base their work. However, historians have not always queried their sources for who the Indians were, instead taking it for granted that the past observer understood the dimensions of belonging and culture that marked someone as an Indian. The observers on which historians faithfully rely rarely asked themselves who the Indians were, or more pointedly, *what* was "Indian."[2] What does this term "Indian" mean to us as historians or to those whose observations we depend upon for source material?

Much of the historical literature on Indian ethnicity has implicitly defined an Indian as an individual who is racially different from American immigrant groups; who has a historical, continuous attachment to a particular place; and who belongs to a community that shares a common political organization and set of rituals different from their neighbors. In fact, geographic movement (rather than attachment to one specific place) and expansive attitudes about adoption and cultural exchange (resulting in racial mixing and cultural adaptation) more accurately describe Indian groups historically. Yet their identities as Indians do not dissipate as a result of these changes. Indian identity, then—indeed, all identity—is a historical process, not a fixed constant from which we measure change. Identity can include seemingly organic features of an Indian tribe, but those markers change over time as well, both for those inside the community and for those outsiders who interpret Indian identity.[3] Identity is therefore a conversation between insiders and outsiders; these categories themselves are not fixed, and the labels represent heterogeneous populations. Hence, the conversation is not always polite and rarely achieves consensus. Indian—and American—identity often involves conflicts, threats, selfishness, and silences as much as trust, loyalty, sacrifice, and freedom.

This book tells the story of how the Indians of Robeson County, North Carolina, have crafted an identity as a People, a race, a tribe, and a nation. They have done so not only as Indians but also as southerners and Americans. And they have done so against the backdrop of some of the central issues in American history: race, class, politics, and citizenship. Indeed, this story is set in rural North Carolina during the height of segregation, and its characters inhabit a broad spectrum of ethnicities and classes. Segregation and white supremacy might have homogenized those varied ethnic and social experiences by simply relegating anyone who refused to assimilate to a "colored" status. But in Indian history, we find that such homogenization did not occur. People living in tremendous tension with American identity took that tension and used it to carve out their own sense of nationhood. The Lumbee, in particular, did this by adopting (and adapting to) racial segregation and creating political and social institutions that protected their distinct identity.

My own relationship to this story explains some of the tensions behind identity formation. I am a Lumbee, a southerner, and an American. My husband, who is also Lumbee, and I attended a wedding in Pembroke in October 2007. Most of the guests were related to one another. Before the ceremony, an older gentleman, a preacher, approached me.

"Who's your people?" he asked, sitting down.

Some of my husband's relatives were at this man's table and they had pointed me out to him. I get pointed out a lot in Pembroke. It might be because of my mixed-up accent (part southern, part nowhere); when people hear me talk, they can't figure out where I'm from. This man knew something about me by who I "favored" (meaning who I looked like, in the Lumbee patois) and to whom I was married. But it still was taking some effort for him to place me.

Lumbees refer to themselves collectively as "our People," a term I grew up taking for granted. I knew first and foremost that I was part of a People; that I had family and that my family connected to other families; and that all of these families lived in a place, what for us was a sacred homeland: the land along the Lumber River in Robeson County. Even though my parents raised me about two hours away in Durham (making me a "diasporic Lumbee," an "urban Indian," or even a "Durham rat," according to my cousins), Robeson County—and especially Pembroke—was our "Home-Home," the place where our People lived and were buried.

"You're not from here, are you?" the preacher asked.

"Yes, I'm from here!" But then I started over. "I mean, my family's from here—my mother is Foy and Bloss Cummings's daughter and my father is Wayne and Lucy Maynor's son."

The man nodded, smiling in polite recognition, but his eyes squinted slightly, telling me he thought he knew me but wasn't sure.

"You know preacher Mike Cummings?" I continued.

"Yes," he said.

"That's my uncle, my mom's brother."

"Oh, yes . . . Foy and Bloss." He turned in his chair to face me, and his eyes brightened in recognition. "Well, your grandmother . . ."

And so began another story telling me who I was and where I had come from, a story that transformed me from an outsider to an insider. This conversation was not only about identity; it also shaped identity when it reminded me of my dual status. Indeed, none of the perspectives on identity formation are homogenous; even the insiders don't all hold the same view. Yet some themes and patterns emerge, particularly when we include conversations like this one in the story. This conversation showed how kinship and place are the foundational layer of Indian identity in Robeson County.

But the documentary record on which this book is based commented most frequently on Indian divisions, not Indian cohesiveness. I hope to explain how those divisions can coexist with a relatively coherent, though not unchanging, set of identity criteria. Those criteria had kinship and place at their foundation, but layers accumulated as the internal and external conversations changed. Robeson County Indians adopted four different names between 1885 and 1956, not because they didn't know who they were or what constituted their identity but because federal and state officials kept changing their criteria for authenticity. New names, and internal tribal debates about the legitimacy of those names, fostered political factions and class distinctions. The four names were "Croatan," "Cherokee," "Siouan," and "Lumbee." Each was recognized by the U.S. Congress, the Office of Indian Affairs, and/or the state of North Carolina. Two of the names, Cherokee and Siouan, became labels for different political factions in the 1930s. A fifth name, "Tuscarora," formally emerged in the 1960s and applies to a smaller proportion of the overall group who claim that tribal affiliation as their dominant ancestry; it has yet to be acknowledged by the outside establishment. Today, the largest group of Robeson County Indians call themselves Lumbee, while a smaller group claim Tuscarora.

This story demonstrates a link between factionalism and identity. It acknowledges the destruction to a People's aspirations that factionalism engenders, yet it also considers factionalism's strategic utility in the formation of identity. Many historians and anthropologists have described factionalism as a driving force in Native societies, though they have differed in their views of its origins. Some scholars attribute it to external events, such as the intrusion of the market or white settlement, or to what they perceive as innate biological differences between "full-blood" and "mixed-blood" Indians. These writers tend to view factionalism as destructive to Indians' sense of community and a reason for that community's failure to effectively combat white intrusion and absorption. Those that view it as a product of Indians' agency, rather than their victimization, have more commonly attributed it to internal dynamics that sometimes predate European contact and always reflect Indians' own political, economic, or social agendas. These writers have seen factionalism as an important part of Indian persistence.[4]

Anthropologists Gerald Sider and Karen Blu discuss these issues, among others, in their studies of the Lumbee and Tuscarora. They use the Lumbee as a case study in theories of identity formation and definitions of culture, two central concerns of anthropology. Their contributions to this book are found throughout the text, although I am less concerned with demonstrating that the Lumbee are Indians and more concerned with excavating the category of "Indian" itself and how that category shifts, both over time and within moments and conversations. Blu and Sider also began their fieldwork from the assumption that the South is unique in its fixation on race and its manifestation of white supremacy; I hope that this work demonstrates that such obsessions resonated throughout Indian policy as well.[5]

In particular, this book focuses on watershed policies known collectively as the Indian New Deal. I examine that era's role in shaping self-determination, governance, and the ideas about race and identity with which we wrestle today. Robeson County Indians demonstrated that factionalism in the 1930s predated the Indian New Deal and was, in fact, an important component of Indians' social and political organization. Indian victimization did not produce all political disagreements; many were the product of Indian agency. To conclude that victimization motivates disagreements implicitly denies that Indian people can legitimately disagree and asserts that "Indians [are] passive objects responding to white stimuli rather than . . . individuals coping creatively in a variety of ways with the different situations in which they found themselves," in the words of historian Robert Berkhofer. Rather than permanently rupture their social fabric, the political disagreements among Robeson County Indians demonstrated a creative response to the disempowerment they faced under segregation and contributed to new markers of identity.[6]

I argue that factionalism for Robeson County Indians was, first and foremost, strategic. Names and factions emerged as responses to specific sets of political circumstances put forth by Congress and the Office of Indian Affairs (OIA), today known as the Bureau of Indian Affairs. Congress and the OIA disagreed about what constituted Indian identity; Congress tended to rely overtly on racial definitions, while the OIA used the concept of "tribal" culture to stand in for race. I view race as a layer of identity that springs from inherited characteristics but is primarily used to rank and divide the human population into groups. This purpose of race gives it a situational nature, like all categories of identity, and the book demonstrates that race is not merely ascribed by dominant groups but also claimed for strategic purposes. Yet, its influence changes in the course of the identity conversation between insiders and outsiders, and it rarely existed as the only layer of identity that Robeson County Indians articulated.

Factions adopted these racial or tribal criteria and added new layers of identity to a foundation of kinship and place. Despite these contradictory messages from the federal government, Indians in Robeson County maintained a coherent identity as a People connected by family and place. I do not mean that their existence was always cohesive, however—politics, especially, divided rather than united them. The layering of Indian identity markers allowed for disagreement within the group while they preserved their common identity and their distinctiveness from their black and white neighbors.

This overlap between "race" and "tribe" introduces the very firm connections—so evident in the Lumbee experience but missed by much scholarship in Indian history—between the modernist impulse of white supremacy and the implementation of Indian policy, most particularly the Indian New Deal of the 1930s and the termination policy of the 1950s. For Indians, embracing segregation, the Indian New Deal, and termination was like embracing a boa constrictor: the snake squeezed back. At the very moment the civil rights movement might have slain this enemy, federal, state, and local interests instead combined to strengthen white supremacy and the boa's grasp. The Lumbee struggled to adapt and affirm their distinct identity as Indians. This struggle was not for identity itself; Lumbees have had few existential crises about who they were. Rather, they struggled for sovereignty, for a right to function autonomously, determine their own ways of knowing and being, and live free of constraints on opportunity. Political factionalism emerged as a strategy to uphold autonomy against white supremacy.

The written record cannot tell the whole story of Lumbee identity and factionalism. Oral histories, photographs, and my own recollections and family narratives open a door to the motivations of historical actors that we simply cannot know or guess from the documentary record alone. Some of the memories are the result of specific questions I asked family members when I was conducting research. I gathered others through formal oral-history interviews and informal conversations with community members. I have collected some of these stories without reference to this book; they are simply the tales that explain my own place in the world. Selecting these stories was shaped by autoethnography, a method of exploring one's own relationship to research that begins with questioning how culture and society have affected one's experiences. Autoethnography is different from autobiography; these vignettes are not strictly autobiographical because often I am telling someone else's story and not my own. Rather, I have examined my own place in my family and culture and deployed stories, like fables, to teach a lesson or address a historical question.[7] Those fables interrogate the documentary record, allowing a Lumbee way of seeing the world to enter the more conventional narrative of political history.

Why is that Lumbee way of seeing important for academic scholarship? Leaving it out reinforces an old colonial agenda to silence Indian people. Further, the historical evidence makes little sense without a Lumbee perspective.

For example, the experience of Lumbee factionalism would simply look like pointless infighting if I did not try to understand the cultural meanings behind Lumbees' articulation of their identities. Without those ways of knowing, the Lumbee experience—indeed, the Native American experience as a whole—appears fractured and nonsensical, and it bears no relationship to the larger story of the American nation.

Though it is difficult to separate neatly the layers of identity as they have taken shape over time, I have tried to tell the story in a roughly chronological fashion. The introduction explains the coalescence of the Robeson County Indian community in the seventeenth, eighteenth, and nineteenth centuries. A history of displacement, acculturation, and change made it difficult to define "Indian" in a way that pleased those who would later act as arbiters of Indian identity, but this period laid the foundation of kinship and settlement that influenced Indian politics through the late nineteenth and twentieth centuries. Chapters 1 and 2 then describe that boa constrictor of white supremacy and segregation and how it restricted Indians' options socially, economically, and politically. Chapter 1 also introduces the importance of names to Indian identity, a theme that becomes a point of factional dispute between Cherokees and Siouans when Congress and the Office of Indian Affairs begin to enter the lives of Robeson County Indians.

Chapters 3 through 7 delineate how political identity operated during and after the Indian New Deal and how new markers of Indian identity developed. Chapters 3 and 4 discuss the conflict between Congress and the OIA over the criteria used to recognize Indians during the 1930s and the Indian New Deal. For congressmen, recognition was a political favor doled out to Indian constituents, but officials at the OIA believed a petitioning Indian group had to prove its authenticity according to anthropological standards. This conflict between federal-level definitions of Indian identity plagued Robeson County Indians through their recognition as Lumbee in 1956.

Chapters 5 and 6 detail the Siouan faction's efforts to work within the Indian New Deal and federal agencies to achieve recognition. To secure a land base, Siouans brought a Farm Security Administration resettlement project called Pembroke Farms to the county's Indian sharecroppers. To qualify as Indians under the Indian Reorganization Act, the centerpiece of Indian New Deal policy, the Office of Indian Affairs encouraged tribal members to enroll under the act's "half-blood" requirement using anthropometric tests. Neither Pembroke Farms nor anthropometry resulted in federal recognition for the group, due in part to the federal agencies' misunderstandings of Robeson County Indians' society and the agency leaders' unwillingness to confront the racial and economic discrimination of the Jim Crow system that disempowered Indians. In these ways, the New Deal emboldened white supremacy rather than undermined it.

Chapter 7 discusses how Indians seeking affirmation of their identity as Indians also affirmed their identity as Americans. Ironically, perhaps, their Americanness confirmed the kind of disempowerment they had experienced under segregation. After World War II, members of the former Cherokee faction, along with some Siouans, reemerged as the "Lumbee Brotherhood" determined to gain federal recognition by returning to a congressional strategy. A new policy of tribal termination at the federal level made an assimilationist rhetoric most attractive to the Indian leadership, a rhetoric that alienated many Indians, including war veterans and others who chose to deal with segregation differently. Termination policy and the pressures it exerted on recognition divided the group yet again, but Congress finally granted a nominal and ambiguous recognition in 1956. Tuscarora then emerged as an alternate tribal name that represented another approach to affirming identity. The political divisions present in the tribe's only successful attempt at federal recognition ensured that the political realm would remain an easily fractured aspect of Lumbee and Tuscarora identity.

This book concerns four layers of Native American identity: People, race, tribe, and nation. How the first three developed in the Robeson County Indian community are fairly clear from the historical record, but the last remains an open question. "Nation" is a European idea that emerged during the Enlightenment period, but Indians all over the United States have adopted it to better portray their existences as political, not just social or ethnic, entities. So what does this category of nation mean for Indians and, by extension, for Americans? Especially in times of crisis, politics can easily and quickly divide members of a nation who otherwise generally agree on many things. This is true of both Native nations and the American nation: they are politically divided (sometimes bitterly so), but citizens consent to these disagreements and share a sense of their value. On one level, Indians are citizens of an American nation, while on another level they are citizens of their own nation; Robeson County Indians' emphasis on affiliations with families and places gives the group the kind of "deep, horizontal comradeship" that Benedict Anderson discusses as an aspect of nationhood.[8]

Yet conflict is an inherent part of nation building, and the nationhood status of Robeson County Indians bears comparison to that of the United States. In the United States, disagreement is a fundamental part of the political process, but since the Civil War it has not actually torn the nation apart. Likewise, members of the nation of Robeson County Indians, whether Lumbees or Tuscaroras, Cherokees or Siouans, consented to these disagreements and maintained a fundamental sense of themselves as a People. Factionalism does not destroy that comradeship, and it may assist nation building by incubating creative solutions and reminding citizens about what they share. Citizens recognize that political division moves the nation forward, even though it may not often result in social harmony. At the heart of the political differences and identity distinctions are certain overarching attachments. Indian citizens may have been alienated from the American state, but they have been, and will continue to be, Americans—residing on the land and connected in every way to the fortunes of the nation. Lumbees and Tuscaroras, Cherokees and Siouans, though alienated from one another, shared a love for their People and their land.

Acknowledgments

My attempt to thank the people who have helped me with this book will undoubtedly be inadequate. But I will try, and I beg the forgiveness of those I have neglected. I've often wished I could write poetry; if I could, this book would be an ode to my ancestors, who dreamed much for their descendants. I hope I have not disappointed them. To my grandparents, Wayne and Lucy Maynor and Foy and Bloss Cummings; they were great readers, storytellers, bakers, teachers, farmers, and hard-working pilgrims. To my parents, Waltz and Louise Maynor, whose help, encouragement, sacrifice, and persistence I owe an unpayable debt. Thank you. I only hope to pay the debt forward.

Generous funding for the project dates back to 2003 and includes the Royster Society of Fellows at UNC–Chapel Hill, the Ford Foundation Dissertation Fellowship, funds from Harvard University's Faculty of Arts and Sciences, the Harvard University Native American Program, and the Post-Doctoral Fellowship in Southern Studies at the Center for the Study of the American South at UNC–Chapel Hill.

Over the years, I have relied on many colleagues for input, and this book is the result of discussions in various forums. I have presented the arguments from this book in lectures at Brandeis University, the University of Massachusetts–Boston, the Center for Documentary Studies at Duke University, the Environmental Protection Agency in the Research Triangle Park, the University of Georgia, and UNC–Chapel Hill. Many ideas were refined through exchanges at conferences, including the Society for Ethnohistory Annual Meeting (2005), the Japan Society for the Promotion of Science symposium, "Genocide and the World Today" at the University of Tokyo (2006), the Western History Association Annual Meeting (2007), the Southern Historical Association Annual Meeting (2007), the Native American and Indigenous Studies Association Annual Meeting (2008), and the American Historical Association Annual Meeting (2009). Thank you to colleagues who participated with me in these forums and made the events possible: James F. Brooks, David A. Y. O. Chang, Jessica Cattelino, Phil Deloria, Michelle Dubow, Laura Edwards, Donald Fixico, Joseph Flora, Jun Furuya, Susan Hill, Jacquelyn Jones, Jane Kamensky, Barbara Krauthamer, Melissa Meyer, Mary Jane McCallum, Tiya Miles, Amy Den Ouden, Tom Rankin, Nancy Schoonmaker, Circe Sturm, Charlie Thompson, and Jace and Laura Weaver. Portions of this book have been published in *American Indian Quarterly* and *Native South*, and I am grateful to James Taylor Carson and Amanda Cobb for those opportunities. Passages from those articles ("Telling Our Own Stories: Lumbee History and the Federal Acknowledgement Process," *American Indian Quarterly* 33, no. 4 [Fall 2009]; and "Indians, Southerners, and Americans: Race, Tribe, and Nation during Jim Crow," *Native South* 2 [2009]) are reprinted here courtesy of the University of Nebraska Press. Thanks also to editor Ulrike Wiethaus and Peter Lang Publishing for permission to reprint a portion of the article "Practicing Sovereignty: Lumbee Identity, Tribal Factionalism, and Federal Recognition, 1932–1934," which appeared in *Foundations of First Peoples' Sovereignty: History, Culture and Education* (New York: Peter Lang, 2008), 57–95.

Mark Simpson-Vos at UNC Press envisioned and crafted this book along with me, and I appreciate his faith in me, as well as that of the staff and board of UNC Press. Special thanks also to Tema Larter, Jay Mazzocchi, and the folks in marketing. Three readers—Melissa Meyer, Tiya Miles, and Alexandra Harmon—were generous, wise, patient, and exacting in their reviews of the manuscript. Thank you for making it much better.

I could not have asked for better friends and colleagues at Harvard University, several of whom read the manuscript and all of whom provided encouragement or support at critical times: Vincent Brown, Patricia Capone, Joyce E. Chaplin, Lizabeth Cohen, Bill Fash, Janet Hatch, Walter Johnson, Jill Lepore, Mary Lewis, Diana Loren, Kay Kaufman Shelemay, Werner Sollors, Hue-Tam Tai, Laurel Ulrich, and John Womack. Rachel St. John and Alison Frank, cofounders of the "have your cake and eat it too" writing group, deserve great thanks for provocative and detailed readings that pushed my analysis much further than I would have taken it on my own. My Native colleagues at Harvard, most especially Lisa Brooks and Carmen Lopez, gave me an intellectual home that is irreplaceable in my heart. Thanks to the students who helped on this project—Jessica Righthand, Emily Pierce, Kelsey Leonard—and to all of my students. You have taught me much more than I have taught you.

Theda Perdue and Michael Green saw the potential of this book and would not leave me to my own devices, and for this and many, many other favors, I am deeply grateful. Other readers, mentors, and friends—especially Harry Watson, W. Fitzhugh Brundage, and Jacquelyn Hall, but also Bill Andrews, Danny Bell, Brandi Brooks, Sandra Hoeflich, John and Joy Kasson, Clara Sue Kidwell, Townsend Ludington, Beth Millwood, and Joe Mosnier—all inspired me in different ways. I have colleagues in the field of Native American, southern, and U.S. history, folklore, and anthropology whose contributions are seen throughout the book. They answered my slow-witted questions and freely contributed their own hard-earned insight: Anna Bailey, Lee Baker, Karen I. Blu, Margaret Bruchac, Jack Campisi, Jefferson Currie, Virginia De-Marce, Jean Dennison, William McKee Evans, Bill and Marcie Ferris, Angela Gonzales, Barbara Hahn, Ann Kakaliouras, Judy Kertesz, Stanley Knick, Cary Miller, Megan McDonald, Christopher Arris Oakley, Blair Rudes, Gerald Sider, Tim Tyson, Rachel Watkins, Ulrike Wiethaus, David Wilkins, Walt Wolfram, Peter H. Wood, and Cedric Woods.

Special thanks to Ryan K. Anderson, Randi Byrd, Susan Gardner, Rayna Green, Josephine Humphreys, Chris McKenna, Jean O'Brien, Katherine M. B. Osburn, Linda E. Oxendine, Claudio Saunt, Rebecca Seib, Paul Spru-han, Daniel Usner, and the redoubtable Rose Stremlau for going beyond the call of duty.

I lived in Pembroke while writing the first drafts of these chapters and revising much of them. There, I could always gain insight and inspiration from Bruce Barton, Cynthia Brooks, Sherman Brooks, Ed Chavis, Tina Dial Cummings, Mark Deese, Maureen Dial, Willie A. Dial, Arlinda Locklear, Carnell Locklear, Dave Locklear, Elisha Locklear, Garth Locklear, Susan Lowry, Carol Smith Oxendine, Maggie Oxendine, and Blake Tyner. They selflessly spent many hours teaching me what I wouldn't find in the documents. Pura Fé, Billy Tayac, and Gabrielle Tayac also shared their families' stories. Derek Lowry and Robert Locklear started me on this path. Thanks also to Darlene Jacobs, Cynthia Hunt Locklear, Ruth B. Locklear, and Wes Taukchiray.

I would have run into many dead ends were it not for the expertise of archivists and librarians, in particular Jerry Clark, Joe Schwarz, and Selina Davis from the National Archives; Lillian Brewington and Carlene Cummings from UNC-Pembroke's Livermore Library; Janet Graham from the

Robeson County Public Library; Mike Van Fossen and Antoinette Satterfield from UNC–Chapel Hill's Davis Library; Jeannie Sklar from the National Anthropological Archives; and Alison Scott from Harvard University Library. I want to express my tremendous appreciation for the work and personal commitment of Glenn Ellen Starr Stilling at Appalachian State University, whose bibliographies of the Lumbee are works of art and treasures for researchers.

My immediate family and dear friends let me stay with them, fed me, hugged me, and told me it would be okay and that they were proud of me. Thank you especially to Ivy Gordon, Cynthia Hill, Gail Huddleson, and Anna Smith. I want to thank the Lowery and Tyler families, the descendants of Buddy and Margie Lowery, especially Miranda, Dustin, Clint, and Corey Lowery; Alice Tyler; and Laura Bradley. To my siblings, their spouses, and their children: Cherry, Zeb, Mary Joyce, Cindy, Lisa, Matt, Andy, Kevin, Connie, Eli, Keagan, Josie, Cara, Elizabeth, Dane, Kris, Kaelyn, James, Ian, Ben, Heather, Jake, and Chris. I know I can call on each of you when I need help. My aunts and uncles, especially Jeff and Sue Maynor and Mike and Quae Cummings, have not only provided me with lots of information and introductions but also have told me they loved me when I needed to hear it the most. My daughter Lydia is my inspiration. My deepest, wordless gratitude goes to my husband, Willie French Lowery. He is on every page.

A Note on Terms

At the beginning of every semester, a student will ask me, "Should we use the word 'Indian' or 'Native American'? Which is correct?" I always look forward to the question, as it signals a unique opportunity to talk about how words are constantly shifting symbols of larger categories of knowledge. The query is understandable; these particular words are insufficient and confusing, historically speaking; their meanings and use depend on context and varied cultural perspectives. I tell the class that one way to sort it out is to use the word that people use to describe themselves, but to be aware of the context or audience to which one is speaking. I use "Indian" and "Native American" interchangeably because I grew up calling myself an Indian, and I have since come to see how the term "Native American" also acknowledges a group's status as the original inhabitants of a place. In the United States, most Indians I know use the term "Indian" freely when talking to one another. The same people will use Native American or "Indigenous" when speaking to a multitribal, multiethnic, or international audience or when speaking about tribes and Native nations generally. I have followed those same conventions in this book.

I have also used the word "People" when discussing Indians. To me, People is a general identity label, but one used more often by Indians to talk about members of their own group. Using People acknowledges that Indians have a history and sense of self that goes back to before the colonial relationships that labeled us Indian, Native American, or Indigenous. But that does not mean that the meanings behind People are immune to change; indeed, I have sought to demonstrate in this book that a group can change considerably—and experience intense internal conflict—but still not lose its sense of itself as a group.

Though it may surprise some scholars, as I worked on this book, I also encountered no small amount of questioning from Lumbees and Tuscaroras regarding my use of the term "Jim Crow." Indians who had grown up at the height of southern segregation and were deeply entwined in that system would ask, "Who's Jim Crow?" "Precisely!" I thought. "Why does that term get applied so freely?" Jim Crow originated with white Americans as a fictional character popularized in the 1820s by a white comedian who wore blackface in his song-and-dance routines. Through generations of blackface performers' cruel mockery, Jim Crow became a pejorative term for African Americans and a symbol of their inferiority under white supremacy. In the twentieth century, Jim Crow referred specifically to the laws passed by southern states to segregate the races. On the surface, the term has little to do with Native Americans, but Indians in the South were scarred by the abiding division between black and white that Jim Crow represented. I have chosen to use it to remind us that even though this is a story about Indians, it is also a story about every southerner and every American.

Lumbee Indians in the Jim Crow South

INTRODUCTION   Coming Together

In June 1936 Carl Seltzer, E. S. McMahon, and D'Arcy McNickle were sent by the Office of Indian Affairs (OIA) to Robeson County. They were well-educated and accomplished men: Seltzer was an anthropologist from Harvard, McMahon was an attorney from Washington, D.C., and McNickle was a novelist who had attended Cambridge University. Only McNickle, who was then serving as the administrative assistant to OIA commissioner John Collier, had visited the county before. He had come earlier that spring on what was probably one of his first assignments for Collier. McNickle was of Metis (Cree) and Irish descent, and he had been raised on the Salish-Kootenai reservation in Montana.[1] Unlike most of the OIA staff, he was deeply familiar with the contours of contemporary Indian life.

As they got closer to the town of Pembroke, a gateway to the Robeson County Indian community, they likely saw a settlement that looked on the outside like any other small southern town. Corn and tobacco grew in the fields. Farm families also planted cotton, their only other source of income. The town hosted a small assortment of businesses, dominated by Pate's Supply, the local dry-goods merchant. Other prominent features included Old Main (the historic edifice of the Cherokee Indian Normal School) and churches—Methodist, Baptist, Free Will Baptist, and others. School, church, and the credit lender—the pillars of any farm town in the 1930s.

But on the inside, Pembroke was quite different from other southern places. The town lacked some of the obvious signs of racial segregation. No "white only" or "colored only" placards hung in cafés, and Indians regularly refused to sit with blacks in the balcony of the segregated movie theater, whose white owners also ran Pate's Supply.[2] Pembroke was the only town in Robeson County that was dominated by Indian-run businesses, churches, and schools. Here, Indians could afford to resist the arbitrary divisions embodied in those placards. This soft edge to Jim Crow became a sharp blade, however, when Indians asked for increased funding from the all-white county school board or for fair credit terms from corporate landlords.

Perhaps the most punishing aspect of segregation for Indians was completely invisible. White supremacy subjected Indians to two kinds of prejudice. On the one hand, they were nonwhite and vulnerable to formal and informal discrimination and humiliation. Jim Crow linked equality and civic inclusion to whiteness, and Indians possessed a "double consciousness" that also frustrated African Americans' attempts to overcome white supremacy.[3] But white supremacy wasn't just a local phenomenon. This visit from the OIA brought a new standard for inclusion and a new group to join. If Robeson County Indians met the OIA's criteria for primitivity and purity, Indians believed they could become a federally recognized tribe and mitigate the damage of local racism. Acknowledgment would mean more funding for the Normal School, opportunities to attend postsecondary schools outside North Carolina, and perhaps even land of their own, where their kin wouldn't be beholden to a landlord. They quickly learned, however, that the OIA's work promoted white authority as much as Jim Crow did.

Joseph Brooks and Jim Chavis were the first Indians to meet the OIA delegation. They were spokesman and secretary, respectively, for the General Council of Siouan Indians, a representative government organized to obtain recognition from the United States. Both Brooks and Chavis watched their crops that day; Chavis, who also taught school, was probably enjoying his first few days of summer break, when he could focus his energy on the plot of land he owned and farmed. Brooks and Chavis were also well-educated men; that is, both had about as much education as an Indian could get in 1930s North Carolina. For Brooks, this meant graduation from high school, while for Chavis it meant an additional two years studying to be a teacher at the Normal School.

Chavis and Brooks—along with their siblings, in-laws, cousins, and neighbors—had spent three years working to pass a bill in Congress to recognize all the Indians in Robeson and adjoining counties as "Siouan Indians of Robeson County" rather than as "Cherokee Indians of Robeson County," the name approved by the state of North Carolina in 1911. Siouan, they believed, more accurately described the People's ancestry, and Commissioner Collier had convinced them that the right name could open the door to federal acknowledgment of their identity as Indians. Acknowledgment had eluded them in previous decades due in part to federal and state officials' confusion over their tribal name. But a name wasn't the only factor involved in recognition. Their ancestry, or "blood," was important too, and so they had agreed to a visit from an OIA delegation that would conduct scientific tests to determine how much Indian blood their People had. McNickle, Seltzer, and McMahon were there to examine various physical features of local Indians, such as the color of their skin, eyes, and hair and the shape of their noses, lips, and cheekbones.

The written record does not tell us where this June 1936 meeting took place, though I imagine it was at Saint Annah Church, a Free Will Baptist church on Prospect Road just outside of Pembroke. It would have been easy for a visitor to spot, and Joe Brooks also attended church there. The church, and the community surrounding it that went by the same name, was an important location for the Siouan Council, which held their meetings there. But the OIA delegation almost surely missed the cultural significance of place for the Indians. Instead, they immediately set about explaining to Brooks and Chavis how their study of Indian blood (what scientists called "anthropometry," or the study of the proportions of the human body) would work. But no one, neither the insiders (Brooks and Chavis) nor the outsiders (McNickle, Seltzer, and McMahon) would have anticipated that this study would fail and actually come to undermine the Indians' goal of affirming their identity and alleviating the burdens of segregation.

McNickle might have suspected it would go wrong, for right away the Siouans did not meet the OIA delegation's expectations. "Our task was made difficult at the outset," the men recalled, "by the fact that these people did not have a clear understanding of the term Indian."[4]

A bizarre statement: Indians who had no idea what the term "Indian" meant? But to the OIA, "Indians" were people who had at least one "full-blood" Indian parent and who exhibited features that conformed to a physical stereotype. Some of the features on their list were obvious: reddish-brown skin, straight hair, and brown eyes. Only a physical anthropologist could discern the others, which included tooth shape, skull size, and height. Phenotype, the delegation believed, revealed one's degree of "Indian blood"; sufficient amounts of "Indian blood" assured the OIA that an individual had enough "Indian culture" to be considered "Indian" and thus deserving of recognition. This standard depended on genetic and cultural characteristics that developed in isolation and remained static over time.

Indians in Robeson County had lived as Indians in that place for hundreds of years, but they were hardly isolated, and aspects of their culture and community had evolved and changed over time. The Lumbee and Tuscarora populations are the offspring of nearly 300 years of migration and cultural exchange between the varied Indigenous communities that inhabited Virginia, North Carolina, and South Carolina. These modern-day tribes trace their pre-Columbian ancestry to Eastern Woodlands peoples—farmers, hunters, and fishermen whose lives revolved around their extended families and their small, politically autonomous, villages. Archaeologists and anthropologists have grouped the Indigenous people of this region into three language families: Siouan, Iroquoian, and Algonkian. Members of all three language groups resided and traded within the coastal and piedmont regions. Autonomous villages made economic, political, or military alliances with one another based on mutual interest, adoption, and kinship. Leadership in these small communities, which ranged between fifty and perhaps several thousand residents, adapted to specific situations. These communities were not "tribes" in the way we think of them today; members did not declare allegiance to governments that exercised control over a specific, bounded territory.[5]

Instead, kinship ties governed Indigenous people and influenced Indians' identification with their group. Both before and after European contact, an individual belonged to a People because he or she was born into or adopted by a clan that had specific roles within the larger society. Indeed, during the seventeenth and eighteenth centuries, few people—even Europeans—would have assumed that identity was exclusively linked to racial ancestry. Race had little to do with Indian identity until the Removal era of the nineteenth century, when European Americans began to declare Indians racially inferior in order to justify the United States' expansion.[6] Throughout the colonial period, Indian communities commonly incorporated members of other races and ethnic groups through marriage or captivity rituals.[7] The area's cultural and linguistic diversity and the nature of Indian political and social organization thus make it difficult for historians to define *one* particular group from which the present-day Lumbee and Tuscarora descend.[8]

Constant migration due to disease and war contributed to this diversity. Between 1550 and 1750, the destructive impact of smallpox and warfare reduced many Native villages to just a few inhabitants in the Carolinas. Likewise, these events damaged knowledge of Native languages, religious traditions, and other markers of Indianness that would be obvious to Americans today. Survivors became refugees, moving to find others like themselves and escape the dangers of European contact and war waged by other Indigenous groups. In this context, they must have minimized the value of a name for their emerging communities, a point that only became important as colonizing entities such as the U.S. government and the state of North Carolina confronted their "Indian problem." Like the Catawbas, Creeks, Choctaws, Seminoles, and other Indian groups in the East, Robeson County's Indians are a "nation of nations" for whom a formal name ultimately became necessary primarily for negotiating with colonial, state, and federal authorities.[9]

The oral tradition of Robeson County Indians reflects these migrations of Indian peoples and reveals how they formed a coherent group upon their arrival in what is now Robeson County. Oral tradition consistently points to their origins in three regions: the Roanoke River in northeastern North Carolina and southern Virginia, the Pamlico Sound and Outer Banks of North Carolina, and the piedmont region south and west of present-day Robeson County. In the sixteenth and seventeenth centuries, Indian groups in these areas included the Cheraw, Waccamaw, and Peedee (Siouan speakers) in upper South Carolina; the Tuscarora (Iroquoian speakers) and Saponi (Siouan speakers) in piedmont and eastern North Carolina; the Hatteras (Algonkian speakers) on the North Carolina coast; and small Indigenous communities such as the Yeopim, Potoskite, Nansemond, and Weanoke in the Roanoke River region along the North Carolina–Virginia border.[10] Cheraw and Seneca groups traveled through the swampy, remote area around Drowning Creek in Robeson County, but a Waccamaw community resided there as well, and Cheraw settlers joined them later (Map 1).[11]

While Siouan-speaking Indians lived in and traveled through the present-day home of Robeson County Indians prior to the eighteenth century, oral tradition also speaks of the migration of Indians from the Roanoke area. In the first half of the eighteenth century, a group of families, composed of both Indians and non-Indians, coalesced in areas near Saponi and Tuscarora settlements. These families are the ancestors of the majority of today's Lumbee and Tuscarora tribal members.[12] Genealogical research has revealed that they were most likely refugees from Yeopim, Potoskite, Nansemond, Saponi, and Tuscarora groups who lost land in the wake of the Tuscarora War of 1711–15. Many of the refugees migrated to the Drowning Creek area between the 1730s and the 1780s and joined the Cheraw and Hatteras peoples who also had made their way there. Anthropologist Karen Blu believed that English may have been a convenient *lingua franca* for refugees from different Indian communities, explaining the lack of an aboriginal language among Robeson County Indians.[13]

The Indians who migrated to Drowning Creek shaped their identity not

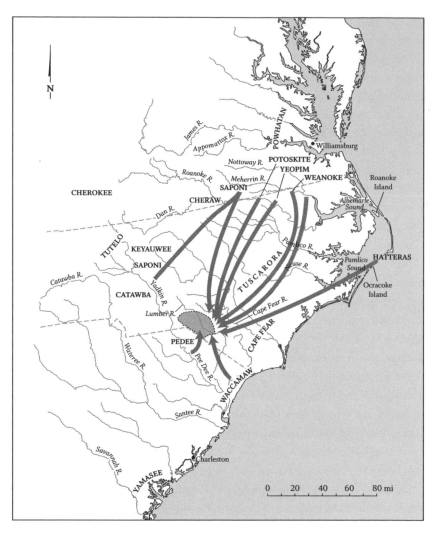

MAP 1. Carolina and Virginia, 1700–1730, Showing Migration of Indian Groups
to Drowning Creek (Lumber River)

around a tribal name but around kinship. Families from Roanoke had likely
formed social and kin alliances prior to moving to Robeson County, creating
the kin networks that would later become a "tribe" of Robeson County Indians. Many of these families probably reckoned kinship through their mothers as their ancestors had done, meaning that a child of an Indian woman
would be a member of her mother's clan or family; the ancestry or clan affiliation of her father did not matter to the child's ethnic identity.[14] Retaining
a matrilineal kinship system allowed an Indian community to persist, even

in a multicultural, multiethnic group like the one that coalesced in Roanoke and then in Robeson County. Even as ways of reckoning kinship changed to bilateral—with children recognizing the families of both their mother and father as "blood" relatives—the centrality of kinship to identity remained. Migrations into the Robeson County Indian community continued into the nineteenth century, as Indians from other parts of North Carolina and South Carolina relocated to be with their kin and preserve an Indian identity.[15]

The pattern of Robeson County Indian coalescence makes it difficult to establish precolonial landholding traditions. The first records we have of Indian landholding in the English sense emerged in the eighteenth century. Between the 1730s and the 1790s, Indians became landowners in one of three ways. First, Indian families received land grants from the English monarch prior to the American Revolution or from the state of North Carolina after the Revolution; second, Indian families were bequeathed a right to purchase land by a European settler; or third, Indian families had simply occupied and altered the land from its natural state prior to European settlement and continued to do so after whites came into the area. Because no record existed of a prior occupant or owner, by law these last families held a fee-simple title; their occupation of the land was simply so old that it predated English law and deed making, and the early U.S. government recognized their title because they had made what the English considered to be "improvements" on the land. European settlement and slaveholding was relatively sparse in Robeson County prior to the American Revolution, and the dense swamps and forests made the land unattractive to most white farmers. Most of the non-Indians coming to the area at that time were probably interested in escaping the law themselves, and they had little interest in establishing large farm operations. By the time the formation of the United States exerted pressure on Indian-held lands, the local and state governments considered these Indians private property owners and did not regard their lands as subject to the kind of usurpation visited upon the tribes that were removed from the rest of the Southeast. Shielded, in a sense, by historical accident from the danger of land theft, Indians in Robeson County developed intimate attachments to places and bounded them tightly with their attachments to family.[16]

In 1936 McNickle and his OIA colleagues knew none of this history and would not have recognized the ways that Indians defined themselves. Rather than deciphering percentages of "Indian blood," Indians used connections to family and settlements to identify one another. By the time of the OIA visit in 1936, most Indians traced their ancestry back to one of the following "forefathers" who had migrated to Robeson County in the 1700s: Major and John

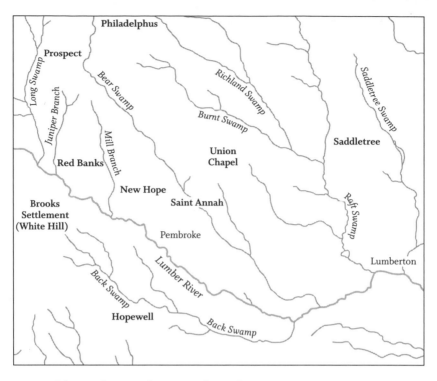

MAP 2. A Selection of Nineteenth-Century Indian Settlements

Locklear, Ishmael Chavis, James Lowry, John Brooks, or Charles Oxendine. Evidence indicates that some of these men were members of the Cheraw and Waccamaw groups who lived in and around Robeson County in the second half of the seventeenth century, but it seems that all of them married Indian women and their children then founded the community that coalesced in Robeson County. Later, other men moved into the community and married Indian women; or Indian families from other parts of the state, particularly Sampson County, brought surnames such as Emanuel, Maynor, Brewington, and Hammonds into the community.[17] But it was the "core families" from the eighteenth century that launched the development of the Indian settlements that determined much of life in the 1930s (see appendix charts 1–5). To be a Hammonds from Saddletree, a Lowry from Pembroke, a Brooks from White Hill, or an Oxendine from Union Chapel meant something to other Indians (Map 2). It was their way of identifying another Indian's family and thus his likely reputation, economic background, political influence, and overall social "place" in the larger community. Locale thus reinforced family relations and cultural values and shaped the social cooperation and conflict that occurred within the Indian community.[18]

The Brooks Settlement, about four miles southwest of Pembroke and across the Lumber River, provides an example of the affiliations created by kinship and place in Robeson County. Residents of the Brooks Settlement descended from both Lovedy Brooks, the daughter of John Brooks, and Peggy Locklear, John Brooks's second wife (see appendix charts 2 and 3). The Brooks Settlement had a reputation for violently defending its autonomy and fiercely attacking those who tried to encroach on its lands or threaten its women. "We looked at them as the . . . old-timey Indians, the real Indians," my father once told me. "Crazy, but smart. They'd fight and cut you to death."[19] Maintaining the settlement's "Indian" quality was of supreme importance to the elders, and they allowed cousin marriage more frequently than other Indian families. Elders wielded absolute authority over their offspring, and children rarely questioned them. Some members of the Brooks Settlement were landowners, teachers, and devout churchgoers who had established the churches and schools at Harpers Ferry and White Hill.[20]

The community's determination to maintain its connection to its cultural heritage may have made members particularly receptive to a Mohawk Indian delegation that arrived from St. Regis, New York, in 1928. Led by Chief Snow, the visitors helped brothers Colan, Ralph (also called "Releford" or "Pikey"), and Lawson Brooks, along with their first cousin Will Brooks, establish a Haudenosaunee longhouse adjoining Colan Brooks's land. Since the Mohawk and Tuscarora both belonged to the Six Nations council in New York, Chief Snow and the others may have recognized a long-standing kinship connection with the Brooks Settlement community and its historical ties to North Carolina's Tuscarora population, even if Robeson County Indians' state-recognized name at that time was "Cherokee." Taking up Robeson County Indians' official name, the community dubbed their longhouse the "Cherokee Indian Longhouse," but they held Haudenosaunee ceremonies—what they called "powwows"—on Saturdays. The longhouse operated until 1951; in its final years, Indians from Pembroke pressured the Brooks Settlement to shut it down. A member of the Brooks Settlement explained to me that the New York Mohawks had intended to remind Indians in Robeson County of their ancestors and their proper rituals; calling it "Cherokee" simply connected it to the larger community's officially recognized name and mattered little in terms of the actual rites that took place there or the identity that those gatherings reinforced. The longhouse represented a visible Indian institution that belonged to a distinct people who occupied a unique social and geographic place.[21]

As we will learn, McNickle and his colleagues discounted the kinds of "blood" ties that Indians in the Brooks Settlement and other places upheld. The insiders knew, however, that even though names and family structure had changed significantly in the recent past, Indian identity markers remained relatively stable. Robeson County Indians' adoption of Christianity and their widespread landholding in the nineteenth century transformed the matrilineal relations that had characterized eastern native societies in the eighteenth century. Indian children thus came to trace their kin relations not only through their mother's line but through their father's as well. The influence of Protestantism and the inability of married women to own land reduced women's visible roles in community governance. Although the system of reckoning kinship changed, gender roles continued to uphold kinship networks in Robeson County. Men and women tended to identify positively with their respective roles, each accepting responsibility for distinct areas of family and community life. A father claimed his role as the head of the household, the family's primary provider, and the person most responsible for negotiating with outside institutions. These duties corresponded with whites' recognition of an Indian man's status as a landowner, but they also coexisted with an Indian mother's position as mistress within the home. In addition to providing for the family through her work in the fields and the garden, mothers made the decisions regarding children's discipline and socialization. Women also transmitted the oral tradition and kept kinship connections intact by caring for in-laws and by keeping the family in church.[22]

Women's ability to exercise authority helped preserve the community, both socially and politically. Women wielded considerable influence in families in which a child was born out of wedlock or the father was an outsider, either an Indian from another place or a non-Indian. In both cases, children typically knew little of their father's ancestors, and mothers raised them as full-fledged members of the Robeson County Indian community; they often took their mother's surname.[23] Women also appear to have had some political power in the nineteenth century, providing guidance for the group's efforts to perpetuate their identity through acknowledgment. For example, when Robeson County Indians mounted an effort in the 1870s or early 1880s to gain federal recognition through Congress, they sent George Washington Lowry to Indian Territory in Oklahoma to learn as much as he could from the Indians who had removed there from the Southeast. Records show that Lowry's aunt, Clarissa Lowry Chavis—granddaughter of "forefather" James Lowry—granted him permission to undertake the journey. Her authority may have stemmed from her status as an elder or her knowledge of the community's history, or she may have had a more formal role, such as clan mother.[24]

By the early twentieth century, Indian men and women used their authority to consolidate their families within rural settlements. In the process, reciprocity became an indispensable feature of Indian identity; sharing and generosity ensured the community's survival. Settlements consisted of several extended family groups linked through marriage. Typically, the dominant families owned land, and children, spouses, grandchildren, and great-grandchildren clustered around the family's holdings and worked the farms as a cooperative unit. Families came together to help one another build barns, shuck corn, cut wood, and even plow if one of the family members was injured or sick. I learned part of this reciprocity ethic when I was younger, listening in on adult conversations about land. Adults seemed inordinately focused on finding a way to keep land in families or at least to avoid it passing out of Indian hands. Keeping the land for Indians ensured a cycle of give and take that would keep future generations together. Community members used marriage ties to keep this ethic alive. Women would sometimes find a spouse from another settlement and move if he owned land, or her husband would become part of his wife's parents' farm. Marriages outside the home settlement increased the family's ties to other settlements, though in the lean economic times prior to 1900, marrying one's second or third cousin was an acceptable way to enhance family solidarity and consolidate the family's economic resources. Oral history interviews with elders who remember those times confirmed that generations stayed close to home and beyond the reach of significant white contact and commercial engagement. Being near one's family and sharing in the obligations of child rearing and elder caregiving was of paramount importance to the survival of the community.[25]

Lumbee and Tuscarora ancestors formed the deepest layers of their group identity between their early eighteenth-century coalescence in Robeson County and the end of the nineteenth century. Social attachments to family networks, Indian-owned land, and settlement communities fashioned a layer of identity that survived even the most bitter political conflicts. If Robeson County Indians lived in isolation from non-Indians, kinship and settlement markers might have been the only ones needed to determine who was and who was not an Indian.

However, Indians in Robeson County have shared their homeland with non-Indians since shortly after merging. This shared environment and the group's focus on kinship raises questions about interracial marriage and Indians' social relationships to whites and blacks. McNickle and the OIA sought to clarify these questions. Lumbees seem to have a particular reputation for multiracial ancestry. Perhaps our seemingly anomalous position in the South raises the question: because Lumbees were considered nonwhites, the argument goes, whites must have classed them socially with African Americans; therefore, Lumbees must have married African Americans extensively because they could not have married anyone who was white.[26] Such reasoning is a product more of scholars' own impressions of a black-and-white color line than of the historical reality of earlier times. While it may not have been the norm for whites to marry or have offspring with partners outside of their own communities, it certainly happened with enough frequency to generate a wealth of lawsuits over miscegenation.[27] That body of law also indicates that although whites benefited from lumping blacks and Indians together legally as "nonwhite," Indians and blacks did not always see themselves in those terms and actively resisted such homogenization.[28] Throughout the United States, whites, Indians, and blacks certainly interacted, had relationships, conducted business with one another, and shared political aspirations. Some families and individuals choose to identify with their multiracial heritage and some do not. Such choices had little to do with whether a *group* articulated a black, white, or Indian identity.[29] Rather, that articulation was based on layers of identity that evolved over hundreds of years.

For example, Lumbees tend to discuss ancestry and kinship as somewhat distinct layers of identity. I was taught that our mixed racial ancestry doesn't make us any less Indian; an outsider who marries in is able to stay in because he or she can live with and even adopt some of the symbols and attitudes that Lumbees have used to maintain our community. The children of such unions are Lumbees because they have Lumbee family and perhaps because they and their descendants stay in the community and contribute to it for generations, upholding the values their non-Indian ancestor initially embraced. This view, I think, generally sums up Lumbee attitudes about our mixed-race ancestry.

As other historians have pointed out, there is a difference between kinship and race. Oklahoma has been fertile ground for studies that explained race as a concern of the tribal government and kinship as a concern of tribal citizens. The Creek government, for example, embraced Jim Crow and rejected black Creeks as a means to enjoy the benefits of whiteness in a state that legally classified Indians as white.[30] The "Five Civilized Tribes" have long histories of slaveholding, treaty making, and bureaucratic interference with their kinship systems, necessitating an intense public conversation about multiracial tribal members and political fractures between the government and the people.

Relationships between Indians and blacks received the most scrutiny in these communities because of this history. We will learn how Lumbee political leaders instituted various kinds of government to arbitrate these discussions and eschew any ties to blacks, but there are some important differences between North Carolina and Oklahoma. As discussed in chapter 1, the state of North Carolina gave Indians a separate legal classification as Indian, thereby sanctioning, to a degree whites could tolerate, Indians' own identity markers. The United States did not attempt to bureaucratically define and control kinship and race in Robeson County until McNickle's visit in the 1930s, well after Lumbees began to adjust their own ideas about these matters. When the OIA did become involved, their preference was not for white blood ties, as it had been in Oklahoma, but for "pure" Indian blood. On a local level, Robeson County Indians have received pressure to "forget" about black ancestors and kin while embracing their white relatives, but we will see that such pressure was far more arbitrary and fluid than it was among Oklahoma tribes. This pressure stemmed from short-term political agendas on the part of Indians and whites; amnesia was a strategy to affirm Indianness in a society where whites' attitudes about race dictated social and cultural relations. Further, whites who mixed with the Indian community in Robeson County often received negative attention as well; the debate concerned more than the impact of black ancestry on Indian identity. As such, Lumbees have not divided in the same way over race and kinship; the two coexist, perhaps somewhat idiosyncratically.

Yet much scholarship about the Lumbee has taken ancestry as its central question rather than one among a number of factors to consider in identity. These authors have reinforced the idea that Lumbees are unique in their multiracial roots. Typically, outsiders have overestimated the extent of Indian-white or Indian-black offspring in Robeson County, while Indians themselves have underestimated it. Thanks to the U.S. census's highly obscure and constantly changing definitions of race, as well as the silence of nineteenth-century local marriage records on the subject of race, we have little written evidence to back up either assertion.[31] But two of my undergraduate students—Jessica Righthand, with help from Emily Pierce—decided to see what they could find. They combed through the census and Robeson County marriage records from 1790 to 1880 (with the exception of 1840) in the quest to uncover, to the extent possible, the degree of intermarriage between Robeson County Indians and non-Indians.[32]

The most openhanded estimates of intermarriage based on the census, which included households that showed any indication whatsoever of a possible interracial relationship, demonstrate that the rates were highest in the earliest decades after the American Revolution and steadily declined through 1880. In 1790 the highest percentage of Indian households, 16 percent, contained members described as different races, while by 1880 that percentage had shrunk to 2 percent. The vast majority of these households contained a person with an Indian surname and a person who the census enumerator described as white. The marriage records, which are arguably more reliable because they included both spouses' surnames, present a somewhat different picture. Between 1799 and 1868, the Indian/non-Indian intermarriage rate was 24.4 percent. Further research in marriage records may determine how that rate changed over time and whether the marriages were predominately Indian-white or Indian-black. Despite the reassurance provided by numbers, the reality of "crossblood" love and marriage is still unknown, but we can be certain that Indians determined their own criteria for whom to marry while being influenced by a growing bifurcation of race in the South and a stigma attached to blackness.[33]

After the American Revolution, whites in the South struggled to protect political, social, and economic supremacy against nonwhites' claims to equality. The freedom to associate with members of other races and the apparent rough political and economic equality that Indians had enjoyed in the eighteenth century had practically disappeared by the end of the nineteenth century.[34] Segregation was constructed at odds with America's racial history, and it is against this backdrop that race became truly significant for Robeson County Indians.

Whites marked Indian identity in direct relation to that ebb and flow of racial equality. Questions of citizenship and race were at the forefront. For example, the 1776 North Carolina state constitution did not specifically prohibit nonwhite free persons from voting, and in some counties, including Robeson, nonwhites apparently voted and exercised other aspects of citizenship. This local custom ended in 1835 after North Carolina revised its constitution and declared that "free Negroes, free mulattos, and free persons of mixed blood descended from negro ancestors to the fourth generation inclusive (though one ancestor of each generation may have been a white person)" could not vote.[35] Read literally, this provision did not apply to Indians in Robeson County; after all, most of the convention delegates had no awareness of Robeson County Indians. But by the 1870s, at least some Indians and whites had come to believe that local whites used the amendment to prevent Indians from voting.[36] Local whites may or may not have used the possibility of black ancestry to eliminate Indians' voting rights; the written record simply does not say. In any case, this racialized citizenship category became a tool to exclude Indians and other free persons of color. The 1835 constitution also encouraged Indians, in resistance to this racial classification, to distance themselves from their mixed-race ancestry (both black and white) and any social or economic association with blacks, whose mutual association as "free persons of color" they came to fear and denigrate.[37] Over the next thirty years, more restrictions were placed on the Indian community. In 1854, for example, the state General Assembly passed a law voiding all marriages between a white person and a free person of color to the third generation that had taken place since 1839.[38]

Indians responded to these and other restrictions in a rebellion led by Henry Berry Lowry, great-grandson of forefather James Lowry. During the Civil War, the Lowrys and other families around their settlement suffered Confederate conscription; they were sent to build an earthen fort at Wilmington, North Carolina.[39] Afflicted with malaria, yellow fever, and dysentery, Indian men returned from their service only to face the violence of the Home Guard. Brantley Harriss, the Home Guard's conscription officer, murdered Henry Berry Lowry's first cousins while they were at home on furlough. A few weeks later, in January 1865, Lowry allegedly killed Harriss in revenge. Tensions rose as Sherman's army approached; by February they were preparing to cross the Lumber River.

Meanwhile, Henry Berry Lowry's father, Allen, sheltered Union soldiers who had escaped from a nearby Confederate prison. Allen was the wealthiest Indian in Robeson County at that time, a landowner and church leader with a large family. But even this prosperity did not keep his smokehouse full, and white neighbors with plenty to feed themselves schemed to take his land. Henry Berry and his brothers, hiding out in the swamps to avoid conscription, collaborated with the escaped soldiers to raid wealthy white farms for food. After one particularly profitable raid where the bandits outgunned Confederate soldiers, 100 men surrounded Allen Lowry's home and kidnapped Allen, his wife Mary, his sisters, and a guest. They took the group to a nearby white farm, where they met another posse that had captured several of Allen's sons, including William, the eldest. They locked the women in the smokehouse and questioned everyone; after a short "trial," the mob loaded Allen and William into a wagon and drove them back to the Lowry homestead. From the smokehouse, Mary and the other women heard distant gunshots, and their worst fears materialized: Allen and William were dead. For the next two days, the posse kept the women in the smokehouse and threatened them with the same fate if they did not reveal information about the raids and the hiding places of Allen and Mary's other sons. Receiving no information, however, the mob finally let the women return home.

These events sparked a seven-year war between a gang led by Henry Berry Lowry and the perpetrators of Allen and William Lowry's murder. Henry Berry's band included his maternal kin and close neighbors—his brothers, brothers-in-law, first cousins, and the spouses of his female cousins, including two African American freedmen and one poor white. Lowry and his gang murdered nearly two dozen of the most prominent white men in the county, including former Confederate officials, the sheriff, state militia officers, and the head of the local Ku Klux Klan. Henry Berry Lowry himself was a man of few words and said little to indicate that his war was political in nature, but his actions spoke loudly enough to whites: nearly all of the victims were conservative Democrats opposed to black and Indian voting. The Lowrys did kill two Republicans, but reportedly they did not intend to. During the Lowry campaign, the state constitution of 1868 restored the franchise to Indians (who had been allowed to vote prior to 1835), and freedmen held it for the first time.

In contrast, authorities captured, tried, and executed only one member of the Lowry gang: my great-great grandfather Henderson Oxendine. He was Henry Berry's first cousin; their mothers were sisters. The state executed Henderson for murdering the high sheriff, but I was taught that he hadn't actually done it; rather, he had decided to give himself up so that the rest of the gang and their families could live in some peace. The written record also points to this family memory. After years of successfully eluding the authorities, suddenly Henderson was easy to find; they apprehended him while he visited his sister's house. Henry Berry Lowry himself disappeared mysteriously in 1872 and the authorities never captured him. Other gang members eventually left Robeson County or were shot by bounty hunters who sought the reward the state offered on the Lowry gang members. The "Lowry War" proved that white supremacy would not go unchallenged. The story Lumbees tell each other about it explains a great deal about the qualities we value in ourselves.[40]

The Lowry War helps us tie together the foundational aspects of Indian belonging—reciprocity, kinship, and settlement—with a political battle over the level of supremacy that white elites should maintain in the presence of an enormous nonwhite and poor-white electorate. Largely characterized by nonwhites committing violence against whites, the Lowry War seems to contradict the standard narrative of the racial and political dynamic of the post–Civil War South. But what seems like a contradiction can also reveal the underlying systematic nature of white supremacy in rural areas and help explain why Indians would later embrace segregation.

An omnipresent paternalistic and personal social system characterized Robeson County and much of the rural South. A photograph (Figure 1) illustrates this point. These white men killed Tom Lowry, Henry Berry Lowry's brother and a member of the Lowry gang. Lowry's lifeless body is in the foreground, a patch of blood on his chest. The photograph would have been submitted as proof of the hunters' deed, necessary for them to collect the $6,000 reward. Tom Lowry's killers knew him personally and stalked him until they found the right time to kill.[41] The fact that Lowry was an outlaw and likely also guilty of personal crimes against his killers' families perhaps helps us rationalize the death depicted; it was not arbitrary violence, but vengeance for specific acts. This is the image of the personal, paternalistic South.

Tom Lowry's killers showed that whites demanded deference from non-whites rather than the distance they came to insist upon in urban areas. Sometimes that deference led to violence, but more often it led to accommodations. For example, nonwhites consistently used paternalism to their own advantage by seizing available opportunities to ask for favors from whites. Further, paternalism did not preclude continuing the many interracial intimacies that characterized southern race relations through the eighteenth and nineteenth centuries. Expectations of deference *did* maintain the authority of elite whites to control the political and economic structures of southern society, despite Indians' ability to retaliate against oppression and resist economic subjugation. Therefore, when the Lowry War ended, whites may not have believed it was necessary to exact violent retribution on Indians.[42] As historian Mark Schultz writes, private relationships characterized by deference "humanized white supremacy without effectively diminishing it" and undermined nonwhite solidarity against white privilege.[43] In a culture of deference, people like Henry Berry Lowry broke rules without breaking the system of authority itself.

For Robeson County Indians, the end of the Lowry War was their Wounded Knee massacre. Their nation didn't die, but it did become subject to state, local, and federal authority in many ways. The Lowry War left Robeson County Indians a separate social identity, but they spent the next seventy years, through the 1950s, gaining acknowledgment of their political autonomy. This effort often tore them apart, even as it brought them together in a shared quest to affirm their identity in the segregated South.

FIGURE 1. The Wishart brothers, bounty hunters of Tom Lowry (Wishart Family Papers, Southern Historical Collection, Wilson Library, University of North Carolina at Chapel Hill)

My family photographs ring with layers of belonging; we have one of the Pembroke "graded school," or elementary school, that features my dad's sister Faye (Figure 2). She is on the left end of the front row, and my great-uncle Theodore Maynor is the teacher (third row, left end). Aunt Faye was in the first grade, but some of those children on the top row don't look like first graders—they're preteens but most likely in their first year in school. Each child in this picture came from an Indian household; they had two Indian parents and lived within a few miles of Pembroke, close enough that they could walk to school. Few Indian children had access to a school bus, but the Pembroke graded school did have a sturdy brick building, evincing their modest prosperity compared to more isolated communities. I can imagine my grandmother Lucy mending the special collar she had sewn for Faye's dress the morning this picture was taken; I can picture Faye practicing an appropriately serious expression in front of her mother's dresser mirror—the only mirror in their five-room house, which was large for that time and place. My grandfather Wayne, a schoolteacher like his brother Theodore, was probably in the yard feeding the hogs; or maybe he was plating a few biscuits with molasses for my dad, Waltz, then only five years old. In a few years, Waltz, Faye, and their siblings would rise before dawn to pick cotton so they could go to school that day.

But this scene is just a fiction to me; my grandmother died before I was born and my grandfather died when I was three, so I don't recall their voices or personalities or the atmosphere in their home. In fact, just trying to access

FIGURE 2. First-grade class at Pembroke Indian Graded School, circa 1937 (Dorothy Blue and the Lumbee River Fund Collection, Livermore Library, University of North Carolina at Pembroke)

1938 is difficult. I didn't go to a segregated school, but the faces in my class pictures looked just as varied as these do. This photo poses some questions: How did the segregation era, marked by a supposedly iron-sided wall between the races, evidence so much variety? What were the contours and boundaries of racial segregation for Native American southerners? How did their identities function, and how did the concept of race become institutionalized out of an identity based on kinship and settlement?

These are questions that historians now ask, knowing that race and color became definitive categories in American society in the twentieth century. But at that time, Indians asked another question, one that had little to do with their position in the racial hierarchy and everything to do with their identity as a People: how do we maintain our autonomy while promoting opportunity and prosperity among our people? Faced with the challenge of an emerging color line and whites' defense of it, the answer was no less ambiguous than the social and political air they breathed.

By 1910 white supremacy dictated the separation of racial groups in urban public facilities—schools, churches, restrooms, drinking fountains, movie theaters, buses, streetcars, hospitals, and other places. In Robeson County, that separation was threefold in the county seat of Lumberton. There were different facilities for whites, blacks, and Indians. In the county courthouse, each group had its water fountains and restrooms, while the Lumberton movie theater boasted a balcony divided by wooden partitions for the Indian and black patrons. In the county's private places and in rural areas and small towns, however, the picture is less divided and more like the one of my aunt's school class: variegated, but with a certain logic once one looks below the surface. White supremacy was at once arbitrary and systematic.

Indians took step-by-step advantage of the post–Civil War racial environment to add another layer to their strategies for maintaining identity. Segregated schools and churches, along with the growing obsession with a hierarchy of color and ancestry, fostered a racial identity and helped Indians affirm their identity as fundamentally different from whites and blacks. However, adopting segregation to preserve distinctiveness proved to be a double-edged sword: excluding blacks and whites from their community assured Indians control over some of their own affairs, but it also conceded whites' power to govern race relations. Indians operated within the constraints of white attitudes about the racial hierarchy and, to a certain extent, had to determine their social boundaries according to what whites were willing to accept. Even so, they employed their own values in monitoring social contact with both whites and blacks.

The state evidently approved of their expressions of Indian identity, and in 1885 the legislature recognized Robeson County Indians as a "tribe." Unlike *racial* minorities in the late nineteenth century, Indian *tribes* were acknowledged entities that had independent political structures and historic claims. Under U.S. law, Indian tribes primarily had political identities, not racial ones. "Tribe" and "race" were not synonyms; rather, both words reconstructed a People and imposed rules on its opportunities, prosperity, and social mobility in different ways. However, when legislators recognized Robeson County Indians as a separate group in 1885, ideas about the racial hierarchy and a political identity converged for whites. Increasingly, Indians would struggle to use both to their strategic advantage. Being a legally recognized "tribe" created new opportunities for organizing to preserve autonomy, while being a socially acknowledged "race" authorized white power and control.

The 1885 law established Indians' right to separate schools and complicated their political identity through the exercise of that right. Indians also retained the ballot—in contrast to their black neighbors, whom Conservative Democrats disfranchised in 1900. With a tribal identity and the right to vote, Indians could use separate schools and churches to gain political influence. Indian leaders debated the best way to handle whites' power over their schools and churches. Should whites or Indians pastor Indian churches? Should Indian children with darker skin and curly hair be admitted to Indian schools? Indian-only social institutions then precipitated conflict within a community already characterized by a decentralized political and social structure. As this conflict became entrenched, Indians began to look beyond kin and settlement identification to institutionalize race and assert their tribal identity. The coexistence of "race" and "tribe" as identities fostered a degree of internal community disagreement as social and political ties between Indians and whites expanded and as ties between Indians and blacks diminished.

THE LOWRY WAR, characterized by a multiracial alliance, had a profound impact on the Republican and Democratic battle for power during Reconstruction. Historian William McKee Evans demonstrates that the Lowry gang's aggressive and violent resistance to oppression divided Republican Party supporters between those who supported fighting violence with violence and those who believed that deferring to whites was the most productive political route. These divisions stalled Republican momentum significantly enough to allow Democrats to achieve consistent, though not complete, victories in North Carolina elections throughout the 1870s and 1880s.[1] The multiracial coalition that Henry Berry Lowry assembled lost its political effectiveness amidst Republican divisions and a culture of deference that reinforced paternalistic white power.

If the Lowry War left a lasting political legacy, it was that Democrats could not take their victories for granted; Indians, blacks, and some whites still allied at the ballot box in favor of Republicans. Democrats thus began to court Indian voters as Robeson County became critical to the party's recapture of control in North Carolina. Democrats observed the county's tiebreaking participation in the election for delegates to the state 1875 Constitutional Convention, and they saw a unique opportunity to use the racial divisions in the county to their advantage. This convention was called to amend the Republican 1868 state constitution, which gave nonwhites the right to vote. To Democrats, the 1868 constitution represented "carpetbagger" and "Negro" rule, and when they regained control of the state legislature in 1870, they were eager to rewrite it. The two convention delegates from Robeson County gave the Democrats a one-vote majority at the convention. One Robeson attorney who later wrote about these events recalled that those two Democratic delegates only won Robeson by "the slimmest of majorities" and implied that the county's party leaders rigged the election to provide the convention with two Democrats. Though officials denied such chicanery, Democrats achieved victory by throwing out the votes from four county districts because the

TABLE 1. Robeson County Population, 1860, 1870, and 1900

	1860	1870	1900
White	8,572 (55.34%)*	8,892 (54.67%)	19,556 (48.46%)
Free persons of color/colored	1,462 (9.43%)*	7,370 (45.33%)*	3,877 (9.62%)*
Negro	N/A	N/A	16,917 (41.92%)
Slaves	5,455 (35.21%)	N/A	N/A
TOTAL	15,489 (100%)	16,262 (100%)	40,350 (100%)

* Includes Indians

Notes: The kinds of data collected by census enumerators varies from census to census. It is impossible to directly compare the numbers of voting-age males across racial groups across decades; only the 1900 census contains data specific enough to allow comparisons of voting-age males. These general population numbers thus only give the reader an indication of how the county was divided.

Sources: University of Virginia Geospatial and Statistical Data Center, United States Historical Census Data Browser (University of Virginia, 1998), available online at *http://fisher.lib.virginia.edu/census/* (18 August 2004 and 7 December 2006); Ernest D. Hancock, "A Sociological Study of the Tri-Racial Community of Robeson County, North Carolina" (master's thesis, University of North Carolina, 1935), 36.

poll books did not include the vote count as the law required. At least one of these districts, Burnt Swamp, had a majority of nonwhite voters. Voters from the discarded districts protested at the county courthouse as the votes were being counted, but election officials gave the victory to the Democratic candidates.[2]

Demographic changes in Robeson County before and after the Civil War demonstrate the relationship between voter populations and the Democratic and Republican contest. Emancipation had tremendous political significance in Robeson County. In 1860 whites dominated the electoral process because Indians and slaves were not allowed to vote. But in 1870 whites held a slim majority in the population as a whole. Republicans could change the balance of power if they could convince a few whites to join Indian and black voters. The 1900 census for Robeson County reveals that there were more Indians and blacks in the county than whites (Table 1). This reality indicates why Democrats believed they had to use a campaign of terror to win support at the polls.

Had Indians and blacks continued to vote together as they had during and immediately after Reconstruction, white Democrats would have lost every election if just a few poor whites joined Indian and black Republicans, which was the voting trend in many parts of the state through the 1890s. Historian Kent Redding argues that Republicans successfully employed racial identity politics long before the Democrats engaged their white-supremacy campaign. Although Conservative Democrats gained a majority in the state legislature as early as 1870, local races remained hotly contested and black Republicans continued to hold offices in many eastern counties. In Robeson County, for example, Republicans comprised the majority of registered voters, but the Lowry War divided them sufficiently to prevent them from gaining permanent control. One Democratic politician remembered that Indians were "chiefly Republican" through the 1890s.[3] The ruling status of Democrats was hardly secure, but the presence of the Indian population gave Robeson Democrats an opportunity to secure a clear majority. If they convinced Indians to join their cause and distance themselves from black voters and the Republican Party, Robeson Democrats could potentially eliminate any meaningful Republican opposition.[4]

Indians probably saw that this arrangement could work to their own advantage as well. In the aftermath of the Lowry War, some Indians likely recognized that their own political voices might be silenced, and they therefore sought to maintain what power they had. With an immovable place in this emerging race-based political system—guaranteed by their white Democrat friends—Indians could maintain some control over their own affairs while not threatening whites. Establishing Indian-only schools and churches secured this autonomy and also served another purpose: maintaining kinship networks. Schools and churches drew extended families closer together. Prior to the Civil War and during Reconstruction, Indians had learned and worshiped more informally, without attachments to outside sources of funding or church denominations. At least a few Indians attended school with blacks in the county seat of Lumberton during Reconstruction; a white Presbyterian minister and prominent Republican activist ran the school.[5]

When North Carolina established its public schools in 1875, they provided for white and black children only. Whites expected Indians to attend schools with blacks or not attend school at all. In response, some Indians founded family-based, privately funded "subscription" schools, but historian Anna Bailey has shown that Indians also operated schools within the publicly funded "colored" school system. Each school was governed by a "school committee," a group of three men who controlled admission to the school and made hiring and firing recommendations to the Board of Education. In some areas of the county with larger Indian populations, school committees were all Indian, but in other areas of the county, whites, blacks, and Indians served on school committees together. Bailey has also demonstrated that Indian and black children attended school together in some areas with smaller Indian populations. These interracial partnerships did not exist everywhere, however; some Indians apparently objected to admitting black children to their schools. In one district, the county Board of Education had to order an Indian school to admit "colored" children; when the school committee refused, the board renamed the district "colored," although it had formerly been called "Indian."[6] Perhaps the board punished noncompliance by changing racial labels and classifying Indians as "colored," an act that indicated the flexibility of racial categories in this time period and the tensions that ideas about race produced. Despite this instance of racial antipathy, Bailey's research shows that to some degree, Indian, black, and white cooperation survived the Lowry War; Indians clearly worked with both blacks and whites in education, and their approach to these issues was decentralized and likely varied among different settlements. Through decisions about school attendance and control, they affirmed the centrality of kinship and settlement to Indian identity.

In 1885 Conservative Democrat Hamilton McMillan, a state legislator who represented Robeson County and lived in the town of Red Springs, recognized that the school issue presented an opportunity for gain in the contested political and social arena of Robeson County. McMillan successfully lobbied for legislation to recognize Robeson County Indians as a "tribe" of "Croatan Indians" and to create an Indian-only school system. The state instructed the Robeson County Board of Education to establish districts for Indian schools and to provide Indian children their share of the general school funds. The act created Indian-only school committees and allowed Indians to select their own teachers for their schools.[7] McMillan's law not only promised educational advancement; it also would contribute to Indian autonomy. Indians welcomed this segregation act because it affirmed their identity to non-Indians. By supporting Indian-only schools, McMillan divided the Indian and black vote, which had favored Republicans, and he helped secure Democratic political power and social supremacy.[8] The multiracial political and educational coalition that surged during and after the Lowry War decayed when Indians chose to support the Democrats in exchange for their own schools.

The 1885 law recognizing the Indians of Robeson County as Croatans only partially institutionalized racial separation in Robeson County. Segregation mandated that Indians teach Indians, but prospective Indian teachers could not attend the state postsecondary institutions unless they agreed to enroll in black schools. In 1887 McMillan sponsored additional legislation to fund a Normal School to train Indian teachers. Indians wanted their own teachers because they functioned as role models for students, and their kin connections helped Indian parents feel secure that the teachers understood their children's values. The legislature appropriated $500 to pay instructors for the school. Recognizing the value of a teacher-training institution for Indians, Rev. William Luther Moore, an Indian minister from Columbus County, raised the additional funds to construct the facility, even donating $200 of his own money. After purchasing an acre of land, the Indians built the school at New Hope Church.[9]

Hamilton McMillan's theory of a Croatan identity for the Indians in Robeson County stemmed from his research and from conversations with Indian elders and local whites. During the Lowry War, he had been the editor of the local newspaper, the *Robesonian*. An amateur historian, McMillan interviewed Indians and published a full-length article about them in the *Robesonian* in 1877.[10] Indians told him about their Roanoke ancestors and their Hatteras ancestors, while local whites deduced that the acculturated farming habits of the Indians in Robeson County meant that their ancestors must have been Englishmen. McMillan thus linked the tribe to North Carolina's first English settlers—the Lost Colony—and the tribes that supposedly offered them refuge. McMillan gained state recognition for the tribe as Croatan, the name of the place to which the English colonists are said to have gone after they abandoned Roanoke Island. The name assured whites that Robeson County Indians had a history distinct from other southerners.[11]

Recognition as Croatan, however, served a dual purpose for the Indians of Robeson County. In a society increasingly segregated by law, Indians had to have their identity legislatively recognized in order to express that identity through separate schools. McMillan accomplished this goal by ascribing an origin to the tribe that had a historic aura, one that convinced his fellow legislators of the distinctiveness and worthiness of Indian people. For most non-Indians at this time, being "Indian" depended on what "tribe" one descended from. Identifying a historic lineage was necessary in the minds of white North Carolinians, who desired assurance that these Indians *were* a distinct racial group and not in fact African Americans. An identification as Croatan provided not only a tribal name but also a noble heritage. Hidden behind the name "Croatan" was a legend of white ancestry, white sacrifice, and white heroism. For a society obsessed with race and the traits that blood supposedly transmitted, emphasizing the tribe's white ancestry gained much-needed support for separate schools.[12]

McMillan's move ensured racial segregation and created new avenues for Indian leadership in the form of Indian schools. In subsequent years, the relationship between Indian leadership and segregation politics began to trans-form Indian identity. In the context of segregation, "tribe" and "race" became synonymous for Robeson County Indians. This new confluence of categories only created more political ambiguity for Indian leaders. Being a "race" secured the "tribal" prerogative of separate schools; schools sustained Indian kinship networks and settlement affiliations while also supporting the logic of white supremacy and emerging segregation law. Adopting a race-based under-standing of identity meant accepting the right of whites to define social, po-litical, and legal practices and norms; in turn, Indians had to cease political cooperation with blacks or risk toppling their precarious place in the power balance. The white mayor of Pembroke observed that Indian leaders consis-tently supported white supremacy even four decades later. Writing in 1929, the mayor described the Indian men who were trustees of the Normal School as "good Democrats that want good government," men who stood among "the highest element of the leading and outstanding whites of the County."[13]

That balance of power entered a new phase when the statewide battle be-tween Republicans, Populists, and Democrats ended in the disfranchisement of black voters in 1900. Robeson County residents formed North Carolina's first local unit of the Farmer's Alliance in 1887, forming an important base for a potential Populist revolt in the county.[14] Many local farmers remained Democrats, but in the early 1890s, white farmers all over the state flocked to the Populist Party and joined with Republicans to create a Fusion ticket, which captured a majority of legislative seats in 1894 and the governorship in 1896. In the wake of these victories, blacks continued in positions of political power. Their future threatened, Democrats engaged in a violent campaign to restore white supremacy.

The political campaigns that secured Democratic victories in the late 1890s would have made a particular impression on the Indian voters of Robeson County. The first so-called Red Shirt rally in North Carolina was held in Fayetteville, forty miles from Pembroke, just a few weeks before the November 1898 elections. The rally included 200 white men wearing "the red shirt badge of southern manhood"; their attire evoked the Confederacy's bloody losses during the Civil War and represented the return of white men to political power. Twenty white women, dressed in white to connote their purity, followed the 200 men. Delegations of Red Shirts from the Robeson County towns of Lumberton, Lumber Bridge, Red Springs, and Maxton also marched in the Fayetteville parade. The keynote speaker was "Pitchfork" Ben Tillman of South Carolina, the leading spokesman for black disfranchise-ment. Two days after the Fayetteville rally, white citizens of Red Springs, a town bordering the rural Indian settlements, welcomed Tillman and gave his message a standing ovation. On 1 November, the town of Laurinburg, fifteen miles from Pembroke, held another enormous rally and parade that included the Maxton Red Shirt Club. Nine days later, North Carolina witnessed its worst episode of political racial violence: the Wilmington Race Riots, which resulted in the deaths of as many as sixty African Americans and the exile of thousands of others. In one Robeson County district, Red Shirts kept blacks away from the polls with Winchester rifles.[15]

In 1898 Democrats regained control of the state legislature, and in 1899 they launched a campaign to pass a constitutional amendment to disfranchise those who could not pass a literacy test. They started their campaign in Laurinburg, the seat of Scotland County, which partially borders Robeson County.[16] To prevent the disfranchisement of 20 percent of the white voting population, lawmakers inserted a "grandfather clause" decreeing that if a man's ancestors voted prior to 1867, he could also vote, regardless of the literacy requirement. As a result of the constitutional amendment and white terrorist violence, blacks stayed away from the polls in large numbers in 1900, and they continued to do so until the 1960s.

Many Croatans could not pass a literacy test, nor had their grandfathers been allowed to vote, but Democrats nevertheless protected their right to vote in exchange for their support at the polls. In fact, Croatans were a special target of Democratic pressure. Democratic congressman John D. Bellamy, who represented Robeson County, "devised a scheme," as he put it, to secure Indian support. Bellamy financed a series of meetings in Indian settlements, where he spoke to them "about the necessity of education and pride in their ancestry." As Anna Bailey has explained, he and others explicitly linked the survival of Indian schools to Indian votes for the Democratic Party.[17] As W. H. Humphreys, a white Democrat, told a Croatan group assembled at a schoolhouse: "You are in duty bound to support the amendment. It will not disfranchise a one of you. . . . [A]ccording to the promises made in the last campaign and in view of what has been done by us for your race, you are bound to support it." Democrats saw an opportunity to gain further loyalty from Croatans with the disfranchisement amendment, and they specifically cited all that the Democrats had done for Croatans to prevent them from being legally classed with blacks. "If you will stick to [the Democrats] they will lift you out of the mire and clay," Humphreys told the crowd. "But if you turn your backs on us . . . I shall not know what plea to carry to my party for you again."[18]

Fearing that their schools and political privileges would be taken away, Indians supported black disfranchisement and white supremacy. As Oscar R.

Sampson, a teacher and trustee at the Normal School, put it: "[The amendment] will stimulate education to a higher degree in North Carolina. It will . . . establish White Supremacy. . . . It will solve the race problem in the State and the people can be thinking of something else. I think all teachers should support the amendment."[19] Naturally, Indian teachers agreed with Sampson because they wanted Indian schools and desired to continue to make a living. Yet these educated Indian voters had no reason to believe that their voting privileges would be permanent.[20] The Democrats' explicit threat against Indian schools raised the possibility that those schools might later be jeopardized. "Don't you want a share in the pie?" Indian teacher A. N. Locklear rhetorically asked other Indians in a newspaper editorial.[21] Democrats had portrayed support for education as a limited resource doled out in exchange for votes, and Indians acquiesced, eager to maintain the educational, economic, and political benefits they possessed.

Robeson County was not the only place where Democrats took advantage of a local Indian population to ensure political dominance. Even federally recognized tribes, not normally viewed as subject to the machinations of local politicians, experienced this pressure. Democrats intimidated voters from the Eastern Band of Cherokees, for example. Local whites prevented Eastern Band members from registering to vote in 1900, arguing that their status as noncitizen wards of the federal government did not entitle them to exercise the franchise. However, Cherokees had voted freely during Reconstruction, and local whites commonly contested their status as wards when they wanted to try Indians in state court. In fact, Democrats realized that Cherokees had Republican sympathies, just as Robeson County Indians had; but rather than secure Cherokees' support for Democrats by granting them some privileges under white supremacy, whites searched for a justification for their total disfranchisement. They found one in Cherokees' political relationship to the federal government—not as individual citizens, but as a tribe. Although Congress passed an act in 1930 that explicitly confirmed Cherokees' rights to vote, only extensive protests and lobbying by Cherokees themselves pressured county election officials to register Cherokees in the 1940s.[22]

The Mississippi Choctaws also had close ties to Democratic politicians throughout the early twentieth century. Democrats in Congress helped Mississippi Choctaws argue for access to allotments of land granted to their kin who had removed to Oklahoma in the 1830s; the Choctaw Removal Treaty established their right to the allotments. To gain land, Mississippi Choctaws had to prove descent from persons entitled to land under article 14 of the treaty. The government set up an Enrollment Commission to hear evidence of Choctaw descent from claimants, and the commission established the "full-blood rule of evidence" that determined, in essence, that only Mississippi Choctaw full-bloods could legitimately claim land. The evidence for full-bloodedness was largely visual in nature but also included the maintenance of language and distinct cultural customs. Choctaws themselves readily asserted claims of full-bloodedness and eagerly opposed individuals from other areas of the state who also sought enrollment and access to land. Historian Katherine M. B. Osburn argues that Democratic congressmen supported the Mississippi Choctaws perhaps because the Choctaws' self-identification as full-bloods helped solidify racial segregation. "Their allusion to blood may have imitated an idea of racial purity adopted from the racialist ideology of Jim Crow, perhaps a shorthand way of saying that the Choctaw were not 'colored' and did not deserve the disadvantages of discrimination," Osburn writes. But Choctaws were still disfranchised, indicating that white Democrats in Mississippi shaped segregation by elevating Choctaws above blacks in some respects but not others. According to Osburn, "Federal Indian policy during the allotment era intersected with the segregated society of the Jim Crow South to create a market for Indian identity; the discourse of Indian blood was the currency of this realm."[23]

The ties between race, local politics, and federal Indian policy did not end with the allotment era. In the 1930s Democrats again allied with Mississippi Choctaws to make claims on assistance from the Indian New Deal; by that time, the Office of Indian Affairs had established a relationship with Choctaws that amounted to their acknowledgment, making them eligible for assistance. In the crisis of the Great Depression, Democrats saw the Choctaws' status as a federally recognized tribe as an opportunity to increase federal funds to their districts.[24] During the era of federal allotment policy, Choctaws' "race" secured the alliance with Democrats, while during the self-determination era of the New Deal, their status as a "tribe" proved influential.

The white-supremacy campaign of the Democrats convinced Robeson County Indians that their place in the racial hierarchy was more vulnerable than ever; they had to support white supremacy if they wanted to protect their Indian identity. To maintain that place and their autonomy within it, Indians took strategic advantage of white perceptions of Indian identity to organize politically as a tribe. For white officials constructing a biracial society, "tribes" had distinct names and bloodlines that may be in part European but should never be *any* part African in origin.[25] The Mississippi Choctaws encountered this same belief from the allotment Enrollment Commission, which ruled that "where any person held a strain of Negro blood, the servile

TABLE 2. Indexes of Educational Access for Robeson County Schools, 1933–1934 (All Figures Percentages)

Race	Schools Built of Brick	One-Teacher Schools	Children Transported by Bus
White	63	3	54
Indian	7	30	29.3
Black	5	37	3.3

Notes: Whites had twenty-one schools built of brick (out of thirty-three schools); Indians had two brick schools (out of twenty-nine); and blacks had three brick schools (out of fifty-five).

Source: Ernest D. Hancock, "A Sociological Study of the Tri-Racial Community of Roberson County, North Carolina" (master's thesis, University of North Carolina, 1935), 81–83, 89–90.

blood contaminated and polluted the Indian blood."[26] The public, political presence of Robeson County Indians in this new society required them to embrace this criterion and eschew the civic cooperation with blacks, whether in politics or in education, that the Lowry gang had embodied during Reconstruction. This process of adopting segregation to affirm their distinctiveness resulted in an additional layer of identity for Indians who had previously thought of themselves as a People. They now began to express their intentions as a race and as a tribe. The political participation that the Lowry gang sought during Reconstruction had been achieved, though the Red Shirt campaigns and black disfranchisement reminded Indians of the precarious nature of that achievement. The question became how to secure autonomy in this political climate; in response, Indians became increasingly comfortable with an identity as a "tribe" as well as a "People" and a "race."

ACCORDING TO SOME INDIAN AND WHITE federal government officials, the political patronage afforded by Indians' loyalty to the Democrats resulted in county Indian schools comparing favorably with local white schools and ranking far above black schools.[27] By 1910 Indians ranked above blacks in funds spent per student ($1.76 for Croatans and $1.21 for blacks; whites received $2.75 per student). By 1915 the spending disparity had widened between Indians and blacks but not between Indians and whites. That year the county spent $3.06 per white student, $2.03 per Indian student, and $1.09 per black student.[28] Some statistics indicate that Indian children had access to better school facilities than African American children. In addition to the low number of brick schools for black children (Table 2), 27 percent of black

TABLE 3. Socioeconomic Indicators for Robeson County
Schoolchildren, 1933–1934

Race	Total School Census* (Percentage of Ethnic Population)	Percentage of Children Who Enroll	Percentage Enrolled Who Attend	Percentage of Population Illiterate (1930)
White	8,119 (25.9%)	92.8	85.1	8
Indian	5,168 (41.7%)	87.7	81.6	30.7
Black	7,257 (31.8%)	94.1	85.5	23.4

* Number of children in the general population of school age

Source: Ernest D. Hancock, "A Sociological Study of the Tri-Racial Community of Roberson County, North Carolina" (master's thesis, University of North Carolina, 1935), 39, 86, 88, 94.

schools were rated as being in "poor" condition in 1939, while no Indian or white schools were rated as "poor."[29] Other measures of student access to education that relate to school funding (school bus transportation and the presence of one-teacher schools, for example) ranked Indians higher than blacks. By the 1930s, some aspects of schooling in Robeson County began to reach parity between the races. For instance, schools for every race operated for 160 days, representing tremendous improvement in educational access for all children. In 1900 the average length of the Indian-school term was 2.4 months per year, in comparison with 2.5 months for blacks and 2.75 months for whites.[30] The state of education for all of Robeson County's children was deplorable at the turn of the century. But after Democrats achieved uncontested control, politicians seemed to dole out favors to their supporters, at least in limited ways.

But in this ambiguous political atmosphere, Indians' educational opportunities were mixed at best. Other measures indicate that Indians had access to education that was equal to or less than that of African Americans. School attendance was not compulsory at this time, and fewer Indian children than black or white children received an education. The percentage of Indian children enrolled in school was the lowest in Robeson County, and an even lower percentage of Indians actually attended school (Table 3). While these statistics described the entire Indian population, I doubt that these patterns were uniformly distributed throughout the community. Certain Indian settlements may have faced economic obstacles to attending school because of the demands of landlords who insisted that children stay out of school to work in the fields. Other Indian families had better facilities and more consistent educational opportunities. Even in the late 1940s, Indian parents in the Brooks Settlement complained that 150 Indian students were crammed into a frame building with only three teachers, while the Pembroke Graded School experienced no such overcrowding, according to its principal.[31] Chapter 2 will describe these differences within the group in more detail.

Particularly for more isolated communities, the high proportion of children in the Indian population combined with the lower percentage of Indians attending school meant that many Indian settlements had leaders who could not read and write, even in the 1930s. Indeed, Indian illiteracy rates were higher than any other group in the county (see Table 3). Whatever advantages some Indian students may have had due to the political patronage system under segregation, those advantages did not reach the majority of the Indian population. Indian and black children together suffered other hardships that doubtless interfered with their ability to learn. Like their Indian counterparts, black parents in Lumberton complained that their children suffered from overcrowding, condemned buildings, and lack of school buses.[32] As of 1939, no Indian schools had lunchrooms, and only one black school did. Consequently, no Indian children and only a few black children could qualify for state-funded school-lunch programs since, to meet the requirements, their schools had to have lunchrooms.[33]

Structural discrimination of this kind particularly affected Indians. For instance, Indians fell far behind both blacks and whites in higher education. There were two colleges for whites in Robeson County—one for women in the town of Red Springs and one for men in Maxton. Until the early 1930s, the Thompson Institute for Negroes operated in Lumberton. After that school closed, blacks still had the option to attend colleges throughout the state, such as Shaw University (incorporated in 1875), the Negro Agricultural and Technical College (which had been conferring degrees since 1898), and the State Colored Normal School (which had been receiving state funding since 1877). Unlike these schools for African Americans, which had received both private and state support since the late nineteenth century, the state did not provide substantial funding to the Indian Normal School until 1913, nearly two decades after its founding. In the interim, the school's trustees raised funds "door-to-door" in the local community, and the institution operated as an ordinary elementary school with two years of high school work. The Normal School did not provide full teacher training until 1928, a situation that significantly retarded the progress of Indian students because segregation dictated that only Indians could teach Indians.[34]

Indian and black education could also be compared in terms of their impact on community life and on empowerment under Jim Crow. For both groups, education represented a profound opportunity for self-sufficiency and independence, and Indians and blacks seemed to establish schools with equal fervency in the late nineteenth century. Many of these schools were privately supported, and they functioned as community centers as well as places of learning. Segregation required that teachers share their students' identities—Indian teachers for Indian students, and black teachers for black students. In these settings, Indians and blacks exercised greater control over the classroom and the curriculum while promoting solidarity among the students. Both groups evidenced a strong desire for community control over education. But in order to gain support for their schools, blacks were forced to engage in and accept white supremacy, just as Indians were, and teachers consequently became unelected political leaders who spoke for the community to whites.[35]

Important differences also existed between Indian and black education. For example, black education in Robeson County received support from outside the South. This included thirteen schools funded by Sears, Roebuck and Company chairman Julius Rosenwald that benefited from a steady stream of teachers who were educated outside the Robeson school system and likely had more updated teaching methods and higher expectations. Unlike Indian Normal School graduates who could only aspire to teaching or preaching as professions, black college graduates had further educational opportunities, becoming doctors, lawyers, college professors, and bankers. Aside from one Indian who earned a medical degree in the late nineteenth century, Indians did not begin earning medical, law, or doctorate degrees until the 1960s, and the first Indian-run financial institution did not open its doors until 1973.[36]

But perhaps most importantly, Indians and blacks developed different objectives for education. As articulated by the most influential black leaders, writers, and educators, education should promote progress toward racial equality. Leaders such as Charles N. Hunter (who taught blacks in Robeson County at different times during his fifty-year career as an educator and activist), Booker T. Washington, and W. E. B. DuBois disagreed about the speed and manner by which this equality was to be gained, but all generally agreed that equality with whites was the ultimate goal.[37] Black leaders articulated this view to counter a specific agenda of discrimination concerning black education; whites debated the extent to which their tax money should be used to support black education, for example. But no specific discriminatory agenda existed with regard to Indian schools. Elected officials had created them in a paternalistic moment to persuade Indians to vote with the Democratic Party. Therefore, the discrimination that Indian children encountered might be regarded as a by-product of white supremacy's role in education rather than as a specific intent of lawmakers. Indians in Robeson County occupied an ambiguous space where they could use education not only to achieve racial equality but also to enhance the fundamental layers of their identity—kinship and settlement—while gaining necessary skills to augment their economic and political autonomy beyond white control. In the words of historian Anna Bailey, "Indian leaders worked to convince their community that these were institutions of *distinction* rather than *discrimination*."[38] With an awareness of their long-standing tenure on the land and their well-developed identity as a People, Indians saw education as a means to enhance their political position as a "tribe" with claims rightfully separate from their status as a "race."

For Indians, "race" proved to be a category whose definition became most clear when they set themselves apart from African Americans. Some Indians did not receive an education at all due to the complexities of negotiating a racial identity under the system of white supremacy. The history of recognition as Croatan, and whites' corresponding expectations about blood ties, surely activated the stance of Indian leaders on the question of which Indians to educate. In 1887, the same year that the legislature created the Normal School, the state outlawed marriages between Indians and persons "of negro descent to the third generation." Two years later, the General Assembly barred children "of the negro race to the fourth generation" from attending Indian schools.[39] Under these restrictions—designed to construct a solid wall between the races—Indians acted in ways inconsistent with their own identity markers.

For example, soon after the state created Indian schools, the Prospect community school received a request for admission from the children of a freedman who had married an Indian woman prior to 1887. The mother of the children was a member of a prominent Indian family; her brother belonged to the local Indian school committee that oversaw admission into the school. The County Board of Education had assigned the children to Prospect School, but the local committee ignored the mother's Indian identity and refused to admit them, based on their father's African American ancestry. The father sued the school committee, and the committee won the case, an affirmation of their right to control admission to Indian schools.[40] The case represented a wedge between brother and sister and contradicted Indians' own deep markers of identity. I can only speculate that following the passage of these crucial

Jim Crow laws, the committee members believed they had to deny links to African Americans in order to secure their continued ownership over their schools. They affirmed the racial categories that segregation imposed and helped clarify Indians' own racial identity in the process. A generation later, however, whatever rift existed seems to have been healed; future generations of children in this family have since attended Indian-only schools.[41] Their mixed-race ancestry did not banish the family forever, but the politicized atmosphere of education under Jim Crow catalyzed a decision that threatened the maintenance of the community's fundamental identity markers.

These decisions frayed families and forced the community to cede a good degree of authority to white supremacy and the system of segregation. Denying kinship with African Americans for the purposes of school admission continued into the twentieth century as well. In 1913 the Goins family, who came from an Indian community known as the "Smilings" in South Carolina (named after another dominant family surname), petitioned to enroll their grandchildren in the Indian Normal School; one of their children, Fannie, had married a Robeson County Indian and been admitted to the school. But the school's Board of Trustees excluded the grandchildren. Local Indian leaders claimed they had accepted Fannie on a probationary basis and ultimately felt they could not determine the Indian ancestry of the Goinses. They justified their decision on the fact that the family group had migrated into Robeson County from South Carolina relatively recently. The Goins parents sued, and in court the school trustees also based their defense on the physical appearance of one of the family patriarchs who, one Indian witness said, "is according to the way I look at it . . . of the Negro blood." Further, the defense called witnesses who testified of known associations between the men in the family and the African American community. The defendants thought they could prove the ineligibility of these Indians in court through evidence of appearance and associations, but the court was unconvinced. Other witnesses from the Robeson County Indian community, including Fannie's husband and several Indian preachers who had personal knowledge of the "Smiling" settlement in South Carolina, supported the Goinses' evidence of Indian identity. Their willingness to testify implies that at least some Indians did not approve of the school leaders' strategy to exclude kin based on purported black ancestry. Ultimately, the defense failed to prove that the plaintiffs had black ancestry and *did not* have Indian ancestry. The state supreme court upheld the Goins children's right to attend Indian schools. However, the Robeson County Board of Education decided to establish a separate school for the family in their settlement, which became known as the "Smiling" or "Independent Indian" school. Until the 1960s, Robeson County had four different segregated school systems.[42]

Opportunities for all of the county's children suffered under this administrative albatross, but some Indian leaders persisted in their efforts to preserve segregation at all costs. Knowing how difficult it could be to prove identity through markers of appearance, associations, and ancestry, Indian educators and white elected officials and experts collaborated to find a way to enforce what was unenforceable. It seems that Indian leaders most feared that families who had no kinship ties to the community might relocate to Robeson County and try to "pass" as Indian in order to enroll their children in school. They knew that the existing phenotypic diversity in the Indian community likely confused whites, who also had no knowledge of kinship connections and could not identify which children legitimately belonged. No written evidence confirms my speculations, but James Chavis, a leader of the Siouan faction, remembered in 1971 that his ancestors had to "cut a line" between Indians and anyone who whites might perceive as black. "They were just simply afraid to take anyone in, afraid it was a mulatto or something other slipping in," he recalled.[43] I can only imagine that Indian school leaders were in a difficult position; they did not want to exclude children who had legitimate ties, regardless of their appearance, but they could not include children whom whites might question. They had to seek some means of outside help to assert their authority, and they found that assistance in experts whose own agendas made them eager to help. Like their white counterparts who created the system of segregation itself, Indian leaders feared anonymity, the prospect that people whose kinship ties they did not know might intrude on their privileges and threaten their control. Segregation was a means to prevent this, and Indians embraced it as a tool to promote their interests.

Indians explored the potential of eugenics to police these boundaries. At the height of its popularity in the 1920s, eugenics was fostered by laws on both the state and federal levels that restricted immigration, banned interracial marriage, and promoted mandatory sterilization based on the idea that race and class defined an individual's worth in society. Eugenicists believed that breeding out deficiencies would advance society as a whole; correspondingly, they thought that government should actively engage in this breeding process. As an arm of government, public schools played a prominent role in the dissemination of eugenic ideas and in the collection of data that confirmed these notions. Eugenicists believed that intelligence was inherited, and they could make their case with data from mental tests performed on children. Through these tests, children would ostensibly learn where on the scale they and their race stood; they could better understand their proper place in society and what, if anything, they could do to improve their standing. If a child belonged to a racial minority or immigrant group, he would doubtless learn that his intelligence was unavoidably inferior to those of native-born white students. Indeed, eugenics redefined the social uplift that education promised: many children learned that such uplift was not for them, but for others. The political consequences of this lesson were startling and national in their scope. As education scholar Anne Gibson Winfield writes, "testing provided the moral equivalent to absolution when it came to access to education and, by extension, wealth and power." Even as the North Carolina Teacher's Association, for instance, told educators that identifying "deficients" was a "civic, charitable, and personal duty," eugenicists also provided "scientific" justification for white supremacists' campaign to limit the educational, economic, and political opportunities of Indians and other poor and nonwhite people.[44]

North Carolina's white teachers and school administrators were active in the eugenics movement.[45] I do not know the extent to which their ideas directly influenced Indian teachers, but it seems likely that eugenicists' desire to weed out "deficients" resonated with some Indians' fears of imposters. Further, the sequence of court cases concerning the race of prospective students must have encouraged some to believe that their schools were under siege, whether by racial imposters or white supremacists. In any case, eugenics came to them in the form of sociologist Arthur H. Estabrook. Educated at Johns Hopkins University, Estabrook spent most of the 1920s working for the Eugenics Records Office of the Carnegie Institution in Washington, D.C. He coauthored *Mongrel Virginians: The WIN Tribe* (1926), a volume that purported to demonstrate the intellectual, physical, and social deficiencies of Indians in Virginia and simultaneously alert Americans to the threats to "racial integrity" in the nation's oldest English colony. Estabrook colluded with Virginia's notorious vital statistics registrar Walter A. Plecker, who "pronounce[d] all 'Indians' in the state of Virginia 'Negroid,'" according to Estabrook's coauthor Ivan McDougle.[46] The ability to change racial identity by the stroke of the pen indicated how truly undefined "race" could be.

Mongrel Virginians also contains brief treatments of Indian groups from other states, including Robeson County Indians. But Estabrook apparently had trouble drawing any new conclusions in Robeson. "They resent questioning as to the probability of the negro having come into their blood and cooperation so far with them has been impossible," he wrote in the book. Contrary to his assumptions, he did learn that "the skin color of the people seems to have little to do with their economic or intellectual level, some of the very dark people being of very high grade ability."[47] But Estabrook did not give up; after the book's publication, he renewed his efforts. He apparently saw an opportunity to advance his social and research agenda (and get better cooperation from Indians) by capitalizing on Indians' anxieties about the perilous state of their schools. Estabrook launched his fieldwork in 1924, when a white Normal School teacher, A. F. Corbin, hosted him in the county. Estabrook took pictures at the school, and trustee Oscar R. Sampson objected strongly to the photo taking; he told Corbin to request that Estabrook send the film back to prevent "folks from suspecting [Corbin] of underhand[ed] dealing." Apparently, Sampson did not want the photos published as representative of students at the school.[48]

But even though Estabrook had an awkward start, Indians did not reject his work entirely. He encouraged the measurement of Indians' physical and mental traits "to assist them in keeping their race pure, and to aid them in the promotion of legislation to this end." Estabrook's hope for legislation was consistent with eugenicists' broader goal of involving government in the achievement of racial integrity. Further, Estabrook probably believed that the results of these tests would give him data on "negro blood" that was unavailable from Indians themselves; certainly it would demonstrate the extent of "feeblemindedness" among the group, a trait that Estabrook and other eugenicists associated with mixed-race and Indian groups.[49]

But Estabrook gave Corbin a slightly different justification for the tests. He said that the tests would judge the aptitude of students to determine what intellectual qualities would lead to success in college. "Both Tecumseh Brayboy and Doctor Fuller Lowry want their boys to go to college, and others will go when schools are opened to them," Corbin wrote.[50] Higher education mattered deeply to Brayboy, Lowry, and other Indians; in 1904 Lowry was the first student to graduate from the Normal School with a diploma. They apparently hoped that segregation would one day abate sufficiently to allow their own children to attend college, and Estabrook took advantage of their vulnerability under Jim Crow. Such data, he argued, "can be used for direct requests not only for bettering the present schools but even college opportunities for many who now cannot have them."[51] If Indians showed special abilities, perhaps they might prove their worth and receive better funding for their schools and even opportunities for higher learning.

Estabrook's rationale intrigued Oscar Sampson and A. N. Locklear, who had both been vocal supporters of the white-supremacist disfranchisement amendment in 1900. In addition to being a trustee of the Normal School,

Sampson served as principal of the Pembroke Graded School, and Lock-lear was the fourth-grade teacher there.[52] Locklear told Estabrook, "We are putting forth every effort possible to eradicate the undesirable blood found among some of the Indians here. . . . This blood, it is true, crept in during the days of Darkness and Ignorance." Obviously the blood in question was African American; the "days of Darkness and Ignorance" likely referred to the era before the Democrats established segregation. Locklear was cautious, however. "It is wise to move slowly in this matter," he wrote; perhaps some community members would object to his "purifying" agenda.[53]

Indeed, Locklear could expect objections from at least one Indian family: a group of brothers who had formed a successful gospel quartet. Their father had a black parent and an Indian parent, and their mother was Indian. The group identified themselves as Indians, and apparently they were good singers because they had gotten some publicity. But this public attention prompted Locklear and others to form the "Indian Betterment Society" to promote racial purity. This example shows how the community experienced some internal tensions over unions between Indians and blacks. But had the family not been so visible, I suspect the society probably would never have cohered around racial purity as a goal. The prospect that whites might learn of an Indian family with black ancestry clearly gave urgency to the society's mission. But despite Indian educators' anxiety about Indian and black families, some Indians nevertheless continued to value kinship above race.[54]

Locklear and others saw eugenics as a useful tool but also had some concerns about how the group as a whole would be represented. They articulated those concerns, for example, in their desire to have another Robeson County Indian actually conduct the tests that Estabrook proposed so no more "strangers" would need to come in, according to Corbin.[55] "Our people are very suspicious," Indian minister Lonnie W. Jacobs told Estabrook, "because of their misrepresentation by many visitors coming for pictures and other information."[56] Black strangers were not the only outsiders that Indians feared, apparently; white strangers raised alarm as well. While the state education superintendent, the Normal School superintendent, Oscar Sampson, and a few other Indian educators advocated for the tests, not all were in agreement about how the tests ought to be conducted. Lonnie Jacobs, for example, perhaps knowing that eugenicists sought evidence of deficiencies in nonwhite groups, wanted to ensure that "the more intelligent ones as well as those of inferior mentality" would be examined. He cautioned that his People needed more time to grasp what might be involved in the tests.[57] Nevertheless, Estabrook persisted and succeeded in having one test done as a sample; and finally Corbin secured the agreement of teachers at the Hopewell school, where the Lowry family resided, and the White Hill school at the Brooks Settlement.[58] Unfortunately, the documentary record stops there, and I do not know if Estabrook ever actually conducted the tests. It seems unlikely, however, because Indians were clearly skeptical of eugenics as a meaningful tool. After all, as Lonnie Jacobs suggested, it might ultimately disfranchise them further.

Having found eugenics unsatisfactory, Indians may have turned again to their Democratic friends in the state legislature to help enforce racial boundaries. In 1929 the General Assembly established an admissions committee for Indian schools and gave it "original, exclusive jurisdiction to hear and determine all questions affecting the race of any person" attending Indian public schools and the Normal School. Locally, the group became known as the "Blood Committee" and functioned to screen applicants for black ancestry.[59]

The legacy of Indians' embrace of segregation to root out racial imposters is ambiguous. White supremacy demanded that Indians avoid blacks both politically and socially and deny inclusion to community members who might possess African ancestry. For Indians, excluding blacks from their community may have preserved some autonomy, but it sometimes required Indian leaders to forswear their own kin ties and the value they placed on family. At the same time, Indians who did not directly deal with whites, or who simply did not accept the exclusion of their African American kin, continued to exercise caution when deciding which tools to embrace to promote their autonomy. Indian leaders faced a true dilemma concerning the role of race in the maintenance of their identity.

The ambiguities of segregation created tensions within the Indian and black communities, but I am not certain about the extent to which those tensions spilled over into overt competition between the two communities. Surely black leaders and Indian leaders tried to gain advantage with their white supporters by elevating their own cause above that of the other, and white leaders likely responded by playing one group against the other and encouraging mutual dissatisfaction. But the impact of these discussions was the appearance of better Indian school facilities alongside lower quality of education for Indian children. These gains were miniscule at best and set the stage for Indians' attempts to involve the federal government in their quest for recognition; affirmation of their identity as a "tribe," rather than as a "race" in competition with other minority "races," might begin to address Indians' quest for autonomy under Jim Crow.

Although Indians supported segregation and accommodated the internal conflicts it precipitated, they recognized that the system institutionalized racial inferiority and economic discrimination. Members of the Indian community may have seen recognition by the federal government as a way to escape the restrictions of white supremacy. They used Hamilton McMillan's Croatan theory to seek educational assistance from Congress; they believed that federal recognition would compensate for the state's unequal funding of the Normal School. Their appeal reflected the continued identification pattern of kin and settlement but indicated how the larger Indian community used the notion of itself as a tribe to get what it wanted. In 1888 a group of Indians signed a petition to the U.S. Congress asking for financial assistance for the Normal School. The Prospect community encompassed the largest number of petitioners, with additional signers from New Hope, Union Chapel, Burnt Swamp, and Harpers Ferry—communities tied to Prospect through marriage. Typically, a father and several of his sons and sons-in-law signed the petition. Therefore, heads of families influenced political activities: the father was a settlement leader and his male relatives followed their elder. But the issue of educational improvement drew Indians from different settlements together to form a consensus. They forwarded that consensus to Congress, representing themselves as a tribe of "Croatan" Indians.[60] Regardless of how well the name or McMillan's history fit their own oral tradition, they recognized that using the name in the presence of outsiders gained the desired outcome of separate schools. As evidenced by how Indians organized themselves to submit the congressional petition, the name did not appear to change how Indians reckoned identity on a day-to-day level to one another. In Robeson County, being Indian depended on the family and settlement one came from, not what "tribe" one descended from. The name "Croatan," by itself, did not alter this reality.

Croatan did, however, radically alter the political presence of Indian people in Robeson County, in the state of North Carolina and in the nation as a whole. It became the basis for a collective political identity, as well as a source of debate within the tribe and with outsiders about the historic tribe or tribes from which the Robeson County Indians descended. For Indians, being named Croatan and identifying with a tribe made the organization of a political body to represent the people all the more important. The name also made the question of historical authenticity an internal point of discussion. Which of their ancestors should they claim as their historic identity? These discussions and their national impact began to alter the political and social structure of the community. Indians began to see identity markers other than kin, settlement, and social institutions as their tribal name became more prominent. But the idea of a "tribe" did not fundamentally change the primary layer of identification as a People through their families and settlements. Even as their tribal identity developed and new ways of identifying themselves gained prominence, Indians continued to monitor their home communities and search for ways to display their "Indianness" in a society increasingly divided by the racial categories of "white" and "colored." In a segregated society where white supremacists had the power to reclassify Indians as "colored," Indians began to distance themselves from both blacks and whites. This strategy became a successful way for Indians to distinguish themselves.

BUILDING INSTITUTIONS WAS A PRIMARY WAY for Indians to express their own boundary lines under white supremacy. Even prior to the Democrats' manipulation of Indian votes, Indians, blacks, and whites had begun to construct separate venues for social interaction, particularly in churches. Before this time, Indians met for religious gatherings as they had for centuries: in brush arbors, on riverbanks, and in homes. Indians and non-Indians often worshipped together until after the Civil War. Soon after emancipation, freedmen in Robeson County established their own Baptist churches in the towns of Fairmont and Lumberton. Lumberton witnessed its first black Presbyterian church in 1875. Black Christians organized a formal church association in 1900, when they formed the Robeson County Missionary Baptist Union.[61] The Hammonds family in Saddletree established the earliest documented Native American church in Robeson County in the eighteenth century. Between the 1850s and 1880s, Protestant Indian congregations emerged in Union Chapel, Hopewell, Prospect, Burnt Swamp, and many other settlements.[62] Few Indian churches had a denominational identity at first, though Indians seemed to actively eschew the Presbyterian faith—perhaps as a way to distance themselves from local whites, who had predominately Scottish ancestry and strong affiliations with the Presbyterian church. Like many other rural southern communities, whites, blacks, and Indians continued to visit one another's churches even after strict racial separation was established.[63]

Building Indian-only schools and churches strengthened Indian identification with one another through kinship and place. Church trustees included prominent men and women from a settlement whose landholding Indian neighbors granted them title to property for the church building. Many of these church founders descended from the "core" families of the community, including the Lowrys, Locklears, and Brookses. Each settlement and kin group had one or more churches that served as the focal point of social and religious activity. Over time, church buildings emerged as visible settlement markers located at a central crossroads. The community built its school across the road from the church and sometimes on the same property.[64]

Both Baptists and Methodists gained significant footholds in the Indian community during this period. The first formal Indian Baptist association emerged in 1881.[65] Churches formalized their associations with outside denominations around the same time schools attached themselves to the state. These affiliations allowed some Indians to leverage outside influence to enhance their own status as leaders and engender divisions within the community. But Indians' preferences, not white demands, ultimately characterized these divisions. While Indian leaders eagerly adopted segregated institutions and acquiesced to white supremacy concerning schools, they mitigated, and some ultimately rejected, white control in their churches. Indians gained power and influence from family and settlement connections and through leadership positions in schools and churches. But schools relied more heavily on white patronage than churches did, giving leaders some flexibility to oppose white dominance in religious settings. When the opportunity arose to develop the Normal School and to create an Indian-only Methodist conference, leaders institutionalized race to demand that non-Indians, especially white Democrats, recognize their distinctiveness.

The relationships between Indian schools and churches reflected the social structure of the Indian community, and the power of white supremacists heavily influenced the development of both institutions. Understanding the actions of Indian leaders from the perspective of cultural and historical relationships among those leaders reveals that Hamilton McMillan and the actions of the Democrats catalyzed Indian divisions. The establishment of the Normal School reflected the community's priority of organizing according to family and settlement. Indians built the school in the New Hope community because of the family connections of the initial Board of Trustees. Members of the board had deep kinship connections that stemmed from the eighteenth-century "core" families of the Indian community, especially the Oxendines and the Lowrys.[66]

The connections between family, place, church, and school are longstanding in the Lumbee and Tuscarora communities. The Prospect settlement, about five miles northwest of present-day Pembroke, exemplifies these ties between community and social institutions. James Moore, now eighty-eight, owns a gas station at the heart of Prospect—across from the church and the volunteer fire department, next to the historically Indian school, and kitty-corner from his cousin Harbert's small-engine repair shop. His grandfather was Rev. W. L. Moore, who had originally worked with McMillan to establish the Normal School. His grandmother was Mary Catherine Oxendine, the conduit to W. L. Moore's transformation of Indian education and a niece of "Big Jim" Oxendine. Big Jim probably got his nickname as much from his standing as from his physical stature. He was equivalent to a principal at the Prospect community subscription school, known as the Cooper Shop. Big Jim funded the school and taught there; it was located at a workshop for barrel makers (or coopers), who made the barrels for the turpentine that Robeson County's pine trees produced. Mr. Moore told me that Big Jim was a Robeson County commissioner during Reconstruction, the only Indian elected official at that time. I also found from the census records that he was one of only eight Indians who owned more than $1,000 worth of real estate in 1870, giving him the means to support Indian education.[67] Big Jim and W. L. Moore became friends when Moore, one of the only Indians who had received any formal schooling, began teaching at the Prospect school. Soon afterward, Moore became pastor at the Prospect Methodist Church, and Big Jim introduced Moore to his niece Mary Catherine. Moore must have recognized the wealth and influence of the family he had married into, and he capitalized on that influence to establish an institution that the whole community badly needed.

These kinship connections were not coincidental; they had a purpose in institutionalizing the school, and they influenced the development of Christian denominational associations as well. The Normal School's Board of Trustees were all related through blood or marriage, and it is also not surprising that Prospect played a large role in founding the school. Some considered Prospect the heart of the Indian community, and its reputation as a center of Indian churchgoing and landowning exceeded that of any other settlement at that time. Another Prospect community leader and trustee, Preston Locklear, was married to Emmaline Lowry from the New Hope area; Big Jim's wife, Delilah, was also a Lowry—connections that probably made it possible for them to locate the school at New Hope, where the Lowrys owned land.[68] Kinship connections formed the basis of these racial and tribal institutions in the late nineteenth century. This fundamental layer of identity ensured that schools and churches operated outside the purview of whites to a great extent, even as whites imposed segregationist values on how those institutions were supported. Indian kin ties continued to play a major role.

The administration of social institutions among Indians varied depending on how their leaders chose to adapt or resist white control. Indian leaders divided initially over whether whites would be involved in the leadership of these organizations. The factions that emerged in the early years of the Normal School reveal the impact that segregation politics had on Indian institutions. W. L. Moore, then teacher and principal of the Normal School, led one faction. Hamilton McMillan described the leaders of the other faction as "cling[ing] to Radicalism." By "Radicalism," of course, McMillan meant the Radical Republicans, who still held some sway among Robeson County voters. "This disaffected element still adheres to the Negro churches," McMillan told the state superintendent of public instruction, "and is intensely radical in politics. It is composed of the worst class." McMillan thought these political alliances should close down the school and told the superintendent as much. McMillan described Indian churches as "Negro churches" because they were influenced by the Republican Party—the party of "Negro rule," according to white Democrats.

These tensions erupted in 1887, when several churches and an Indian school were burned, perhaps by Indians who disagreed with Moore and McMillan's request of funds for the Normal School from the legislature.[69] This form of protest likely made sense to an Indian community that spawned the Lowry War and knew that such extreme measures could help them reach their goals. We don't know who initiated the burnings, but they likely protested not merely the request of funds but also Moore's alliance with McMillan. As a result of these violent actions, McMillan suggested that the superintendent follow the suggestion of at least some of the members of the board and replace Moore, who appeared to be divisive, with a "wide-awake white man . . . to give the school a new start."[70] By "wide-awake," the trustees perhaps meant that they wanted a principal who was sympathetic to Indian community needs rather than a "boss" who would direct the community away from its roots. The superintendent replaced Moore with Ezra Bauder, but the atmosphere around the school remained divided "mostly on the religious question," according to Bauder.[71]

The "religious question" of the day involved the actions taken by the Methodist Episcopal Church (now the United Methodist Church) to exclude nonwhites from worship. Like other Protestant denominations in the nineteenth century, the Methodists had divided in the 1840s over the issue of slavery. The church formed two distinct branches, one in the North and one in the South. In 1870 the southern Methodist Episcopal churches "separated out" their nonwhite members, excluding them from church worship, but the northern church continued to minister to nonwhite members. The actions of the southern church affected several of the Methodist churches in Robeson County in which Indians and non-Indians worshipped together, including the church of Normal School trustee Isaac Brayboy at Union Chapel.[72] The Indian members of Union Chapel joined the northern Methodist Episcopal Church, reputedly under the influence of the radical Republicans. The Hopewell community, populated by the Lowrys, also joined the northern church along with Union Chapel. The Allen Lowry family had good reasons for opposing the actions of the southern Methodists: in the 1830s white church members at Hopewell had asked them to sit in the balcony with African American slaves. They refused and left the church.[73] Union Chapel and Hopewell became associated with the Republicans, Hamilton McMillan's political enemies. However, no members of W. L. Moore's church in Prospect had been separated out, and Moore and his in-laws continued to work with white ministers of the southern Methodist branch as well as Democratic politicians.[74]

Frustrated by Methodist factionalism and the destructive influence of segregation, Methodist minister Henry H. Lowry, Allen Lowry's grandson, led some Indian churches to withdraw from the Methodist Episcopal conference. He and others built a conference of Indian churches in which Indians controlled their own affairs, including the appointment of Indian pastors, bishops, and superintendents.[75] Given the dangers of appearing socially connected to blacks, Lowry's desire to disassociate from what McMillan called the "Negro" church of the North undoubtedly influenced his efforts to create a separate Indian Methodist conference. Lowry's association became known as the Lumber River Holiness Methodist Conference, and it still thrives today.

Indians reacted to their internal disagreements by dividing into two groups with different views about how best to respond to the challenge of segregation. The Prospect faction, led by Moore, remained unaffected by the Methodist exclusion of nonwhites. They saw nothing amiss in aligning with whites and working with white leadership to promote Indian progress. That progress, they believed, enhanced the educational and religious institutions of Indians and thus helped to maintain Indian identity. The Hopewell and Union Chapel faction, led by Lowry, believed that the path to progress required Indian leaders. After all, Indians had experienced discrimination within the white-run Methodist Church and had seen how white power could hurt Indian autonomy. Indian mentors and guides reminded Indians of their community connections and urged them to preserve Indian identity. The division between Henry H. Lowry and W. L. Moore was political, not personal. In fact, they remained lifelong friends, refusing to allow their differences of opinion to disrupt the alliances that their families had created over the previous decades.[76] Perhaps the men recognized that a family squabble did not create their differences; instead, the actions that white Methodists and white Democrats took to separate Indians and whites created them. With such actions, race became the central issue in the institutionalization of the Indian Methodist Church and the founding of the Indian Normal School. McMillan also stoked the fire by characterizing Indian factionalism as destructive, perhaps in an effort to divide the Indians and consolidate his own political influence over his Indian constituents.

McMillan's role in fomenting Indian disunity presages state and federal officials' roles in aggravating Indian factions several decades later. Indians turned those divisions, however, into a creative dialogue about how to manage white supremacy and resist the attempts of whites to exercise total dominance over Indian institutions. That dialogue prompted a new religious association—the Lumber River Holiness Methodist Conference—and sustained considerable social and political empowerment for Indians as they continued their quest to gain recognition for their identity. However, as leaders followed their principles of redressing injustice, Indian children and Indian parishioners lost something: their school and churches were burned to the ground.

THE DIALOGUE OVER SEGREGATION'S INFLUENCE in the Indian community extended into everyday relations among Indians, whites, and blacks. The idiosyncratic yet pervasive nature of white supremacy sometimes empowered Indians in these relationships, and sometimes it did not. Whites often ascribed their own racial attitudes to Indians. To whites, the reluctance of Indians to identify themselves with African Americans meant that Indians hated blacks as much as they did. McMillan described his view of Indian-black relations in 1914: "Since their recognition as a separate race they have made wonderful progress. Their hatred of the Negro is stronger than that entertained by Caucasians."[77] Federal supervisor of Indian schools Charles Pierce wrote of Robeson County Indians in 1912, "They do not associate with the Negre [sic] race, looking upon them in about the same way as do the whites of their community."[78] James Henderson, agent for the Eastern Band of Cherokees, observed in 1923 that "the Indians dislike the Negro population to the point of bitter hatred."[79]

While some Indians were undoubtedly as racist as whites, evidence of this fact most often comes from whites, who had every reason to shape the discourse of race in terms that would support their own supremacy. McMillan's statement, in particular, must be read in light of how he himself treated Indians as inferiors. For example, McMillan never asked Indian visitors to sit down; instead, McMillan expected them to stand up, even when he was not in the room. This personal treatment of Indians demonstrated McMillan's belief in his own superiority and his fear that Indians would aspire to his position in society. His daughter Cornelia reinforced that fear when she told a visitor that she believed "in treating the Indians fairly, not so that they would think they were your equal, but fairly." McMillan and other outside observers paid no attention to the efforts of Indians to preserve their community; instead, they characterized Indian-black relations in terms of progress toward their own racial goals. Whites accepted the distinction between Indians and blacks only if they could preserve deference from Indians.[80]

Indians, however, probably saw race relations differently in the context of the "white" and "colored" binary. White supremacists only recognized Indians if they visibly disassociated themselves from blacks. This insistence on separation between Indians and blacks had produced Indian-only schools and legal acknowledgment of their separate status. Maintaining social distance from blacks was just one way to express an Indian identity in the early twentieth century, and it was "particularly likely to occur in the presence of whites," according to anthropologist Karen Blu.[81] If Indians had exhibited consistent hatred of blacks as whites claimed, then historians would see evidence that members of the Indian community with black ancestry had experienced wholesale exclusion. I have cited here cases where the offspring of Indian and black couples could not attend Robeson County schools, and I have been told about Indian women who married black men and were forced to leave the community. But people have also told me about individuals with known black ancestry—what my cousin called "roots"—who became community leaders and school committee members. The families who had been legally barred from Indian schools, for example, were fully embraced by the Indian community a generation later.[82]

If Indians bore the kind of hatred that McMillan and others claimed, at the very least historians might expect to see Indians dividing into darker-skinned and lighter-skinned castes, as some tribes have. But as Blu points out, no such division has occurred.

> Robeson Indians appear always to have had many factions, but
> none has crystallized along color or imputed-ancestry lines clearly
> and definitively enough to result in a community split that counts
> some people as members of the group and some as nonmembers. . . .
> In refusing to define membership in terms of presumed biological
> ancestry, either in degrees of Indian "blood" or in notions of "racially"
> determined appearance, the Indians have rejected White criteria

and set up their own. Physical appearance is obviously significant to Indians because they know that Whites evaluate them on that basis, but Lumbees today refuse, and insofar as can be determined in the past refused, to characterize themselves as a group according to physical appearance.[83]

As the observations above illustrate, disassociation from blacks seemingly pleased whites and likely contributed to the proliferation of Indian schools.[84] What appeared to be "hatred" of blacks was a more subtle attempt to create and protect an "Indian-only" sphere, which Indians in Robeson County considered essential to their identity.

Indians recognized that cooperating with blacks might mean compromising their identity as a "race" and a "tribe," but they also recognized the social risks of associating with whites. For example, local whites had exhibited a consistent, historical tendency to erase Indian identity and attempted to classify Indians as blacks socially and politically. After the state recognized Robeson County Indians as Croatans, whites shortened that name to "Cro," with the derogatory association of Jim Crow. In response, Indians petitioned to have their legal name changed to "Indians of Robeson County" in 1911 and "Cherokee Indians of Robeson County" in 1913.[85] The latter name change bore some resemblance to the initial acceptance of Croatan. Angus W. McLean, an influential white Democrat, obtained and publicized the tribe's Cherokee ancestry the same way McMillan propagated the Croatan name. McLean—a Lumberton lawyer, Democratic Party activist, amateur historian, and later governor of North Carolina—was born and raised in Robeson County. He had long been acquainted with the Indian population, and elders such as George Washington Lowry relayed their People's oral tradition to him. He became convinced that their true ancestry was Cherokee and advocated this name when tribal members exhibited dissatisfaction with Croatan.[86]

While some Robeson citizens recognized Indians, others, both black and white, continued to express open contempt for Indians' insistence on their identity. A young black delivery man overheard Indians saying they refused to attend the segregated movie theater in Maxton; he told sociologist Guy Benton Johnson that "the Indians say they are as good as anybody, good as the whites. . . . They money good as anybody's. If they can't sit with whites, they ain't going." The boy then whispered, "But I tell you, they ain't nothing but Croatans. But you better not let 'em hear you say that." The boy implied that Indians might exercise retribution if they were treated as "Croatans"— which by that time had acquired a pejorative meaning—rather than as Indians. Another black domestic servant told Johnson that she resented Indians' positioning themselves as equal with whites: "I think there ought to be just two people, white and colored. It would be a lot better that way." The white Atlantic Coastline Railroad agent in Red Springs sold rail tickets to Indians who sat in the white waiting room and rode coach class with whites. He did not seem particularly puzzled or concerned, simply commenting, "Seems funny, but they do." To avoid this kind of equality, the mayor of Pembroke requested that the railroad build three separate waiting rooms at the town's train station. Mayor McInnis noted Indians' refusal to wait in the "colored" waiting room, remarking that Indians sat in white train cars "without being asked there, or without being ejected . . . by the Railroad conductors." But he insisted that Indians were not good enough to sit with whites, as "there are some of the Indians who are very nice and good people and there is a large majority of them who are otherwise."[87] No doubt some whites sympathized with those blacks who felt that Indians' insistence on their separate identity complicated matters, and they attempted to force Indians to accept a "colored" identity. For these whites, displaying an Indian identity did not show appropriate deference. For example, as late as 1947, Pikey Brooks, head of the Brooks Settlement longhouse, insisted that the post office at Maxton, a nearby white town, did not transmit all of their mail, "particularly anything that indicates that the sender is treating them as Indians. The people [whites] prefer to think of this group as Negroes."[88]

Treatment "as Negroes" was not universal in white-Indian relations, but few consistent "rules" existed for white-Indian interaction. Degrees of social segregation and exclusion varied depending on the gender, race, and even the class status and political influence of the Indians and whites who interacted. For example, a white auto salesman and farm owner in Red Springs, whose wife was a schoolteacher, objected to Indians' political influence, saying, "The white politicians down in Lumberton are spoiling [Indians], treating them as if they were white folks—letting them come into their homes, entertaining them. . . . And the Indians are getting so they feel they are just as good as white people. Some even think they are better. They're getting so they want to sit on the jury."[89] Given his wife's dependency on political favor for her job in the schools, this man may have believed that Indians had greater political influence than he did and resented that fact. Whatever the circumstance of their treatment, Indians objected to the efforts of whites to remind them of a second-class status, and they set their own standards for contact with whites.

Whites discriminated against Indians in political and civic affairs. Democrats wanted Indians to vote as long as they voted for white candidates, but party leaders silenced Indian voices when they might elect an Indian. For example, whites prevented Indians from participating in the town government of Pembroke, established in 1895. In 1917 the state legislature passed an act to appoint the town mayor and commissioners rather than hold a general election. Later, the town attorneys explained to North Carolina governor O. Max Gardner that "a majority of the voters of Pembroke belong to the Indian race and in order to see that the government of the town did not fall wholly into the hands of the Indians, the act in question was passed."[90] This practice continued until the late 1930s, when Indian petitions to state legislators finally resulted in Pembroke residents electing their own government. All the mayors of Pembroke subsequently have been Indians. Although whites acknowledged a difference between Indians and blacks by permitting Indians to vote, county courts prohibited Indians from serving on juries. "There are plenty of good white men to do this sort of thing, so we just use them," the clerk of superior court in Lumberton remarked. This exclusion resulted in numerous miscarriages of justice in the minds of Indians, especially in the harsh sentences to Indian offenders. Indians responded with persistent complaints to the Office of Indian Affairs and petitions to court officials in Lumberton. Eventually they succeeded in forcing whites to appoint Indian and black jurors in 1937.[91]

Socially, Indian families responded to white prejudice in different ways. Some parents encouraged their children to marry whites—in spite of the legal restrictions against such marriages—in the hope that children with lighter skin would have greater success in society. Not all Indians, however, encouraged their children to marry whites. In the matrilineal system of the past, the kinship ties of children were linked to the mother, regardless of the father's ancestry. Now, Indian children reckoned kin through both sides of the family. It became more important for both mother and father to be members of the Indian community so the child felt secure in his sense of belonging. For example, when asked in 1936 whether he had ever heard his grandmother mention anything about clans among the Robeson County Indians, a sixty-two-year-old man said, "I don't know that I did. They [our elders] didn't want you to marry Negroes or white folks so that we wouldn't get mixed up." According to his son Colon, Aaron Brooks, a member of the Brooks Settlement, told his children "to marry [so that] we wouldn't be ashamed of our marriage, that we wouldn't be ashamed to associate with them nowhere."[92] Indians recognized that marrying whites could endanger their autonomy, self-esteem, and group cohesiveness, but marrying blacks carried even greater penalties.

White actions gave Indians good reasons to discourage their children from socializing with or marrying whites. Whites avoided using titles of respect for Indians, except for those Indians who had attained some wealth or influence or who whites considered "nearly white" in attitudes or class standing. Whites also used these forms of personal labeling to make distinctions between Indians and blacks. For example, some whites avoided calling Indians "uncle" or "aunt," as they would blacks, because such a title would make Indians "fighting mad." In the aftermath of the Lowry War and in light of their loyalty to the Democrats, Indians undoubtedly felt that they did not deserve the kind of paternalism that whites inflicted on African Americans.[93]

Whites and Indians also clashed over intimate relationships. Whites ostracized Indian-white couples; white families disowned their daughters who married Indian men, and local whites refused to address such women as "Mrs." Conflict often arose between a white man and the family of his Indian wife if the man tried to force the woman to sever connections with her family. In addition, extramarital sexual relations between white men and Indian women generated tensions. White women generally characterized this activity as taking place between Indian women and "poor white trash," while white men of every class openly acknowledged their lust for Indian women and correspondingly believed that Indian women reciprocated their desire. Indian families, on the other hand, typically tried to control the social interaction of their daughters with all white men, hoping to avoid an unintended pregnancy and ostracized child.[94]

Other Indian families took pride in their white ancestry and their lighter skin color and encouraged their children to marry whites if possible. Some Indians, particularly families in Prospect and Pembroke, appeared to adopt the same prejudice as whites against dark skin tones. "My husband's real light and all his sisters have yellow hair and blue eyes," said one Indian woman in Prospect to sociologist Guy Johnson in 1937. "We've got more white blood than anything else. You ought to come up here to school commencement. [The girls] are real beautiful and intelligent too. They have pink skin just like my baby here and my husband. If they were to get away from this section, nobody would ever think they was anything but white." "Pink" skin, as opposed to the varied olive and brown complexions of most members of the Indian community, equaled greater beauty, heightened intelligence, and more opportunities in life—in particular, the ability to leave Robeson County and pass as white. Ironically, the woman also pointed out the reality of having white ancestry in the Indian community: lighter-skinned, blue-eyed Indians remained Indians while in Robeson County. Local whites did not permit them to cross the line, regardless of their appearance. She may have emphasized the white ancestry of her family to please the white man to whom she was speaking, but other Indians echoed her views when they spoke freely about a family's "good blood" (meaning white) and "bad blood" (meaning black). Some made efforts to highlight their "good" ancestry. These attitudes served to perpetuate kinship knowledge as a primary criterion for Indian identity, but they also prompted social differentiation within the community, leading some Indians with lighter skin to feel that they were "better" or "more accepted" than those with darker skin. Although Indians had identity markers other than racial ancestry and skin color, they knew that whites evaluated them on such criteria, and they turned those prejudices on themselves as much as they did on outsiders.[95]

The sensitivity to skin color in the Indian community reflected the color lines that whites drew for southern society. But those color lines were hardly impermeable. Rather, a culture of deference could accommodate contradictions, and exceptions to the general "rules" of white supremacy flowered in Robeson County. Furthermore, not only whites developed and monitored this interaction; Indians had their own understandings, desires, and norms and manipulated the system to their own advantage as much as they could. As such, variety flourished in reactions and opinions about the subjective categories of social interaction, especially ancestry and skin color.

As the lines between "white" and "colored" hardened in North Carolina in the late nineteenth and early twentieth centuries, Indians realized that non-Indians must recognize their distinct identity. They adopted segregation and institutionalized race, as whites did, in their schools and churches. These moves assured that whites would recognize their "Indianness." However, Indians left white supremacy intact in most of their social and political relations. While Indians valued segregation for its support of Indian-controlled institutions, they also saw the ways in which the system disempowered them and permitted whites to govern the ethnic boundaries of their society.

The James and Edna Sampson family lived in the rural Deep Branch community, east of Pembroke. They farmed cotton, tobacco, and corn for a living. Mr. and Mrs. Sampson were among the 20 percent of Indians who owned land in the early twentieth century. Miss Bessie Oxendine, a local Indian schoolteacher, took a picture of the Sampsons in the springtime, on a day when the family was tearing down a sweet potato hill (Figure 3). Some of the children are holding a sweet potato in their hands. To store sweet potatoes through the winter, Mr. James dug a hole in the ground and layered in pine straw, burlap, and maybe fifty pounds of sweet potatoes. Then he covered the potatoes with more pine straw and burlap and mounded dirt to make a hill. The survival of any Indian family through the winter depended partly on their sweet potato hill. Winter was a "season between," coming after the crops had been sold and before creditors would advance the family food or supplies on the potential value of their next year's crop. Tearing the hill down in the spring meant a new beginning.

Atelia (nicknamed Addie) Sampson is sitting in front of her father, her hands over her mouth. She was nine or ten years old and had just started working in the fields for the family. She brought this picture to a community gathering in Pembroke and told me the stories that welled up in her. Unlike the children at the Pembroke graded school pictured in chapter 1, much of her education took place at home and at church. Her father ensured that his children had the opportunity to at least learn the basics. "We could go to church on Sunday and to the field during the week," she said. "When we

FIGURE 3. James and Edna Sampson sitting on their front porch with their children, circa 1922 (Atelia Sampson Chavis and the Lumbee River Fund Collection, Livermore Library, University of North Carolina at Pembroke)

weren't working [Daddy] would tell us to go get our Sunday school books and go sit down and read them."

I imagine that this moment was, in hindsight, one of the last easy times for this family. Addie's mother, Edna, died two years after this photograph was taken. A few years after that, Addie tried to enroll at the Indian Normal School, which at that time wasn't a postsecondary institution but only offered a high school education and two years of teacher training to Indians. She wanted to start in the eighth grade; her father could help her get to school, but he couldn't help her pay the tuition. "At that time we did not have any money," she remembered, "and you had to pay a $2.50 fee to go to school and I did not have any to pay, and they had the [entrance] exams that day and they would not let me take it. . . . That would not be like that today. If you did not have any money they would try and help you. Back then something just weren't right." Later she told me, "Crops back then did not bring nothing. You got ten cents for your tobacco. People did not make nothing."

One of the reasons Addie's family had so little was because white creditors cheated her father out of his land. She remembered, "They would just take it. I don't know how they would do it but they did. And my daddy didn't owe them nothing. He had paid them but he didn't get a receipt to show it and he wouldn't give them a receipt. He got a lawyer from Fayetteville to come here and fight it in court. And they ran the lawyers out, [they] would not let them come here. That is the way the white man done in Lumberton." She added, "If Henry Berry Lowry . . ." She paused and began again. "There should have been enough of Henry Berry Lowrys in this part of the world. We would have had a better living. He would have got rid of them."[1]

When this photograph was taken, Addie Sampson had taken her place as a provider for her family and had her own dreams of mobility, of taking advantage of the opportunities she thought were available to her because of her Indianness. But in a few years she found out that the institutions her People had built—landowning and education—were not available to her. In the thirty years before this family moment, the institutions and power centers created by Indians' identities as a People, a race, and a tribe had engendered changes in their senses of place. While Indians accepted segregation for the system's support of institutions that reinforced the value of place in terms they accepted, they struggled with the economic discrimination that accompanied the system's social structure. Their struggle revealed itself in the community's internal economic and status differences.

"Place" continued to have its connotations of settlement affiliation and geography. Addie Sampson firmly identified with Deep Branch as her home community. Like many Indian settlements, Deep Branch derives its name from the swamp that runs west to east and lies north of the Lumber River. The land was fruitful, naturally irrigated by the river and its "branches," or swampy streams that sprung from the central channel. The extended Sampson family, including James and Edna and their children, was the settlement's core. With the help of white missionaries from Ohio, their elders established the community's church prior to the 1860s, followed by a school several decades later. The Sampsons and other families in Deep Branch were also known for their political leadership as far back as the 1840s, when they opposed antebellum laws restricting Indian gun ownership.[2] Community members named both church and school after their lifeblood: the swamp. Through these connections between people, places, and institutions, Indians used locale and tenure on the land to gauge group membership.

For example, when an Indian asks "Where do you stay at?," he or she means where on the land are you living. The answer conjures up a whole host of associations for the questioner, based on knowledge that has been passed down over generations. If Addie answered "Deep Branch" to that question, the listener would likely associate her with the Sampson family, assume that she went to the Indian-only school and church there, and think about Deep Branch's reputation as an old, prosperous, and hard-working community that generated educational and religious leaders. The answer identifies how long one's People have belonged to this land and where one belongs in the wider Indian social network. Such information comprises internal identity markers, and Indians established an easy dialogue of kinship among people and between places. In the 1920s these aspects of place had profound influences on Indians' social organization by tempering the Indian community's decentralization and, to a large degree, preventing the formation of rigid status hierarchies that have been seen in other Native communities.

These internal markers of kinship and place were not enough to assure the community's future under white supremacy. "Back then something just weren't right," Addie said regarding her rejection from the Normal School. That "something" was the failure of her People to deliver the meager promise of segregation: giving children the basic educational skills they needed to maintain independence from white landowners, creditors, and others who sought to sustain their power through economic means. In that moment, the strong, impersonal forces of white supremacy revealed themselves to the fourteen-year-old Addie Sampson—even though it was an Indian and not a white person who stung her with the poison of discrimination. Her place in her family and community, reinforced by hundreds of years of cultural development, had acquired a second dimension. For her, like so many other Indians in the Jim Crow era, the meaning of "place" came to mirror the connotations that "place" had in a society of white supremacy.

The rural southern power dynamic that allowed Indian protest through violence like that of Henry Berry Lowry also placed profound restrictions on Indians' economic opportunity. After whites failed to defeat Lowry, they perhaps recognized that a slow but steady weakening of Indians' economic power would ultimately serve their interests more than confronting Indians' physical power. But even prior to Reconstruction, whites had organized this system of oppression by classifying citizens according to "race" or by social categories that are marked not only by phenotypic observation but also by smell, taste, touch, sound, language, genealogy, and other measures.[3] After slavery ended and nonwhites became economic actors in their own right, fictions of biological inferiority acquired a necessary urgency if whites were to maintain economic and political power. By the early twentieth century, race had become an undeniable factor in the southern agricultural economy; to a certain extent, race limited opportunities to earn even the most modest living.[4]

Though Indians maintained the power of self-defense, the threat of political disfranchisement encouraged them to assert their voice through segregated institutions. Despite their embrace of segregation, Indians could do little to transcend their disadvantaged economic place in southern society. This social ambiguity and economic subordination stimulated political factions within the Indian community. These factions were characterized by varying philosophies on how best to maintain autonomy and affirm their Indian identity under dire economic circumstances. But given the enduring and powerful attachments to kinship and settlement that Indians exhibited, those political factions resonated with places, not just philosophies.

Between 1900 and 1930, Indians increasingly lost land through foreclosures. This land loss made the politics of place especially fierce. Land loss turned most rural Indian families into sharecroppers, but some Indians began to settle in the emerging railroad town of Pembroke. "Town" Indians acquired a lifestyle that augmented their income and encouraged further cooperation with the local whites who governed the town and county. The "progressive" values that town Indians asserted appealed to whites and positioned town Indians to have greater influence in the group's affairs. But rural, or "swamp," Indians had little contact with whites and continued to organize their social interaction around kin and settlement. Addie was likely very surprised, then, that her own People would reject her based on her inability to pay; "on the swamp," Indians helped one another more freely. This division, exacerbated by the economic realities of segregation, influenced how and with whom Indians negotiated for federal recognition. An identity as a "tribe," distinct from their identities as a People and a race, thus emerged from the process of recognition by governments. But the dialogue between age-old internal priorities and local external circumstances also shaped tribal identity.

In Robeson County's Jim Crow economy, Indians and blacks could not occupy certain jobs that included standard wages and contributed to more available cash and access to consumer goods. Manufacturing, in particular, was one sector where nonwhites rarely occupied positions that paid hourly wages or salaries. Indians had access to nonfarm occupations only through entrepreneurship, preaching, and the public schools. Other than teaching, such "public jobs" included positions in small businesses or, later, as members of a school's custodial or cafeteria staff. In the 1930s some relief work finally became available to Indians, which will be discussed in chapter 5.[5] Thus, Indians competed intensely for the few jobs that were available outside of farm work. Competition created by segregation resulted in economic and social tensions that had profound implications for both the Indian community's leadership structure and their economic divisions.

OVER THE PREVIOUS CENTURIES of settlement and development in the swampy territory around the Lumber River, Indians constructed a decentralized and temporary leadership pattern. Achieving a tribal organization promised to be difficult in this context. Extensive swamps separated communities that kinship linked and common concerns occasionally brought together, such as the congressional petition for recognition discussed in chapter 1. An Indian's sense of "Indianness" stemmed first from his family and locality and second from the group as a whole. At the end of the nineteenth century, their identity as a People did not reside in a governmental body that exercised influence over all group members. Rather, particular issues and particular leaders stimulated an Indian's sense of identification with the group. Indians looked to a variety of individuals as sources of authority on different issues, while several institutions—including lodges, school committees, and churches—often served as political forums.

Attached as they were to kin, to church, and to settlement, Indian leaders pulled apart more often than they pulled together on many issues. Leadership was individualistic and entrepreneurial, heavily influenced by family or personal charisma. Having no single spokesperson, Indians tolerated a wide diversity of opinion within the community, and tribal members placed great emphasis on respect for the opinions of family patriarchs and matriarchs, as well as pastors and teachers. Each community had its own set of acknowledged leaders who influenced individual conduct, religious doctrine, voting, school admission, employment, and a host of other issues. Leaders routinely challenged one another's authority. Though not strictly hereditary, some families held status as "leading families" for several generations.[6] Overall, the words "decentralized" and "contested" best described Indian leadership.

Yet despite the situational nature of leadership, the community's segregated social institutions brought Indians together across kin boundaries and gave some Indians greater political influence, both within and outside the community. For example, the Red Men's Lodges assembled settlement residents to discuss community matters. The Red Men's Lodges, which were fraternal organizations, developed around the turn of the twentieth century and exercised political and social influence. The lodges monitored social behavior. One Robeson County resident remembered that the lodges discouraged dating and marriage between Indians and non-Indians. They called mass meetings and held fund-raisers for causes such as education and federal recognition. Prior to the 1930s, the lodges sponsored political-strategy sessions to bring Indian concerns to the federal and state governments.[7]

Indian-only institutions like the Red Men's Lodges served as one kind of internal political structure, while schools provided a level of organization that also affected external events, especially local and state elections. School committees, for example, were composed of several leading men in an Indian settlement, initially appointed by the Robeson County Board of Education and then replaced by committee members themselves. Appointments were often made at the recommendation of other influential Indians. The school committee directly controlled the flow of resources from county government to the Indian settlements and depended heavily on segregation politics.

The committees made some Indian leaders more powerful than others and encouraged a patronage system within the group. With their ability to make employment decisions, school committees controlled the economic fortunes of Indian families and ostracized those who disagreed with their decisions. They also influenced votes for county and state elections, and white politicians depended on them to bring in Indian votes. Conversely, Indian voters appealed to their local school committeemen for help in finding a job, solving a legal conflict with local officials, or digging a drainage ditch on their farms. In exchange for assistance, committeemen expected Indians to follow the leader on election day.[8] The connections between Indian school committees and white county or state government officials gave them particular success in both granting favors to other Indians and securing support for white candidates.

Like their black and white neighbors, Indians envisioned education as the great economic equalizer under the "progressive" politics of the early twentieth century, which promoted better schools for every child, regardless of race. Such a platform made embracing segregation logical and attractive since Democrats did not separate segregation and schooling as political issues. Although Indian teachers did provide superior education for some of their students under segregation, improved literacy and math skills did not seem to advance economic gain. After 1900, Democrats in North Carolina adopted a regressive tax system that was based not on the "progressive" ideal but on the idea that one should receive benefits from the state in accordance to what one contributes. In reality, the poor were taxed at a higher rate than the rich, but the state justified low allocations of funding to nonwhite education by arguing that it was simply cheaper to run nonwhite schools; counties spent less money on teacher salaries and facilities for Indians and blacks. Disfranchised, blacks had no means to protest politically, and though Indians could vote, viable candidate alternatives were few and far between. Furthermore, Democrats had already warned Indians that their schools would be dismantled if they objected to the Democratic program. To shore up their power, Democratic "progressives" depended on black disfranchisement and on their ability to convince Indian and poor white voters that absolute gains from generation to generation in education improved those voters' welfare, even though they were not receiving an equal education. But "this notion fundamentally mistakes the nature and function of education in a competitive society," historian J. Morgan Kousser writes. "In the struggle for jobs, or, more broadly, increased economic welfare, it is relative, not absolute, levels of education that count." It mattered little that an Indian had a better education than his father if he was competing for jobs against a white of the same generation; that white person was unarguably better prepared because the state allocated more resources to white education.[9]

Indians' sacrifices for education did not mean greater economic empowerment, even though Indian leaders profited politically. They allied with white Democrats to promote the belief that educational improvement meant elevated standards of living for the community. Rural Indians felt these inequalities keenly, especially when they confronted the improved educational opportunities that town Indians held. Because the structural problems that fostered inequality were so distant and obscure, eventually rural Indians turned their protest toward local town Indian leaders. Town schools received the greatest benefit from their leaders' connections with white Democrats, even though that benefit was marginal compared to what middle-class whites received. Teachers and school committeemen functioned in the Indian community as "double agents." Historians Glenda Gilmore and Adam Fairclough use this term to describe black teachers who appeased whites for the larger purpose of serving the black community, and Indian teachers were caught in the same trap. Their actions were a source of division among the Indian community. Some community members decried their apparent privilege and demanded tangible evidence of the benefit they brought to underprivileged Indians. Others applauded their cumulative achievements for Indian education and saw benefits in the political connections they distributed to others. In this climate, Indian leaders were often held responsible for discriminatory economic and social conditions that existed entirely independent of them, or they were given credit for gains to which they themselves did not contribute. The structure of education for Indians—but not of education itself—was a source of factional tension and identity during segregation.[10]

While influenced by questions of resource distribution under "progressive" white supremacy, Indian leadership patterns also helped to ensure some insulation from economic subordination for ordinary Indian people, giving the community a coherence despite decentralization and internal conflicts.

Indian life largely rested on the rhythms of subsistence-level agriculture. Indians also exercised immediate authority over other Indians, whether in the fields, in the classroom, or in the pews. This social structure had the effect of an overall feeling of equality among Indians, even among those of different economic fortunes; regardless of his own wealth, an Indian had kin or schoolmates or church members who were richer or poorer.[11] The economic pressures of segregation created social and economic distinctions within the Indian community, but one's standard of living and relative wealth had comparatively little influence on those distinctions, and a sense of themselves as a coherent people persisted.

What enabled a sense of coherence to continue even as economic distinctions flourished was that an Indian's livelihood depended on a variety of factors and not just on his family's status and wealth. Those factors included an Indian's place of residence, his own "rank" in the agricultural ladder, and his relative political influence among leaders. Just as Indians had created a dialogue between kinship and place to mark their identity, the economic dimensions of white supremacy prompted residence, rank, and leadership to exchange positions of importance in the quest to affirm Indian identity. No one was "rich," and few thought of themselves as "poor," but all acknowledged that there existed significant social differences within the Indian community. One's status as "middle class," a concept which emerged with the settlement of Pembroke and the economic limitations of the Jim Crow economy, had more to do with perception than reality.[12]

I remember learning about this element of Lumbee class structure one afternoon while riding in the car with my parents on one of our many, many journeys through Robeson County. My mother, who was born in 1943 in the Saint Annah community north of Pembroke, was describing how little her family had to eat sometimes and how she aspired to a middle-class standard of living because the large number of children in her family made it difficult to study, eat, sleep, and do everything else. She said that they were "poor," though she did not realize it until she was older and living away from Robeson County.

My father, who grew up in the New Hope community adjacent to Prospect and is ten years my mother's senior, responded, "But your father owned twenty-two acres of land! He was on the school committee!" My father's father, on the other hand, did not own any land of his own until my father was an adult; and though he was a teacher, he had a controversial relationship with the Pembroke school committee, having been fired on at least one occasion for disagreeing with a committee decision. My mother said that his father's income as a schoolteacher made all the difference in his family's standard of living. (My father and uncle had cars, for example, and my father was one of five children who were raised in a large house with electricity; my mother grew up in a house that had two rooms and no electricity until the 1960s; it was home to twelve children and several grandchildren.) My father felt that, despite my mother's relatively poor living conditions and his relatively middle-class conditions, her family had more power and influence than his did and were thus of a "better class."

But despite these distinctions, which are very meaningful when Indians speak to other Indians, the Indian community's class demarcations blur when you look at the big picture. Both my parents had a lot in common economically. My mother's twenty-two acres was hardly enough to feed a family of fourteen; the fact that her father owned it impacted her daily life only in that they didn't have to move around from farm to farm, renting or sharecropping. Landownership didn't seem to give her a lot of status in her own settlement. She used to tell me that the neighbors would gossip about her family—what an odd bunch they were, how many children and how little they had. But she knew her family had more than many. Both my parents spent a lot of days out of school because they had to take care of younger siblings, do household chores, or plow or harvest crops. The outspokenness of my father's father did not make his children's lives any easier when they did go to school. Both of my parents worked in their own family's fields and for other families in the community's reciprocal-exchange network. Sometimes they were paid for this work, and sometimes they were not. They did it because families helped one another. Each family appeared to have different standards of living, but in fact memory and perception drove my parents' different class status; economic and social coherence prevailed in the Indian community.

Prior to the segregation era, Indians had largely avoided internal competition and differentiation by focusing their economic resources on opportunities that sustained their kinship networks: subsistence farming, seasonal wage work in the turpentine and lumber industries, and land ownership. Before 1900, swampland pervaded Indian settlements; whites did not compete for this land because they saw it as untenable for farming. Typically, whites settled on higher ground suitable for cash crops, while Indians held title to low-lying land that they farmed according to the seasonal rhythms of swamp floods. Before Reconstruction and the agricultural transitions that took place in the South, Indians did not use farming to build capital to invest in farm improvements, farm equipment, and the like. Rather than focusing on profit, subsistence and maintaining the ability to stay on the land was the main priority. In addition to farming corn and other vegetables, Indians also harvested fish and game from the swamps and timber from forests in their area.[13]

Young men and some women worked for part of the year on the county's massive turpentine plantations, and some took their families to other states and worked there. Turpentine provided the closest occupation to wage labor for Indians and blacks in Robeson County. Some Indians used the income gained from turpentining to advance their educational opportunities. For Rev. J. J. Blanks, who aspired to become a teacher, turpentine work funded his schooling almost entirely. Writing in the third person, Blanks reminisced, "[H]e had to chip boxes morning and evening to pay his way" for two months of school, at the conclusion of which his father decided to help him pay his board. But according to their deal, Blanks had to furnish his own clothes; he went "into the woods . . . and dipped turpentine enough to purchase his clothing" and then attended school for another two months. To pay for his intermittent four months of schooling, Blanks likely worked in turpentine for over a year.[14]

Blanks and his coworkers obtained turpentine with backbreaking labor. They cut a box-shaped cavity into a pine tree during the winter months, "chipping" between seventy-five and 100 trees per day. Through the summer and into November, the sap collected in the box. Periodically during the summer and fall, Blanks collected sap from the box, likely working between 600 and 1,200 trees daily on a 10,000-tree plantation. Other workers distilled the sap into turpentine. As profitable as the industry was for owners and for Indians who could transform its wages into better opportunities, the industry steadily declined in North Carolina, and workers who refused to travel with it had to find land or labor on another farm.[15]

Some Indians continued to work in turpentine, and, in the process, they recrafted their identity as a People. For example, in the 1890s a group of approximately 100 Indians migrated from Robeson County to Bulloch County, Georgia, to work in the industry. Without Robeson County Indian settlements and extended kinship networks to bond them together, they perpetuated an identity as a People by establishing regular contact with home and creating an Indian-only school and church. They embraced Georgia's segregation and mimicked tactics their relatives in North Carolina used. In this case, kinship and place identifiers could change to accommodate a new circumstance, but Indians did not lose a sense of themselves as a People. In fact, that tie was so strong that almost thirty years later, Indians left Bulloch County and returned to Robeson, where most of their descendants live today. Other Indians, such as my great-grandmother Malinda Brooks Chavis, migrated as individuals to work in turpentine. Some never returned, and today their descendants are not Lumbee; but most went back and forth between work in other states and home in Robeson County.[16]

Indians who did not leave for work typically aspired to own their own farm. Landownership was widespread but not universal among Indians in the nineteenth and early twentieth centuries. Significantly, owning land reinforced the markers of kinship and reciprocity. In the Indian community, families often had economic security even when they did not own land themselves. The adult children and grandchildren of Indian landowners worked their parents' farm cooperatively, and sometimes they purchased land from the head of the household or from aunts and uncles. Even as cash-crop farming and sharecropping began to take over the Robeson County economy, Indians found a way to keep their cooperative farming intact. Fathers and uncles rented to sons and nephews, and children worked alongside parents. Keeping land and labor within the family may have been a way for the community to maintain women's authority, even though the matrilineal system of descent had disappeared. White males controlled banks, auction markets, access to credit, farm supply stores, and every other economic institution a farm family needed to get through the year. Whites expected to negotiate with Indian men, and men increasingly dominated the family's economic decision making. But continuing the ethic of sharing and reciprocity carved out a place for women's continued influence. Families shared labor and farm equipment between relatives and neighbors, and they shared food as well. With their vital work in the vegetable garden, women provided for the extended family and the settlement's elders. Some families grew more than enough to feed themselves in order to have a surplus to redistribute.[17] By the 1930s, a typical Indian farm had most of its acreage in cash crops—cotton and corn—with a few acres in wheat and oats and an acre for a vegetable garden to feed the family. Many farmers had small tobacco allotments as well. Women and children also earned income by raising chickens and selling their eggs, and women prepared for the winter months by canning and preserving vegetables and fruit.[18]

Landowning had even deeper meanings in the Indian world. Robeson County was their homeland, and to paraphrase anthropologist Karen Blu, landowning, more than a means of livelihood, was an end in itself. Owning land took precedence over the money that could be made from the land. For example, James E. Chavis bought a twenty-acre farm in 1933 and admitted to a government agent that his land "was not so good as other, more expensive places" in other parts of the county.[19] This land was not the best—not even good enough to feed his family—but the farm sold at a price Chavis could afford and gave him a material stake in the community.

Typically, landowners in the 1930s owned small parcels of five to ten acres. Some Indians dedicated a large portion of their income to buying land, even small amounts, in order to preserve their connection with past and future generations. When Indian agent Fred A. Baker spoke to Indians about the possibility of owning land under the Pembroke Farms resettlement project in the 1930s (discussed in chapters 4 and 5), he was startled at the over-whelming response he received: "Many of the old people could not restrain their feelings—tears filled many eyes and flowed down furrowed cheeks. We must confess to the fact that our own feelings were deeply touched as the old people expressed so deep a longing to have a piece of land on which they could live in peace without fear of ejectment by a landlord."[20] Owning land in Robeson County was an important part of how Indians identified one another and how Indians maintained their identity over time. With land, one could always provide a place for one's children to grow up, for one's grandchildren and great-grandchildren to identify as the "homeplace." On their own land, Indians could nurture and preserve their values.

Landholding by itself did not insulate an Indian family from an economy shaped by segregation. In 1935 about 200 Indian families owned land, but only twenty-five of these were "independent farmers" who had "money in the bank." One of these was Chesley Locklear, a farmer in the Saint Annah com-munity near Pembroke. Maggie Oxendine, who knew the family well, told me that everyone called him "Rich Chesley Locklear." He had enough land to support several Indian tenant farmers. He lived in a six-room brick house— the only one of its kind outside of Pembroke—and he drove a Lincoln Zephyr instead of a mule and wagon. Chesley took in several of his wife Mary's rela-tives as house servants, who worked in exchange for room and board. One of Chesley Locklear's house servants was my grandmother Bloss, Mary's niece, who spent almost all of her childhood there while my great-grandmother Malinda worked in the turpentine camps in Georgia. I never spoke to my grandmother about her time at Uncle Chesley's, but my mother has talked about it as a lonely time in Bloss's life, during which she was treated as an or-phan. While my grandmother was clearly there to clean house, raise children, cook, and help Aunt Mary, there are indications that she was not regarded as a some sort of indentured servant; she was allowed to go to school and com-plete her education, and when she fell in love and married at age sixteen, no one prevented her from doing so and leaving.[21]

Although owning a little land may have reassured Indians that their livelihood and identity would persist, owners still faced financial uncertainty similar to that of tenant farmers and farm laborers. Most Indians who worked in agriculture found themselves dependent on credit, living in substandard housing, and facing economic discrimination. Creditors foreclosed Nathaniel Dial's sixty-acre farm in 1935 for a $2,000 debt, on which he owed 10 percent interest (4 percent over the legal rate). Dial was simply unlucky enough to get in debt to the wrong lender, for whom "nothing would satisfy the debt except the land." In fact, this lender made a regular habit of buying Indian farmers' debts and foreclosing on their farms.[22] Farmers typically paid 20 to 25 percent more than the cash price on items they bought on credit. Credit imprisoned farmers all over Robeson County and enriched local white merchants, who also often acted as landlords. These merchants increased their land holdings by foreclosing on indebted farmers. The McNair Corporation, for example, notoriously foreclosed on farmers who got into debt with them, and the company acquired a large amount of land in Robeson County this way. Landowners did not escape financial difficulties, although ownership reassured most families that they would be able to save something for their offspring, and owners typically had more control over their labor and their economic future. Landowning families also relied heavily on loans and credit for supplies such as fertilizer and farm equipment.[23]

A decline in Indian-owned land in the decades after 1900, due to bank foreclosures, drove Indians into sharecropping and reduced their economic opportunity as farmers. Government projects to drain the pervasive swampland made the largest impact on Indian landholding. As laws began to consolidate economic and political power in the hands of the white elite before the Civil War, the state of North Carolina confiscated any land whose owner had not registered it in the deeds office and had not paid property taxes. In Robeson County, much of this confiscated land was Indian-owned swampland. The state drained the swamps, cut down trees, and sold the newly cleared, fertile land to the highest bidder. Widespread drainage occurred again between 1914 and 1918, when the U.S. Department of Agriculture drained the land around Back Swamp, south of Pembroke, at the behest of local white landowners. This drainage project affected nearly 33,000 acres of Indian-owned land. The government required Indian farmers to pay for the initial cost of ditching the portion of the swamp that ran through their land, as well as an annual maintenance fee for the ditch. Farmers who had no cash on hand took out loans to pay these expenses, with their land as collateral for the loans. When the agricultural depression hit in the early 1920s and crop prices dropped, Indian farmers fell behind on their loans and lost the land.[24]

Indians readily believed that the drainage projects just gave white land-lords and creditors another excuse to buy Indians' mortgage loans and fore-close on their farms. Indian landowner and teacher James E. Chavis named the responsible parties in an appeal to the Senate Committee on Indian Af-fairs: K. M. Biggs, Pates Supply Company, the McNair Company, and "various lawyers in Lumberton." "They take [Indian] homes, make out such papers as they please, go have them recorded and make the people move," Chavis complained. "I believe you can advise or help me," he wrote to Senate staff member A. A. Grorud. "I believe if we could have an impartial investigation by the relief administration it would bring to light some of the most deplor-able conditions and most crooked work done in the United States along this line." Doubtless many southern farmers of all races would have liked such an investigation in their communities, but Indians in Robeson County were beginning to recognize the unique potential of the federal government to ad-dress their problems as Indians.[25]

These episodes of land loss turned most Indian landholders into tenant farmers and sharecroppers. The 200 estimated Indian landowners in Robeson County were greatly outnumbered by the 1,800 tenant farmers. Tenant farm-ing was the most restrictive system; landlords controlled the farmer's labor and severely constrained his ability to produce a crop that could feed and clothe his family. Three kinds of tenant arrangements existed in Robeson County: renter, half-cropper, or third-cropper. A renter simply paid the land-lord a flat fee for his land every year rather than a percentage of the crop. Sharecroppers, on the other hand, made an arrangement with the landlord whereby the landlord provided certain things in exchange for a portion of the harvest. A third-cropper usually received a house for his family, tools, livestock, seed, and fertilizer from the landlord; then, at harvest time, the landlord kept two-thirds of the crop and the farmer kept one-third. A half-cropper usually received just a house, seed, and fertilizer from the landlord. The farmer owned his own tools and livestock and received half the crop at harvest time.[26]

Tenant farmers sometimes made a profit on their farms, but usually they were so deeply in debt that they had little to carry into the next year. A land-lord typically restricted the amount of food he permitted a sharecropper to raise so that the farmer could grow a maximum amount of cotton on the land. In some cases, the landlord exercised total authority over the family's labor; if he wanted the farmer to keep his children out of school to work, the farmer had to obey the landlord. Similarly, if a wife had tasks to do, such as canning or making clothes, and a landlord or overseer sent her to the field, she had to go. Consequently, families bought clothes and canned food on credit, which usually trapped them in peonage.[27]

The sharecropping system made it impossible for every individual in the agricultural market to participate equally. Landlords' practices—and sometimes their prejudices—made farmers vulnerable to their control. For example, landlords did not allow tenants to rotate crops; landlords wanted the most money from the land in the short term, and this farming method exhausted the soil's nutrients. Many tenant farmers did not have tobacco allotments, further reducing their ability to turn a profit. Tenant houses were often in poor repair. Some did not have windows, and perhaps ten or more people lived in a two- or three-room house. Diseases such as pellagra, pneumonia, and malaria were common, and some tenant families had only rags to wear. Ellen Jacobs, a third-cropper in the Red Banks community, produced an excellent cotton crop in 1935 for the Fletcher Plantation, but she had no shoes or stockings for herself or her children. One third-cropper on the Fletcher Plantation, however, cleared $700 in 1935; he had a ten-acre tobacco allotment. Farmers who paid cash to rent their land, rather than paying a portion of the crop, tended to have more disposable income. Clarence Lowry, for example, paid $3 per acre per year on fifty-five acres of land and made enough to purchase a car.[28]

As the Depression deepened in the early 1930s and crop prices dropped further, circumstances worsened for Indian tenants. President Franklin D. Roosevelt's New Deal agricultural programs implemented policies designed to bolster crop prices while mitigating overproduction, which New Deal policy makers blamed for the low prices. The Agricultural Adjustment Act (AAA) of 1933 mandated reduced crop production and total acreage farmed, which encouraged landlords to reduce their tenants' productivity and shore up their own income. Landlords restricted the amount of fertilizer a farmer could use and consequently diminished his crop yield. Indian third-croppers encountered difficulties obtaining a farm because landlords did not want to make the investment in tools and livestock for the farmer. Indian landowners also faced hardships due to the AAA. After the crop allotments of these landowners were reduced, officials at the local AAA office refused to make fair adjustments for farm size, and they then withheld refunds for overpayment of tax to punish farmers who tried to solve the problem by planting more than their stated crop allotment.[29]

Indian farmers also faced local competition from white and black farmers, dating back to the turn of the twentieth century. For example, in 1910 the Lumberton National Bank offered three prizes for the best corn in the county; the second year, Indians won all three prizes and the bank subsequently cancelled the contest, refusing to highlight Indian farmers' superior techniques. Some whites freely praised Indian farming skills but did not want to employ Indians as sharecroppers. One man said, "If you get an Indian on your place with mules, etc., working on halves, he really takes care of it and makes money for you. But I tell you this: I'd rather have a Nigger tenant because he knows his place and I can make him do as I please, but you can't do an Indian that way." This attitude became even more harmful starting in the late 1920s, when white-owned merchant-landholding companies, such as the McNair Corporation, began traveling to other tobacco-farming counties in North Carolina and inviting white tenant farmers to come to Robeson County. A superintendent at McNair's claimed that they brought in white farmers because they could "drive a better bargain" with them than with Indians. Even though the county's large population already made sharecropping places competitive, white landlords believed that recruiting additional tenants would force Indians to negotiate yearly contracts in the landlords' favor. Further, landlords may have simply preferred to give needy white families jobs during the Depression. Tobacco allotments were taken from Indians and given to whites, and landowners simply dispossessed some Indians entirely.[30]

As bad as the economic future looked for Indian landowners and sharecroppers, farm laborers probably faced the most difficult day-to-day circumstances. Many sharecroppers who failed to get farms in the 1930s became day laborers. They supported large families for only six or eight months out of the year. Most laborers lived on the farm where they worked, making fifty cents per day, and only a few had a small garden of less than a quarter of an acre.[31] Lawrence Maynor, for example, was a thirty-three-year-old resident of the Philadelphus community north of Pembroke. He had a crippled leg, worked as a day laborer, and supported seven children. His letter to the commissioner of Indian Affairs demonstrates the plight of an Indian laborer and also reveals Indians' strategy for coping: "I need some Help in some way in which I can Live. I am trying to get some Help through the State or county But they puts me off and wont help me non[e] worthwhile. I am living on the other man's farm in an House not fit to Stay in."[32] Laborers like Lawrence Maynor probably faced the most dire economic circumstances among the Indian community in Robeson County. Not surprisingly, he and men like him sought assistance from the federal government to escape the economic ills under Jim Crow.

Just as Indians probably had someone in their family who struggled economically on the farm, they also were likely to be close to someone who earned a living in a trade or profession. Some Indians moved to Pembroke after the wave of land loss in the early 1920s and took advantage of the availability of education at the Normal School for their children and themselves. A new group of Indian teachers emerged, and the community schools quickly became overcrowded with teachers trying to use their kin and church connections to gain favor with the school committees. Segregation prevented Indians from teaching in non-Indian schools, and, consequently, "some who want[ed] appointments literally [paid] for the votes of the school [committee]." Educated Indians typically could not go into factories. Companies only made manufacturing jobs available to white workers, with the rare exception of John R. Lowry, who lived in Pembroke and drove to the larger town of Laurinburg for his job as superintendent of a flour mill. Similarly, whites dominated New Deal relief work. Some Indians opened small businesses such as garages, gas stations, and blacksmith shops. Income from these establishments and from teaching usually supplemented farming for Indians; a trade did not take the place of farming, even for Indians who lived in town. The middle class remained involved in agriculture—although their income from professions may have been better—because one's siblings and cousins continued to farm. Mixed incomes from farming and teaching not only sustained tradition; it also elevated the family's standard of living. James E. Chavis, for example, bought his farm with his teaching income. Other Indians used teaching to build houses, buy cars, or pay for their children's education.[33]

In the two decades prior to 1930, the town of Pembroke increasingly became a focus for Indians who aspired to a better lifestyle. The town was built in 1895 at a north-south and east-west railroad crossing. Initially white residents dominated the town, and they insisted on keeping control out of the hands of the surrounding Indian population. Despite political restrictions, the town became the center of Indian educational activities after the Indian Normal School relocated there in 1909. Soon it developed into the only town in Robeson County where one could patronize an Indian-owned business, such as a dry cleaner or a movie theater.[34] Families began moving closer into town to take advantage of the school there. Rev. Tommy Swett, for example, a minister in the Lumbee Holiness Methodist Conference, used his church connections to H. H. Lowry, the conference founder, to buy land near Pembroke. He moved his family from the Rowland area so that his children could go to school in Pembroke.[35] Pembroke had a reputation for having the best-funded and maintained Indian schools and churches in the county, and many families who lived outside the town limits sent their children to the public schools there and identified themselves with Pembroke. In the tradition of contesting leadership, however, residents of Prospect, Union Chapel, and other older Indian communities disputed Pembroke's sense of itself as the "center" of things. They more often pointed to Pembroke's reputation as a violent community, where it was "not uncommon to see bodies in the street" as a result of violence related to personal feuds or bootlegging.[36]

Settlements outside Pembroke also made and sold illegal liquor. Indians in Robeson County had a reputation throughout the South for moonshining. One author estimated that there were more illicit stills in Robeson County than anywhere else in the country. As one federal agent reported, "We could go to the Lumber River and chop up ten to twelve stills on any afternoon. . . . They were lined up beside the road. I had never seen moonshining in western North Carolina carried out to that extent." To make more money, Indian moonshiners formed a network and pooled their whiskey in cooperative fashion to sell in large quantities. They then split the profits. While this income could mean greater political influence and wealth, it did not necessarily create a social hierarchy in those settlements. For some, distilling alcohol meant survival. Widows and single women, in particular, made liquor to support their children. Other families with land parcels under forty or fifty acres— the minimum amount needed to run a self-sufficient farm—made and sold alcohol to supplement their income.[37]

Bootlegging has always been a much-discussed phenomenon in the community, but little has been written to document it or its effects. I started asking questions and learned that for some Indians, bootlegging or moonshining brought the same "extras" to a family that public jobs brought. Some bootleggers acquired significant property holdings; they diversified their business by renting farms to Indian sharecroppers and owning gas stations and cafés. Others invested their profits back into their farms, purchasing advanced machinery or more land. Bootleggers may have exercised political influence as well by using their money to back political candidates directly or funneling money through relatives who had political connections and influence in both the Indian and white communities. They reportedly also gave money and land to churches, earning an instant and powerful, if not widely acknowledged, following within the church congregation.[38]

Certainly, bootleggers could hamper projects they did not want, even when whites initiated them. For example, one member of the Brooks Settlement told me about his ancestor Dockery Brooks, a landowner and bootlegger who halted the construction of Highway 74 through the settlement in the 1920s.

When the state government tried to obtain his land for the highway's right-of-way, he refused to sell out, and no amount of pressure changed his mind. Finally, a government agent took advantage of his reputation as a bootlegger and planted whiskey underneath his house; authorities subsequently arrested him for illegally selling liquor. He went to jail for a year, during which time the state went to court and confiscated his land to build the highway. Bootlegging may have given Brooks an advantage over his fellow farmers: he did not have to go deeply into debt to operate his farm, and he knew he would not lose his land to an unpaid debt. But Brooks's bootlegging gave the government another way to take his land, essentially using his own power against him.[39]

Bootlegging's gateway to a better standard of living did not make the enterprise a route to membership in the town community of Pembroke. Some of the most powerful bootleggers in the Brooks Settlement, or in more rural communities like Shannon and Saddletree, stayed in those communities and did not move to Pembroke. Their own settlements and the white community felt their influence, but they did not believe themselves to be connected to the Pembroke professional class. The power that bootleggers wielded, however, signaled that class status within the Indian community hinged on more than power, wealth, and lifestyle. Being "middle class" also centered around "progressive" values and proximity to the town of Pembroke.

In contrast to the bootleggers, the law-abiding Indian population of Pembroke endeavored to maintain a reputation as a temperate, pious, thrifty, and, above all, "progressive" community. These values prepared Indians for participation in the Jim Crow economy, where whites set the standard for achievement. The rules for students at the Normal School embodied these values. "The school seeks to encourage each student to form the best habits, cultivate uprightness of character and conduct, and to give due attention to spiritual adjustments and relations in life," according to the school's 1935–36 catalog. School officials dismissed students who got drunk, broke any civil laws, left campus without permission, or participated "in any unwarranted criticism of the policy of this institution." Furthermore, they expelled "any student known to associate himself or herself with parties or places which would cast reflection on the institution."[40] Like the African American progressives of this era, Indians surely thought that whites interpreted their behavior as a reflection of their capability and fitness for advancement in society. Educational institutions passed this precept on to younger generations, particularly to those from other Indian settlements who had had less contact with whites.[41]

Indians who adopted a middle-class identity in values and lifestyle presented an image that they thought would be acceptable to whites. Depicting Indian people as "progressive" had become, by the 1930s, a powerful way to articulate Indian identity to non-Indians. Segregation and racial subordination made white middle-class values the ideal to which some Indians aspired; those Indians believed that appealing to white values helped them escape white prejudice. White values, coincidentally, also reinforced the ethic of self-reliance on which most Indian families depended to earn a living on the farm. In this way, the Indian middle class did not lose its sense of itself as connected to other Indians. Rather, the Indian middle class saw itself as leading the Indian people in a direction toward greater autonomy and freedom from white control.[42]

The future of the Indian people as a whole mattered more to the middle class as Indians became increasingly characterized as a "tribe." A tribe needed leaders, and from the perspective of the goals of town Indians, this tribe needed leaders who had friendly, rather than antagonistic, relationships with the whites in power. The Pembroke leadership that emerged in the 1930s derived their power from older sources of Indian identity: schools and churches. However, they channeled that power in new directions. Rather than using their influence to uphold an Indian identity based on kinship and settlement, they used it to address the challenges that a segregated economy and social subordination posed to Indian identity. Those challenges placed Indians in a second-class position relative to whites, and the Pembroke middle class refocused their articulation of Indian identity around proving that they were equal to whites. White values, then, became the standard to which they appealed; increasingly, white ideas about society and who Indians ought to be became the basis for an Indian identity. While Indian leaders enhanced Indian autonomy and strengthened identity through these values and the Indian-only institutions they supported, their success in having their Indian identity recognized ultimately depended on whether their appeal to white values worked.

As it had been in the nineteenth century, the church and church leadership were focal points of this "progressive" awareness. In the 1930s or 1940s, my Uncle Mike Cummings told me, a delegation from the Burnt Swamp Baptist Association (BSBA) visited the Baptist State Convention of North Carolina to ask permission to join. My uncle is a Baptist preacher himself, now the director of the BSBA, and he also served as president of the state convention. He knew the men who went to the convention and heard from them what happened. BSBA was the only association of Indian Baptists in the state and was a cornerstone of the Robeson County Indian community. The Baptist State Convention was a committed whites-only organization, but these men petitioned the convention for inclusion to increase their institutional networks. The convention agreed to extend Christian fellowship to Indians on the condition that they be careful "not to embarrass the Convention." Uncle Mike said, "Those of us now that hear that statement feel like it has everything to do with the fact that [Indians] are different, we look different, we are different. . . . [A]t that time [we] may not [have been] as well educated or not as affluent." Even now, the convention's paternalism stings Indian preachers whose "progressive" values make them no less Indian.[43]

Pembroke's small Indian "power structure" epitomized this relationship between segregation and leadership. Pembroke hosted a special group of leaders in the 1930s, 1940s, and 1950s who lived on Fourth Street, one block off the town's main street. The "Fourth Street Power Structure" included James C. "Sonny" Oxendine (a business owner and mayor of Pembroke in the 1940s), Clarence E. Locklear (a Baptist minister and mayor of Pembroke in the 1940s), John R. Lowry (superintendent of a flour mill in Laurinburg), James R. Lowry (dean of the Normal School), Martin Luther Lowry (a Holiness Methodist minister and member of the Normal School's Board of Trustees), Lonnie W. Jacobs (a Baptist minister and member of the school's Board of Trustees), and Elmer T. Lowry (principal of Pembroke High School in the 1940s). Doctor Fuller Lowry, a Methodist minister, teacher, postmaster, and member of the Normal School's Board of Trustees, did not live on Fourth Street but might be counted among the number of influential, middle-class Indians in Pembroke.

The Fourth Street Power Structure is my own term to describe groups of men who ran things locally. These men all had the power to make or break another Indian's leadership efforts. When Dakota anthropologist Ella Deloria visited Robeson County, she described perfectly what members of a power structure do. For example, of Martin Luther Lowry she observed: "Everyone says or implies that until he is for anything, it can't go, because he can make or mar a thing simply by backing it or bucking it." Such individual power came partly from family connections (five of the eight men were grandsons or great-grandsons of Allen Lowry) but also from their involvement in serving the community through its churches and schools. These men also embodied the trend of middle-class migration to Pembroke; the Lowrys' home settlement was Hopewell, south of Pembroke, and L. W. Jacobs, Sonny Oxendine, and C. E. Locklear also came from outside the Pembroke area. But kinship and place receded in importance as these men established a new power base and source of identity in Pembroke. My father remembers this group and identified them as the ones who "generally ran things around Pembroke."[44]

These eight men embodied "progressive" values and middle-class wealth, and they commanded followings, whether through preaching, employment in business or the schools, or elected office. Their followers based their allegiance on the economic realities of segregation. If an Indian wanted a public job, he had to obey the rules set down by Jim Crow. Segregation mandated that Indians only work at certain jobs in specific places, and these men held the keys to many of those sources of income. D. F. Lowry, in particular, was well connected with white politicians and lawyers in Lumberton, the county seat and home of the local white "power structure." He was also a political protégé of Angus W. McLean, a Lumberton lawyer and North Carolina's governor from 1925 to 1929. This relationship to McLean, who believed that Robeson County Indians had Cherokee, not Croatan, ancestry, embedded Lowry in the efforts to recognize Robeson County's Indians as Cherokees in the early part of the twentieth century. Those who came to support a Cherokee designation in the 1930s and 1940s identified most closely with this group of Pembroke leaders, who had developed a symbiotic relationship with local whites which linked Indian votes for Democrats with state funding to the schools that provided one source of the leaders' power.[45]

Other Pembroke leaders, however, equally identified with the values of the middle class but rejected the idea that cooperating with local whites would gain Indian autonomy. They did not hold such politically sensitive occupations as the men of the Fourth Street Power Structure, but they nevertheless placed value on education and civic duty and aspired to earning comfortable livings for their families. Men such as Joseph Brooks, Chesley Locklear, and James E. Chavis would come to lead the Siouan movement. They viewed local whites as political adversaries, and whites therefore excluded them from their patronage. And unlike the Fourth Street Power Structure, Brooks, Locklear, and Chavis held no obvious authority within the community's Indian social institutions. Their power derived from the settlements lying outside of Pembroke—from Indians who maintained kinship as a basis for identity. Regardless of how it affected their relations with whites, these men believed that an improvement in Indians' economic situation could only be achieved under Indian leadership and with full Indian autonomy. They inherited, in some ways, the vision of the Holiness Methodist leader H. H. Lowry, and they followed in the footsteps of their ancestors, who consistently rejected association with blacks and whites. But their vision for Indian autonomy still depended on whites—just not the local ones who promoted segregation. These Indian leaders needed the favor of white policy makers and legislators in Washington, D.C. While their power flowed from an older marker of Indian identity, they used their power to transform the basis of Indian identity beginning in the 1930s.

In the 1930s in Robeson County, one could find as many wealthy, well-educated Indians who resented white intrusion into their community affairs as wealthy Indians who cooperated eagerly with whites. Likewise, poor Indians took up both sides. The Indian middle class did not cohere ideologically on the issue of tribal identity, federal recognition, and segregation, however much they may have agreed on the values of education and respectability. The factions that developed within the leadership in the 1930s indicated that town leaders constituted a different class unto themselves, one defined by their influence both within and outside of the Indian community. Class formation in the Indian community hinged on place and power, not solely on ideology or wealth.

Indians who lived in areas more distant from Pembroke had little contact with these leaders and likely mistrusted their self-styled leadership. Rural Indians did not automatically identify with the middle class simply because these men considered themselves to be their leaders. Instead, they continued to call on settlement leaders closer to home, who, regardless of their wealth, may not have considered themselves part of the middle class around Pembroke. The emergence of a middle class and of Pembroke as a predominately Indian town precipitated a new kind of division in the larger Indian community. Rather than pinning one's identity to a settlement, school, and church, the 1930s heralded a new identity boundary: a political, not simply place-based, division between town and rural Indians. Indians based this division partly on wealth but also on access to whites' power and influence. While many town Indians sought cooperation with whites, rural Indians continued to adhere to old suspicions and to identify closely with families and settlements. Landowners, bootleggers, and other wealthier Indians in places such as Saddletree, Prospect, and the Brooks Settlement looked for leaders other than those they found in the Pembroke middle class.[46]

Beginning in the 1930s, the existence of this leadership class within the Indian community began to affect the ways in which Indians identified themselves to one another and to outsiders. The leaders' dependence on white favor, whether local or national, began to shift the identity discussion away from kin, settlement, and Indian social institutions and toward the issue of a tribal name, a tribal history, and a tribal government. As the economic discrimination inherent in racial segregation intensified, claims of Indian ancestry became increasingly important. Negotiations between the leadership class and local and national powers—who demanded that an Indian group identify itself a certain way to receive its due recognition—hastened these developments.

The photographs in Figures 4 and 5 are of the same man. Someone, however—perhaps the photographer, an archivist, or an anthropologist—has
given the man different labels. In blood he is "mixed," in name he is "Croatan." How do we know which label is right? Can they *both* be right?

In 1911 many Robeson County Indians viewed neither label as correct
descriptors of their identity. Labels presented classificatory challenges, especially for the professional "outsiders" charged with speculating on Indian
identities. A host of choices had been made for me as a historian before I
found these photographs. Apparently, no one recorded the subject's personal
name, and only a little effort went into defining other aspects of his identity,
ancestry, and tribal affiliation. It seems that the subject himself had no input
into the choice of labels. But who else did the choosing?

In fact, this man may have been the first Indian from Robeson County
that anthropologist John R. Swanton ever met. Swanton was a noted expert
on Southeastern Indians. In 1933 he recalled, "My first encounter with a
Robeson County Indian was in the office of Mr. Mooney a few years before
his death. He called me in on this occasion, pointed to a tall swarthy individual standing near and asked me if I did not clearly recognize the Indian
features."[1] In 1911, when these photographs were taken, James Mooney was
the leading anthropological authority on North American Indians and had
written several reports on Robeson County Indians.[2]

This gentleman might have presented himself at Mooney's office door in
the Smithsonian Institution. His name was Aaren Spencer Locklear, editor

FIGURE 4. "Portrait of Man (Mixed Blood)," by Delancey W. Gill, Washington, D.C., January 1911 (National Anthropological Archives, Smithsonian Institution [NAA INV 06194800])

FIGURE 5. "Profile of Croatan Man," by Delancey W. Gill, Washington, D.C., January 1911 (Human Studies Film Archives, Smithsonian Institution [BAD GN 866 B])

and publisher of Pembroke's only Indian newspaper at that time, the *Indian Observer*. Surely his three-piece suit, silk cravat, and pocketed pen made as much an impression as his Indian features. He may have simply looked to engage Mooney as a fellow teacher and scholar, expecting a lively and learned chat about Indian history. Locklear wasn't simply an "Indian," a "mixed blood," or a "Croatan." Although we know nothing for certain about what he intended in presenting himself this way, we can also look to what he didn't do for some clues. He didn't borrow a headdress, buckskins, moccasins, and face paint for the occasion. He might have therefore intended to assert his similarities with the men he met in Washington, D.C., not his differences. He was not a stereotype, a mimic, or a minstrel.[3]

Mooney had concluded that Robeson County Indians were of "mixed blood," as many other Indians were; he wrote as much in reports to the Office of Indian Affairs (OIA). But the day Locklear presented himself, Mooney called Swanton into his office to show him what a "real Indian" looked like. Perhaps Mooney then summoned photographer Delancey Gill to record the man's looks for posterity. Mooney and Swanton's politics of knowledge included the idea that Indians could be tribally Indians with distinct identities and still have "mixed" ancestry. Yet, even as they recognized this complexity, these and other scholars created labels and terms that implied fixed and discrete categories of identity. Congressmen in turn used those tools to uphold white supremacy in the South.

As a Lumbee, I have no doubt that I have ancestors from the Americas, Europe, and Africa. In a modern world of DNA testing, I might even be able to find out what proportion of my ancestors come from these places. Would knowing damage my identity as an Indigenous person, or would it have damaged Locklear's identity? I doubt it, because one cannot easily equate "mixed-blood" or "mixed-race" ancestry with a group identity. But names are part of this alchemy of identity as well. Blood and names are linked in the political realm, when having identity conversations with outsiders; but insiders separate them easily. "Insider" discussions of identity and authenticity do not originate with tribal names, nor do they change only because a name alters. But "outsider" discussions of identity and authenticity can vary quite a bit as tribal names change.

In these photographs, we meet the "outsiders"—photographer, anthropologists, and archivists—and the "insiders," represented by the man photographed. Each group was distinguished not so much by their differences in dress, ethnic origin, or class status but by the categories of knowledge they used to interpret the other. "Outsiders" typically relied on relatively abstract, fixed notions in explaining the Indians they encountered. Anthropologists saw a tribal name, a culture, and physical features that matched a class or type of person. White supremacists, some at the local level and others in Congress, saw ancestry, place, and proper expectations constructed to support their own power. "Insiders" interpreted their worlds through an experiential and situational lens; where a person was from and who his people were all spoke to the relationships that person had and informed the actions that revealed how identity was formed. In these photos, a Lumbee might see someone prosperous and knowledgeable—perhaps a bit amused at the exercise of ethnographic photography but also aware that he is representing his People in a forum of knowledge that will have a profound effect on their political and economic fortunes. A Lumbee might see a moment of opportunity, a strategic window to garner greater political and economic authority and autonomy in the world of Jim Crow. Even though a Lumbee historian is both inside and outside, what I see is only part of the picture; there is so much about the past that we don't know. Identity formation is a process that in some ways mirrors the historian's process, identifying and mediating a conversation between the insiders and the outsiders.

FOR SOME OUTSIDERS, the social order that names and categories produced was racially segregated, with whites making the decisions for blacks and Indians. North Carolina state senator Hamilton McMillan had introduced "Croatan" to help protect the political future of the white-supremacist Democratic Party in 1885. Croatan explicitly referenced a history of Europeans mixing with Natives on the wild shores of Roanoke Island. Even Democrats thought the state of North Carolina should be proud of this experience and give this People a unique name and their own schools. Later, Indians retained the right to vote when their black neighbors, who were probably equally racially mixed, were denied that right. For whites in the late nineteenth century, mixed racial ancestry was not the hinge on which this door to white privilege opened and closed. Nor should it be the hinge on which our own door to understanding identity opens and closes. Identity, not ancestry, was the category of experience that needed definition so that white supremacists could use it properly to their advantage. At first, Croatan connoted a certain degree of inclusion in the privileges of whiteness, but such inclusion did not mean that whites treated them as equals.

After blacks had been fully disfranchised, local whites moved to secure their superiority by shortening Indians' tribal name into a sneer—"Cro," or "the Cros."[4] "Jim Crow," the blackface minstrel character so popular throughout the nation in the nineteenth century, symbolized whites' perceptions of African American inferiority. That notion had triumphed in the South by 1910, and white and Indian voters made sure blacks remained powerless to challenge Jim Crow's social, political, and economic consequences at the ballot box. "Cro" explicitly referenced the mixing of white colonists with red peoples *and* black slaves. The name was local whites' way of banishing people who did not have supposedly "pure" white ancestry to the same caste, regardless of their cultural differences and identity distinctions or the history of whites' own partial acceptance of these same people. Some African Americans used Croatan as a racial slur—as did the previously mentioned young black man when he whispered to sociologist Guy Benton Johnson, "They ain't nothing but Croatans. But you better not let 'em hear you say that."[5] Despite local whites' insistence on grouping Indians and blacks together after 1900, both Indians and blacks recognized distinctions between themselves and acted accordingly; in this case, blacks also insisted on Indians' difference and inferiority. Jim Crow subjected everyone to some degree of disempowerment.

The 1910s witnessed the beginnings of the struggle over names and recognition among Indians in Robeson County, local whites, members of the

North Carolina legislature and U.S. Congress, and the staff at the OIA. In the political sector of identity discourse, Indians created internal factions to deal strategically with external notions of identity. These factions reproduced, in some ways, existing divisions and disagreements among a highly decentralized group. Indians engaged in this process of identity formation with full awareness of the power that whites held over them and with a simultaneous awareness of their own identity markers. Blood and name had contested meanings for scholars and local whites and blacks, but Indians also embraced those markers and manipulated them to their own ends. The leaders of Robeson County's Indian community perceived a different social order from that inscribed by the "Croatan" slur. They were not able to envision a world entirely without white supremacy, and to a degree they resigned themselves to work within its boundaries. But Indians also sought to hold whites accountable for the economic and educational disempowerment of Indians and to affirm their distinct history and identity as Indians, not simply as nonwhites.

Robeson County Indians responded to whites' misuse of the Croatan name with a political solution designed to take away local whites' power to make these classifications. They appealed to the state legislature, to the U.S. Congress, and to the OIA. This strategy used their voting power and attempted to position themselves as the authorities on their own identity. In the four decades between 1913 and 1953, Indians abandoned the Croatan designation and renamed themselves "Cherokee," "Siouan," and "Lumbee." Each name change reflected a political strategy, a difference of opinion, and a retelling of history, and both Indians and white politicians and bureaucrats engaged in the renaming. But the names did not reflect a consensus, either on the part of the federal and state governments or on the part of the Indians themselves. Congress used this lack of consensus to deny Indians federal recognition of their identity.

Other Indigenous peoples were routinely caught in this same colonial trap. As historian Ned Blackhawk writes of Indians in the Great Basin region of Utah and Nevada, "No timeless ethnographic categories or political definitions characterize these Native peoples. Indeed, in this region, precise band names, territorial locales, and stable political designations are often unreliable."[6] Native peoples, no matter where they reside or what political regimes they face, are not accurately or wholly described by fixed categories determined by outsiders. Rather, when those categories are used to describe Native peoples, they often serve a specific political purpose, one designed to shape knowledge to fit a hoped-for outcome. In the case of Robeson County

Indians, the names and categories of identity used to define them reflected the agendas of white supremacists in Congress, of officials at the OIA trying to avoid responsibility for another group of Indian people, and of Indians themselves seeking greater educational and economic opportunity. Indians defined their own categories, even though non-Indians rarely granted them the epistemological authority to do so. But Indians never doubted their own such authority to determine who they were and what they would be called, and so they clashed powerfully—with one another and with non-Indians—in the struggle to do so.

By the 1930s, Indians in Robeson County expressed their identity in one or more ways: as members of a kin network, as residents of a settlement, as attending an Indian school or church, as town or rural Indians, or as members of a tribe called the "Cherokee Indians of Robeson County." Between 1932 and 1933, they verbalized their existence as a tribe by asking for federal recognition from Congress, first as "Cherokee" Indians, the name the state of North Carolina had given them, then as "Siouan" Indians, the name suggested by the OIA. Neither bill brought recognition to Robeson County's Indians, though the negotiation process revealed the contentious politics of federal policy, local white supremacy, and Indian leadership. These congressional bills exposed divisions between town Indian leaders; both groups believed they were the community's rightful representatives. Though segregation reinforced some aspects of their identity, Indians feared that their right to vote and their ability to control their schools—the political and social institutions that enforced their racial boundaries—could be taken away by the state at any time. Both groups sought federal recognition to shield them from the uncertainties inherent in the Jim Crow system. The factions disagreed, however, on how to achieve federal recognition. "Cherokees" believed that Indians should reinforce their support of white supremacy to gain congressional favor, while "Siouans" looked to prove their identity to the OIA directly and avoided ingratiating themselves with white politicians. The factions also reflected preexisting social divisions between kin and settlement groups. Ultimately, neither group proved willing to compromise on its agenda.

But the failure of recognition did not solely rest with the tribe's internal divisions. Within the federal government, Congress and the OIA disagreed. Robeson County Indians' attempts to gain acknowledgment revealed the historical conflict between the two branches of government about the purposes and assumptions of federal recognition. North Carolina's congressional delegation saw recognition as a political matter. They aimed to please their white and Indian constituents and satisfy the concerns of other congressmen about questions such as racial purity and legitimate Indian leadership. Staff members at the OIA, on the other hand, approached recognition from an academic and bureaucratic perspective, measuring Robeson County Indians' identity against intellectual and legal categories of "Indianness" that included evidence of particular tribal ancestors and whether their descendants qualified for federal services. Fearing budgetary strain and reluctant to interfere with the South's Jim Crow system, the OIA expressed ambivalence about these questions as they regarded Robeson County Indians. Their indecision gave Congress opportunity to listen to the interests of white supremacy's supporters, both Indian and non-Indian, who wished to uphold the status quo in Robeson County.

SUFFERING HUMILIATION FROM LOCAL WHITES who used the "Cro" slur, Indians began this journey by appealing for protection to a higher authority: the North Carolina state legislature. In 1911 Indians petitioned the state to change their name simply to "Indians of Robeson County," a name that seemed neutral. Within two years, however, Indians realized that this name still left them vulnerable to losing their already fragile social autonomy, since the name itself provided little insight into the issue the federal government cared most about: the tribe's connection to historically documented people with recognizable "tribal" names and affiliation.[7]

A group of Indians representing various families and settlements decided to lobby for congressional legislation to secure their status as Indians and obtain better funding for their schools. In 1912 North Carolina congressman Hannibal Godwin, a Democratic lawyer from Harnett County, introduced legislation to recognize Robeson County's Indians as "Cherokee Indians." The new name presumably represented an attempt to claim a historic identity that whites would associate not with racial inferiority but with a noble and authentic Indianness. Angus McLean, an influential white Democrat and future governor of North Carolina, obtained and publicized evidence of the tribe's Cherokee ancestry. He had been long acquainted with the Indian population and was a friend of Doctor Fuller Lowry, a member of Pembroke's Fourth Street Power Structure. In previous years, McLean had listened to elders relay the tribe's oral tradition, and he became convinced that their true ancestry was Cherokee. The bill requested $50,000 for construction of a federal Indian school and $10,000 for its maintenance, though nothing for salaries and other costs.[8]

Godwin's interest in the matter is unclear. Perhaps he simply saw an opportunity to serve his Indian constituents with an effort that was not terribly taxing politically. Godwin also had political allies, such as Angus McLean, who had demonstrated an interest in Indians and who may have pressured him to act. Over the next twenty years, McLean remained committed to helping Indians obtain federal recognition from Congress, consistently using his political connections to do so. His own motivation to stay involved may have been old-fashioned southern white paternalism, or it may have had a more complex relationship to his role as the state's leading political visionary and fiscal conservative. McLean believed that the federal government, not the state, had "discriminated" against Robeson County Indians because it provided funding for schools for other Indians but left the state of North Carolina to carry the financial burden of an Indian school for Robeson County. In helping Indians become federally recognized, McLean was trying to alleviate a budgetary concern for the state while not sacrificing Indians' continued support of the Democratic Party. Godwin's assistance in this quest would surely be repaid. The bill passed in the Senate but encountered more challenges in the House.[9]

McLean testified on the Indians' behalf before the House Committee on Indian Affairs in 1913. One exchange between a congressman and McLean illustrates Congress's assumptions about federal recognition. Segregationists' racial agenda played a major role in how Congress viewed Robeson County Indians' request. White southerners and their sympathizers in the federal government marked Indian identity according to how Indians distinguished themselves from blacks. Representative Charles H. Burke of South Dakota, a Republican real-estate developer, explicitly linked Robeson County Indians' status with that of blacks in the hearing: "It is my belief that these Indians have no right to enter any Indian school because they are not full-blooded Indians. I will also say that I have great sympathy with people in the South in dealing with the Negro. You refuse to recognize them. I presume that it is due to the prejudice that exists in the mind of the people on account of color." McLean replied, "The Indians themselves recognize this feeling and respect it."[10]

Burke's assertion that "these Indians" were not "full-blooded," followed by his comment on southern racism, implied his suspicion that "these Indians" were actually "Negroes," or in any case they did not have enough "Indian blood" to justify federal interference with the South's race problem by recognizing them as a separate group with separate rights. McLean, a southerner and conservative Democrat, dodged any question about the tribe's Indian ancestry and appealed to Burke's prejudice, telling him that these Indians felt the same way as whites did about blacks. McLean told Burke that he should recognize Robeson County's Indians as Indians, not because of their pure Indian ancestry, but because they were as prejudiced as he was.[11] Racial prejudice lay at the core of southern whites' view of Indian identity, one that Indians expressed in the previous decades by ostracizing blacks, at least in the presence of whites.

A month following the 1913 House committee hearings, the state legislature changed the Indians' name to "Cherokee Indians of Robeson County." McLean's political muscle clearly outweighed the objections of the Eastern Band of Cherokees to the bill, who, according to a reporter, had nothing against the Croatans but believed that they simply had no claim to the name "Cherokee." One Robeson County Indian who confronted them at the state capital said they objected because "they seem to think if the Government recognizes us it would entitle us to some of their little rocky ground there and they don't want us. . . . [B]ut we did not want to do anything like that."[12]

What this Robeson County Indian thought was "rocky ground" of little value was in fact large tracts of very valuable timber. The Cherokees' state-chartered tribal corporation owned this timber and prevented individual Cherokees from commercially cutting it. But timber trespass was the most prevalent crime on the Eastern Band's reservation, and tribal leaders surely wanted to prevent others from having access to it. Further, the Eastern Band Cherokees had a perplexing legal status: for some purposes (criminal trials, for example), they were citizens of the state of North Carolina, like Robeson County Indians. In other cases (when local Democrats wanted to prevent them from voting for Republicans), they were noncitizen wards of the federal government who could not exercise the rights of citizenship. Eastern Band Cherokees perhaps believed that recognizing the Robeson County Indians, a group whose citizenship was not in flux, as Cherokees might have aggravated this problem, with detrimental results for the tribe's timber holdings. Eastern Band Cherokees' status as quasi citizens, with timber owned by the tribal corporation, prevented the OIA from allotting their reservation under the 1886 Dawes General Allotment Act. Allotment, the practice of dividing reservation land into tracts held by individuals, probably would have hastened the loss of land, as it had for so many tribes in the West. Keeping Robeson County Indians well away from their lands might have been a strategy to help them protect those lands, not so much from other Indians but from federal intrusion.[13]

Although they were from different regions of the country and were members of different political parties, Angus McLean and Charles Burke had a great deal in common. Both men sought out political patronage for Indians as a means of protecting whites' access to economic and social privilege. Seven years before these hearings, Congress passed the 1906 Burke Act, named for its sponsor. The Burke Act amended the federal Indian land-allotment policy and rapidly accelerated the loss of almost 90 million acres of Indian-owned lands in the western United States. White landlords in Robeson County who were eager to take Indian and black farms might have learned something from this master architect of foreclosure; he accomplished it with the blessing of the U.S. Congress, whereas white landlords in the South largely relied on Indians' and blacks' voicelessness in the justice system to accomplish their schemes. The different tactics used to achieve such chicanery were in fact part of the same trend that was unfolding on local and national levels.

Both Congress and local whites were committed to achieving prosperity for white Americans by using economic resources—namely, land—that were unsteadily held by populations overwhelmed by colonial domination. To these populations, the federal government must have seemed like an authoritarian state; after all, Indians did not fully consent, or were not fully included in, their governance. As anthropologist James C. Scott has observed, social disaster follows even well-intentioned state projects that combine an authoritarian state's willingness to coerce its designs onto a civil society unable to engage in a movement to resist them. For Indians in the United States, this process unfolded not solely at the behest of one branch of government, but in a collaboration between many people in various layers of society who were often not even aware of one another's actions. Occasionally, however, these interests converged, as they did in that House committee hearing room when McLean and Burke spoke.[14]

The Burke Act was part of a package of Indian legislation passed in Congress that allowed the secretary of the interior to declare an Indian "competent and capable of managing his or her own affairs" and thus gain title to his or her allotment. This provision removed all restrictions against the sale of that land, restrictions that had been ostensibly established to maintain the land for Indians' economic survival. The act also made all "competent" allottees subject to the jurisdiction of the United States and the state in which the individual resided. Further, the secretary of the interior's implementation of the act evolved into a de facto racial standard of "competency": "mixed-blood" Indians were declared competent more often than "full-bloods." Burke's law not only facilitated fraudulent sales of Indian lands; it also made Indians subject to the same race-based discrimination to which state laws subjected African Americans.[15]

Such a counterintuitive policy—making the "competent" powerless—

demonstrated the authoritarian nature of the United States when it came to Indian policy and questions of inclusion for racial "others." Making Indians and blacks politically and economically powerless was a precondition for the achievement of Burke's philosophy on assimilation and economic prosperity. The link between Indians and blacks in Burke and McLean's interaction in the 1913 hearing says more about the attitudes of lawmakers than it does about the actual identity or ancestry of Indians in Robeson County. Their exchange also speaks volumes about the shared situation of Indians and blacks throughout the South and West. The role of the federal government at this time was to protect white privilege, just as it was the role of state governments.[16] That privilege was economic as well as legal and social, and it conveniently classed Indians and African Americans together in order to ensure white dominance.

McLean's testimony indicates that southern whites did not care what kind of Indians the Robeson County Indians were; for the purposes of taking their land, exploiting their labor, and controlling their social behavior, it was sufficient simply that they were Indians, or rather that they were not white. Their status as Indians needed no special historical or biological reinforcement for whites at the top of the racial hierarchy, other than a tribal name; designating them as Indians simply required that Indians prove that they were not black, which the distinct tribal name helped to accomplish. In this way, a separate Indian identity reinforced the legitimacy of the racial hierarchy in the minds of powerful whites because Indians themselves acquiesced to it. Indians adopted this method of reckoning identity in the presence of their white neighbors—partly because it achieved concrete gains in social autonomy and partly because it did not threaten their own markers of family and place, which had little to do with tribal affiliation and everything to do with social organization and behavior. But there was an unintended consequence of this embrace of state authority: the social needs of whites, rather than their own needs, largely governed Indians' actions.

ALTHOUGH CONGRESS AND LOCAL WHITES colluded to maintain white supremacy by using Indians' unique status, the OIA had a different strategy. McLean's reasoning at the 1913 House hearing reveals a basis for Indian identity that appeared logical under the nation's white supremacy yet remained far outside the mainstream of OIA definitions of Indianness. His answer to Burke—"the Indians recognize [white prejudice] and respect it"—indicates why Robeson County Indians and other Southeastern Native communities have had so much difficulty gaining federal acknowledgment. As historian

Anna Bailey has pointed out, "national" markers of Indian identity have not necessarily conformed to "local" markers.[17]

Historically, the federal government and Indian nations had a political, rather than a social, relationship. That is, their relationship was between two governments. From the perspective of federal law, an Indian's identity was intrinsically linked to his tribal affiliation *and* whether that historic tribe had a relationship to the U.S. government. Congressmen, who preferred to deal in political favors and did not want to concern themselves with the intricacies of federal Indian law, assigned the OIA the task of legitimizing the petitioning tribe's claim. Accordingly, OIA officials concerned themselves with the historical origins of the Indian group that applied for assistance so that they could determine the authenticity of these appeals. They based their findings on historical and anthropological research that established links between the contemporary Indian group and a past people who the government considered a "tribe." The OIA's judgment included assumptions about racial ancestry and a proper "Indian" phenotype, but such assumptions did not form the exclusive criteria for Indian identity. Prior to the 1930s, OIA staff found the key identity test in whether the "tribe" had a historic relationship with the United States and the right to treaty-based assistance. For an Indian group to receive assistance or recognition under this regime, they would have to demonstrate that their ancestors had signed a treaty with the United States.[18]

In their congressional lobbying efforts, Robeson County Indians discovered that Congress and the OIA had different standards of identity. North Carolina's delegation to Congress cared primarily that tribal members would support white supremacy. OIA officials, however, sought to verify a tribal identity according to anthropological standards, particularly the presence of "Indian blood" (as opposed to the absence of "black blood," which mattered to Congress). The OIA also concerned itself with the Indian community's treaty relationship with the United States. While Indians in Robeson County had become comfortable with accommodating the politics of white supremacy, the OIA's measure of identity was new to them. Correspondingly, OIA officials had little experience with circumstances like those faced by Robeson County Indians in the early part of the twentieth century. These challenges left the OIA uncertain about how to handle Robeson County Indians and their request for federal recognition.

Conflict arose between southern white politicians in Congress and the Indian Office over federal acknowledgment of Robeson County Indians' identity. The problem started when the state of North Carolina recognized Robeson County Indians as Cherokees in 1913 but officials in the federal government were unaware of the change. In 1915, after Indians had lobbied to submit yet another bill for federal recognition and educational assistance under the name "Cherokee," the Senate ordered Indian Commissioner Cato Sells to report on the "tribal rights and conditions" of Indians in Robeson County. Sells sent Special Indian Agent Orlando M. McPherson to Robeson County to investigate. Sells wanted to know whether these Indians had any claim on assistance from the federal government, not whether they were Indians per se. To make a judgment, McPherson had to determine whether "Cherokee" was the appropriate tribal affiliation of these Indians; as an agent of the OIA, he focused his investigation on anthropological, not political, criteria for Indian identity. The state of North Carolina's position made no impact on the OIA's inquiry.[19]

McPherson included an extensive historical section and numerous documents to draw some conclusion about Robeson County Indians' tribal affiliation, but the report reads like a catalog of information that is ultimately contradictory and confusing. He seemed unable to deploy the OIA's definition of Indian identity—a tribe's historic relationship to the federal government—in order to reconcile Indians' anomalous status in the South and provide a history that reflected both their oral tradition and their contemporary social context. McPherson concluded that the tribe did not have much, if any, Cherokee ancestry; instead, he believed that their ancestors were Hatteras Indians and the Lost Colony survivors. Yet he did not doubt their Indian ancestry or that they had maintained an identity as Indians, and he also emphasized their poverty and their desire for education. Consequently, McPherson's only recommendation involved the establishment of an agricultural and mechanical training school for Indians in Robeson County to redress the lack of institutions of higher learning for Indians in North Carolina under Jim Crow.[20] This recommendation must have been welcome news to Indians, who had asked for the same provisions in their congressional petitions.

Essentially, McPherson found Robeson County Indians' tribal ancestry difficult to determine and their historic relationship to the federal government impossible to trace, but their needs as Indians were, in his mind, indisputable. He believed that their poverty alone justified their recognition from Congress. In response to McPherson's report, the secretary of the interior recommended that Congress appropriate funds for a school, but Commissioner Sells rejected the proposal. Sells doubted "the wisdom of the Government's assuming this burden" and chose to demur on the question of tribal ancestry. To avoid additional administrative obligations, Sells neglected to provide Congress with a ruling on the tribe's affiliation, and as a result, Congress did not act on the question of federal acknowledgment for Robeson County Indians. The rationale for federal recognition that McPherson and the secretary of the interior endorsed did not satisfy the OIA's criteria, leaving no federal authority prepared to assess the issue. As a result of this intergovernmental disagreement over the nature of Indian identity, the priorities of white supremacy determined the outcome of Indians' claim to federal recognition. Disappointed, Indians waited nearly ten years before they organized once again to gain assistance from the federal government.[21]

When Indians led by A. B. Locklear asked Congress to introduce another bill for recognition as Cherokee Indians of Robeson County in 1924, Indian Commissioner Charles Burke, who had suspected in 1913 that Robeson County Indians did not qualify for federal Indian schools, objected to the bill. As a member of Congress, he had expressed doubt about their ancestry, but as Indian commissioner, Burke based his objections on other criteria consistent with that of past commissioners and OIA staff: Robeson County's Indians were self-sufficient, they did not live in a tribal state (meaning that they did not hold land in common and seemed fully assimilated to white ways), and they had never been recognized by the Indian Office (meaning that the already-scarce funds for Indian assistance were not available to them).

The OIA never questioned their identity as Indians. Rather, it rejected them because of policy considerations and the lack of funds, never ruling on the question of tribal affiliation. In its official opinions about legislation, both in 1913 and in 1924, the OIA left the question of tribal affiliation for Congress to decide, while Congress consistently referred the issue back to the OIA's agents and anthropologists for an "expert" opinion—which they never provided. OIA officials had multiple reasons to reject recognition of Robeson County Indians. The assimilation policy made assistance unattractive, and neither branch of government wanted to interject itself into white southerners' control of race relations. But both rationales reflect the federal government's use of Indians to establish white political, social, and economic dominance.[22]

The Indian Office's stance on race relations was consistent with their assimilation policy. Upholding white supremacy through Indian assimilation had been the avowed goal of Indian policy since the 1880s. After 1900, OIA policy viewed Indians as members of an inferior race destined to remain unequal to whites, ostensibly admitted to citizenship but confined to "proper" roles on the periphery of a "white man's world." In this context, the OIA and southern whites both agreed to marginalize Indians economically and exploit their labor and land. As Commissioner Francis Leupp said in 1906, "Even the little papoose can be taught to weed the rows just as the pickaninny in the South can be used as a cotton picker." In the following decade, Commissioner Sells pursued a "termination principle," eliminating Indians who did not appear to need government assistance from the responsibility of the OIA. This trend culminated with the Indian Citizenship Act in 1924, the same year of Burke's report on the Cherokee bill. In an atmosphere where policy makers pushed for "dependent wards" to become "independent citizens," Robeson County Indians probably seemed to have already achieved the goals of Indian citizenship. The OIA's rulings on these Indians conveyed its attitudes about white supremacy to Congress.[23]

But Indians in Robeson County were determined to hold the federal government to its previous recognitions of their Indian identity, even if Congress and the OIA had refused to make a ruling in their favor. Their next strategy involved establishing a form of self-government that could represent their people's interests directly to the federal government. In 1931, following a meeting with Senate Indian Affairs Committee staff member Albert A. Grorud, the Cherokee Indians of Robeson County elected a business committee and leadership council in a meeting held at Mount Airy Church.[24] A long-established place of spiritual and political leadership, the church stood at the center of a prosperous Indian community outside the town of Pembroke. Mount Airy Indians were known for "keeping to themselves," often not marrying outside the settlement and maintaining kinship and place affiliations as the highest priority.[25] Grorud may have suggested the formation of the council, or Indians may have recognized the strategy as one that many Indian groups employed.

Whatever the motivation, employing a self-government strategy placed their efforts in line with those of other Indian communities and with changes in federal Indian policy. In 1928 the Department of the Interior published a landmark study of Indian Affairs titled *The Problem of Indian Administration*, which came to be known as the Meriam Report after its lead author, Lewis Meriam. The report found nothing new and did not question the assimilation program; OIA and interior officials had known for decades that federal services for Indians were deficient, obsolete, and negligent. But the report recommended some small changes that, with the help of a shift in leadership at the OIA, intensified into larger changes in the philosophy behind Indian policy. Recommendations in education, health, and land policy all trended toward decentralizing the assimilation effort and removing Indians' isolation from the larger American society. In the hands of John Collier, who would become commissioner of Indian Affairs in 1934, these recommendations meant that Indians' futures would be placed increasingly in the hands of Indians themselves.[26]

The Meriam Report recommendations did not apply to Robeson County Indians, but they seized the opportunities afforded by a trend toward greater self-government. At Mount Airy, an assembly of men elected B. G. "Buddy" Graham as chief councilman. Graham owned land in the Saint Annah community and likely went to church with "Rich" Chesley Locklear. Another business committee member, A. B. Locklear, had led a community group known as "the lodge" in Union Chapel during the 1920s (possibly a Red Man's Lodge), and he had lobbied for the 1924 Cherokee bill.[27] None of these men belonged to the Fourth Street Power Structure, though all of them probably owned land and farmed. Indians outside of Pembroke may have recognized that the strategies of their leadership in 1913 had not worked and gave other men a chance. In any case, the Indian town leaders who derived their influence from the community's segregated social institutions did not appear to play a significant role in the effort to become federally recognized as Cherokees in 1932.

Graham immediately established a gift-giving relationship with leaders in the U.S. Senate. In December that year, he sent Senate Indian Affairs Committee staff member Albert Grorud a ham, which Grorud enjoyed at Christmas dinner with Senator Burton K. Wheeler, a prominent member of the Indian Affairs Committee.[28] Following their gesture of friendship, the business committee asked for action on the 1914 McPherson report and for the Senate to send another representative to update the report. The Cherokee business committee expressed their wishes in terms of their historic relationships—not to the federal government, but to things that were deeper and more meaningful to them: their land, their identity, and their struggle. Moreover, they expressed themselves as representatives of a sovereign people. "We represent the interest of some 12,000 Cherokee Indians, men, women, and children," they wrote. "Our forefathers occupied this particular country before any white man visited it, and their descendants have continuously, down to the present time, occupied it. Neither we nor our forefathers have ever received any compensation from their government for the lands of which we were deprived." Such a statement acknowledged the OIA's preference for dealing with Indians who had treaty relationships and explained why this group would seek recognition, even though no such treaty existed. The group continued, "We are in need of help and earnestly ask that our government, which we respect, and to which we are loyal, now come to our relief and, after careful investigation, do us that justice to which, we believe, we are entitled." The Cherokee government based their entitlement not only on their historic rights and claims as Indians but also on their status as loyal citizens of the United States, citizens who had been discriminated against and were in need of relief.[29] The Senate committee, however, did not respond to these appeals.

Perhaps perceiving that the committee's lack of action stemmed from their prior conflicts with the OIA, Indians in Robeson County took yet another approach to federal recognition in 1932. Indians went directly to Washington and discussed their situation with the foremost Indian policy activist of the day, John Collier. In March 1932 a delegation of Indians met with Collier, who at that time served as executive secretary of the American Indian Defense Association (AIDA). The AIDA had a reputation as the most controversial organization lobbying for changes in Indian policy. The group advocated reversing the devastation induced by the government's goal of allotting Indian lands and assimilating Indians to white norms.

With Collier, Robeson County Indians reviewed a new draft of a bill for recognition as Cherokees, and he agreed to help them introduce it. Collier then contacted Senator Josiah W. Bailey, North Carolina's senior senator. "Being myself from Georgia," he wrote, "I am able to appreciate the desire of these Indians for some status by which they would be, at least in their own thinking, clearly distinguished from Negroes. And as a matter of fact, my impression of the group who came here was that they had strong Indian characteristics."[30] Collier's reference to vague "Indian characteristics" indicated the ways in which definitions of Indian identity had become less certain since the OIA began questioning the assimilation policy following the 1928 Meriam Report. Whether Collier meant that the delegation looked "Indian" or behaved like "Indians" is unknown, but his assessment joined a long line of "outsider" views of Indian identity, such as those articulated by anthropologist James Mooney. But whatever his meaning, Collier recognized that segregation drove Indians' new attempt to gain federal assistance, and he sympathized with their position.

After their meeting with Collier, Buddy Graham and the Cherokee Business Committee forwarded Senator Bailey a petition signed by more than 600 Indians requesting introduction of a Cherokee recognition bill. With the exception of Rev. L. W. Jacobs, none of the members of the Fourth Street Power Structure signed the petition that the Business Committee sent to Senator Bailey, signaling a change in the community's designated leadership, or at least an emerging faction that refused to go through local whites to demand recognition.[31] This Cherokee bill proposed three types of assistance: recognizing the Indians formerly known as Croatans as Cherokees (as the state had done), permitting these Indians to attend federal Indian schools, and reexamining Robeson County Cherokees' circumstances to update Orlando M. McPherson's 1915 study. The bill also forbade any change in the Indians' current property rights or "present status" as citizens and denied them any tribal rights or monies due to the Eastern Band of Cherokees or the Western Cherokees in Oklahoma.

Like the other recognition bills, this one emphasized education as one of the tribe's needs for assistance, but it also requested another report that, in Collier's words, "would lay the foundation for subsequent action" by the government to support Indian education in Robeson County.[32] The Meriam Report had documented dismal conditions at federally supported Indian schools. But Indians in Robeson County probably perceived that compared to their current situation, a sustained source of funding from the federal government would improve their educational opportunities. After all, such funding was based ostensibly on a relationship defined by federal law, not by the changing priorities of white supremacy. They also probably did not know how much other Indians had suffered at the hands of this legal relationship, which negligent OIA officials disengaged from financial support.

Philosophically, this legislation fit squarely in the tradition of the group's previous attempts to gain federal recognition: the bill declared a historic tribal affiliation and asked for educational assistance. The measure intended to secure an Indian identity through enhancing educational opportunities for Indians, a strategy that had worked well at state and local levels in the past and reinforced the social institutions that Indians already used to monitor their community's boundaries. Yet the approach involved an important strategic difference. Rather than soliciting the help of white Democrats, Indians asked for assistance from a white activist—John Collier—perhaps believing that his experience with federal Indian policy would prove more effective in Congress than segregationist logic. This strategic difference reflected the alternative leadership that had emerged to carry these concerns forward. The Fourth Street Power Structure, Indians who had earned their community standing through their connections to white segregationists, appeared to have little part in this new movement.

Perhaps reluctant to ally with Collier, a vocal critic of Congress, Senator Bailey checked with his white supporters in Robeson County before acting on the bill. He used his congressional power to reinforce local whites' influence over the affairs of Robeson County Indians. His role here was similar to that of Angus McLean two decades earlier: he was the nexus of federal and state collusion to maintain whites' privileged access to economic and political power. Bailey asked L. R. Varser, a Lumberton judge and state legislator, whether or not the bill was "acceptable to all the Indians."[33] Varser replied that he thought that the legislation "ought to be" acceptable to Indians and that "it would be of considerable value to them," provided that it did nothing to affect their current status as citizens of North Carolina. Varser approved of the legislation but did not want it to impact Indians' place in the racial hierarchy. Reiterating the "progressive" values that upheld white supremacy, he wrote, "It will make them feel that they have the recognition from both the State and Federal Government, and ought to inspire a spirit, and ambition, to accomplish the best as citizens."[34] Those "progressive" values of civic duty, economic ambition, and educational advancement encouraged Indians to "accomplish the best as citizens"—meaning as citizens of the larger segregated society.

Because of his position as an elected official who depended on Indian leaders for votes, Varser was likely well acquainted with the influential town Indians who espoused such "progressive" values themselves, such as the members of Pembroke's Fourth Street Power Structure. As citizens, Varser believed, these Indians "knew their place" in the racial hierarchy and did not seek to elevate their status to the level of whites. To him, increased access to education, which federal recognition provided, only advanced the "progressive" portion of Robeson County's Indian population and the white southern "progressive" agenda as a whole, without necessarily giving Indians the power to challenge white supremacy.

Bailey introduced the "Cherokee" bill in May 1932, including all the provisions set forth in the original draft except the request for an additional investigation.[35] The investigation, as Collier indicated, would have paved the way for future assistance from the federal government and might have empowered Indians to see their interests as separate from those of North Carolina's white citizens. Bailey sent a copy of the bill to McLean, who replied approvingly and commented that "the Indians in this County desire this Bill passed and I hope you will succeed in having that done."[36]

The Senate Committee on Indian Affairs asked Commissioner of Indian Affairs C. J. Rhoads to report on the bill. Rhoads's concerns echoed those of earlier commissioners, and he did no more to establish a tribal affiliation than did previous investigators. In fact, Rhoads's report clouded the issue of tribal ancestry and unintentionally deepened the confusion between OIA and congressional criteria for federal designation. Like Commissioner Burke in 1924, Rhoads left the ultimate decision about tribal ancestry up to Congress, but his articulation of Indian identity alarmed white southerners.

In his memorandum, Rhoads quoted ethnologist James Mooney's 1907 writings about the Croatans. Mooney wrote, "The theory of descent from Raleigh's lost colony of Croatan may be regarded as baseless, but the name itself serves as a convenient label for a people who combine in themselves the blood of the wasted native tribes, the early forest rovers, the run-away slaves or other Negroes, and probably also of stray seamen of the Latin races from coasting vessels in the West Indian or Brazilian trade."[37] This portrayal of Robeson County Indians' ancestors provided no definitive evidence of their tribal affiliation and simultaneously introduced the notion of miscegenation, about which Charles Burke questioned Angus McLean in 1913.

But we must read Mooney's statements in light of his own assumptions as an ethnographer and the assumptions of the federal officials for whom he wrote. Mooney knew that Robeson County's Indians were not exceptional among other Indian communities in their multiracial ancestry; in another, later memorandum, he stated that "Indian blood" predominated in the tribe and compared the Croatans' ancestry to that of other acknowledged groups in the Southeast, citing the Nanticoke, Pamunkey, Chickahominy, Creek, Catawba, Shawnee, and Cherokee.[38] To Mooney, mixed ancestry did not mean that the Robeson County Indians were not actually Indians. Accordingly, Rhoads did not explicitly deny their Indian identity. Rather, he discussed identity in terms relevant to the OIA in order to answer the question about eligibility for federal services. He used Mooney's assessment to establish that they had never entered into a treaty relationship with the United States and were therefore ineligible for assistance.

Rhoads added another warning to his report: "We believe that the enactment of this legislation would be the initial step in bringing these Indians under the jurisdiction of the Federal Government." The text of the bill asked for nothing more than for "Cherokees" to be admitted into federal Indian schools and did not ask for an additional report to be made. Rhoads's warning was unnecessary, but he added it because he wanted to make certain that his office assumed no responsibility to these people. To substantiate his reasoning, Rhoads might have denied that Robeson County's Indians were Indians at all, but he chose not to. Instead, Rhoads acknowledged their identity repeatedly in the report but left the question of their specific tribal affiliation to Congress.

He avoided a definitive statement because he knew that if he affirmed the historic identity they claimed, Congress could recognize the Robeson County Indians and make Rhoads responsible for the education and welfare of another 8,000 to 12,000 people. Alternately, if he expressly denied any Indian identity on the part of Robeson County Indians based on their mixed ancestry, he would be going against an eminent scholar's assessment and setting a double standard for federal relationships to Indian tribes, none of whom had "pure" Indian pedigrees. Furthermore, he would be critiquing the racial order that North Carolina's congressmen supported. Like his predecessors, Rhoads did not commit to the subject of Robeson County Indians' historic tribal affiliation and "passed the buck" back to the Senate Committee on Indian Affairs. Not surprisingly, Congress adjourned and the committee did not act on the bill.[39]

McLean responded to Rhoads's report with confusion and outrage. He revealed the ways that North Carolina politicians' impressions of Indians differed from the notions of the federal government. McLean thought that Rhoads had misunderstood the purpose of the bill. In McLean's view, Robeson County Indians did not want to come under the jurisdiction of the government; they simply wanted permission to attend federal Indian schools. McLean saw this provision as a simple matter, but Rhoads envisioned larger budgetary problems. McLean also reacted to James Mooney's words. He did not read them as Rhoads had, but instead he saw them in the light of southerners' obsession with miscegenation and racial hierarchy. McLean told Bailey that "this article . . . by James Mooney . . . is wholly unjustified and unreliable. . . . From all I know personally, and from history and tradition, it is complete slander to say that these Indians are in any way amalgamated with the Negro race." McLean saw the Mooney and Rhoads reports not as subtle affirmations of Robeson County Indians' identity but as a threat to the racial order that Indians "recognized" and "respected," to quote his words to Representative Burke in 1913. From McLean's perspective, limited congressional recognition of Robeson County's Indians secured that racial order and Indians' place in it. "I am anxious to do everything possible to help them," McLean wrote. "No people in our County have made greater progress in agriculture, in education and in general improvement than these Indians." For white southerners such as McLean, federal validation of Indians' identity affirmed that Indians were not black and thus were capable of the kind of progress white politicians had helped them achieve through supporting Indian schools.[40]

Indians in Robeson County were also displeased by the decision of the commissioner of Indian Affairs. Their dissatisfaction partly stemmed from the evidence cited in the decision—Mooney's statements about the group's racially mixed ancestry. A. B. Locklear vociferously protested the Rhoads decision, arguing that McPherson's report, which affirmed mixture with whites but not blacks, was not only more recent but more authoritative. In Locklear's words, McPherson "put it in a book and laid it on a shelf," unlike Mooney, whose report he had never heard of. "I [know] that the commissioner is agenst my people[.] I am demanding something [done] about the McPherson report[,] not James Mooney's report."[41] Locklear was simply unwilling to grant Rhoads the authority to make a determination based on a report that he found unsupportable when another report, McPherson's, was available and obviously more popular within the Indian community.

Interestingly, Locklear's objection seems to be based not on the idea of racial mixture itself but on which races did the mixing. Mixture with English colonists had been sanctioned by white supremacy, but mixture with African slaves had not been. The state of Virginia had removed this concern about miscegenation in 1924, when its Racial Integrity Act declared that Virginians with one-sixteenth or less "Indian blood" who descended from Pocahontas and John Rolfe were legally white.[42] In contrast to the historical memory of the Jim Crow period, where any and all miscegenation between whites and nonwhites was banned, it seems that both white supremacists and Indians made some exceptions when it came to Indian-white relationships—at least those that had taken place in the past.

Indeed, Senator Bailey claimed that Mooney's statements about the group's racial mixture with African Americans had prevented the Senate from scheduling a hearing on the bill. But Locklear suspected that Bailey was not a true ally and was making an excuse for his unwillingness to act. Even before Congress adjourned, Locklear appealed directly to the Indian Affairs Committee through committee staff member Albert Grorud and the committee's chairman, Senator Lynn Frazier. Locklear anticipated Bailey's unwillingness to push the bill, writing, "Mr. Bailey might wait until Congress is out and then say that he did all he could for [us]."[43] So when Bailey informed them that Mooney's report was to blame for the bill's failure, Locklear and other Indian leaders probed deeper and questioned Grorud on the matter. Grorud told them that the negative report from Rhoads should not worry them. Often, he said, bills are passed by the Senate and House "in spite of [unfavorable] reports" from the Department of the Interior.[44] If Grorud's assessment was correct, senators routinely cared more for what their political supporters wanted than what the "experts" at the OIA had to say. Bailey himself was likely waiting to make sure the "Cherokee" bill would meet with the approval of local whites in North Carolina before using any of his own political muscle to ensure a hearing on the bill. In the realm of politics, blood and names were inextricably bound. The labels used to identify the ancestry of Robeson County Indians, and the relative weight given to those labels, made all the difference in whether their concerns were addressed in political forums.

Faced with the obvious conclusion that Bailey needed the reassurance of his white counterparts in the state, Locklear accepted another offer of help from McLean.[45] But McLean's advocacy became a bone of contention within the Indian community in the summer of 1932. More Indians recognized the ways in which McLean's segregationist logic differed from the OIA's reasoning. As a result, Locklear's support within the Indian community began to unravel. Locklear continued to pressure Grorud for some accurate statement of why the "Cherokee" bill had not passed. He felt intense pressure from his community to get something done on Capitol Hill. "My people will 'buse me out if I don't show some reason why that bill did not go through Congress," he wrote.[46] To Senator Bailey, Locklear took a more conciliatory tone and asked for advice on McLean's involvement. "Some of me people is afraid that [McLean] would not Doe[.] I think he is the man and I think that he could Doe us a Lot of good." Bailey replied to Locklear and was supportive of McLean's assistance. But he told Locklear that the prospects for the bill's passage at that session were not good and that he hoped to reintroduce it in December.[47] In November 1932, voters elected Franklin D. Roosevelt as president, and Bailey knew that changes in the Interior Department would follow, giving him an excuse to stall the "Cherokee" bill. Bailey put Locklear in an awkward position relative to his own people. Locklear was willing to appease his followers, who did not want McLean's assistance, but he needed Bailey's help to do it. Bailey declined to support a hearing, however, and he left Locklear with no choice but to appeal to McLean and risk displeasing Indians who disagreed with McLean's involvement in their affairs.[48]

In March 1933 Robeson County Indians received the news that their campaign had again failed, and they immediately demanded new leadership. Rather than withdraw their support from Bailey, however, Indians' suspicion of McLean's and Bailey's involvement turned into hostility toward Locklear. "People got mad with him [Locklear]," remembered one ninety-nine-year-old resident of the Saint Annah community. "[They] claimed that he was just after money, taking their money and spending it on something else."[49] True to the Indian community's tendency to challenge their leadership, Indians transferred their support to Buddy Graham and Joseph Brooks. Brooks had grown up in the Saint Annah community near Graham and was a brother-in-law of "Rich" Chesley Locklear. Brooks apparently took Locklear's place as "spokesman" for Graham; perhaps the Cherokee business committee felt that a team of representatives more closely tied to each other by kinship and settlement affiliation would be more effective.

The two men launched a direct appeal to Bailey to gain support for the bill, traveling to Washington, D.C., themselves to secure his support and that of the Senate Indian Affairs Committee.[50] They organized a letter-writing campaign, and over 100 Indians from various settlements urged Bailey to reintroduce the bill in exchange for their votes in the next election. They structured their campaign according to families and settlements, a method inherited from their forebears who had appealed to the federal government for assistance in 1889. This sense of kinship and attachment to place formed the basis of their identity as a People, but their leaders' trip to Washington and exchanges with outsiders also shaped these fundamental layers of identity. Indians' sense of themselves as a People became an organizing tool, one that ironically augmented the political fragmentation of the community in some ways.

The letters from Indians reminded Bailey of his vulnerability as an elected official and let him know that Indians expected benefits in return for their support of his career and of white supremacy in general. The letters outlined Indians' reciprocal relationship with white supremacy and segregation and showed how they used their distinct identity as a People to enforce this reciprocity. Shaw Deese, a tenant farmer in the Brooks Settlement and husband of Joseph Brooks's sister Margie, wrote, "I am an Indian of Robeson County and has never been recognized by the US Government, even though I am a voter and has been for a number of years. . . . [Y]ou has never represented me as a Cherokee Indian of Robeson County, I have tried to show my color for you and thought was empressing me that you would do something for me. . . . [U]nless [you do] something in the behalf of us as a tribe of Cherokee Indians, your Hope for votes will be in vain."[51] Political party loyalists "showed their colors" in support of their party. For Indians, their place in the racial hierarchy was tied explicitly to their loyalty to the Democratic Party. "Showing his color" may have another meaning as well: in exchange for Bailey's support for recognition, Deese may have implied that he accepted segregation by "showing his color" and assuring Bailey and other white politicians that he knew his place in the racial hierarchy. Deese's letter disclosed disap-

pointment that Bailey did not honor his part of the bargain and help mitigate Deese's tenuous place in southern society by granting Indians greater
autonomy.

Colon Brooks, a landowner and member of the Brooks Settlement Longhouse, also wrote to Bailey, emphasizing his identity as an Indian and his
respect for the color line. He admonished Bailey for not representing their
interests as Cherokee Indians: "I am a real Indian of Robeson County and
always have been a citizen of our country and voted as our white friends[.]
. . . [O]ur [congressmen] has never represented us as a tribe of Cherokee
Indian and I think we should be recognized and cared for as much so as any
Indians in the USA[.] Unless this is done no Indian in Robeson County and
adjoining ones will never throw another vote for a [congressman]."[52] Bailey
received over 100 letters like these, with most authors representing themselves not just as voters but also as Indians who had a right to recognition.
The principle of reciprocity, so important for gauging Indian identity within
the group, also extended to their congressmen. Rather than protest the system that oppressed them, Indians demanded that the system keep its part of
the bargain.[53]

Armed with community support, Graham and others again traveled to
Washington to meet with government officials. Desperate to shore up his
own support from elected officials, A. B. Locklear told Bailey that "the President of our committee, Mr. B. G. Graham . . . [has] joined in with a bunch
of folks who are enimies [sic] to white people and are habitual fighters."[54] To
accomplish his goal, Locklear planted mistrust in Bailey's mind about the
intentions of Graham; Locklear intended to characterize the faction led by
Graham and Brooks as against the "progress" that his own faction promoted
and therefore as unreliable representatives of the Robeson County Indians.
While we do not know the exact outcome of Graham's meeting, Graham did
give Bailey a strong message: Graham, and not A. B. Locklear, now spoke for
the Indian community.[55]

Negotiating the 1932 legislation for Cherokee recognition divided the Indian community along ideological lines. The issues involved in passing the
bill—maintaining the racial hierarchy and determining a tribal affiliation—
mandated cooperation from white segregationists such as Angus McLean.
But the strategy did not work when confronted with the concerns of the
OIA, and Indians suffered another delay in their long-sought goal of federal
recognition. In response to that disappointment, some Indians looked for
new leadership and a new strategy, while others remained confident that
McLean would serve their interests. Congress's and the OIA's different atti-

tudes about federal recognition undoubtedly strengthened the group's internal factionalism.

IN ROBESON COUNTY Indians' next attempt to gain federal recognition, this division, rather than the racial hierarchy, dominated the negotiations. Kin differences and residency patterns, not just ideological disagreements, characterized these internal tribal divisions. Kinship, settlement affiliation, and disagreements on strategy separated one faction from another; these distinctions developed into different ways of articulating identity within the Indian community.

Having authority to speak for the community, Graham and Brooks began lobbying for another recognition bill. They asked Bailey for another meeting in order to present "information which we have obtained from public records and History" regarding "our original and ancient Name" that "we believe will be of great help in behalf of having favorable action taken" on the bill. They thanked Bailey for "past favors" and assured him that they were his "supporters," reminding him, as so many other Indian constituents had, of his duty to them as voters. Their evident efforts to research their documentary history demonstrated their acquiescence to the OIA's criteria for Indian identity, and their confidence in their own case for federal acknowledgment grew. Brooks supported the name "Cherokee," James E. Chavis recalled, "because that was the name we had in Robeson County, in the state. If we were not Cherokees, the state was in error." Robeson County Indians displayed a willingness to work with whatever name the state and federal governments accepted, regardless of how foreign it was from their own approach to identity.[56]

After their meeting with Bailey, the delegation met with John Collier, whom Harold Ickes, the new secretary of the interior, had recently appointed commissioner of Indian Affairs.[57] Collier knew of the group since he had met with some of them in 1932, when he seemed convinced of their Indian ancestry and their eligibility for federal recognition. He may have pointed out to the delegation that "Cherokee" would not satisfy the OIA as a tribal affiliation, however, since ethnologist James Mooney had debunked the name and the Senate Committee on Indian Affairs had rejected it as well. Nevertheless, Collier seemed to accept their "Indian characteristics," as he had indicated in 1932. Whether these characteristics were phenotypical, cultural, or behavioral, the only question to be answered was their name, their historic tribal affiliation. The delegation's encounter with Collier asked the community to contend with a set of evolving assumptions behind the OIA's definition of Indian identity.

To arrive upon a suitable tribal affiliation to recommend to Congress, Collier sent the delegation to see John Swanton, an anthropologist who specialized in Southeastern Indians in the Bureau of American Ethnology (BAE) at the Smithsonian Institution. When he met the delegation in 1933, he apparently recognized their Indian ancestry. Swanton gladly accepted the challenge and spent "a few days" looking into the Robeson County Cherokees' true tribal heritage. Apparently he never visited Robeson County but instead interviewed the delegation and conducted documentary research in government and anthropological records in Washington, D.C. He investigated the community's genealogy, their oral tradition as put forward by McMillan and McLean, the colonial records of North Carolina, the census records, and old correspondence in the BAE files.

Swanton's extant notes reveal little about his thought process or methodology, but they do indicate that he looked into the surviving records of every major Indian community in colonial North Carolina and South Carolina for evidence related to the contemporary Indian group in Robeson County. He then made some logical deductions based on indirect evidence that placed particular Indian groups at certain locations during the colonial period. He concluded that the core ancestors of the Robeson County group came from the Keyauwee and Cheraw tribes, two Siouan-speaking groups that had migrated to the swampy area around Drowning Creek. He disavowed the Cherokee and Croatan theories, arguing that the former represented a confusion with the name "Cheraw" and that there was simply no evidence for the latter. He did acknowledge, however, that other Iroquoian or Algonquian groups probably made "contributions" to the Robeson County Indians. Swanton declared that Cheraw would be the most appropriate name for the group, since it was well known to whites.[58]

Senator Bailey and Representative J. Bayard Clark introduced companion bills on behalf of the Robeson County Indians on 1 May 1933. Rather than recognize the community as Cherokees, the bills proposed recognition as Cheraw Indians, a change that reflected Swanton's conclusions. The bill was nearly identical to the previous Cherokee bill, including the stipulation that the legislation not "affect the present status or property rights of any such Indians or prohibit the attendance of children of such Indians at Government Indian schools"; furthermore, it prevented the Cheraws from having any rights to "the tribal lands or moneys of other bands of Indians in the United States."

According to James Chavis, Joseph Brooks drafted the bill naming them Cheraws and returned home to confirm the legislation with his followers in

Robeson County. Both congressional and Indian leaders had reason to think that the name satisfied at least some of the OIA's concerns, since the OIA's anthropological consultant suggested the tribal designation. The Committee on Indian Affairs requested that the Department of the Interior report on the bill.[59] But Brooks was uncertain whether the name would satisfy Indians in Robeson County. Perceiving some opposition from the new name, he asked Albert Grorud to write an official letter to "help me to settle any argument that might come up about the old Cherokee bill," possibly from A. B. Locklear and his followers.[60]

As Brooks predicted, the community divided into two opposing groups on the question of which name best served their interests in the South's racial hierarchy. The groups differed over how best to sustain an Indian identity in the context of white supremacy. Those who favored keeping the name "Cherokee" believed that that name would protect their hard-fought victories for education in the state, victories secured by white supremacists' notions of Indian identity. Those who favored the name "Cheraw," however, looked to the federal government's standards of Indian identity to support their social autonomy in the Jim Crow South.

That summer, Joseph Brooks and others began organizing a new representative council of the Indians in Robeson County. Referred to as the "Cheraw Indians of Robeson and Adjoining Counties," this entity of self-government demonstrated to the OIA the Indians' serious desire to gain protection for their schools by asserting tribal self-rule. They elected a "Business Committee" consisting of B. G. Graham as president, Joseph Brooks as vice president, and James E. Chavis as secretary. The Senate Committee on Indian Affairs accepted their government and Joseph Brooks as the duly elected representative of the group to the federal government. The Senate committee expected the council to govern democratically in order to be legitimate. They warned, for example, that Brooks should honestly represent the council and that the council should "stand by" the majority of tribal members.[61] The Cheraws then met to elect their representatives to the council and passed a resolution declaring their affiliation with the Cheraw Indians, based on their belief in the research of John Swanton. They also appointed B. G. Graham and Joseph Brooks to proceed to Washington "to foster the passage of certain bills to recognize and enroll us as Indians by the U.S.A." They then gave Graham and Brooks sole authority to transact business in the council's stead, perhaps anticipating challenges from other members of the tribe.[62]

The Senate Committee on Indian Affairs held hearings on the bill in late January 1934. Harold Ickes, secretary of the interior, told the committee in a letter that he did not favor the bill in its present form but that "legislation to clarify the status of these Indians is desirable." Without explanation, Ickes asked that the name "Cheraw" be changed to "Siouan Indians of Lumber River." James Chavis remembered that this change was a result of the Senate committee chairman's knowledge of the multiple tribal ancestors of the Robeson County Indians; he felt that "Siouan" would "cover all the small tribes and groups represented in and among the Siouan people."[63]

Furthermore, Ickes recommended that the Senate strike any provisions regarding education from the bill. Ickes suggested that they replace those provisions with the following: "Provided, that nothing contained herein shall be construed as conferring Federal wardship or any other governmental rights or benefits upon such Indians." Such language accommodated both Congress's and the OIA's agendas; it acknowledged Robeson County's Indians as Indians while still making them subject to state laws that upheld the racial hierarchy, but it also preserved the OIA's historic policy of refusing responsibility for their education and welfare. Ickes concluded, "As the Federal Government is not under any treaty obligation to these Indians, it is not believed that the United States should assume the burden of the education of their children, which has heretofore been looked after by the State of North Carolina." The committee recommended the bill's passage, with Secretary Ickes's amendments.

Unlike previous reports from the Department of the Interior, this one affirmed a tribal ancestry for Robeson County Indians and satisfied at least part of the concerns of Bailey's constituents. The bill did not, however, provide for federal assistance in education, a key provision to protect Indians' control over their schools in Robeson County. While previous bills did not reconcile congressional and Indian Office definitions of Indian identity, the approved bill represented a compromise with white supremacy by the OIA and Senate Committee on Indian Affairs. They gave Robeson County Indians nominal recognition but left control of Indian schools in the hands of the state of North Carolina.[64]

As with the previous Cherokee bill, the Robeson County Indian leadership was not satisfied with Ickes's ruling. With a great deal of emotion and frustration, they appealed to Grorud to help them get a hearing before President Roosevelt, "without sending [it] through our representatives of the state," who they no longer trusted. "This is the crisis of our race," James Chavis wrote. "I am in this with my whole heart, for I have worked with my people here night and day. . . . We sure need help for it seems that this race has been under this curse 99 years and the state intends to hold us there."[65] While we cannot know whether Chavis used the words "people" and "race" with some specific intent here, his frustration likely arose out of how his tireless work for his People bore no fruit, because the state of North Carolina—and officials at the federal level—continued to label them as a race. Grorud was noncommittal in his response.[66] Indian leaders in Robeson County had no choice but to accept the Senate committee's version of the bill with Ickes's amendments. Their acquiescence may not have seemed like an utter failure, however, because this was the first time a bill had been successfully pushed through the committee in the twenty-one years that Indians had been engaged in this process. Brooks, Graham, and others likely felt that in some measure, at least, it secured their authority as effective leaders and representatives of their People.

But the factionalism that began with the Cherokee bill did not abate with the partial success of the Siouan bill. Instead, internal divisions only shifted slightly. Other Indians in Robeson County disputed the new Siouan government's authority and challenged the bill and the new name. Their motivations centered on preserving the state's authority and Indian control of admission to Indian-only schools. Although their overriding concern was the conflict between the state-sanctioned identity as Cherokee and the federal identity as Siouan, they attacked the authority of Graham and Brooks to speak for the tribe and resurrected the Lost Colony history, propagated by white Democratic "friends" of the tribe. Graham and Brooks's opponents became known as the "Cherokees" because of their insistence on that designation for the tribe. Cherokee leaders not only disagreed with the Siouans ideologically, but their leadership also came from different kinship and settlement communities. The Lowry and Oxendine families in Pembroke dominated the Cherokee leadership. These families' home settlements were in Hopewell and Prospect, and the leaders descended from some of the community's most active nineteenth-century religious and educational leaders (see appendix charts 1 and 4).

Clifton Oxendine, principal of Pembroke's Indian elementary school, wrote to Senator Bailey and raised objections to the Siouan bill. "The majority of the Indians in Robeson County are absolutely opposed to the passing of such a bill by congress," he wrote. Furthermore, he argued that the bill "ignored" the Lost Colony connection as supported by Hamilton McMillan: "The persons . . . who are in Washington trying to get this bill passed are not the leaders of our race. They are of that class that believes that the government owes us something. . . . I realize that our privilege[s] are very meager and limited as it is, but with the passage of the proposed bill we will be in much worse shape than we are at present. It's true that we as a people need help from the Federal Government but I feel that the bill which is before congress concerning us would be very detrimental to us if passed." While Oxendine saw the obvious need for and benefits of federal assistance, he opposed the bill in its present form because, as recommended by the committee, the legislation did nothing to alter the situation of Robeson County Indians other than changing their name. Oxendine also objected to the persons who proposed the name change and the unforeseen effects the change might have on Indian schools.[67]

Worried that direct appeals would prove ineffective, the Cherokee faction engaged older tactics and solicited help from two white contacts—former Lumberton district attorneys and state legislators T. A. McNeill and E. J. Britt, who forwarded their opinions to Senator Bailey. A delegation of Indians "who represent the best element of their people" visited Britt and registered their objections to the bill. "They say that at least 90% of the best element of the Indians of Robeson County are opposed to the passage of this Bill," Britt reported. "They are satisfied with their present status and desire to remain as Cherokee Indians of Robeson County." Consequently, he hoped that Bailey would "see to it that the Bill is not passed."[68] Britt emphasized the middle-class status of the Indians who opposed the bill, hoping that Bailey would see the interests of this class as benefiting the Indian people as a whole. Though he does not say so directly, Britt also knew that this "best element" of Indians controlled a large bloc of votes that could turn for or against a white politicians' campaign. Such knowledge made him particularly sensitive to the interests of that group, whether or not they represented a true majority of Indian opinion.

A similar delegation of thirty self-styled Indian "leaders" also visited T. A. McNeill. McNeill assured Bailey that the Indians "who have been for years engaged in building up their race, and who are the educated ones among them, are opposed to the bill." McNeill implied that the Siouan faction lacked knowledge of their situation and therefore did not represent the best interests of the Indian community. Further, McNeill's visitors saw the Siouan name as a threat to the Indian-only educational system they had worked so hard to achieve. As McNeill explained, these men

> have for forty years labored faithfully to get some status for their
> people, and have succeeded in having the state recognize them in a
> creditable manner as a race. . . . They have had considerable trouble
> keeping the mulatto people from adjoining counties, and particularly

from South Carolina, from moving into Robeson County and entering their schools under false claim of Indian blood. They have had many law suits about this, and it is now generally understood that none but Robeson County Indians, or Indians of that descent can enter these schools. . . . They feel . . . that this connection with this supposed tribe of Indians [the "Siouans"] will again open the flood gates to South Carolina and adjoining counties.

For the Cherokee faction, the Siouan name clouded their status in the eyes of the state politicians and judges who for many years had protected their schools from "mulattos" and other people they considered to be non-Indians. McNeill, like Britt, probably had a vested interest in seeing that Bailey addressed these men's concerns. "I unhesitatingly advise that you follow their suggestions to kill this bill," McNeill told Bailey.[69]

Kinship marked community membership, but settlement affiliation and, by extension, one's association with the settlement's school and church were just as important. Whether one belonged depended in part on whether one attended an Indian-only school. According to McNeill, these Cherokees feared that if "Siouan" became the federal tribal designation, imposters might claim that affiliation and threaten opportunities for other Indian children. Children might begin enrolling from two different groups; while these leaders could predict that those who claimed to be Cherokee would be from known families, they apparently could not confidently predict the eligibility of those who might claim to be Siouan. Given their precarious situation under white supremacy, their reasoning likely involved a feared association with "mulatto" children, and they logically emphasized this reasoning to white elected officials.

But here the racial hierarchy intertwined with issues of political autonomy and identity. These leaders could not predict the actions of Indian families under the proposed law, nor could they predict the actions of state officials. Ultimately, the name change might cast doubt on Indians' power to determine their own community membership. After all, a name change on the state level had not preceded a federal name change, and leaders did not know how the state government would react to Congress's decision. State officials might decide to only allow Cherokee children to attend the schools and ban Siouan children because Cherokee was the name the state approved. The local authority of school committees to determine which children belonged to the community and therefore qualified for attendance could be compromised, further damaging the little bit of autonomy that Indians had under white supremacy. The state, not the federal government, funded the school system, and the maintenance of those schools depended upon the state's recognition of a separate Indian identity.

Cherokees articulated their Indian identity through their work to preserve Indian-only schools, which in turn required a negotiation with the state government and white supremacy. From their perspective, the Siouan bill threatened their identity as Indians, especially since the bill made no separate provision for federally funded schools and left their education at the mercy of white supremacists at the state level.

O. H. Lowrey, an Indian, articulated the Cherokee position even more clearly in terms of the racial hierarchy and the benefits of miscegenation with whites. "[Y]ou . . . know of our status in Robeson," he wrote. "We, as a people, have been set a part a separate race based on Indian and white Blood. We know our place and hope to maintain it[.] We expect our Representatives in Washington to help us Progress not retard." Like the Indians who had written in support of the Cherokee bill in 1933, most of whom became Siouan supporters, Lowrey also expected Bailey to keep his part of the bargain in return for Indians' acquiescence to white supremacy. His letter reveals that both factions sought recognition for their Indian identity and Indian autonomy, but while Siouans looked to the OIA's definition of an Indian in this quest, Cherokees wrestled with white southerners' approach to racial identity, confident that what had worked in the past would continue to work.[70] In this way, white supremacy and segregation functioned to aggravate internal divisions in the Indian community.

Bailey threw his definitive support to the Cherokees late in February 1934, when a committee that included D. F. Lowry and his nephew James R. Lowry proposed another bill to designate them as Cherokees. They wrote the letter on stationery from the Indian Normal School, where James R. Lowry was dean of students: "We are unanimous for National recognition in accordance with our present State recognition i.e. Cherokee, with the same rights and privileges of other citizens." They wanted federal recognition as much as the Siouan group did, but they felt more comfortable with a bill and a history that pleased southern whites. The bill they proposed was identical to the one that failed in 1932.[71] In spite of the same bill's previous failure, Bailey replied, "This is entirely agreeable to me. I shall have the Siouan Bill killed and withdrawn from the Senate."[72]

The Siouan Council called a public meeting a month after Bailey had killed their bill. The crowd gathered at Saint Annah, a rural community just north of Pembroke and the home community of some of the Siouan leadership, which included Buddy Graham, Joseph Brooks, and Chesley Locklear. The settlement's eponymous church was probably filled to capacity; the turnout was especially high because so much controversy had surrounded the various congressional bills. Cherokee leaders came to the meeting as well, perhaps seeking to explain their position. Brooks called them "politicians," a derisive word in some Robeson County Indian settings. I have heard Lumbees and Tuscaroras use it at the kitchen table as a direct insult, and for Brooks to directly confront people with that insult implied that the fracas in the halls of Congress had noticeably damaged the community's political fabric. Brooks then reportedly followed the insult with a threat. "Go on home," he told them, "or we'll make it hot for you."[73]

Brooks's outburst was probably uncharacteristic. Whenever I ask people to describe Joe Brooks, they first say something like, "Everybody loved him." By all accounts, he and his fellow Siouan Council leader Jim Chavis were typical of Robeson County Indian men—not taciturn or particularly stoic, but ready to smile and laugh, extend a hand, and sit down to chat. The Lumbee men I know love to gossip and "politick," to discuss the affairs of the day and conquer one another in debate. Joe was my great-great uncle, my maternal grandmother's uncle; Jim's family were close neighbors with my mother's family. The heated exchange that apparently occurred at Saint Annah that day reflected the considerable political heat generated by Senator Bailey's actions.

Bailey's role in killing the Siouan bill did not alleviate the internal controversy of the community, so the Senate Committee on Indian Affairs called a meeting of the two factions in Washington, D.C. Representative J. Bayard Clark from the House and Angus McLean were also present at the conference. Graham and Brooks claimed that 90 percent of the Indian population approved of the name "Siouan," and they believed that duty called them to stand by the majority. Representatives of the minority Cherokee faction did not dispute the claim of the Siouans in the meeting; perhaps they simply believed that regardless of the majority's opinion, they better understood the community's situation under state law and white supremacy. According to committee staff member Albert Grorud, "The attitude of the delegates who represent the minority . . . would not yield." Grorud thought that John R. Swanton's Siouan designation was the most appropriate for the tribe, but because the Cherokee faction would not compromise, nothing came of the conference.[74]

The delegates from both sides returned to Robeson County and held meetings with their supporters; the Cherokees met in Pembroke, while the

Siouans met at Saint Annah Church. Gertrude Bonnin, a Sioux Indian and president of the National Council of American Indians (NCAI), spoke to the Siouan group and urged them to continue to fight for federal recognition. The group voted to join the NCAI at the meeting, sending a message to the Cherokees and non-Indians that they would use outside resources in their cause.[75] Grorud was also present at this meeting, lending his support to the Siouan faction. Surely, the other Indians present at the meeting saw his presence essentially as an endorsement by the Senate Indian Affairs Committee.[76] A Robeson County sheriff's deputy arrived to police the 2,000-person meeting; Saint Annah's capacity was probably about 200, and people must have been blocking the road in front of the church. Asserting his authority and the community's autonomy, Joseph Brooks told the deputy, "We'll run our own affairs."[77]

The locations of these meetings sent a powerful message to other Indians. In some ways, the locations reflect typical distinctions based on kin and settlement that had existed for decades in the Indian community. But the negotiations with the federal government in the early 1930s gave these distinctions a new political importance for how the tribe maintained its identity and its autonomy. Leaders of each faction believed they held the key to a federal process that would moderate the crippling social, political, and economic effects of segregation. Cherokees saw themselves as closely affiliated with the town of Pembroke and the Normal School, places that were Indian-controlled but heavily dependent upon white patronage. Siouans, however, met in the church, another symbol of Indian autonomy and power over which whites had less control; furthermore, their seat of power was a rural community that was close to Pembroke but dominated by Indian landowners.[78] Each faction defined itself in opposition to the other. For an Indian who was not a member of the leadership class, then, choosing to attend a meeting at the Normal School or at the church signified which faction he preferred and with which of the tribe's growing social classes he most identified. The identity markers embedded in these political events hardened the distinction between town and rural Indians that had developed in the 1920s.

These differences implied that there were wide, irreconcilable gulfs between supporters of the Cherokee and Siouan names. However, the two groups had a great deal in common. Leaders of both sides were landowners and relatively well educated; both sides embraced education for their people—as indicated by the text of the bills that they proposed—and both sides clearly saw the limitations that poverty and segregation placed on their people. Both sides recognized the value of federal acknowledgment; validation from the federal government as a "tribe" with a distinct history could empower them to assert greater control over their own affairs and perhaps gain positions of influence in the segregated South. Furthermore, both sets of leaders saw value in making contacts with whites outside their community to improve their circumstances and enhance their own influence within their kin networks and settlements.

Despite these broad areas of agreement, two main factors separated the groups. Kin and settlement patterns, and an ideological disagreement concerning the role that white supremacy should play in their affairs, divided them. As indicated by the names of those involved in the negotiations, at least three of the members of the Fourth Street Power Structure, as well as other influential educational leaders, promoted the Cherokee name. These men, almost without exception, resided in the town of Pembroke and belonged to that town's middle class. Several of them were also close kin to one another, descendants of Allen Lowry of Hopewell or James Oxendine of Prospect. The Cherokees appeared to have no formal political council and did not keep membership or registration lists.

The Siouan group counted only one member of the Fourth Street Power Structure among its supporters, while their other leaders came from Pembroke and Saint Annah. The Siouan faction also included many members of the Brooks Settlement, who were also distantly related to Joseph Brooks's family but constituted their own kin network. As indicated by the letter-writing campaign that Brooks and Graham had organized to support the Cherokee bill, their network reached beyond Pembroke to include many communities north of Pembroke (such as Philadelphus, Saddletree, Rennert, Red Banks, and Prospect) but fewer communities south of Pembroke.[79] By the spring of 1934, what was formerly the Cheraw Council had become the "General Council of Siouan Indians of Lumber River," with 2,181 members who elected councilmen representing seventeen Indian settlements. Graham, Brooks, and James E. Chavis continued to serve as the group's executives.[80] These divisions reflected the political diversity that had been an ongoing feature of community life.

These kin and settlement differences did not by themselves mean disagreement on the question of which tribal name they would accept. After all, many of those who supported the 1932 Cherokee bill, including Joseph Brooks and B. G. Graham, became Siouan supporters in 1933 and 1934. To the majority of those who desired federal recognition, the origins of the different names in the group's history or ancestry did not matter. But the meanings embedded in the names changed a great deal over time, and Indians recognized that whites and their notions of identity controlled the meanings of the names. They persistently pushed for support in the face of the injustices of segregation under whatever tribal name whites wanted, whether they were local southerners or federal officials.

Kin and settlement differences became significant when Indians factored attitudes about segregation into the discussion. Pursuing a name with which whites felt comfortable resulted in disappointment, due to the federal government's ambivalent attitude about southern segregation and its consistent refusal, until 1933, to recognize a tribal affiliation for these Indians. No single name pleased everyone at any one time, and neither the Indian Office nor Congress acted on the question because of two factors: uncertainty about how it would affect southern white power and an ongoing reluctance to establish a relationship with another Indian group. Prior to the 1930s and during the assimilation era, these agendas were intimately related. In the meantime, Indians had their own reactions to the names, and when the government finally applied a definitive label in 1933, Indians themselves divided on the question based on their various opinions about how best to deal with segregation.

The primary disagreement between the Cherokee and Siouan supporters was not over whether the federal government should recognize the group but over what strategy should be used to accomplish this goal. Cherokees put their faith in their political contacts in Congress, the local white community, and state government, while Siouans followed the lead of the OIA in Washington. These political actions affected how each group articulated and chose to maintain their identity as Indians. The Cherokee leadership called on their forty-plus years of experience working within the Jim Crow system, in which proving they were Indians depended on proving they were "not black" and, at least in some ways, aspired to "be white." Maintaining Indian-only schools, where it was evident to non-Indians that Indians were a distinct and socially autonomous People, was critical to maintaining an Indian identity in this context. They saw the Siouan name as a potential threat to their schools because the state government had not recognized that name, and they feared losing control over their ability to determine their membership.

Siouan supporters, on the other hand, called on their experience with Jim Crow and decided that they could maintain their schools with the federal government's help rather than the state's. They sought to distinguish themselves from blacks and whites, not just on the basis of values that local whites thought were important but on markers that whites in Washington thought were important—namely, a tribal name. Believing that an inconclusive tribal affiliation was the main obstacle to federal recognition, they pursued a name that federal government representatives suggested. They also created a representative tribal government to signal to the Congress and the OIA that the Robeson County Indians functioned politically and socially as a distinct Indian tribe, similar to other tribes that the federal government assisted. Siouans organized politically as a tribe in order to prepare themselves for what they believed was near-certain government assistance to alleviate their precarious position under Jim Crow. Unlike the Cherokees, who believed that persons of "doubtful" ancestry assaulted their Indian identity, the absence of equal opportunity most threatened Siouans' sense of themselves as Indians. Thus, they allied themselves with another set of powerful policy makers in Washington.[81]

These conflicting views had ramifications for how Indians expressed their identity in the 1930s, 1940s, and 1950s. The two factions agreed on many things, and the community's social organization, which revolved around kinship and place, encompassed all sides and continued to give their identity an important coherence that political disagreements could not destroy. But the differences between how Cherokees and Siouans expressed their identity became the source of much conflict within the community. Cherokees demonstrated a "progressive" attitude that appealed to white middle-class values and also helped convince whites that Indians were a unique People, deserving of separate status from blacks. This expression of their "progressive" qualities—the fact that they represented the "best class" and the "best educated" of the Indian population—reveals a certain resignation to the Jim Crow system. In the face of segregation and a pervasive racial hierarchy, these men saw the power of white standards as inescapable. But the Cherokee leaders also kept their Indian community and Indian identity in mind. There is no evidence that they tried to escape being Indian, and they thought carefully—more than the Siouan leadership did—about how federal law might endanger their autonomy within the state. They articulated their Indian identity in terms of the Indian community's "progressiveness."[82] Ultimately, Cherokee supporters after 1933 believed that self-help was the key to maintaining Indian identity, a view that prompted Clifton Oxendine to deride "a class that believes the government owes them something." Cherokees wanted to be self-contained and self-supporting, and they believed that receiving direct benefits from the federal government would constrain their own power and their community's opportunities to become equal to the whites among whom they lived.

Siouans also wanted to be self-supporting, but they envisioned using the federal government to help them attain that status. In contrast to the Cherokee leadership, they did not appear resigned to segregation or anxious to assert their "progressive" values. Instead, their communications to federal officials reveal an insistence on their tribe's sovereignty and right to self-rule, objectives that were antithetical to a segregated system in which whites ruled everyone (although they permitted Indian social autonomy). To a certain extent, the emergence of an identity expressed by membership in a tribal organization was a reaction to the "progressive" identity put forward by the tribe's Cherokee leaders and by earlier generations. But Siouan leaders' rejection of segregation politics did not make them necessarily less self-interested than Cherokee leaders. The Siouan leadership surely recognized that connections to the OIA benefits in Washington augmented their own standing within the Indian community; furthermore, federal assistance put them on the same playing field with other Indians across the nation, such as those who founded the NCAI. They did not know whether those connections would eventually yield resources, or whether federally acknowledged tribes actually exercised any meaningful autonomy, but their experience had given them hope and instilled hope in their followers. Such hope of escaping the realities of Jim Crow seemed enough to carry forward. With this in mind, they continued to cultivate outside contacts and resources to make their existence and their cause known.[83]

The period 1932–34 was the climax of factional bitterness. In subsequent years, neither faction triumphed over the other, and neither surrendered. The Siouans continued their strategy of appealing to the OIA for assistance with the problems brought by the Great Depression, while the Cherokees continued to work within the local political context to maintain the tribe's social institutions. Both types of activities transformed the ways in which Robeson County Indians articulated and maintained their identity in the latter half of the twentieth century.

4 Confronting the New Deal

At age twenty-one, my father dropped out of college and started work in a local furniture factory in Robeson County; he had a wife and three children to support. Fifty-three years later, one morning over breakfast, he recalled the layout of the factory's segregated restrooms—White, Indian, and Colored.

"When I started there I was working at night," he said. "And the plant manager showed me the White bathroom to use, he didn't show me the Indian bathroom."

"Did he think you were white?" I asked, thinking how lots of people mistake my family members for Italians or Jews.

"No, he knew I was Indian. Mama worked there and everyone knew we were Indian . . . but I was the only Indian male that worked there at night, so I guess he thought it was okay for me to use the White bathroom. When I went to work in the daytime, I had to use the Indian bathroom."

My father believed that the proximity of his mother—his kin—at the plant made his identity visible to the plant manager. The manager might have known my father was Indian by this marker, or the manager's knowledge might have been based on my father's appearance. Some alchemy of appearance and known ancestry dictated the separation of races under Jim Crow, but the manager seemed perfectly willing to defy custom when no other Indians might notice. At this furniture factory and for this manager, social association was as important an identity marker as appearance. We might conclude that whites in Jim Crow Robeson County recognized the same kinds of identity criteria that Indians did, which was probably the case. But when my father continued his story, I began to realize that the plant manager may have also had a political motive behind his seeming act of tolerance.

My father wasn't just an employee; he was also a union organizer. He was no revolutionary, but the local carpenters-union representative chose him as the plant leader "because I didn't know any better," he said. Nevertheless, he tried to get the workers, mostly Indian and white with a few blacks, to organize a union. The plant manager may have allowed him a small privilege of whiteness—using the white restroom when no one else was looking—to encourage him to side with the management rather than the union. It didn't work, and the plant manager fired everyone who was involved with the union, except my father. Instead, the manager assigned a man to follow my father around the factory as he worked, surveilling him; then my father quit. After a National Labor Relations Board (NLRB) hearing about the firings, the plant manager hired everyone back. But he reassigned my father to a "bad job" in the metalworks part of the plant—where blacks worked—hoping that a threat would work better than a promise. The NLRB also required the plant employees to hold a referendum on establishing a union. After workers voted down the union, my father walked out "and never looked back," he said. His past behind him, he decided his future lay in a college education.

Industrialization in the style of Daystrom Furniture accompanied legal segregation in the South. In many ways, segregation arose from the quest to categorize and order what the industrial economy had made into a rather anonymous, impersonal South. This kind of economy is a hallmark of modern society, and the spaces associated with it were typically cities. "Modernity" is a sociologist's shorthand for industrial civilization; U.S. historians often use it to talk about the nineteenth and twentieth centuries, when many people worked within manufacturing and market-cash (rather than informal-barter) economies. The temporal and regional boundaries of the modern United States are vague and subject to debate, but it seems that in some ways segregation marked the visible emergence of a modern South. The systematic rules of segregation arose from the anonymous social interactions typical of urban spaces, where a black person's inferior economic status could not be assumed. Several scholars have shown how such a social-structuring enterprise was evidence of the South's modernity. Modern spaces and states were legible to outsiders; defined strict categories and hierarchies of people, ideas, and things; and valued administrative simplification. Segregation essentialized the South's spectrum of ethnicities and economic statuses and made white supremacy a seemingly natural device to keep society peaceful, prosperous, and "progressive." As people moved into industrialized spaces, those in power found it necessary to make new rules and create exceptions to old ones. Law and policy reflected those rules, which aimed to reinforce white supremacy. Indians were not simply passive victims of these changes, however; they rejected and accommodated modern America as well.[1]

With the exception of historian Philip Deloria's work, little has been done to understand Indians' relationship to modernity. In his book *Indians in Unexpected Places*, Deloria argues that whites stereotyped Indians as premodern or "primitive," not because Indians did not participate in modern society but so that whites could better measure their own modernity; they could be scientific, rational, and wealthy if Indians were superstitious, incompetent, and poor. In other words, the dichotomy of premodern and modern did not exist without white privilege.[2]

This dichotomy was part of the foundation of white supremacy in its twentieth-century form. The system's authority lay in its power to include or exclude based on whether a group or individual fit the modern mold. White supremacy's authority lay not in the system's power to ban all nonwhites completely but in its power to control the gateway to the status that accompanied a white identity. Whites, and no one else, controlled who had what kind of access to the privileges of whiteness. Being modern was one of those privileges. The creation of segregation required that white supremacists engage in modernity and see the world in terms of essentially "white" and essentially "black" people; Indians fit neither category but had to be rationalized in some way to be subject to the system's rules.

My father's experience was modern in the sense that industrial priorities regulated his work and segregation boxed his identity into a racial hierarchy. But it was also premodern in the sense that the factory manager invoked personal knowledge of my father's identity as an Indian and a union organizer, and he used that knowledge to apportion my father reward or punishment for his adherence to Jim Crow's rule of economic subordination for plant workers. His reward was the privilege of using the white bathroom, his punishment a "bad job" working alongside blacks. The dichotomy of modern and premodern is often false, but those people with less power—in this case, my father—must reckon with it anyway. Often they find ways to subvert the dichotomy, or they don't bother trying to manage it; my father did so by quitting his job and following his mother's advice to go back to school.[3]

Indians in Robeson County engaged this modern system of segregation and began to add layers to their identity to maintain some degree of autonomy within it. In the 1930s they took their negotiations with the federal government to a new level and further capitalized on the modern notions of identity and policy held at the Office of Indian Affairs. The relationship between Jim Crow and federal Indian policy may seem unexpected, but only if one expects that Indians belonged outside the framework of southern race relations or that southern Indians belonged outside the framework of federal Indian policy.[4] With a political association to the federal government (defined by "name") and a racial relationship to the state of North Carolina and local proponents of white supremacy (defined by "blood"), Indians in Robeson County had to affirm their identity by negotiating the ideologies of both systems. The engagement with the OIA during the New Deal also generated additional identity markers, demonstrating how Indians creatively pursued modern trends to affirm their sense of themselves as a people. Indians' identity created change in their society.[5]

For Indians in Robeson County, their functioning social order revolved around identity markers of kinship, settlement, and a decentralized, contested political structure. New Deal Indian policy did not match Robeson County Indians' social order, nor the order of most tribes that came under its purview. OIA officials hoped to develop self-governing Indian communities so that Indians could determine their destinies according to their own cultural traditions, "but only in the sense that communities followed the basic ideological guidelines the [OIA] established," according to authors Vine Deloria Jr. and Clifford Lytle.[6] These ideological guidelines contained certain assumptions about Indian identity, and in Robeson County, the OIA used the same criteria that white southerners had established: ancestry and appearance.

SOUTHERN WHITE SUPREMACISTS based identification by ancestry and appearance on ideas that they believed were scientifically legitimate. "Blood" and ancestry were important aspects of white supremacy because maintaining the system without slavery necessitated a more rigid definition of who belonged to what racial group—especially important for classifying people with mixed racial ancestry, those whose ancestry was unknown, or others who were not obviously "white" or "black."[7] Without slaves as property, white males conceived of family and ancestry as property interests, with whites holding the sole right to construct "normal" families and thus regulate who would benefit from property ownership through laws of marriage, inheritance, custody, and divorce. The "science" of race, which gained coherence around the same time as emancipation, dictated that ancestry was the only reliable marker of whiteness.

To ensure that no one trespassed on white privilege, one's white ancestry, or "blood"—a supposedly quantifiable, measurable substance, not unlike money in an industrial age—had to be "pure." In many states, blood composition became the marker for measuring the degree of inclusion a nonwhite person or group received. But how would society measure blood? For all the scientists' insistence on the promise of ancestry as a definitive racial marker, most southerners could only measure it by the most unreliable of markers: appearance. Most of the time, courts and the general public fell on common-sense understandings of racial origins that everyone "knew."[8] The bureaucrats at the OIA relied on these same "scientific" understandings in implementing the law.

At the OIA, white supremacy was based on a fundamental assumption embedded in Indian law since the nineteenth century and consistently present in anthropological literature of the same era: there is a direct and linear relationship between the amount of "Indian blood" and amount of "Indian culture" within an individual who claimed to be Indian. OIA administrations and Congress have interpreted and reinterpreted the premise that diminishing "Indian blood" accompanies an irreversible loss of distinctive "Indian culture."[9] This view not only ignores the ways in which Native cultures—like all cultures—change over time, but it also ties Indian communities, in the words of sociologist Eva Marie Garroutte, to "stringent notions about ancientness that seldom, if ever, appear in the identity definitions related to other racial populations."[10] Garroutte points out that the dominant society has allowed African Americans, in particular, considerably greater leeway to express an identity as "black" while exhibiting cultural characteristics that are far removed from their African tribal roots.[11] The inconsistency in treatment of blacks' and Indians' identity definitions was one example of the role of white privilege in asserting a distinction between modern and premodern peoples. Whites visited these inconsistencies on blacks as well. For example, whites valued African Americans as premodern people when they consumed black "primitive" art during the Harlem Renaissance of the 1920s.[12] Defining groups as modern or premodern assisted white supremacists at the federal and local level in exploiting each population's resources for the benefit of whites.

WHEN AMERICAN VOTERS elected President Franklin D. Roosevelt in 1932, Roosevelt took his mandate to alleviate the Great Depression to every corner of government. In the Department of the Interior, Secretary Harold Ickes appointed activist John Collier to the position of commissioner of Indian Affairs and directed him to fix the problems in the federal government's assimilation policy. These policies had led to the dissolution of tribal landownership and the partial destruction of Indian languages, religions, and traditional lifeways. Collier had worked against these policies in earnest for over ten years.

Collier was the grandson of a Confederate veteran on one side and, on the other, an army soldier who had assisted in the Removal of the Cherokees; he grew up in Atlanta and later moved to New York. A social worker interested in using anthropological theories of culture to benefit the poor and needy, Collier first encountered Indigenous cultures as a young man on camping expeditions through the North Carolina mountains around the turn of the century. His guide was a twelve-year-old Cherokee boy who had never seen the mountain range they explored but "in some mysterious way he knew all of the old trails and was perfectly at home."[13] From a young age, then, Collier believed that Indians could provide solutions for problems. While participating in an influential circle of activists and intellectuals in New York, Collier visited Taos Pueblo in New Mexico in 1920. After observing Taos's ceremonial and communal life, Collier became convinced that this approach to community could heal the wounds created by the Western industrialized world. Indian communal life, he believed, provided an example for an America on the brink of social disintegration. Furthermore, the approach offered by the social sciences—particularly anthropology—could engineer a communal democracy that valued both reciprocity and individual choice. Having seen the injustices perpetrated upon Indians by policies that furthered their destruction rather than their preservation, Collier set out to remake Indian policy and Indian communities in the image of a democratically run corporation capable of effectively managing economic resources.[14]

Congress passed the Indian Reorganization Act (IRA; also known as the Wheeler-Howard Act) in May 1934 to end the cultural and land loss that the assimilation policies had brought about. The preamble established the act's intent: "To conserve and develop Indian lands and resources; to extend to Indians the right to form business and other organizations; to establish a credit system for Indians; to grant certain rights of home rule to Indians; [and] to provide for vocational education for Indians." Congress accomplished these provisions by abolishing future allotment of Indian lands; authorizing the restoration of remaining surplus lands to tribal control; providing funds for the acquisition of more land; granting tribes the right to incorporate or write constitutions and by-laws and form other organizations; establishing a loan fund for economic development; and expanding the civil-service requirements to include and give preference to Indians.[15]

Congress and the OIA collaborated on writing the IRA; congressmen made law, but OIA officials made policy by deciding how to implement the law.

While Congress's final law departed in significant respects from Collier's original bill—a debate described in detail by Deloria and Lytle in their book *The Nations Within*—both documents had certain fundamental features in common.

First, Collier's bill and the final IRA both defined an "Indian." The definition relied primarily on the political relationship to the federal government that had been enshrined in judge-made Indian law dating back to the 1830s, which in some cases eschewed blood quantum as a standard. "Blood quantum" refers to the practice of measuring a person's identity by equating their racial ancestry to a proportion of blood in their body; for example, a person with an Indian parent and a non-Indian parent may have been thought to possess a blood quantum of one-half "Indian blood." But the act embraced blood quantum in other cases as an identity marker that was measured by ancestry and appearance. An Indian, according to the act, was a member of a recognized tribe "*whether or not* residing on an Indian reservation and regardless of the degree of blood"; or an Indian was a descendant of a member of a recognized tribe *and* living on a reservation "regardless of blood." Alternately, an Indian could be "a person of one-half or more Indian blood, whether or not affiliated with a recognized tribe, and whether or not they have ever resided on a reservation."[16] Robeson County Indians were members of this final class of persons, provided they could prove their blood quantum eligibility.

Collier originally proposed that Indians with one-quarter or more "Indian blood" qualify for this recognition. But Montana's Senator Burton K. Wheeler, chairman of the Committee on Indian Affairs, changed the provision to one-half or more "Indian blood." His rationale demonstrated a political merger of economic concerns and supposedly scientific markers of identity. The Senate committee left discussion of the provisions for nonreservation Indians until the last day of the hearings about the IRA bill, indicating policy makers' general neglect of these Indians. Wheeler remarked, "If you pass it to where they are quarter-blood Indians you are going to have all kinds of people coming in and claiming they are quarter-blood Indians and want to be put upon the Government rolls, and in my judgment it should not be done. What we are trying to do is get rid of the Indian problem rather than add to it."[17]

Wheeler wanted to prevent the government from bearing any additional burden from nonreservation Indians. He apparently thought a one-quarter "Indian blood" requirement would tempt imposters who could not prove the kinds of political relationships the federal government otherwise recognized. He perhaps calculated that a one-half requirement was so difficult to meet that Indians who did meet it had undoubtedly maintained some cultural and residential distinctiveness as well. To underscore this point, Wheeler indicated his belief that Indians with lower blood quantum were totally assimilated and therefore not really Indians at all. Speaking of California Indians, he said to Collier, they "are no more Indians than you or I, perhaps, I mean they are white people essentially."[18] Regardless of the ancestry or cultural connections of California Indians, Wheeler viewed them as "essentially" white, just as white supremacists in the South had constructed people of various ethnicities as "white" or "colored," transforming blood from a kinship metaphor to a property interest. Both revisions of identity were partly motivated by the same economic goal: reserving Indian economic resources for whites' benefit.

Second, both the OIA and Congress fundamentally believed that Indian groups had no political organizations of their own, an assumption that ignored the functioning social order that Indians themselves had established in favor of a centralized, schematic policy that effectively treated all groups the same.[19] But while Congress simply authorized tribes to "organize for [their] common welfare," elect their leaders, and write constitutions, Collier micromanaged Indian self-governance when he implemented the law.[20] He believed that land allotment and the assimilation policy had destroyed whatever governments existed in Indian communities, with the exception of those found in the southwestern Pueblos. Accordingly, he believed that Indians on reservations were victimized by OIA agents and needed a relationship to the federal government that approximated the "indirect rule" or "home rule" found in British colonies around the world. Very little evidence supported the assumption that Indians had no functioning governments, but Collier promoted Indian governments that the federal government viewed as acceptable and legitimate. The IRA did not prohibit Indian communities from organizing (or maintaining) governments that reflected their own social and political traditions. But in implementing the act, attorneys within the Department of the Interior drafted the actual constitutions—many of which "had a distinct Anglo-American flavor," according to Deloria and Lytle, and subjected important tribal powers to the approval of the secretary of the interior.[21] The constitutions brought concepts of "Western-style democracy," such as majority rule, to Indian political organizations that operated under very different assumptions.[22]

Sometimes these measures had positive results; among the Blackfeet in Montana, for example, leaders took advantage of the IRA's democratic tools to increase self-determination and incubate creative responses to cultural threats.[23] But in other cases, the OIA actually blocked self-government. According to anthropologist Richard Clemmer, the Hopi tribal council adopted a "boilerplate" legal code suggested by the Interior Department. These ordinances contravened the tribe's own way of doing things and resulted in the dissolution of the IRA government. The Western Shoshone in Nevada adopted the IRA and wrote a constitution that matched their own governance patterns, but the OIA rejected that constitution in favor of a system that ultimately undermined Western Shoshone land claims. The impact of the IRA's self-government provisions varied, and the OIA's implementation of the act sometimes contradicted the IRA's stated purpose.[24]

In hindsight, these contradictions seem predictable in light of Collier's conviction that Western-style governments improved Indians' chances of lobbying effectively for their needs and curtailed the destruction of Indian life. He intentionally chose this method of organizing "tribes" over the alternatives of family, settlement, or other preexisting social structures in Indian communities. According to historian Wilcomb Washburn, "Collier chose the tribe [as the primary organizational structure] because that was the way Whites saw Indians, and he could use the term to convey a favorable historical and romantic image to justify the preservation of Indian cultures and group organizations to a potentially unsympathetic Congress." The "tribe" was a social and political unit convenient for government officials, but not for Indians. Furthermore, Collier expected these governments to unify families, villages, or other subgroups so that Indians could pursue their interests in agreement with one another. As Washburn writes, "The United States had not in the past been willing to deal with every Indian village, pueblo, or band and this was unlikely to change. Collier's solution was to take advantage of the White perception of tribal unity, create that unity where it did not exist, and strengthen tribal power where it was lacking."[25]

Collier theorized that a unified, centralized political organization would provide the best conduit for government services to tribes and the most effective means of economic development. But he did not anticipate the ways in which such organization, particularly on reservations with more than one tribal community, might create additional political divisions. Collier's legislation might have solved this problem by asking Congress to explicitly recognize that governments existed in tribal communities, but his blindness to this fact prevented this obvious solution. Amidst these predicted problems, Congress agreed to organize reservations, not tribes, as governing units. Asking reservation governments to deliver services to Indians gave sovereign powers to administrative units rather than Indian-defined societies and arguably contributed to the undermining of traditional Indian political organizations.[26]

Implementing the IRA among the Mississippi Choctaws provided a good example of what might happen under these circumstances. The Indian agent established a Tribal Business Committee and charged them with approving the IRA, but Choctaws themselves, many of whom served on the Business Committee, formed a parallel government: the Mississippi Choctaw Indian Federation. The federation did not represent another faction of Choctaw leaders but instead served particular needs that the Business Committee could not. Choctaws themselves did not object to the Business Committee but to the Indian agent's domination of it. The federation, on the other hand, acted somewhat more autonomously—though in open cooperation with local white politicians—and served to expand democratic principles. Despite Choctaw support of the federation and Collier's rhetoric of Indian self-determination, Collier was not willing to undermine the agent's authority. He refused to recognize the federation and backed the Business Committee as the legitimate Choctaw government. Choctaws refused to back down, however, and it took another eleven years—and the interests of Shell Oil Company in Choctaw lands—to organize a tribal government in Mississippi. Historian Katherine M. B. Osburn argues that unlike Collier, Choctaws had no difficulty embracing two legitimate governments.[27] Collier's belief in tribal unity and his denial of existing tribal governments were fatal flaws in the IRA, flaws that stemmed from his conviction that Indians' premodern existence had been destroyed by intervention from the modern state. While his policies unquestionably provided a new foundation for Indian self-government, his inability to see beyond this dichotomous view of society did not advance Indian self-determination and autonomy.

In practice, Collier's emphasis on political unity and other modern trappings of government was not new to Robeson County Indians, who had been dealing with whites' view of Indians, Indian unity, and an Indian "tribe" for quite some time. Collier assumed that once Indians organized governments, a particular set of threats would confront tribes and force them to unify politically. But he did not anticipate the ways in which forming those governments and recognizing Indian tribes exacerbated the fragmentation that already existed in Robeson County and elsewhere in Indian Country. The opportunities presented by the Indian New Deal did not provide Indians in Robeson County with a compelling reason to create a single government that oversaw all tribal members. The potential for change was too great for Indians to immediately agree on how they should handle federal services and tribal organization. As a result, their political disagreements developed into different ways of articulating their identity as Indians. While Robeson County Indians had been able to unite against outside threats, the IRA represented not a recognizable threat but an opportunity to expand and secure their community.[28] As such, the OIA's view of political unity had little relevance to the functioning social order of Robeson County Indians.[29]

Collier held a third assumption regarding the racial hierarchy, which was inextricably linked to the use of economic resources on Indian lands and his modernist preference for expert advice. Throughout his tenure as commissioner of Indian Affairs, Collier attacked what he saw as the root of the previous assimilation policy's failure: land allotment. Allotment gave Indians individual parcels of land. Theoretically, individual land ownership encouraged Indians to adopt Euro-American methods of farming and running households and would, in the long run, rid the government of its trust responsibility.[30] In reality, allotment accomplished little in the way of assimilation and simply made it possible for whites to acquire Indian land more easily. Lawmakers and policy makers accomplished these land transfers with a variety of methods, including a "competency" requirement that lifted restrictions on the sale of allotments owned by Indians of lower "Indian blood" quantum. Politicians in Congress and bureaucrats at the OIA presumed that greater amounts of "Indian blood" made Indians less capable of managing their own affairs; Indians with higher blood quantum were thought to be incompetent. Policy makers therefore sought to put Indian land management in the hands of "experts" at the federal level because they believed that local whites would use every means to defraud Indians of their lands. Conversely, when experts found that an individual Indian had a certain percentage of non-Indian ancestry, they often determined that the person needed less federal protection and rescinded restrictions on the alienation of lands more quickly.

Unfortunately, the category of the "incompetent Indian," determined by blood quantum, made both federal and local abuses even more likely, partly because blood quantum was such an unreliable measurement of a person's capabilities. Further, according to historian Tanis Thorne, OIA officials' determination to control Indian lands created a bureaucratic culture that could not successfully counteract the white majority's desire to release more Indian land into the general economy at the expense of Indians themselves. Under the allotment and assimilation policy, the OIA's "well-meaning paternalism had metamorphosed into an unwieldy and undemocratic bureaucracy." Racial theories therefore conjoined with a bureaucratic mindset to dispossess Indian people and force their cultural and communal destruction.[31]

Collier continued to support racial theories under the New Deal; these theories were inseparable from ideas about a racial hierarchy and modernity. For example, in letters to newspapers, he explained his intentions with the IRA in paternalistic racial terms, perhaps to edify and persuade readers who likely viewed Indians as racial inferiors. He faulted allotment for its failure to assimilate Indians to a "higher stratum of the surrounding white population," he told the *Christian Science Monitor*. He told the *New York Times* that he hoped to "obtain legislative confirmation of a policy which recognizes the Indian as an equal" to the white man. Like many of his modern contemporaries, Collier assumed the existence of a dichotomy between traditional, premodern Indian people and progressive, assimilated Indians who embraced whites' upper-class aspirations to be "self-supporting and self-respecting merchants, mechanics, bankers, lawyers, teachers, etc.; only a small percentage of the mixed bloods attained this goal."[32] This statement implied that mixed-blood Indians would desire to achieve the privileges of whiteness, if it were possible for them to do so. Frequently, of course, this was not the case. Although Collier's words may have been slanted to generate sympathy from a particular audience, his statements reflect a view of Indians as fairly homogeneous, socially inferior, premodern people who would require bureaucratic management to elevate their status in the racial hierarchy.

Collier's embrace of modern approaches emerged through his belief in the need for bureaucracy to carry out administrative functions. He enhanced the bureaucratic culture that delivered services to Indian tribes. Prior to Collier's tenure, assistants to the commissioner acted as overseers of particular divisions of the agency. The human relations division included departments of education, health, agricultural extension, and inspections; the Indian property division included land, forestry, and irrigation branches. When Collier arrived, he added divisions to manage New Deal emergency programs, such as the Civilian Conservation Corps–Indian division and the rehabilitation division. He also established the Indian organization division to manage writing and implementing tribal constitutions. The Washington office of the OIA was responsible for administrative duties, while the OIA's field offices and superintendencies implemented the programs and policies developed in Washington. The Eastern Band of Cherokee reservation in western North Carolina housed North Carolina's only field office. However, this agency had little contact with Robeson County Indians in the 1930s; all of their negotiations took place directly with Collier and his assistants and department managers in Washington.[33]

Thinking about Indians in a democratic way that presumed their cultural, if not political, continuity in contemporary society represented a new departure in OIA attitudes toward Indian communities. But Collier did not abandon all assumptions about Indians as premodern people, inescapably bound by their past, or about federal Indian policy's potential to be a modern alternative.

COLLIER'S STAFF SEEMED UNPREPARED for the social realities in Robeson County. Indians there had never lived on a reservation; they had a contested tribal government, and kin relations, rather than percentage of "Indian blood," defined who was an Indian. Indians in Robeson County, both Siouans and Cherokees, based their identity on kinship and acceptance by Indian schools and churches. This concept of identity created a kind of social unity but left room for contested leadership and political disagreement. Even though these disputes became characteristic of the Indian community, Robeson County Indians agreed on a larger point: they did not require a certain percentage of Indian ancestry to identify themselves to one another. They had developed their attitudes over centuries of strategizing to affirm their community while sharing their homeland with non-Indians and maintaining their distinct place in southern racial politics. The OIA, however, based its attitudes about Indian identity on decades of developing policy for reservation tribes, on Collier's ideas about Indian political and social organization that centered on a tribal government, and on ancestry. Each entity, therefore, saw Indian identity in a very different light, and new markers of Indian identity began to develop in Robeson County as a result of these disparate interpretations.

In early 1935 Indians in Robeson County began responding to the new Indian Reorganization Act. Joseph Brooks, writing as the "Tribal Delegate of Indians in Robeson and adjoining Counties in North Carolina," asked Collier if and how his People could organize under the act. "We have over ten thousand Indians in our group and they all are desirous of having the bill apply to them," Brooks wrote, downplaying the distinctions between Siouans and Cherokees and asserting himself as the leader of all Indians.[34] At the same time, Brooks also renewed the congressional strategy by asking Senator Josiah W. Bailey to meet with him and reintroduce the Siouan bill of 1933.[35] Bailey replied, politely refusing to see him. Cherokees' response to the IRA may have prompted Bailey's reluctance to recognize Brooks's authority.[36]

During this period of negotiation with the OIA, Congress only became involved when Cherokee leaders brought the Siouan activities to the attention of elected officials. D. F. Lowry, representing the Cherokees, had already warned Bailey of Brooks's recent activities. Unlike Brooks, Lowry did not choose to downplay the tribal schism. "We are depending upon you as we did last year to stand for us in case anything should arise regarding the Siouan 'BILL,'" Lowry wrote. Although he did not mention the IRA or the Indian Office specifically, Lowry probably knew that Brooks was in communication with Collier, and he wanted to use his congressional connection to make sure that Brooks failed to gain government assistance through the OIA.

To drive home his point, Lowry disparaged the credibility of Brooks and the other Siouan leaders as official representatives of the tribe. "With all their promises [the Siouans] only enrolled about 2,222 members out of around twelve to fifteen thousand Indians in the various counties," Lowry said, indicating that actual Siouan membership was much lower than Brooks's claim of over 10,000 and that the Siouan Council did not represent a majority of the tribe. Lowry also claimed that Brooks attracted his following by making false promises about government assistance: "Mr. Brooks told in a public address at the beginning of this campagne [sic] that the money was piled up in bags for distribution as soon as they could get National Recognition at Washington." According to Lowry, other Siouan leaders told Indians that "each family would get at least twenty acres of land, a mule and wagon and a Farm house built there on by the Government and a small appropriation." Lowry most likely believed that the IRA provided these kinds of benefits to Indians, and he thought that the Siouans were trying to take advantage of them. Whatever Brooks and the Siouan leadership were planning was entirely against the best judgment of Lowry and the Cherokee leaders. Apparently, Lowry intended to halt their progress using his congressional contacts, who had already expressed their opposition to recognition as "Siouan" for Robeson County Indians.[37]

D. F. Lowry also sought to discredit the Siouans with the OIA. He did so by articulating another version of Indian history based on the kind of "science" that modern policy making at the OIA demanded. OIA staff member W. Carson Ryan asked Lowry to "look at the Indian question from the point of view of scientific information—instead of from . . . personal feelings." In response, Lowry attempted to clarify the Cherokee identity of Robeson County's Indians. He first discounted the report made by James Mooney that claimed that Robeson County Indians had mixed racial ancestry, arguing that "it was collected here . . . from a few unfriendly Whites who were uneducated [and] opposed the progress of us Indians." Maintaining Indians' ambiguous place in the racial hierarchy demanded the renunciation of Mooney's conclusions, which the OIA no doubt believed were "scientific."

Instead, Lowry responded with his own data of sorts, which was based on the community's knowledge of kinship. "[James] Lowry was a nephew of Col. John Lowry, who was once an Indian Chief among the Cherokees, and who signed a treaty in behalf of the Cherokees in 1806," he began, and he continued to recount the ancestors' connections to one another, always labeling their tribal affiliation as Cherokee. He also cited information that indicated that Siouan-speaking communities had no affiliation with the Robeson County Indians.[38] Lowry embraced kinship as a marker of Indianness and used it as a political tool in his campaign against the Siouan leadership's influence in the community. His historical narrative also included a willingness to work with the expectations of white supremacy; he insisted that Mooney's report was fraudulent, implying that Indians had "pure" blood.

Apparently, Collier did not hear about Lowry's concerns over Siouan recognition, because the OIA began to seek sources of funding to help Robeson County's Indians. Indians all over the United States were among the most desperate Americans in the Great Depression, and Collier sought to enable them to gain an economic foothold through the IRA as well as through involvement in many other New Deal programs, such as the Civilian Conservation Corps and the Works Progress Administration. While the IRA provided some support for land purchase for Indian tribes, funding was meager, and Collier had to turn to other federal agencies, such as the Federal Emergency Relief Agency, to help groups that lacked reservation land.[39] For Robeson County Indians, Collier immediately recruited the Resettlement Administration—soon to be known as the Farm Security Administration (FSA)—to provide assistance to them.

The FSA's programs included far-reaching efforts to resettle landless tenant farmers onto more productive land on which they might crawl out of the agricultural depression that had hit the South in 1920. As the FSA developed these farms, they constructed permanent improvements to the rural landscape, such as electrical lines, paved roads, and homesteads that included houses, barns, water wells, and livestock pens. The FSA also created work for the unemployed. In February 1935, Walter V. Woehlke in the OIA's cooperative programs department and Director of Education W. Carson Ryan suggested that the Robeson County Indians submit a request for a resettlement project in the Pembroke area. The FSA and OIA would grant the project on the basis of their status as Indians, provided that they could prove their eligibility. Collier asked Interior Department attorney Felix S. Cohen for an opinion, and Cohen suggested that "a group of landless Siouan Indians of one-half blood or more, recommended by the Siouan Council for their agricultural ability and industry, and approved by the Commissioner of Indian Affairs, [could] purchase a suitable tract of land and surrender title to the United States to be held in trust for the group." Land purchased for a resettlement project could also eventually function as a reservation and make members of the tribe eligible for the full range of federal services. Collier seemed to take charge of the project personally and pushed ahead with Cohen's idea.[40]

Joseph Brooks organized a proposal to enroll Siouans under the IRA and sent Collier an inquiry about a reservation for his followers: "If the Siouan Indian Council will purchase a tract of land, unimproved, and transfer title to the Secretary of the Interior, to be held in trust for the use and benefit of the tribe, restricting the use of such land to Indians that meet the requirements of the Wheeler-Howard Act, who are thrifty farmers, will you accept such a proposition and allow the Indians on such land to organize . . . and incorporate . . . and receive all the benefits of the Act?" Siouans saw a tremendous opportunity in a reservation, one that could shield them from dependency on white landlords. To make his case, Brooks attempted to convince Collier of the justice of the Siouan cause and to demand reciprocity, as other Siouans had demanded from Senator Bailey in their congressional campaign. "With all due respect to past administrations," he wrote, "I do not believe my people have been treated fairly, especially when we take into consideration the part my people played in protecting the early Colonists from hostile Indians. It should also be observed that we have borne arms to protect the United States at every call since its formation." Rather than focus on Indians' acquiescence to segregation, as some Siouans previously had done, Brooks reached further back into history to remind Collier of the Siouans' reputation as "friendly Indians"—the Cheraw had fought with the British against the Tuscaroras in the 1711 Tuscarora War—and of their centuries-old history in Robeson County as Indian people. Aware that non-Indians at the OIA might see Indian history and identity differently than non-Indians in North Carolina and in Congress, Brooks shifted political strategies to secure assistance.

Brooks also articulated a different expression of Indian identity, one that asserted the Siouans' claim to equal status with other Indian tribes rather than their equal status with whites. He argued that the Siouan plan for the reservation alleviated the poverty and dislocation brought on by sharecropping and landlessness. "Our Federal Government has left us without its protection and under such conditions that we have lost nearly all of our land," he wrote, cognizant of Collier's purpose to reverse Indian land loss. Brooks aimed to cast the Siouan plight in terms familiar to Collier, who had worked across the country with tribes that already were receiving government assistance. Indeed, the situation of Robeson County's Indians resembled that of other

Indians, but rather than losing land through allotment, they lost it under a system of racial discrimination. In Robeson County, as in other parts of Indian Country, land loss was intimately tied to racial inequality. "What land we still have is nearly all under mortgage which leaves the Indians only one choice to survive, 'the share crop or 1/3 crop system.' We realize that within a short time, unless there is some drastic change, we won't own any land at all," Brooks predicted.

To address this problem, Brooks proposed that the government purchase a 1,000-acre tract of land to resettle landless Indians onto small farms suitable for subsistence agriculture. Emphasizing their desire to function as a politically and economically autonomous group, Brooks ended his appeal by saying: "We do not propose for the Government to do everything for us but we would appreciate your helping us to help ourselves."[41] Having spent over three years negotiating with Washington officials, Brooks surely recognized the words and ideas that would convince men like Collier of the Indians' legitimate identity, their needs as Indians, and their ability to handle federal assistance.[42] Brooks sent the OIA a copy of the Siouan Council's membership list of 6,000 Indians in Robeson and adjoining counties. He also sent sample budgets for farm provisions for Indian families of various sizes.[43] Collier finally responded to Brooks and asked him to recommend a process by which "members of your tribe half-degree or more Indian blood" would be judged eligible to organize under the IRA. Collier intended to submit the list to the FSA for a project sponsored by the Indian Rehabilitation Program of the OIA.[44]

The Indian Office then assessed the economic and social conditions in Robeson County to determine whether land was available and if a rehabilitation project would meet the program's goals—namely, to encourage Indians' self-sufficiency and remove the local government's responsibility for Indians by placing them under the jurisdiction of the federal government rather than the state.[45] Indian agent Fred Baker conducted the assessment. He met with thousands of Indians and reportedly did not hear a dissenting voice on the subject of the need for a farm resettlement program for Indians. The Siouan Council began urging Collier to make it happen. "I do not know what outcome we can get but we will do our best and I am earnestly hopeful," Collier wrote to James Chavis, secretary of the Siouan Council.[46] For the time being, at least, it seemed as if the OIA would use the Indian New Deal to help Robeson County's Indians.

From the OIA's perspective, finding and implementing this assistance went hand-in-hand with Siouan eligibility for federal recognition and, consequently, a satisfactory determination of their Indian identity. The creation of the Indian Reorganization Act and the efforts of the Siouan Council to organize under its provisions demonstrated three distinct differences between how the OIA and the Siouans conceived of Indian identity. From the OIA's perspective, the Indians of Robeson County did not live on a federal reservation, they had not previously established their blood quantum, and their tribal political organization was fragmented. All of these factors made organization under the IRA a challenge, in spite of the group's obvious "Indian characteristics," as Collier had said of them.

Indians, however, looked at the issue from their own criteria for Indian identity. They had a historic and well-defined land base, which whites had unjustly whittled away in previous decades; they had developed a complex system of social relations, which they determined not by blood quantum but by kinship, residence, and affiliation with an Indian school and church; and they had a contested leadership that did not provide a centralized government but nevertheless made sense to them. These markers of identity had important everyday functions in the life of the community and ran much deeper than whether members of the group looked or behaved like "Indians" to non-Indians.

Between 1935 and 1939, the Indian Office and the Robeson County Indians worked to devise some means for their recognition by the federal government. During that period, the issues of tribal unity, racial ancestry, and the Indians' nonreservation status arose again and again, demonstrating the stark differences between how the OIA approached identity and how Indians regarded identity. These differences revealed that the OIA and the Robeson County Indians could not work together without Indians being asked to change certain aspects of how they expressed their identity.

The OIA insisted on a centralized governmental organization as an essential component of an Indian tribe. Such a tribal government enhanced an Indian group's chances for receiving federal assistance. The Siouan Council existed to serve as a conduit for this assistance, but the OIA became reluctant to recognize the council given the existing divisions within the Robeson County Indian community. In early 1935, for example, J. E. Sawyer, the superintendent of the Indian Normal School, wrote W. Carson Ryan, director of education at the OIA, inquiring about potential scholarship aid for Robeson County Indians. Sawyer expressed concern about the factional dispute within the tribe and wondered whether both Cherokee and Siouan students could receive aid from the OIA. Ryan replied, "My own understanding of the situation regarding the name was that ethnologists . . . had indicated that some other name than Cherokee would be more accurate but I assume that is something for the Indian group itself to determine so far as its own affairs are concerned."[47] Ryan wanted to sidestep the issue of a tribal affiliation, ostensibly in the name of tribal self-rule instead of in an effort to refrain from recognizing the group, as previous OIA officials had done. Collier also expressed a noncommittal preference for the Siouan name, but he acknowledged the existence of a Cherokee alternative as well.[48] This ambivalence prolonged the OIA's reluctance to take a stand on the tribal name of Robeson County Indians, an unwillingness that had contributed to the failure of congressional recognition several years before.

Trying to be helpful, Ryan indicated to Sawyer that he could not assist Indians in Robeson County unless they agreed with one another. "We shall be very glad to have your recommendations for any future action on scholarship aid," he wrote, "but may I suggest that it will be very much easier for us if you folks will agree on some policy and present a united front." OIA officials remained ambivalent on specifying a tribal affiliation for the group and hoped that Indians would unify on their own to provide a conduit for federal assistance. Though the agency did not expressly want to deny recognition to the Indians of Robeson County, such a rejection emerged from their indecisiveness.[49]

Another kind of ambiguity resulted from the OIA's insistence on tribal organization. In spite of the apparent reluctance of the OIA to acknowledge an official tribal government for the group, officials at the agency still preferred communicating with Joseph Brooks and the Siouan Council. Cherokees, it seems, stayed away from the OIA and preferred to keep quiet channels open to members of Congress and other elected officials. Like Congress, which preferred negotiating with Cherokees, the OIA could not escape informally legitimizing one set of leaders over another.

This tendency to take sides revealed the irreconcilable differences between the political and administrative processes involved in federal recognition. In the long run, these disagreements among the branches of government did affect Robeson County Indian politics and ultimately contributed to the failure of tribal recognition. For example, even as Ryan claimed that the issue of a tribal name should be left up to the tribe itself, he legitimized Joseph Brooks and the Siouan leadership as the representatives of the tribe. He advised Sawyer to ask Brooks to recommend students who might be eligible for educational assistance based on the half-blood criterion, because "Mr. Brooks has been generally recognized here in Washington as representing the interests of the Indian group in the Pembroke area." Brooks, however, never gave Ryan any indication that he was the only authority in the county, nor that Cherokees should be ineligible for federal benefits. "Mr. Brooks has never indicated to us that Indians applying as Siouans were to be preferred over any others; as a matter of fact the application presented to us carried both names," Ryan admitted, ignorant of the meaning of Brooks's action.[50] Brooks himself seemed comfortable with the internal division and did not exclude students who claimed a Cherokee identity simply because their families were not members of his group. Instead, by submitting applications from both factions, he acted consistently with his responsibilities as a representative of all of the Indians of Robeson County, regardless of their affiliation. Brooks may have submitted names from both groups to honor the tribe's unifying social organization and to send a signal to the OIA that internal political differences over the name would not affect the Indians' most fundamental ways of reckoning identity.

That fundamental core of identity, however, remained unintelligible to Congress and the OIA. The OIA's reliance on intellectual categories of "Indianness" meant that it sought a tribal government in Robeson County that could deliver services to its members, while congressional action prior to the IRA had depended on a political unity that did not threaten state recognition and segregation. In an atmosphere in which different branches of government insisted on negotiating with different tribal factions, achieving a centralized, unified government was impossible.

BLOOD QUANTUM WAS ANOTHER FACTOR involved in the process of federal recognition. To be eligible for the IRA's provisions, nonreservation Indians had to prove that they possessed at least one-half "Indian blood." While this eligibility standard was, and still is, the most stringent criterion ever applied to an Indian program, it was a breakthrough for nonreservation Indians who had never had a statutory mechanism available to establish their eligibility for federal assistance as Indians. The IRA did not expressly provide for individual nonreservation residents who could prove their eligibility, but OIA policy makers gave them the option to petition the secretary of the interior to establish a reservation for them and, through that land base, gain access to services and benefits.[51]

For Robeson County's Indians, who did not organize their political factions according to blood quantum, the act's half-blood provision became both a blessing and a curse. The half-blood criterion offered a seemingly objective standard by which Indians could establish their eligibility for federal services and circumvent the congressional politics that had previously doomed their efforts. In some ways, the criterion presented a solution to the OIA's historic conflict with Congress. On the other hand, the objectivity of the blood quantum standard was an illusion. The primary method the Indian Office used to determine an individual's blood quantum in Robeson County was to document physically the person's phenotype, a scheme that did not account for the random ways that genes combine in an individual. In most cases, this method proved inaccurate at best and destructive at worst.[52] Collier's best intentions to include nonreservation Indians became a modern exercise that enhanced the power of the state at the expense of Indian communities' own social order.

Collier recognized that the blood quantum requirement raised complex issues, and he struggled with how to implement it fairly. In a 1936 memorandum, he admitted that there "is no known sure or scientific proof" of an individual's percentage of Indian ancestry and that most cases presented to the department contained "reasonable doubt" about the person's identity. To resolve that doubt, Collier suggested that the department use factors "not strictly biological, but which may be fairly indicative of an Indian heritage" to resolve the question of eligibility. He then defined those factors in accordance with the OIA's standards and demands, not according to the identity markers maintained by Indian tribes themselves.

Collier proposed five ways to determine an Indian's blood quantum: tribal rolls "accepted as accurate" by the OIA; testimony of the applicant, supported by family records; affidavits from persons who knew the applicant's family background; a physical examination of the applicant by an anthropologist; and testimony of the applicant and other witnesses showing "that the applicant has retained a considerable measure of Indian culture and habits of living." In all cases, Collier emphasized that the burden of proof was on the applicant and not on the government. When other evidence was scant, Collier instructed the OIA to employ a "competent physical anthropologist" to make a determination, then the commissioner himself would determine what "comparative weight shall be given to the various kinds of evidence." "When the genealogical or biological data still leave doubt as to the applicant's claim," he wrote, "the commissioner will consider whether or not the attitude of the applicant and his manner of living tend to show the inheritance of Indian characteristics."[53] Contemporary anthropological theory, especially that espoused by Ales Hrdlicka at the Smithsonian Institution, assured Collier that ancestry determined cultural characteristics, and that one could define racial ancestry by measuring an individual's physical attributes. Therefore, the policy was fully consistent with the current expert opinion, which Collier believed would transform Indian communities and American society as a whole.[54]

Although Collier attempted to do something new with Indian policy by replacing the old theory of assimilation with a new theory of cultural pluralism, his criteria and methods for determining Indian identity demonstrated an unwillingness to allow Indians themselves, and their own ideas about identity, to govern the process. Ultimately, the reliance on documentary evidence, physical measurements, and Collier's own assessment of whether the applicant "looked like" an Indian did little to promote Indian self-determination. Instead, these criteria gave preference to Indian agents' and anthropologists' judgments of Indian identity and imposed an inaccurate homogeneity onto tribes. Moreover, Indians in Robeson County had experienced an ambiguous relationship with the practice of using biological definitions of race to define Indian identity. Whites' efforts to compare Indians biologically, socially, and politically with blacks made racial definitions questionable and even threatening. On the other hand, Indians used notions of race and the racial hierarchy to their own benefit. While Indians did not embrace rigid measures of biological and cultural inheritance, preferring to mark their identity along lines of kinship, they could not afford to reject the OIA's preference for the blood quantum standard.

Consequently, the inclusion of the half-blood provision and the way the OIA determined it became a quagmire when Collier began dealing with Indians in the South, many of whom he thought had "Indian characteristics," as he said of the Robeson County Indians in 1932. But physical characteristics alone hardly comprised identity. The social and political organization of southern tribes after Removal and their relationships with their non-Indian neighbors were quite different from the western reservation tribes with whom Collier had worked. To Collier, a Robeson County Indian's "attitude" and "manner of living," while fully consistent with their own markers of identity, might not "show the inheritance of Indian characteristics."[55]

Joseph Brooks had vocalized Robeson County Indians' own characteristics to the federal government in 1935. He reminded them that Indians divided their criteria for identity into two segments: how one identified oneself to other Indians and how one identified oneself to outsiders. He told one Farm Security Administration investigator that "Siouans run from 800 full blood to little, if any, Indian, but all are under the same status as *Indian* in the State of North Carolina. All are citizens of the State of North Carolina."[56] To Indians, self-identity had little to do with blood quantum and more to do with their kin relationships; Brooks emphasized that their distinct identity rested on their acknowledgment as Indians by the state of North Carolina. Obviously, an Indian did not have to have a certain percentage of "Indian blood" for the group to recognize him; he or she had to be affiliated with a kin network and an Indian settlement or social institution. Recognition from the state legislature provided another criterion for Indian identity. This acknowledgment gave them no special status above their rights as citizens, but it was significant nonetheless for its provision of Indian schools. This provision made other special rights unnecessary for the purpose of maintaining Indian identity, and their status as citizens of North Carolina and their varied amount of Indian ancestry did not threaten their identity as Indians.

Despite other available criteria, particularly those evidenced by tribal members, the OIA continued its practices of applying blood quantum as the standard for eligibility. D'Arcy McNickle, administrative assistant to John Collier, played a significant role in the execution of the Indian Reorganization Act in Robeson County. As previously noted, McNickle was a novelist, educated at Oxford and Columbia Universities, and a Metis (Cree) raised on the Salish-Kootenai reservation in Montana. He described the racial predicament of the Robeson County Indians and demonstrated his own understanding of their identity markers. "Enrollment for these Indians will mean the first step in the rehabilitation of their dignity as a people," he wrote, linking Indians' desire for federal recognition with their desire to escape the indignities of segregation. He placed their desire for recognition squarely in the context of southern race relations, reminding his colleagues that identity was more than skin deep. McNickle continued, "One realizes after visiting them that race is something more than a social or political complex. Here is a people from whom all native language and tradition have disappeared, yet they keep within themselves an unfailing recognition of their link with the past." He articulated what Collier saw as the essential tension in dealing with non-reservation Indians: their seeming lack of all obvious "native language and tradition." Yet he observed an extant social and political organization among Robeson County Indians in their "unfailing recognition of their link with the past." McNickle saw Robeson County Indians' identity in terms of their pursuit of that link. The factional dispute over a proper name indicates that such a pursuit was relevant to Indian identity maintenance, but McNickle did not seem to see the other side of the coin—namely, that belonging to a living, Indigenous People made one an Indian.[57]

In spite of their recognition of the complexities of racial identity and the evidence that Brooks had provided for them, the OIA continued to insist that the basis for Robeson County Indians' recognition ought to be their blood quantum, which only physical appearance verified. "[T]here ought to be at least several hundred, judging from appearances alone, who are entitled to recognition as of one-half or more Indian blood," McNickle wrote. "Appearances ought not to be entirely deceptive in this instance," he continued, justifying the appropriateness of the blood quantum standard. Referring to a North Carolina antimiscegenation law, McNickle believed that "intermarriage with the white race has been prohibited since 1854, and undoubtedly there has been a gradual recovery of the Indian strain in most families; likewise, the prohibition against intermarriage with Negroes must be dminishing [sic] the degree of that racial mixture." Though McNickle recognized that identity for Indians had more to do with social and kin relations than with blood quantum, he used their absence of stereotypically "Indian" culture to justify the OIA's reliance on blood quantum as an eligibility standard, which, he and others believed, would provide enough evidence of their inherited Indian cultural traits.[58]

This manner of reckoning identity became an outright double standard in cases across the South in which groups other than the Robeson County Indians might have been eligible for recognition under the IRA. Collier decided that while the Indians of Robeson County might qualify for recognition if they could prove their ancestry, "folk groups" in the southeastern and northeastern United States should be excluded from federal guardianship, regardless of their levels of "Indian blood." Interestingly, Collier used their "non-Indian" cultural traits to exclude them, even though the characteristics he cited were nearly identical to the circumstances of Robeson County Indians.

Collier conceded that both Indian and non-Indian blood existed in these groups, as the Siouans themselves declared of their own membership. But Collier also pointed out that "folk groups" had no explicit relationship to the federal government, and "they have lived amidst the general population for hundreds of years," just as Robeson County's Indians had. Finally, Collier justified their exclusion based on the budgetary problems these groups posed for the OIA; he argued that seeking to recognize folk groups would "jeopardize the work with those Indians already under federal guardianship."[59] These expedient reasons for not welcoming folk groups into the IRA's recognition process implied that the link between blood and culture that was so fundamental to the policy makers' views on nonreservation Indians had an economic function as well: it conveniently prevented full acknowledgment for folk groups.

Yet Collier pursued recognition for Robeson County Indians and not for folk groups that possessed Indian ancestry. The obvious double standard hints at a broader philosophical relationship between white supremacy and

Indian policy. By folk groups, Collier likely referred to the "tri-racial isolates" that social scientists studied during the Jim Crow era. Efforts to collect data, catalog, and rank these groups into hierarchies flourished in the academic community and in state governments.[60] Dividing society into categories like "white," "colored," "Indian," "mixed-race," and "folk groups" epitomized the modern mindset that inspired Collier and the so-called progressive policy makers who created twentieth-century segregation. Such essentializing of cultural traits sustained white supremacy because it reinforced whites' abilities to simplify and objectify people, making it easier to demand their subservience. In so doing, powerful whites monitored the gateway to the privileges of being white. By defining Indianness as a collection of essential characteristics, OIA bureaucrats upheld the system of white supremacy that oppressed Indians and other nonwhites.

One of those essential characteristics was "Indian blood." Insufficient amounts excluded Indians from federal assistance, but a stereotyped view of Indian culture was so intertwined with policy makers' assessments of blood quantum that cultural change meant loss of "Indian blood" and therefore Indian identity. To federal officials, evidence of cultural change or non-Indian ancestry "proved" the loss of distinctive Indian culture. As such, the OIA's reliance on blood quantum eligibility standards did not improve Indians' chances for eligibility. Instead, these standards prevented their acknowledgment; Indians would inevitably change, but the eligibility standards did not allow for cultural change.[61] The blood quantum criterion came to be nothing more than a political tool that could be used to deny some people recognition while granting it to others. It did not measure Indian identity in convincing or useful ways for the Indians of Robeson County.

The differences between the OIA and the Siouans concerning the definition of an Indian resulted from a fundamental difference in each group's goals. Even though Collier intended to revolutionize Indian policy to make it more sensitive to Indians' needs, the task of the OIA remained the same as it had been since Robeson County Indians sought recognition as Cherokees in 1913: securing scarce federal resources for Indians who met a test of eligibility. That goal encouraged an atmosphere in which, as Collier outlined in his 1936 memo on blood quantum, the burden of proof was on the applicant. Meanwhile, the OIA had compelling reasons to deny an Indian's application: more Indians meant squeezing more money out of an already stingy Congress.

For Indians, however, identity was a part of their everyday lives, necessary to carry on the community's subsistence, education, religious rituals, and diplomatic relations with non-Indians. They did not see identity as a test one passed to receive benefits or as a legal term subject to OIA interpretation; rather, their identity was their birthright, an expression of their tradition and history handed down from their ancestors.[62] The Siouan Council aimed to petition the federal government for what they believed was protection of that birthright, which their southern white neighbors threatened repeatedly. The conflict between the essential missions of the OIA and the Siouan Council played out in subsequent years as each entity negotiated an agreement that satisfied both parties' conceptions of Indian identity. Ultimately, the process satisfied neither party, and their different views of Indianness deepened the differences within the Indian community about how to articulate and preserve their identity.

The OIA's efforts to implement the Indian Reorganization Act's provisions for tribal organization and nonreservation Indians sparked conflict in the definition of Indian identity. Each provision contained a concept of Indianness that was largely irrelevant to the experiences and traditions of Robeson County Indians, but establishing criteria for Indian identity was critical to fairly and thoroughly applying the act. In defining who an Indian was, the Indian Office only rarely acknowledged the existence of community definitions and never applied them to the policy. Instead, the OIA pursued policies that kept itself and Congress in control of the discussion and kept Indians divided. Collier saw factionalism as a destructive force, but he did not recognize how his own blood quantum criteria was destructive. As a result of these tactics, the federal government dominated Indian affairs in Robeson County Indians through the 1930s. Siouans continued to try to meet the OIA's expectations and to become the kind of Indians the OIA wanted them to be, while simultaneously trying to keep their own social and political priorities intact.

In this quest, Siouans introduced and strengthened three markers of identity that grew in significance to the community long after these events concluded: (1) a desire to articulate the group's "one hundred-percent Indian" ancestry in response to the OIA's insistence on this criteria for federal eligibility; (2) a desire to create and maintain a representative tribal government that exercised authority over tribal members and attempted to unify them; and (3) a desire for economic autonomy, over and above the relationships with local white landlords, bankers, and merchants that they had cultivated in previous decades. Their efforts to acquire land under Farm Security Administration sponsorship and enroll as "half-or-more Indian" under the IRA demonstrated how these identity markers functioned, as well as their relationship to the community's internal divisions.

While Cherokees were not at the forefront of negotiations with the OIA, they continued to operate locally and to influence events in Robeson County. The resettlement project intensified their involvement in tribal affairs, but the Siouan efforts to establish a set of identity criteria in line with the OIA's objectives revealed their differences with the Cherokee faction. With their opposition to the Siouan bill, Cherokees rejected federal government intervention in Robeson County Indian affairs if the government based that assistance on a Siouan history and a Siouan leadership. Cherokees preferred to articulate a history that had brought them a distinct place in the racial hierarchy and the support of local whites. In doing so, Cherokees continued to embrace an identity as "progressive" people; they appealed to local whites who valued the maintenance of the racial hierarchy and segregation rather than to whites in Washington who valued a particular picture of an Indian tribe.

While a relationship with the OIA heightened the differences between how Siouans and Cherokees expressed their identity, it is important to remember that those differences were most apparent in how each group expressed its identity to non-Indians. Between and among themselves, the old markers of kin, place, and social institutions remained important criteria of Indian identity and contributed to factionalism in their own ways. But creating a presence as a "tribe" on a national stage in the 1930s—just as it had on a statewide level in the 1880s—required Indians in Robeson County to develop more elaborate criteria that non-Indians could understand. While leaders in the 1880s and through the early twentieth century had reinforced their identity by reminding whites that they were "not black," leaders in the 1930s asserted their distinctiveness by establishing common ground with the experiences and histories of other Indian tribes. Siouans clearly favored the latter approach to identity expression, but Cherokees continued to base their identity expression on their circumstances in the southern racial hierarchy.

In hindsight, we see a connection between these approaches that the historical actors, whether Indian or non-Indian, likely did not appreciate: both southern segregation and federal Indian policy were driven by a modern mindset that promoted the essentializing and ranking of people and ideas. "Scientific" expertise—whether the science of anthropology or of racism— simplified complex social relations and guided policy making in the Jim Crow South and in federal Indian policy. The significance of this connection lies in how Collier and others made such expertise the basis of their policy, despite the expertise that Indians themselves provided. Furthermore, these manipulations ultimately made Indian resources—land and labor, in the case of

Robeson County Indians—work to the benefit of local whites. The path to this outcome was not straightforward, however, and it was decidedly (and ironically) premodern in its illegibility to "outsiders," those of us looking back at these events.

There is no evidence that Collier exploited Indians in Robeson County, or anywhere else, to promote white supremacy. To argue that he did so would be its own tragedy. Rather, Collier, New Deal officials of the Farm Security Administration, and the southern "progressives" that promoted segregation worked within a framework that took white privilege, all that went with it, for granted, including an assumed dichotomy between the modern and the premodern. In this context, the economics of recognition—that too many recognized Indians, whether "quarter bloods" or "folk groups," would be too expensive—became a justification for denying recognition and imposing identity standards on Indians that negated the cultural systems Collier claimed to treasure. Furthermore, the Siouans' inability to gain recognition for their government demonstrated how a policy that relied on modern ideas about creating political unity and not on the political systems that Indians themselves had created did not sustain Indian self-determination.

5 Pembroke Farms

GAINING ECONOMIC AUTONOMY

The rural Indian family pictured in Figure 6 lived in a one-room, window-less house without running water or electricity, probably in the Red Banks or Prospect communities. They were sharecroppers and candidates for re-settlement onto Pembroke Farms, the Farm Security Administration (FSA) program to assist Indian tenant farmers. This house belonged to their land-lord and not to them; it was probably built sometime after the Civil War. The table and bench are rough-hewn and handmade and might have come with the house. Pictured here is the kitchen part of the room; Mama cooked over the open hearth. The table looks like her work space; her sack of Camel corn-meal and two lard stands sat underneath. Cornmeal was an absolute staple of a farm family's diet. The store-bought cornmeal probably signified that the landlord did not give this family enough land to grow their own corn and take it to the gristmill for grinding. Mama or Daddy must have made regular trips to Pates Supply, the local farm and dry-goods merchant, to get such supplies on credit. She also got the posters on the wall there; the store had likely hung them as advertisements and then given them away when companies shipped new posters. Mama brought them home and tacked them on the unfinished walls to block the drafts coming in between the planks and keep it warmer.

Since no one had telephones, the photographer, Marion Post Wolcott, probably had not announced her visit and so captured this family unawares on an average day. The industriousness and independence of this woman im-presses me. Her floors are swept clean, and she and her children are neatly dressed, the girl in a homemade flour-sack dress. Mama obviously felt con-

FIGURE 6. "Home of Indians (mixed breed) who have not yet been resettled on Pembroke Farms. Maxton, North Carolina" (Photograph by Marion Post Wolcott, December 1938; Library of Congress, Prints and Photographs Division, FSA-OWI Collection, LC-USF34-050379-D DLC)

fident in her house, because she allowed Wolcott to take pictures. Her attachment to her children impresses me also. She comforts her shy, nervous daughter with a hand on her shoulder, and her swelling belly and arched back announce another baby on the way. Her son seems happy and proud to have his picture taken. These were almost certainly not her only children; most farm women had at least five children, and many had ten or more. The rest were working on the farm, or they had possibly gone to school. Farm children often attended school only in the winter months, since the landlord required their labor the rest of the year.

Unlike the town Indian men pictured elsewhere in this book, here is an anonymous woman and her children; not even Wolcott bothered to record their names. Wolcott's choice of perspective—middle-distance—implies a focus on living conditions rather than on individuals. Indeed, the family is an advertisement for the FSA's work, portrayed as if their existence was a function of their poverty. Their names mattered little to FSA officials, who wanted to project the necessity of their work. But as an advertisement, this photo is the exact opposite of the items of high status and luxury depicted on the walls. Note the contrast of Mama's tireless work with the images of leisure and wealth surrounding her—ham that doesn't need parboiling, women swimming, Santa Claus taking a smoke break. She might work her whole life and never afford a pack of cigarettes, a trip, Christmas gifts for her children, or store-bought ham. Odd that this is the picture of poverty, even as the family is surrounded in representations of wealth. Like so many FSA photographs, this one indicts the conditions created by poverty but does not ask for radical change to the system. The overwhelming presence of luxury goods reinforces the attainability of a consumer-oriented economy.[1] Nor did the FSA try to revolutionize the system that kept Indians economically powerless. Rather, agency officials indicted the factionalism that they believed kept Indians from wielding greater political power.

This photograph also symbolizes two obstacles in Robeson County Indians' quest to affirm their identity. One obstacle was the link between blood and names, markers that outsiders used to determine a group's identity. A named photographer recorded anonymous subjects; what Wolcott perceived of their blood quantum was significant for her caption, but she did not include their personal names nor the political faction with which they identified. This woman and her husband probably identified as Siouan since Siouan leaders initiated Pembroke Farms and made every effort to distribute its benefits to their own constituency. This photo symbolized another obstacle: the difference between rural and town Indians. Insiders primarily utilized these identity markers until the Siouan Council drew its membership from rural Indians and thus made the markers visible to outsiders such as FSA officials.

Named male leaders spoke for these nameless women and children, intending to help them but leaving them out of the formal decision-making process entirely. Yet, as we will learn, many of these men had their places of authority through the connections of their wives and sisters. Many tenant farm women insisted on their families' quest for economic independence, but their economic contribution was rarely acknowledged.[2] The FSA reproduced this power inequity in a slightly different way: it privileged Cherokee and white-supremacist views over those of the Siouans, who claimed to speak for rural Indians such as this family. The FSA's paternalistic culture led its staff members to side with those they perceived as being of a higher status, despite the agency's mandate to alleviate the plight of the poorest families.

The Siouan Council believed that Pembroke Farms was the answer to their economic subordination under the Jim Crow system. Siouans initiated the project in 1935 through their contacts at the Office of Indian Affairs, which requested that the FSA study the project's feasibility.[3] For Robeson County Indians, the project promised to sustain their existence, not simply as farmers but as Indians in a predominately black-and-white society. Many aspects of the resettlement program helped Indians affirm their community and culture through difficult economic times. But misunderstandings arose when the FSA's assumptions conflicted with the social and political culture of Robeson County's Indians.

Cherokees were equally interested in Pembroke Farms, but they wanted to control the project themselves. In response to this challenge, Siouan leaders attempted to divert project resources to their own membership, mostly comprised of rural Indians who desperately needed economic assistance. In soliciting support for their members, Siouan leaders also augmented the political power of their governing council and made political allegiance a criterion for Indian identity. The FSA thought that these political contests resulted from social chaos in the tribe, a reaction that stemmed from their minimal understanding of Indian identity in the segregated South and Indians' economic subordination. The FSA's efforts to alleviate political factionalism brought Siouan and Cherokee leaders together. But for rural Indians who depended on town leaders' success in negotiating with white state and national officials for economic and racial justice, the process contributed to their distance from town Indians and intensified a set of divisions that would shape Indians' ways of affirming their identity.[4]

THE FSA'S RESETTLEMENT PROGRAMS epitomized the New Deal's progressive spirit of experimentation and altruism directed at the impoverished of all races. For American agriculture, the Great Depression did not begin in 1929 but in 1920. By 1930, one-third of all American farm families had a standard of living comparable to that of urban slum families.[5] Unlike the agricultural policy of earlier decades, which focused mainly on funneling benefits to landowners and commercial farmers, policy makers turned the spotlight on tenants and sharecroppers during the Great Depression. Officials attempted to address the economic imbalances of the old order and create a democracy that represented the poor as well as the rich.[6]

The FSA constructed permanent improvements to the rural landscape and created work for the unemployed, a mission that did not always produce the cost efficiency that Congress demanded.[7] Ordinary farmers sometimes believed resettlement programs meddled with their own ways of doing things, but they mostly viewed the programs as tremendous opportunities to establish a minimal standard of subsistence. The government built 113 resettlement farms in total; eight of those farms were reserved for African Americans, the largest being at Tillery in Halifax County, North Carolina.[8] Pembroke Farms was one of only two projects for Indians; the other resettled eleven families in the Stockbridge-Munsee community in Wisconsin. The FSA's concern for racial equality provided jobs, a sense of authority over local affairs, and a long-term basis for landownership and political activism within nonwhite communities all over the South.[9]

Rural Indians demonstrated the most critical need among Robeson County's Indian population. This group also comprised the core membership of the Siouan Council. Residents of the rural areas outside Pembroke depended on white landlords or small landholdings to eke out their living, and the Depression, accompanied by landlords' attempts to squeeze out Indian farmers, hit them the hardest. They did not typically identify with Pembroke's middle-class town Indians. Some town Indians identified themselves as Cherokees, but others were Siouan leaders and members of the council. Despite the affiliation of some of its leaders—particularly Joseph Brooks and Chesley Locklear—with the town of Pembroke, the structure of the Siouan Council reflected the identity markers of kin and settlement that originated in Indians' rural settlements. The council had eighteen districts representing Robeson, Hoke, and Sampson Counties; the town of Pembroke did not have a district of its own. Siouans named districts after churches or other traditional settlement landmarks (see Map 3).

By June 1935, male (and some female) heads of families in these communities became members of the Siouan Council; these members represented their kin. The Siouan Council counted 6,000 Indians as members out of a total Indian population of approximately 12,000. Indians who lived "on the swamps" primarily identified themselves by family and settlement, and the Siouan Council reflected the larger community's existing social and political structure.[10] The group's leaders referred to the members as "enrolled members," a phrase they likely hoped would resonate with OIA officials, who were familiar with the enrollment practices of Indians in officially acknowledged tribes. The documentary record does not reveal the specific promises of membership in the Siouan organization. Enrollment was not intended to enumerate property, define rights, or enable access to benefits, as it did on reservations in the West.[11] The roll does not contain blood quantum or other demographic information; it only lists names and settlement affiliation. The Siouan roll was a symbolic document that mirrored Indians' existing social

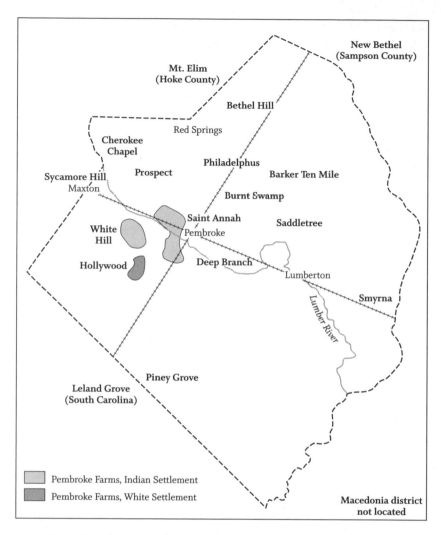

MAP 3. Siouan Council Districts and Location of Pembroke Farms

structure, and, most importantly for the purposes of recognition under the IRA, it legitimized the Siouan Council government to the OIA. One's name on the roll likely entitled one to vote for a council representative and only promised a consistent campaign for federal recognition as "Siouan."

The Siouan Council derived its authority from the communities most linked to the qualities that defined "Indianness" in the 1930s. Their strategy to reach out to the "grassroots" and enroll a majority of the tribe sustained their political authority in the face of threats from Cherokees and anyone else who doubted the legitimacy of their influence. The council tried to avoid

Jhn N. Cummings
Jas.   ,,
Lacy   ,,
Foy   ,,
Ottomis   ,,
Peter Dial
Ransome   ,,
Joe   ,,
Frank Graham
Rufus   ,,
Duncan   ,,

these potential challenges by recruiting members in settlements that Indians
considered bedrocks of their identity, areas that had a reputation for Indian
landholding or for strong kin networks. Accordingly, the council districts
with the greatest representation were also the sites of the largest amount of
Indian-owned land; Saint Annah (Joseph Brooks's home settlement), Saddletree, and Burnt Swamp had the most members, and these districts had the
highest amounts of Indian-owned land in the county. The Brooks Settlement
(or White Hill, as it was called in the council) closely followed these districts
in enrollment. White Hill Indians owned far less land than Indians in the
larger council districts, but White Hill had nearly as many members because
of its reputation for its kin network and its efforts to articulate a sense of
Indianness through the Longhouse.[12] The Siouan leadership wanted to institute a resettlement project to bring the most benefits to the majority of their
members, and the FSA worked with the Siouan Council to link the Indian
community and its markers of identity—particularly kin and place—to the
advancement of economic opportunity.

Those markers of kin and place are very personal for me. The Siouan
Council membership roll (Figure 7) is the only place a direct ancestor of
mine appears in the documentary record. Here is the name Foy Cummings,
fourth from the top; he is my grandfather, and I knew him well and love him
still. His grandfather was Henderson Oxendine, a member of Henry Berry
Lowry's gang during Reconstruction. Henderson had two children with Virginia Emanuel, a member of the Saint Annah community (named after the
church there). Because the state executed Henderson in 1871, he never saw
his grandchild Foy. Foy was also raised at Saint Annah, the son of landown-

FIGURE 8. My maternal grandparents, Hildith "Bloss" Cummings (1917–1998) and Foy Cummings (1907–1997), pictured here with their first child, Donald, in 1935. They went on to have eleven more children and raise another five grandchildren. Foy sometimes called her "Blossie." (Personal possession of Malinda Maynor Lowery)

ers. He inherited a little bit of land, and when he was twenty-six, he married Hildith Chavis, known universally as "Bloss"—short for "Blossom," after her rosy cheeks (Figure 8).

Bloss grew up in Saint Annah, the daughter of Malinda Brooks Chavis and the great-great granddaughter of "forefather" John Brooks. Malinda was Siouan leader Joseph Brooks's sister. Her husband died from gunshot wounds when Bloss was a baby. Bloss never saw him and was thus given the gift, according to Indian custom, of being able to "blow fire," or healing burns by praying and blowing on them. With no husband and no land of her own, Malinda spent Bloss's youth working in turpentine camps in Georgia.

She sent Bloss to her sister Mary, wife of Siouan councilman Chesley Locklear. Bloss was a "kitchen girl" at Aunt Mary's, somewhere between a servant and adopted daughter. Despite having no resources of her own, she grew up in the settlement's wealthiest household and belonged to one of the Indian community's most politically active families. My grandfather had the land, but my grandmother had the family; a husband and wife needed these kinds of complementary strengths to do more than just scrape by farming twenty-two acres.

Perhaps my grandfather saw membership in the Siouan tribe as an avenue to greater economic success, but this seems unlikely; his meager amount of land excluded him from the immediate assistance provided by Pembroke Farms. Rather, I think he signed the roll because of its larger significance to his identity as Indian, based on kinship and place. Uncle Joe or Uncle Chesley probably found Foy at the tobacco packhouse one autumn afternoon and asked him to become a member. Saint Annah had to have members to elect a representative to the Siouan Council, so in signing up, Foy was helping the cause of recognition in Washington, D.C., because he was helping to shape a tribal government. Uncle Joe and Uncle Chesley would have asked Foy, not Bloss, to join, because in the community, men handled such political business. But Bloss is on the roll, too, just not by name; her presence and power lay with her kinship ties to Joe and Chesley. Foy may not have been asked— nor may he have agreed—without those ties. The roll was not about benefits but something greater: affirming identity.

Not that my grandfather sat around thinking about his identity. Identity isn't something that many Indians in Robeson County contemplate. Identity is lived and shared and acted out so thoroughly that it rarely requires discussion in any stable, long-lived community. So if I want to shed light on such a hidden subject, I must look for evidence beyond meaningless names on a page. I must look beyond the ever-changing tribal names as well, names that represented a negotiation with outsiders' ideas about identity. For example, my grandfather identified himself in this situation as Siouan, but when "Lumbee" emerged twenty years later, he and Bloss called themselves Lumbee. Does this mean they were confused about their identity, or making it up as they went along? Perhaps, but there is more evidence that their lives expressed deeper cultural structures of kinship and affiliation with places. I would suggest that they didn't give much thought to tribal monikers because those weren't the names that mattered; rather, the names "Cummings," "Brooks," and "Saint Annah" mattered. Those names were decades or centuries old, were stable, and truly meant something in their everyday lives. Saint Annah meant so much to them that their tombstone features a picture of the church.

Reading this tribal roll is therefore very different from reading the Dawes rolls, the censuses taken of tribes subject to the nineteenth-century allotment policy. Those lists include names, sex, age, blood quantum, and a tribal roll number. The rolls enumerated heads of households, spouses, and children.

They are essentially expressions of a modern ideal of standardization, anonymity, and scientific rationality. The Dawes rolls are vital tools for research in those communities where they were recorded, but they do not necessarily reveal that community's identity markers. The Siouan list of names tells us more only when we can access additional information about the individuals on it, research which is cumbersome if the researcher does not have easy access to the community. Finding evidence of a group's identity formation is tricky, regardless of the sources one uses. Names, in particular, are among the most changeable and situational identity markers.

BECAUSE OF THE PHOTOGRAPHIC RECORD, the FSA's resettlement projects are highly visible, but poor textual record keeping on many projects makes knowing the stories of clients difficult. Information like families' yearly income and progress toward stated goals are not known on even the projects with the best records. The records of Pembroke Farms are incomplete; we do not know the names or backgrounds of all the project staff or clients, for example, nor precisely what benefits they all received from the agency. We know the most about problems the project experienced, because staff, clients, and the Siouan leadership corresponded about these difficulties. The successes, and many facts of the project's basic administration, are less prominent in the records, but some information can be pieced together from the archives. When assisted by some generalizations taken from a 1943 summary report of resettlement projects, the existing records of Pembroke Farms yield a story of good intentions, bureaucratic mishaps, structural flaws, and mixed results.[13]

Siouan Council secretary James E. Chavis began laying the groundwork for Pembroke Farms in 1934, after the Senate failed to consider the bill for recognition of Robeson County's Indians as Siouans. Chavis hosted Albert A. Grorud, an attorney for the Senate Indian Affairs Committee, on a visit to Robeson County in the wake of the bill's demise. Grorud was moved by an encounter with Indian farmer and Siouan Council member D. L. Locklear, who had lost his farm and home to foreclosure. Locklear told Grorud that Indians wanted to take advantage of the New Deal's agricultural programs, the benefits of which were being distributed unequally in the county; white landlords—rather than Indian, black, or white tenants—were receiving most of the benefits brought by the Agricultural Adjustment Act. But Indians also wanted to avoid additional debt, and they believed that their recognition as an Indian tribe was the solution. The government could then take land into trust for the group, and farmers could live there, theoretically debt free. Locklear declared that "if he can redeem his home he intends to have the deed made to the government," because of his belief that Indians' economic security rested in the federal government alone.[14]

Siouans in Robeson County ultimately desired tribal land where the OIA could incorporate the group and bestow all benefits due to them under the Indian Reorganization Act of 1934. Encouraged by Grorud and lobbied by Joseph Brooks, the Indian Office launched the resettlement project and aimed to purchase land to establish such a reservation, provided that the group met the "one-half or more" blood quantum requirement. Interior Department solicitor Felix S. Cohen proposed this plan in April 1935. Cohen suggested that Indians themselves provide funds to assist the government in purchasing the land, and the Indians chosen for resettlement would "adopt a constitution and bylaws and receive a charter" from the federal government, according to the procedure established in the Indian Reorganization Act. This process formally recognized such Indians as a "tribe," and the title for their land remained in trust with the United States. Joseph Brooks specifically recommended a purchase of 8,000 acres, the wooded part of which would be tribally owned.[15]

This desire for a tribal land base, combined with Siouans' ways of articulating their distinctiveness from their neighbors, revealed a strategy for preserving identity that involved more than elevating living conditions. Siouans wanted economic *autonomy*, a measure of control over their own labor, land, and agricultural products that would distance them from racial discrimination and affirm their identity as a distinct people. Indians could not gain true autonomy under a tenant system that left authority over crop sales, credit, and labor to white landlords. Rather, Siouans believed that a relationship with the federal government, whose Indian policies under John Collier appeared receptive to Indian self-rule, better secured their ability to direct their own affairs. However, the possibility of a reservation remained uncertain, since the Indian Office informed the Siouan leadership that the Farm Security Administration had to approve any resettlement project. The OIA implied that they would not take on sole responsibility for the economic and social needs of Robeson County's Indian population. The OIA thereby distanced itself from the Siouan Council's main objective—to have a tribal land base—leaving the council to depend on the FSA to help it achieve its goals.[16]

Overall, the FSA raised Indians' standard of living and their expectations considerably during the life of the Pembroke Farms project. It took nearly four years (1935 to 1939) for the government to plan and construct the project and to choose families for settlement. The FSA invested $623,474 in purchasing and developing over 9,000 acres of land for Pembroke Farms. During that time, the FSA bought large parcels of land from local white and Indian landowners in the Red Banks, Brooks Settlement, and Hopewell communities south and west of Pembroke. Initially, the government rented the land to Indian tenants for a cash price rather than crop shares. The government set the price at between $2.50 and $4.00 per acre per year; typical cash rent in that area was $5.00 per acre. Project administrators later selected some of these tenants as "homesteaders"—recipients of low-interest, forty-year mortgages for the land and its improvements.[17] Ultimately, the FSA chose seventy-five families for inclusion. A committee composed of local Indians and project staff selected the families based primarily on their need for assistance, and they required all families to have experience as farm operators. The committee did not appear to select based on management capability per se, but they did discuss a family's potential for success, which was likely measured by the family's age, size, and their general health.[18]

For the homesteaders, the project augmented their income, standard of living, and overall wealth. Compared to sharecroppers' conditions before the project, when few farmers cleared any profit on their farms, the average Pembroke Farms owner had a yearly net income of $1,585 by 1943. Yearly mortgage payments amounted to approximately $200 for the largest families. Farmers also received short-term loans for farm equipment, seed, livestock, and fencing.[19] These loans had 3–5 percent interest rates and shielded them from the dangers of debt to local merchants, who charged 20 percent interest or more. Low interest rates and a government lender meant that Indians were far less likely to lose the land to the manipulations of a local company like Pates Supply or the McNair Corporation. Pembroke Farms offered some Indian farmers a measure of economic security and prosperity they had not known as sharecroppers. Anthropologist Ella Deloria, who traveled to the county in 1940, witnessed spontaneous and elaborate "thanksgivings" from Indian people for "our government and what it has done for us." She observed, "I believe the Farm Resettlement is looked upon as the very sort of help they were needing to give them a boost and hearten them to go on."[20]

Pembroke Farms also brought a better standard of living to Indian sharecroppers who participated. The government built houses of three to five rooms for each family, painting them on the outside and finishing the walls on the inside. Electricity, outhouses, pump water, and screened windows provided comfort, sanitation, and convenience that many sharecropper families had never enjoyed. Families generally provided their own furnishings. Families also received a smokehouse, stock barn, poultry house, tobacco barn, and pasture fence.[21] The agency hired a community manager who oversaw farm operations and a home management specialist who taught Indian women modern domestic arts—in particular efficient gardening, safe canning, nutrition, and basic health and hygiene. The project also employed a nurse, the farm's only permanent Indian employee. Her duties centered on curbing the area's malaria, tuberculosis, syphilis, and other diseases through treatment and education. The farm also made health insurance available to residents and hosted a Works Progress Administration school that provided literacy education for Indian adults. The government built a community building and elementary school for the project's social and educational activities and organized a National Youth Administration center.[22] The FSA attempted to equalize economic opportunity in Robeson County and to raise the standards of Indians' social and home life.

Indians wanted to use the resettlement program to sustain their family-oriented culture and traditional subsistence patterns while they improved their living conditions and gained control over their own labor and economic resources. In many ways, the FSA helped them achieve these goals. For example, Indians seized the opportunities presented by the need to prepare the land for occupation. The most readily available land for the project was south of Pembroke, where a timber company recently had logged the land. Indians urged the government to purchase at least some of this land and allow their kinsmen to earn money by removing stumps and clearing the land for agriculture. Since this land had not been farmed, it had no tobacco or cotton crop allotments assigned to it. Siouan leaders recognized that newly cleared land had no allotments and therefore precluded resettled families from the substantial income gained by cash crops. During the Great Depression, the federal government instituted the crop-allotment system to restrict production of certain staple crops in order to raise prices on those crops. A county's Agricultural Stabilization Control agent assigned land owners a certain number of acres of tobacco, cotton, or other crops that they and their tenants could grow. Siouans pressured the FSA to purchase additional plantation land so that their farmers could take advantage of existing allotments. Indians wanted more than a mere subsistence living from their government. In the words of one OIA official, Indians desired "to secure the use and control of land" in Robeson County and not just have access to it for subsistence purposes. The FSA obliged them and purchased land of both types on which to settle Indian farm families.[23]

The FSA also supported Indians' desire to enhance the family orientation of their farms. For example, Pembroke Farms families had twice as much land available for gardens as local landlords permitted sharecroppers, enabling them to grow more food. The community manager, H. C. Green, believed that an Indian farmer should strive for "balanced farming" rather than profit. The FSA's approach to farming impressed Elisha Locklear, who was a member of the Brooks Settlement, an enrolled Siouan, and a Pembroke Farms tenant. Locklear told a newspaper reporter, "When Mr. Green came out here this morning the first place he went was to my pig lot. My old boss would have gone to the cotton patch or the tobacco barn." Green emphasized the health and well-being of families through canning food for the winter and purchasing extras like coffee, sugar, and clothes with profits from the sale of hogs, chickens, and eggs rather than with credit from the local merchant. This philosophy served to keep families relatively debt free and healthy and stood in sharp contrast to the sharecropping system, which encouraged families to spend all their time on cash crops and buy necessities on credit, thereby enriching the landlord or merchant. Indians recognized that the landlords for whom they had previously farmed cared little about the physical or social health of a sharecropper's family; instead, the landlord emphasized his own profit from the farm.[24]

Indians also expressed their traditional culture and family orientation through the type of settlement plan they chose. The FSA offered two alternatives: a "neighborhood" plan, in which house lots adjoined fields, and a "village" plan, with houses built close together and fields placed outside the "village." Robeson County Indians preferred the "neighborhood" plan, which was closest to their traditional settlement pattern in the rural communities outside of Pembroke. Furthermore, Indians hoped that the neighborhood plan, with each family having a forty-acre farm, would enable children and grandchildren to build houses close to parents and continue the tradition of working the farm cooperatively. In recent years, Indian sharecroppers had had difficulty maintaining this subsistence tradition because they could not save money to buy enough land to settle and support their large and growing families. Government assistance offered an alternative that could help secure Indian identity, which was so firmly rooted in family.[25]

Indians used the project to gain equal economic opportunity under the Jim Crow system. They told government agents that segregation denied them economic advantages because of their status as Indians, and they expected the government to recognize their distinctiveness and redress such injustices. Indians tied the need for the resettlement project directly to their circumstances under segregation. "We Indians do not have the same chance to work on public works and in the factories as the white people, or even the

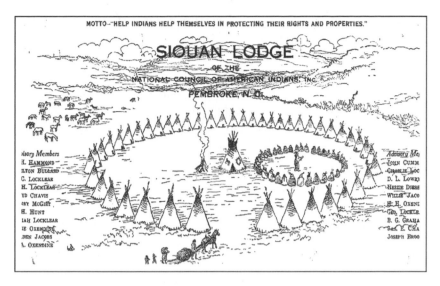

MOTTO—"HELP INDIANS HELP THEMSELVES IN PROTECTING THEIR RIGHTS AND PROPERTIES."

SIOUAN LODGE

OF THE

NATIONAL COUNCIL OF AMERICAN INDIANS, INC.

PEMBROKE, N. C.

FIGURE 9. Siouan Council letterhead (National Archives and Records Administration, Washington, D.C.)

colored race. We must make our living from the land and the most of our employment must be on the lands we own or rent," Joseph Brooks told Commissioner of Indian Affairs John Collier. Segregation, with jobs defined as "white" or "colored," denied Indians employment opportunities off the farm. Brooks's reference to African Americans implied that the government had a duty to assist Indians, not simply because they were economically needy but because Jim Crow had prevented Indians from pursuing jobs available to other races.

Siouans reinforced their claim for a special status as Indians on the letterhead of Brooks's letter to Collier (Figure 9). Underneath the council's motto and name is a large image of a circle of tipis like those found among the Sioux of the Northern Plains. Within the circle is another, larger tipi and a seated group of people with blankets wrapped around their shoulders. One man stands in the center holding a pipe as if he is praying or speaking to the group. On the outside of the tipi circle, a horse with a travois and a small family approach to join the circle. In the background, a herd of horses gather, and in the distance are mountains and a sky with large clouds. The letterhead includes the names of the Siouan Council members on either side of the image. With these images, which the Siouan Council used throughout their official correspondence with the OIA and the FSA in the 1930s, the Siouans intended to convey their status as an Indian tribe and their historic and cultural connection to the Sioux of the West. They reminded government officials that they were indeed a group of "real" Indians, even if their contemporary lifestyle did not match the stereotype.

Pembroke Farms improved Indians' actual standards of living and raised their expectations for achieving some independence from Jim Crow's discriminatory economic system as well. But these gains also carried risks. The FSA did not provide houses and modern conveniences to farm families at no cost. Rather, the government held liens against tenants' personal property and farm equipment, and homesteaders had long-term mortgages to the government on their homes, outbuildings, and other property. Farmers were encountering serious debt to make these advances—albeit debt that theoretically helped raise their families out of poverty rather than sink them further into it. Government policy also did not allow project clients to choose how to allocate their debt. FSA staff thought that housing was the most urgent need for sharecropping families, and indeed, many houses had been deplorable. But given the opportunity, farm families may have chosen to deemphasize housing expenses in favor of other necessities to operate the farm. Or they may have chosen to allocate more of their income to savings. For example, D. L. Locklear had told Albert Grorud in 1934 that debt was his greatest concern, indicating that farmers desired improved economic security in the long term rather than more comfort in the short term. Further, on many projects, the FSA encouraged farmers to take on debt in proportion to their *anticipated* incomes, but farmers ultimately made less than the estimates.[26] Anticipated incomes at Pembroke Farms are not known, but some tenants expressed their concern over these issues when they faced eviction from the property because they had not been selected as homesteaders. In a petition, the evicted tenants said that "the Government has liens on our chattels and farming equipment. . . . and some of us have not made enough to pay off our liens from the proceeds of our crops." The tenants went on to say that other landlords would not rent to them because of their debt to the government, so they had nowhere to go.[27] The FSA's resettlement program tried to address the effects of the single cash-crop system on the farm tenant, but it made these tenants more desperate and left them with no option other than greater debt.

WHILE THE FSA conceived of and executed a plan to revolutionize the economic and social *conditions* that impoverished Indians in Robeson County, cultural assumptions and misunderstandings hampered the project's ability to fundamentally change the economic and social *system* under which Indians lived. While both Indians and the FSA desired to reshape the sharecropping system to Indians' advantage, each group's assumptions differed in meaningful ways. The FSA hoped to improve what its officials saw as a deplorable social situation and destructive factionalism among Robeson County's Indians. The FSA believed that segregation was only one in a series of problems faced by Indians in Robeson County.

Another problem—perhaps the one that was most manageable from the FSA's perspective—was a lack of social harmony and political unity. Their negative view of Indians' social organization revealed the hidden assumptions about race and class behind its program. Whatever belief in the inherent worth of people, regardless of race or class, that individual FSA staff members possessed, their agency's mission hampered their ability to execute this vision. FSA programs indicted the farm-tenancy system and tried to address its effects, but the agency did not try to change the system itself; politically, such a goal would have been impossible to achieve. Clients were therefore subject to the same identity definitions under FSA policy that they were under the tenant-farm system, but FSA officials likely did not understand their own biases. This meant that FSA officials saw Indians' subordinate status as a racial minority as being more meaningful than their identity as a People (as Indians saw themselves) or as a tribe (as the OIA viewed them). As an extension of this view, FSA staff members evidenced a belief that whites were the standard by which all other groups were to be measured, both economically and socially. In a climate of white supremacy, FSA administrators assessed Indians according to the ideals of whiteness.

Indians, on the other hand, did not see themselves as deficient. Their social organizations flourished, with families, churches, and schools growing in number. Their internal fragmentation was deeply rooted in their social network and community organization. But like FSA officials, Indians could not see beyond their own cultural assumptions. They did not recognize how federal bureaucrats were taking advantage of their fragmentation to limit the government's level of assistance and rationalize the FSA's inability to address the fundamental injustices of the economic system under which they lived. Indians therefore responded to the FSA's attempts to push for internal unity with more intense internal disagreements. The refusal of both Indians and the FSA to recognize the limits of their own cultural assumptions gave Cherokees an opportunity to assert control over the project and limited the Siouan Council's ability to achieve economic autonomy through Pembroke Farms.

The FSA's assessment of Indian social life omitted the perspectives offered by rural Indian settlements outside of Pembroke. "The Indians are sadly lacking in social activities and organizations," one FSA official wrote, although he described younger Indians' attendance at local movie theaters and the Normal School's plays and talent nights. Apparently these events did not impress the observer, and his statements reveal his ignorance of Indians' homes, churches, and settlement schools—the community's fundamental social institutions. Other than midnight fights with knives in the rural settlements, he reported, "it appears that the only way to make the Indians have social intercourse is through business intercourse and activities."[28]

This observer's comments suggest that he only viewed the life of town Indians, whose social activities beyond church may have centered around activities like moviegoing and school talent shows. While the community's traditional social units of family, school, and church also engaged town Indians, the observer probably would not have recognized these institutions as distinctly "Indian" without spending time with rural Indians and seeing how these institutions operated in their original settings. The FSA's perception of Indian social life suffered from their misunderstanding of Indians' social networks of family and settlement. If Robeson County Indians did not exhibit a stereotypically "Indian" culture, FSA officials apparently thought that their community was culturally indistinguishable from whites and blacks. Resettlement planners did not recognize an existing, coherent, and distinct social structure in the Indian community.

FSA officials drew on stereotypes of whites and blacks to conclude that Indians divided along lines of racial ancestry. Unlike the OIA, the FSA had relatively little experience working with Indians, and it seems unlikely that the FSA's stereotypes stemmed from "Indian" phenotypes. "The ones with straight hair refuse to be associated with the ones who have kinky hair," wrote A. M. Johnson and R. T. Melvin. "The ones with straight hair prefer to be known as Cherokee and the ones with kinky hair want to be known as Souian [sic] instead of Croatans."[29] These writers also reduced Indian school control to an issue of how Indians physically compared to blacks and whites: "The Indians and Whites and Negroes have their own schools and if perchance an Indian has kinky hair, he either goes to a Negro school or none at all."[30] Johnson and Melvin had only a superficial view of Indian life and apparently missed evidence that contradicted their cursory assessment. Indian schools accepted children who the school committees regarded as Indian according to kinship and settlement affiliation, and skin color or hair texture rarely played a role. After all, intermarriage had not fractured the Indian community, although it sometimes meant personal rejection. Rather, the politics of tribal names under white supremacy cleaved a People who otherwise adhered to the same fundamental layers of Indian identity, kinship, and settlement.

FSA officials did not accept that Indians might have had coherent identity criteria and a functioning, though divided, political organization; they also viewed Indian social organization negatively. The agency failed to look beyond physical traits to recognize the Indian community's existence as a political community and so categorized them according to physical features. In their view, Indians represented a combination of blacks and whites, a perception that dated back to the nineteenth century among southern whites and stemmed from the assumption that "blood will tell," or that one's phenotype reveals one's culture and society. Interestingly, their attitude was similar to John Collier's at the Office of Indian Affairs, but Collier saw "Indian" features in Robeson County's Indians rather than "black" or "white" traits. Federal officials saw what they wanted to see, and those perceptions shaped the government's willingness to promote Indian autonomy. Their assumptions about race and culture by definition denied the possibility of an autonomous, distinct Indian community in the South. In this context, it is not surprising that the FSA expressed a preference for a faction that they viewed as "almost white." White supremacy dictated that whites were the standard by which everyone else was measured.[31]

From the perspective of Cherokees and Siouans, their differences had nothing to do with hair. Instead, their differences centered on power and influence. Both factions were "intensely interested" in Pembroke Farms, according to resettlement planners, but their disagreements centered on who should control the project.[32] Joseph Brooks asserted himself as the "leader in promoting a Resettlement Project for the area," while the Cherokee Lowrys informed investigator A. M. Johnson that if the FSA "[listened] to the pleadings and wishes of the Siouan Tribe that they, the Lowry's [sic], would have nothing to do with the [Farm Security Administration]." When the Siouan Council initiated the Pembroke Farms project, Cherokees did not oppose the project; instead, they objected to the Siouans' claim to be Indian leaders and informed the FSA that unless the agency supported Cherokee claims and rejected the Siouans, the project would fail. The Lowry family, particularly D. F. Lowry, Martin Luther Lowry, and James R. Lowry—all members of Pembroke's Fourth Street Power Structure and town Indians—believed that the FSA should consider them, not the Siouan Council or its rural Indian supporters, to be the Indian community's rightful leaders. These same Lowrys had supported the Cherokee name and successfully defeated the Siouan bill in 1934.[33]

To convince the FSA of their legitimacy, Cherokees tried to appear as if they had the same grassroots support that Siouans had obtained. In doing so, they demonstrated their connection to the Indian community's social structure. These leaders did, indeed, have a reputation for ensuring a project's success or failure, and both town and rural Indians highly regarded their wealth, their achievements, and their service to Indian schools and churches. James R. Lowry, dean of the Indian Normal School and member of the Fourth Street Power Structure, offered his guidance to FSA officials. Lowry introduced them to Indian farmers and businessmen in the area. "The Indian," according to A. M. Johnson, "is by nature reticent and loathes to express himself or even give any information except to bona fide and trusted leaders. . . . We have to have an introductory letter from Professor Lowry . . . to leaders in the different communities before we could get a hearing and even then we did not get much information, except when Professor Lowry was along."[34] Johnson reported that having a recognized leader provide introductions was "common practice" in the Indian community when dealing with whites. These comments reflect the respect that other Indians gave Lowry and his influence with the rural Indians outside of Pembroke. Though they did not express their identity through a formal government, the Cherokees were as connected to the tribe's traditional leadership patterns and social organization as the Siouans.

The FSA told Indians they would be impartial, but they consistently favored the Cherokee leadership. A. M. Johnson told Cherokees that "so far as [he] knew the [FSA] was catering to no class or race in this resettlement work and that . . . they need not fear any partiality on our part to anyone or any faction."[35] But Johnson relied on the Lowrys' advice, believing that they were of a "better class" than the Siouans. In Johnson's mind, the Lowry family was "great in the eyes of the better class of Indians in Robeson County."[36] Johnson and his partner, R. T. Melvin, also called James R. Lowry an "outstanding Indian leader" and the members of the Cherokee faction "well-informed, honest, and courageous."[37] They pledged to depend on Lowry for his advice "in working out this local social problem" of Indian factionalism.[38] The Siouans, on the other hand, "are not as intelligent" as the Cherokees, and their leaders "lead them to believe the impossible in many cases."[39] Farm Security Administration planners invested heavily in the Cherokees' opinions and political network and excluded the Siouans. Like the OIA, which showed a consistent preference for Siouan leaders yet insisted that they had no predilection, the FSA claimed to be impartial but still favored one faction over another and aggravated the existing factional tensions.

When read in the context of investigators' inference that Cherokees were "almost white," the FSA based their favoritism on their own racial prejudices and not on the political realities faced by Indians. From the Indians' perspectives, both Cherokees and Siouans belonged to the same social networks and considered kinship, home settlements, and involvement in Indian-only schools and churches to be important aspects of how they expressed their Indian identity to each other. They did not agree, however, on how to express their identity to outsiders. For Cherokees, Pembroke Farms represented their "progressive" identity, their desire to raise their standard of living and improve themselves through self-help. This articulation of identity sustained local white supremacy and secured Indians' place in the racial hierarchy. On the other hand, Siouans insisted on autonomy and self-rule, traits of an Indian tribe that they believed would earn them a tribally owned land base and that they hoped would alleviate discrimination and powerlessness under Jim Crow. Segregation politics fueled this disagreement far more than phenotypic differences did, but the FSA could not appreciate this fact in light of its own prejudices.

The FSA's favoritism for Indians who expressed a "progressive" identity and who appeared "almost white" allowed Cherokees to successfully challenge Siouan leadership and gain influence over a project they did not initially bring to the community. Because of their partnership with the FSA, Siouans had to bow to Cherokee demands to a certain extent, but they still made every effort to divert project resources to Siouan members, many of whom belonged to the "swamps" and were in desperate need. However, the FSA's inability to distinguish Robeson County Indians culturally from black or white Americans limited Siouans' success. As the project evolved and Pembroke Farms forced Cherokee and Siouan town Indians to work together and resolve their differences, rural Indians became less able to combat the economic inequalities instituted by the Jim Crow system.

The selection of families as homesteaders on Pembroke Farms demonstrated these developments. Joseph Brooks and James Chavis tried to reserve the project for Indian families believed to have one-half or more "Indian blood." The presence of these families ensured the eligibility of the land for designation as a reservation by the secretary of the interior. Settling these families on Pembroke Farms also limited Cherokee influence and augmented Siouan leaders' power because principles of reciprocity demanded deference to them. For the Siouans, affirming Indian identity centered less on the absence of "black blood" (as it did for Cherokees, the FSA, and southern whites) and more on the presence of "Indian blood" (as it did for the Office of Indian Affairs).

But Carl Taylor, FSA director of rural resettlement in Washington, D.C., denied the Siouans' request. Taylor based his objection on the premise that Indian identity was similar to black identity as he conceived it. "A person of $\frac{1}{32}$ Indian blood would and must be given the same opportunity as might be granted a full blooded Indian," he told Joseph Brooks. While the law required that projects be open to members of any race, "it was nevertheless tacitly understood by everyone concerned that the Pembroke . . . Resettlement Project was an Indian Project." Brooks surely wondered why the FSA made a distinction between Indians of $\frac{1}{32}$ "Indian blood" and one-half or more "Indian blood," given that, first, it was illegal to make any distinction between races at all; and second, that OIA policies had always given such benefits to Indians of greater, not lesser, blood quantum. Taylor's decision demonstrated how two federal agencies, the FSA and the OIA, viewed Indian identity completely differently and as such treated Indians differently. Taylor's ruling also makes sense when one considers the ideology of segregation that pervaded the FSA. In Taylor's mind, one drop of "Indian blood" made one an Indian, just as one drop of "black blood" made one black. Other ancestry, particularly white ancestry, made no difference to an otherwise nonwhite individual.[40]

Following the Siouans' attempt to control the project settlement, the FSA proposed Martin Luther Lowry, a Cherokee leader and the brother of Professor James R. Lowry, as family selection specialist, although he was not interested in the position. The Siouan Council objected, fearing that their efforts to control the project would be thwarted by Cherokees. George Mitchell, the FSA's regional director, responded by proposing that a committee composed of a white selection specialist and two other members (one each from the Cherokee and Siouan groups) should conduct family selection. Both factions approved the plan, and Community Manager H. C. Green recommended one Cherokee and one Siouan.[41] For the moment, leaders of both Cherokee and Siouan groups seemed satisfied with their role at Pembroke Farms. Both agreed that white and black tenants who had been living on the land prior to its purchase should be asked to leave immediately, making the project "Indian only." As with the churches and schools, excluding blacks and whites promoted and sustained Indian identity by giving Indians the exclusive chance to take advantage of social, economic, and political opportunities.[42]

Rural Indians, however, who needed the project most, were dissatisfied with the family selection process. Rather than turn on Indian leaders of either faction, however, as they previously might have done, they opposed H. C. Green's involvement in the process. They signed a petition declaring him "incompetent and not satisfactory" to hold the position of community manager. The petition alleged that Green had promised that they would be considered for selection as homesteaders but then denied them the opportunity to apply and simply evicted them.[43] The petitioners also complained that they were now in debt to the government for livestock and farm-equipment loans. Other landlords would not rent to indebted farmers, they said, which left them with no place to go. Green, they believed, was responsible for misleading and subsequently evicting them. In light of the promise that Pembroke Farms represented, rejection must have been deeply disappointing to these men and their families. The petitioners informed the Farm Security Administration that they were sending a delegation to Washington to meet with officials there.[44]

The rural Indians who signed this petition were overwhelmingly affiliated with the Siouan Council, which had served their interests and provided them with opportunities for political organization that extended beyond their traditional kinship and settlement networks. At least 60 percent of the petitioners were enrolled as Siouans in 1935 or were family members of enrollees.[45] One petitioner was a Siouan councilman. Thirty percent of the enrolled Siouan petitioners came from White Hill, and another 15 percent came from Mt. Elim.

These figures represented the ways in which kin and settlement continued to shape Indians' political participation. Rural Indians in White Hill and Mt. Elim, districts that had very low Indian landownership and were relatively far from Pembroke, saw Pembroke Farms as a way to gain a foothold in the segregated economy and preserve their family units without moving to town and identifying with the Pembroke middle class.[46] The Siouan movement enhanced their political power and helped them gain these economic advantages. When the management of Pembroke Farms did not fulfill their expectations, they recruited other Siouans to join their protest. Membership in this political body therefore enhanced rural Indians' economic possibilities and ability to maintain their kinship and settlement networks. In some ways, Siouan membership became a new basis for alliance and wellspring of Indian identity. The petition showed a level of social and political organization that the FSA did not recognize when it responded to the complaint.[47]

FSA officials in Washington were almost certainly familiar with complaints like those issued from Robeson County. Resettlement clients often grumbled about community managers and perceived them as aloof "experts" who knew little about the realities of running a farm. Clients blamed them for problems that were not entirely their fault, and clients felt powerless under the weight of mounting debt and incomes that were often lower than expected.[48] Dealing with complaints was one weakness of the FSA's good intentions; staff members were crusaders and therefore resentful of criticism leveled at them, particularly from the people they sought to assist. Clients typically resented such paternalism but insisted paradoxically that the government should solve their problems for them.[49]

As they might have for any other project, FSA staff members told Robeson County Indians that they would do nothing. "We are of course sympathetic with rejected Indian families, but since the majority of the selection committee was composed of Indians, and since the selection committee and its work have been generally warmly praised, I do not think that charges of personal discrimination by the Community Manager or others could be supported," Mitchell wrote after meeting with a group of Indians who delivered the petition.[50] He offered a superficial assessment of the problem and implied that racial discrimination was not a factor since the selection committee included Indians. His attitude ignored the particular cultural milieu, however; Mitchell said nothing about factional discrimination or promises that project managers allegedly made. Indians followed through with their meeting with officials in Washington, where they confronted further evidence of the FSA's ignorance of Robeson County Indians' unique status.

In Washington, Indians met with L. I. Hewes, an FSA staff member. They recounted their stories only to be informed that the FSA would treat them just like other citizens. "We have a dishonest man in Pembroke to deal with," explained Duncan Locklear. "I am giving it to you fair and square. They will act like angels when you first come in but later they treat you as if you were a brute. They [Indians] are not getting a fair deal. . . . I thought that land was to help Indians." In view of the fact that the selection committee included Indians, Hewes simply refused to believe that any injustice existed. "We are very anxious to see that any group of people, no matter what their race is, their nationality, gets help if they are in trouble," Hewes told the delegation, assuring them that racial discrimination was not part of the government's program.

After eliminating racism as grounds for the Indians' complaint, Hewes decided that they were blaming the government for their own laziness. Hewes treated the delegation with the same condescension they complained of from H. C. Green. "As I see it," Hewes said dismissively, "you came on to a piece of land as tenant. You got a loan. Nobody else [except the FSA] will take a tenant on and give him money to operate. Now the time comes for you to look for a farm. You are having some trouble. . . . Maybe you have looked hard [for a farm], maybe you haven't." Hewes failed to countenance the long history of discrimination against Indian tenants by white landlords and the possibility that the government's assistance had turned into a liability. In fact, on some resettlement projects, farmers did indeed believe that government assistance had led to a serious problem: with the loans they had assumed, they were losing net worth, not gaining it.[51] "I am sure you will get a square deal," Hewes said and concluded the meeting.[52] He and his fellow FSA staff members were unable or unwilling to recognize Indians' unique existence in Robeson County and confront the system that denied them justice. Consequently, they disregarded these farmers' complaints. While the four petitioners whose applications were accepted remained on the farm, the FSA required the others to move.

Siouans renewed their efforts to assert some control over the resettlement project by establishing a cooperative association. The FSA incorporated the Red Banks Mutual Association (RBMA) in 1938 to provide fifteen Indian families with their own supply house, farm equipment, and outlets for cooperatively marketing their crops. Joseph Brooks, James Chavis, and others believed that the RBMA would enhance "tribal life" and free more Indians from dependence on merchants, landlords, and credit. The RBMA settled families on a 1,715-acre tract and leased the land from the government for shares of the association's crops. Families occupied their homes without charge, and in exchange they contracted with the association for their labor; the FSA loaned the association money to make improvements on the cooperative farm.[53]

Red Banks reflected Siouan control in two different ways. First, the Family Selection Committee chose ten families to live at the RBMA, and nearly all of them embodied Siouan emphasis on kinship and reciprocity. The committee selected Joseph Brooks and his sister Margie's husband, Shaw Deese, along with two of the men who had petitioned to remove H. C. Green. Another five farmers had also been tenants on Pembroke Farms.[54] Six of the ten families came from White Hill, and eight of the families were enrolled Siouans. These patterns demonstrated the persistent influence of kinship and settlement in the Siouan movement and the preferential treatment Siouans gave their own.

Secondly, Joseph Brooks and Shaw Deese symbolically exhibited their power to whites and to other Indians by moving into what was called the "Big House" at Red Banks. The Big House was the former home of the white family who had owned Fletcher Plantation, the land from which the FSA crafted much of the Red Banks project. Apparently, the government had appointed Brooks as manager of the project.[55] For Brooks, who had suggested the RBMA plan three years earlier and had fought for the attention of the OIA and the FSA, living in the Big House constituted a display of his power and influence.

The presence of his family members and in-laws also showed that in spite of his town status and political clout, he still practiced rural Indians' ways of living. Finally, his decision to take up residence at RBMA demonstrated his victory—temporarily, at least—over white power and the segregation economy. Some months later, and for unknown reasons, Brooks resigned as manager, and Pembroke Farms manager H. C. Green assumed the position.

The RBMA represented a success in Siouans' quest for economic autonomy. The families at RBMA controlled their own labor, set their own prices for crops, and operated with heavy machinery—particularly tractors, to which other Indian farmers did not have access. Each farmer had two acres of his own for a garden and cash crops, in addition to a share of the profits from the collective. After the selection committee chose the initial families, the group organized a board of directors, which subsequently appointed a new board that selected other families to live on the farm. Each member owned stock in the corporation. In effect, Red Banks represented the Indian-controlled project that the Siouans had hoped Pembroke Farms would be, and the association became the longest-running New Deal cooperative in America, remaining open until 1968. The board of directors used kinship to perpetuate their membership and delivered benefits to their political allies, the other Siouans who were in need. As a result, in the words of Ryan Anderson, "In thirty years the Lumbees who took part in the Red Banks Mutual Association had moved from sharecropper status, living in a system of perpetual debt, to being participants in a solvent business venture."[56] The RBMA symbolized a victory over a discriminatory economy that left Indians largely powerless. Over time, its impact transcended the betterment of the lives of the few families who lived there because Indians had sustained the project by employing kinship, their fundamental layer of identity.

WHILE THE FSA HELPED INDIANS preserve their identity in some respects, the agency's assumption that Indians had no social organization of their own made Pembroke Farms highly susceptible to the influence of white segregationists, who repeatedly reminded federal officials of Indians' place in the racial hierarchy. Even though the FSA intended to lessen the burden of segregation for Indians, its efforts to appease local whites further entrenched Indians' symbolic and actual subordination. The FSA was unaware of this conflict between their goals and their actions because they did not comprehend the particular circumstances of Robeson County's Indians.

For example, the FSA expressed its preference for local white opinion when it hired L. B. Brandon as the first community manager at Pembroke

Farms. Brandon was a former superintendent of the McNair Corporation, which, like Pates Supply, had a long history of lending to Indian farmers at outrageous interest rates and then foreclosing on their farms.[57] According to the Siouans, who protested the appointment, Brandon was personally active in several Indians' farm foreclosures south of Pembroke. Indians favored the appointment of John Pearmain, a Soil Conservation Service agent with whom they had worked closely in the project planning stages, when Pearmain was a community manager. Pearmain wanted the job and recognized that local Indians ought to have some say in the matter. While Senator Burton K. Wheeler, a coauthor of the Wheeler-Howard Bill and a member of the Senate Committee on Indian Affairs, supported Pearmain's appointment, the FSA did not agree; they were mystified that "a senator from Montana" would express a preference in a matter concerning North Carolina. But the FSA did not understand that Wheeler's interest was based on the fact that Pembroke Farms was for Indians and that he was articulating Indian views. Oblivious to the significance of the Indians' request, the FSA informed them that the fact that Brandon had worked for McNair "was no indication that he was not an impartial and thoroughly capable Manager."[58]

Indians sought help from the Office of Indian Affairs, which refused to get involved despite Wheeler's preference for Pearmain and recognition that Brandon might pose a problem for the Indians. Edwin L. Groome, assistant to Commissioner of Indian Affairs John Collier, suggested that Brandon was "so closely affiliated with a State-wide organization in North Carolina that no action should be taken unless some evidence in writing is presented to the Indian Office as a justification for [Siouans'] protest." Fearing that their actions might upset North Carolina's white-dominated economy and politics, the OIA rejected an opportunity to intercede in segregation politics on behalf of Indians.[59] While the OIA might have been sympathetic to Indians' concerns about Brandon's relationship with the largest corporate landlord in the area, neither it nor the FSA proved willing to help Indians gain power in the racial hierarchy.

The FSA further subverted Indian goals when the agency agreed to settle a group of whites at Pembroke Farms. Beginning in May 1936, white civic clubs and churches in Maxton argued that a resettlement project in the county should benefit whites. A white resettlement project, they believed, would help the low-enrollment white schools in the Maxton area remain open, and it would also assist in the growth of the small towns in the western part of the county, which were relatively far from the major tobacco markets in Lumberton and Fairmont. Furthermore, they argued, Indian settlement in the area would devalue white-owned land. They also feared that whites would "abandon" a church bordering land that had been purchased for Pembroke Farms if Indians lived near there. In sum, these citizens believed that a re-settlement project for whites would benefit the county more than an Indian project would.[60]

Congress and the Washington FSA office eagerly interceded on behalf of local whites. Senator Josiah W. Bailey and Representative J. Bayard Clark, who previously had scuttled congressional recognition for Indians, wrote to Resettlement Administrator W. W. Alexander, urging him to consider these white citizens' petitions.[61] At first, the district office of the FSA resisted the request, informing Clark that "if a part of this single Indian project were at this late date assigned to white families, it would mean the break of faith with the Indian community and a source of bitter disappointment to those Indians who have built up their hopes for home ownership."[62] Bailey pressured the FSA's Washington office and it capitulated, reconsidered the request, and reversed the district office's position.[63] Even though the Washington office refused to heed the plea of Indian tenant farmers who the FSA had evicted from Pembroke Farms, they did act on behalf of whites who wanted a share of an Indian project.

The Siouan Council learned of the agency's plans and immediately pro-tested, but Regional Director Mitchell met with whites in Maxton and subsequently recommended that a portion of the land go to white farmers. Mitchell offered five-year leases to seven white families for 450 acres of land, while Indians retained 8,550 acres for eighty families. The FSA's decision pleased no one. Maxton's citizens felt that the compromise was "barely ac-ceptable," but they agreed to it. Indians expressed their disapproval by calling the Indian Office, which requested a meeting with resettlement chief W. W. Alexander. Alexander's staff denied knowledge of the arrangement and said that Alexander would resolve the issue when he returned to the office. While FSA staff stalled the Indian Office, the deal went through. "Mitchell ought to write Cong. Bayard Clark and tell him the good news," wrote one Wash-ington official. Mitchell did so, and indeed, when Alexander returned to the office, Alexander approved the plan.[64] Throughout this ordeal, the FSA never granted Indians a meeting, although they persisted in their requests. Instead, Alexander simply asked Mitchell to "handle this" with the Siouan Council.[65]

Indians recognized that this outcome was a direct result of segregation politics. White citizens had more power and influence than Indians did, and they received a portion of the benefits designed for Indians based on their clout with North Carolina's congressmen. A few years earlier, these same congressmen had abandoned Indians' need for recognition when they posed a threat to local whites' power. Although the concession to whites on Pembroke Farms was relatively small, it had enormous symbolic significance in the context of Indians' previous defeats and the hope that Pembroke Farms represented. Actions such as these demonstrated that while the FSA sympathized with Indians, it was unwilling to disturb the political and economic system that kept them powerless and impoverished.

For the rural Indians in the greatest need, Joseph Brooks's failure to combat, or even delay, the decision to lease land to whites must have signaled the inability of town leaders to defeat the Jim Crow political economy. These events clarified a different sort of division within the Indian community, one based less on political factions and more on class and settlement differences. Thanks in part to the FSA's refusal to challenge segregation directly, divisions in the Indian community centered not on political ideologies about segregation but on how segregation affected one's economic and political opportunities. Town Indians, whether Cherokee leaders or Siouan leaders, were better equipped to get the most out of the Jim Crow system.

But the Great Depression still trapped rural Indians who lacked political connections. They needed direct economic assistance, and preferably economic autonomy, to combat the damage segregation caused. Pembroke Farms and the Red Banks Mutual Association provided this assistance to a certain extent, but for rural Indians, the FSA's failures may have had a larger impact than its short-term successes. While the project provided opportunities for Cherokee and Siouan leaders to work together, the inadequacies of Pembroke Farms contributed to an increased distance between town and rural Indians, whether they fell into Siouan or Cherokee factions.

Even as the interests of town and rural Indians diverged, the Siouan Council endeavored to maintain the sense of kinship it had created among its constituents and fulfill its governmental responsibilities to all of Robeson County's Indians, regardless of their political affiliation. Writing as the "General Council of Indians of Robeson County" rather than as the "Siouan Lodge" or the "General Council of Siouan Indians," council secretary James E. Chavis and others complained to Senator Bailey in 1941 that the FSA's actions made Indians incapable of fighting discrimination. They detailed how promises made by the government had not been fulfilled and accused H. C. Green of employing favoritism among the homesteaders. Indians in Robeson County wanted more local control over the project, meaning that *they* wanted to control it, without the "help" of local whites or the FSA's white managers. "We have been fooled into all kind of cooperation here by the local white people so much until we have lost faith in all such organizations," they said. "We have not been fairly considered by most of the Government agencies here in our locality." They voiced their conviction that both local whites and government officials desired to perpetuate discrimination. Indian control, they believed, would better equip them to fight discriminatory economic conditions under Jim Crow.[66] The council also specifically alleged racism, citing the use of white relief workers and white carpenters instead of Indians on the project. Furthermore, they complained about the lack of Indian staff in the local office. For example, the daughter of Cherokee leader D. F. Lowry made the highest civil-service exam score among the applicants for a clerical position in the project office, but Green rejected her. The Siouan Council's protest suggests that the Siouans had put aside political disagreements to focus on discrimination, but the FSA had ignored the council. As a result, the project had "deviated so far from the original until it doesn't seem real." The council believed that the FSA had abandoned the promise of Pembroke Farms and had acquiesced to discriminatory practices that left Indians, particularly those in greatest need, powerless to fight segregation.[67]

To solve these problems, the Siouan Council revived its original plan to organize under the Office of Indian Affairs: "If the project can be placed with the Indian office let us know how it can be done, if not we want a man who will not be prejudice against the Indians to be sent here instead of Mr. Green, for we are disgusted with him and his whole set up here and at Raleigh." The council saw itself as an Indian government and believed that John Collier's administration could address their needs as Indians better than the FSA could. Such a request expressed their identity as a distinct group in Robeson County with a desire for self-rule and economic autonomy. Their solution also protested against the FSA's tendency to classify Indians with whites and blacks, and Indians demanded that the federal government, rather than local and state governments, recognize and deal with their unique circumstances.[68]

As he had so many times before, Senator Bailey responded to Indians' pleas by consulting his friends in Lumberton, who gave the FSA "a pretty clear bill of health" and insisted that an investigation into the situation was unnecessary.[69] The FSA's Washington office did ask for the district office's opinion, and Assistant Regional Director C. B. Faris blamed self-interest for most of the complaints. Faris cynically wrote, "The 'General Council of Indians of Roberson [sic] County' should have a broader program than to want to run the offices of the 60 families on the project." Faris believed that complaints were illegitimate and unrealistic and were motivated by one person's self-interest. "Joe Brooks wants the job of running the project," he concluded.

The actions of Brooks and the Siouans to control the project alienated the FSA's regional officials. To the FSA, these complaints had no basis in Indians' distinct cultural assumptions.[70]

Indians and the FSA viewed the failures of the project differently because each group had a very different attitude about the nature of Indian identity. The FSA viewed Indians as a racial group, separate from and inferior to whites because of their skin color and ancestry. In the minds of FSA staff members, Indians had no social organization, and their political organization was destructive at best. Hence, Faris and other officials saw nothing other than political self-interest in the complaints issued from the General Council of Indians, and they were unwilling to consider Indians' input and their specific needs. On the other hand, Robeson County Indians, particularly the rural Indians who desperately needed the project, thought that their economic subordination was due to their race *and* to their distinct culture. They did not separate the two and saw their community as vibrant, worth sustaining, and deserving of particular consideration. They were a People connected by kinship and, increasingly, by political bonds. They were not simply a "race," defined by the quality of their hair texture or their political influence. Pembroke Farms did not dismantle the disempowerment inherent in segregation, but it provided a platform for tribal government and gave Indian identity a political impact.

FSA managers and staff chose to see Robeson County Indians as a race, marked by their physical characteristics and socioeconomic standing relative to whites and blacks. They only superficially engaged the categories of knowledge that Indians also articulated about their identity: tribe (a political identity defined by its recognition from the state and the OIA) and People (a kinship identity defined by their shared place and history). FSA officials' actions linked the category of race to the social order of white supremacy; one did not exist without the other. Indians recognized this linkage as well when they argued for assistance based on their economic subordination as a race. But Indians also persistently engaged tribe and People as categories, intertwining the categories into various new configurations that they believed would bring them the strongest advantage under that system of white supremacy. Their actions reinforced white supremacy and intensified their own divisions in ways they could not have expected.

While these actions arguably increased their subordination, Indians also began to build a nation that achieved a degree of recognized autonomy and affirmed their distinct identity. Siouan leaders took the FSA's insistence on racial categories and the OIA's emphasis on blood quantum to establish their difference from whites and blacks; they used town and rural divisions in the Indian community to create a representative tribal government; and they seized on New Deal initiatives to carve out separate economic opportunities for themselves and their constituents. These efforts were not perfectly selfless nor perfectly successful—there were too many voices excluded from the process to achieve a fully integrated, cohesive nation. But we need not hold Native nations, or any nation, to that standard. Indeed, the American nation has not met it. The way forward depends upon a continued commitment by the ones most disfranchised; we see such engagement, and its consequences, in the next phase of Robeson County Indians' relationship to the federal government.

6 Measuring Identity

The individuals shown in Figure 10, along with 200 other people, applied to the Office of Indian Affairs in 1936 and 1937 for recognition as having "one-half or more Indian blood." Referring to "these people," D'Arcy Mc-Nickle and his companions from the OIA said that they "did not have a clear understanding of the term Indian." Anthropologist Carl Seltzer took the photographs as part of anthropometric tests he conducted to determine each applicant's quantity of "Indian blood." The photographs represent one point of view on Indian identity: Indianness is defined by one's head shape, size, skin color, and hair texture.

Each person pictured here had their own story, and together they embodied the community's layers of identity. Brewington, Lowry, Revels, Maynor, and Chavis were all descended from "forefather" James Lowry; Chavis was also a descendant of Major Locklear, as was Beadan Locklear Brooks. "Forefather" John Brooks was another ancestor of Beadan Brooks. Like the other 200 applicants, these six are all connected by kinship, and they testified to that fact in the study; their applications contain genealogy charts identifying their ancestors. For the study, however, each declared that they were "one-half or more Indian blood" to suit the OIA investigators.

Even as this group cohered in kinship, they divided in politics. Two of them were kin to the Siouan leadership: Cloyd Chavis was James Chavis's brother, and Cora Mae Brewington was Joseph Brooks's sister-in-law (his wife Sallie's sister). Chavis hailed from the Saint Annah community, and Brewington was raised in Fairmont but lived with her sister Sallie and Joe around the time she

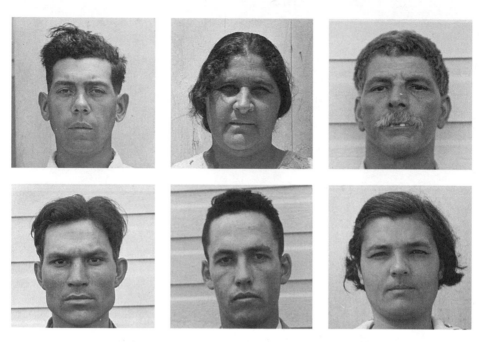

FIGURE 10. Six Participants from the Siouan enrollment study, 1936. Top row, left to right: Cloyd Chavis, Beadan Locklear Brooks, Lindsay Revels; bottom row, left to right: Lawrence Maynor, Kermit Lowry, Cora Mae Johnson Brewington. (Photographs by Carl C. Seltzer; National Archives and Records Administration, Washington, D.C.)

took part in this study. Kermit Lowry was Cherokee leader D. F. Lowry's son; he was raised in Pembroke. Lindsay Revels and Lawrence Maynor were first cousins from the Philadelphus community, and Beadan Brooks lived in the Brooks Settlement. All three became members of a third faction that included the twenty-two individuals whom Seltzer identified as "one-half or more Indian," known locally in the community as the Original 22. Of this group, only Lawrence Maynor was part of the Original 22. Seltzer found that Beadan Brooks was a "borderline" case, and the rest were "unquestionably less than one-half Indian blood." Beadan Brooks's status prompted the OIA to study her family members—another 102 individuals from the Brooks Settlement. Twenty of the Original 22 were kin to Beadan Brooks and distantly related to Joseph Brooks. But kinship to Joe did not matter to their political organization; they sought recognition based on Seltzer's findings of their blood quantum and introduced a new layer of identity formation to the community.

Other factors—age, education, family, and occupation—divided and united this group. The youngest person here was Lowry at age twenty-seven, while the oldest was Revels at age sixty. All of them were farmers—except

Brewington, whose occupation was listed as housewife, and Lowry, who taught school. All were raised in families with five or more children, and each had children of their own. Lowry had the lowest number (only one son), while Brooks had the highest (seven sons and five daughters). Lowry had the most education, having attended graduate school, while Revels had the least; he told Seltzer that he had only attended school in the New Hope community for one month. Indian-only schools would have made the most difference to Lowry, whose father was the first graduate of the Indian Normal School, and the least difference to Revels, who was a teenager by the time Indian schools became widely established. In fact, Revels probably attended the Normal School, located at New Hope, during those first tumultuous years (described in chapter 1) and perhaps dropped his education because of the tensions there. The rest of this group attended Indian schools for between two and nine years.[1] Lowry was the only member of this group married to a non-Indian; his wife, who was white and from Kinston, North Carolina, supposedly refused to annul her marriage when her parents requested it, so they disinherited her.[2]

Divided by name, this group nevertheless all identified as Indians, as a People. Sustaining strongly felt divisions while maintaining coherence is the paradox of identity formation in any community with sharp political disagreements. How does the group stay together? Why doesn't it split apart? Sometimes, of course, it does; many Indian communities have divided along lines of ancestry or politics and become, essentially, different nations. But the imposition of federal policy's intense focus on race served to keep this group together *even while* it was falling apart. For example, today many of the Original 22's descendants would not identify as "Siouan," "Cherokee," or "Lumbee" but as "Tuscarora," recalling the ancestry that many Brooks Settlement members claimed. I have first cousins who are Tuscarora, but I'm Lumbee. Our mothers are sisters, and we all ate at Grandma Bloss's table and sang at Granddad Foy's piano. We don't deny one another, but we pull in different directions over issues of history and tribal names. To say "these people did not have a clear understanding of the term 'Indian'" defies logic and the identity definitions that the People themselves create.

IN 1936 THE COMMUNITY'S INTERNAL CONVERSATION about Indian identity—family, settlement, schools—mattered little to the Office of Indian Affairs. The Indian Reorganization Act's "half-blood" provision had conflated "race" with "tribe," taking a primarily political relationship between Indians and the federal government and converting it into a social relationship not dissimilar from the one that existed in the Jim Crow South. Policy makers at the OIA unintentionally assisted white supremacists. OIA officials proved unable to recognize the legitimate political disagreements of Robeson County Indians because they believed that blood quantum and appearance were accurate markers of identity. Such markers also upheld the system of white supremacy because they defined racial categories, not the political ones that were the foundation of Indian policy. Further, the OIA systematically ignored the realities of Indian people themselves, favoring "expert" opinion instead.

Why did Indians choose to submit their own identity markers to these tests? The answer was complex, involving class, "tribe," racial discrimination, "blood," kinship, and settlement. The Pembroke Farms project proved that economic autonomy and allegiance to a political body—the Siouan Council—brought concrete benefits for some tribal members. However, the Farm Security Administration's failure to address the Jim Crow system left the disempowerment of segregation largely intact, and Indians continued to pursue other means of affirming their identity and improving this situation. When the OIA presented them with the opportunity to gain recognition under the IRA's "half-blood" provision, rural Indians responded with a strategy to enhance their power, influence, and economic situation.

A blood quantum of one-half or more qualified individuals for certain benefits according to the IRA. The OIA employed anthropometric tests that measured and observed a person's physical features to reveal the "Indian blood" of individuals in Robeson County. Robeson County Indians and the OIA each used the tests to express different ideas about Indian identity and "Indian blood." Indians approached the concept of "Indian blood" from a kinship perspective and sought to demonstrate their community's social organization and coherence to the OIA through the tests. Policy makers at the OIA, on the other hand, viewed "Indian blood" as a practical equation that allowed them to apply a scientific theory to social policy. While the OIA's standard seemed objective on the surface, the prevailing racism of the day corrupted their concept of "Indian blood" and enabled science to support racism.[3]

The OIA launched its efforts to enroll Robeson County Indians after the Siouan Council formally requested in 1935 to organize the tribe under the IRA. Had the OIA been able to fund a resettlement project, their involvement depended upon Indians' eligibility for recognition. According to the IRA, nonreservation Indians who possessed one-half or more "Indian blood" qualified for recognition. At that time, anthropology equated Indian ancestry with Indian culture. Based on their predecessors' reports and observations, John Collier, D'Arcy McNickle, and the OIA staff assumed that Robeson

County Indians had mixed ancestry, but they struggled to find an adequate means of proving the percentage of "Indian blood" found in these individuals. Collier and McNickle, in particular, thought that sufficient quantities of "Indian blood" existed among the Robeson County group and proposed enrolling them as "half or more Indian" under the IRA.[4]

Collier and his staff expected to deal with several groups throughout the United States that were "landless Indians of one-half or more Indian blood," as they were termed. Lack of a reservation land base was central to their definition of Indians who could qualify for recognition under the IRA. In some cases, OIA staff expected to relocate Indians onto existing reservations, while in other cases, they purchased land for qualifying Indian groups. As such, the policy tied recognition explicitly to an allocation of resources by the OIA or by Indian groups already on reservations. The OIA was already laboring under inadequate funding for the land-purchase provisions of the IRA and consequently could not help even the reservation-based groups that had too little land to meet their economic-development needs.[5] Although a large number of groups might have qualified for application under the IRA's "half-blood" provision, Collier strictly limited the types of groups to investigate. As discussed in chapter 4, he ruled out many groups along the eastern seaboard (designating them "folk groups") except for Robeson County Indians, for whom he had encouraged the assistance of the FSA. He also reserved special attention for the Chippewa-Cree in Montana and North Dakota, and he further identified Indians in California, Michigan, Mississippi, and Nevada as possibly eligible for enrollment under the IRA.[6] OIA delegations visited only the Robeson County Indians and the Chippewa-Cree in the 1930s, however.

OIA policy makers did not question the Indian ancestry of the Chippewa-Cree, who did not have the long history of OIA investigations into their origins that the Robeson County Indians had. The OIA expressed concern, however, that some applicants did not have the required blood quantum. OIA staff developed an "Application for Registration as an Indian," a questionnaire to determine an Indian's ancestry, tribal affiliation, relationship to the federal government, and degree of assimilation. Legal historian Paul Spruhan pointed out that OIA staff often relied on more than strictly "blood" to determine the identity of Indians under the New Deal. They frequently employed social and cultural definitions alongside evidence of blood quantum.[7] Regarding the Chippewa-Cree, the OIA staff did not employ anthropometry, as they did in Robeson County, to determine eligibility. Instead, they relied on the applications, consequently rejecting some applicants who did not display what officials considered to be proper "Indian habits." For example, officials rejected applicants—sometimes against the recommendation of their Chippewa-Cree advisers—who were married to whites, were perceived as wealthy, or had "a good job." Sources indicated that these applicants were rejected because Collier determined that they did not need or deserve the economic benefits that might have accompanied land purchase. Obviously, OIA officials employed biological criteria loosely, and economic considerations could determine blood quantum.[8]

McNickle traveled to Robeson County in the early spring of 1936; he carried a set of "Applications for Registration as An Indian," but Robeson County Indians' answers to the questions did not satisfy him. The answers "show[ed] no documentary proof of Indian blood. The statements made as to the quantity of Indian blood depend entirely on tradition." The Indian Office discounted "traditional evidence," and the documentary record was a "wasteland" because, according to McNickle, "written records dissolve in mist." McNickle was discouraged by the available oral evidence and considered written records unreliable, as they apparently had no scientifically verifiable origin point with which to determine descent and the group's degree of "Indian blood." But rather than also relying on social and cultural factors, McNickle insisted on pursuing evidence of blood quantum. He proposed that the OIA appoint a commission to hear testimony under oath about the ancestry of Robeson County Indians.[9] The Siouan Council approved this idea and suggested that the OIA include two Indians on the commission.[10]

OIA staff members conferred on the best method for the enrollment commission to authenticate Indians' claims, and they explored both genealogical and anthropometric methods. At issue was the relative reliability of the methods and how to apply abstract theoretical views of "blood" and culture to a concrete policy. They quickly agreed with McNickle that genealogical investigation was too time-consuming and unreliable; OIA officials had tried it at the White Earth Ojibwe Reservation in Minnesota in 1916 and found it unsatisfactory when compared with anthropometry. Harvard anthropology professor Earnest A. Hooton cautioned the OIA that anthropometry was not foolproof, either; the matter of racial ancestry was "not capable of proof." But Hooton assured officials that measurements such as the cephalic index—the ratio of head width to head length—contributed to a racial "diagnosis" akin to the physician's diagnosis of a disease, "a judgment based upon an assemblage of symptoms." The "symptoms," in this case, were measurements of a person's head, skin, hair, teeth, nose, and lips. Ales Hrdlicka of the Smithsonian Institution, who had conducted the anthropometric tests at White Earth twenty years earlier, was more confident than Hooton about the promise of anthropometry to distinguish between races and to reveal mixed-race ancestry. According to Hrdlicka, "it was not only possible to detect and separate all mixed-bloods from full-bloods, but to form a fair estimate of the proportion of white blood wherever mixture existed."[11]

Although Hrdlicka cited field experience in his confident assessment of the utility of anthropometry, determining racial mixture actually had proven difficult. White Earth Ojibwes with curly hair confounded investigators, for example, who were convinced that curly hair could never exist among Indians of a "full-blood" type. But Ojibwes themselves recognized genetic variations better than anthropologists and told Hrdlicka that "it wouldn't make any difference if [someone] had curly hair." According to historian Melissa Meyer, the Ojibwes "objected to establishing fixed physical standards by which to differentiate among Indians because of variations they observed among themselves."[12] As with the Chippewa-Cree in Montana twenty years later, the OIA determined blood status at White Earth by economic considerations more than any "scientific" biological, cultural, or social information. Hrdlicka found very few "full-bloods," paving the way for the theft of allotted lands of the purported "mixed-bloods" and some "full-bloods" as well. Indian-held economic resources were fraudulently transferred to whites, based on Hrdlicka's findings of "mixed blood."[13]

These experiences did not deter Collier and others from using anthropometry in Robeson County, however. "Scientific" information was highly valued, even when it proved vague or faulty. For example, physical traits that anthropometrists considered "of diagnostic value" included skin color, height, the presence of moles, hair form, hair color, nasal profile, and the cephalic index. Anthropometry considered white males to be the standard for many characteristics, and the OIA compared some Indian features to that of the "normal" white male. However, "white" traits were vague relative to "Negroid" and "Indian" types, which were comparatively fixed in nature, according to anthropometry. Typically "Negroid" skin color, for example, was "black or dark brown," "White" was "light," and "Indian" was "red brown to medium brown." "Negroid" hair was "woolly or frizzy" and "Indians" had "straight" hair, but "Whites" could display "straight, wavy, or curly" hair.[14] Ales Hrdlicka himself observed that white Americans were "very mixed" and thus more difficult to accurately characterize. But anthropometrists had no difficulty determining the hair, eyes, and skin color of "primitive tribes," people they assumed were racially "pure." Although Hrdlicka observed in practice that "mixed-blood" Indians could be easily separated out at White Earth, in theory he believed that mixed-race individuals—white, black, and Native American—were unsuitable for anthropometric study because they did not have "pure" ancestry and therefore posed problems for the accurate classification of humanity, which was anthropometry's purpose. In fact, studies of people who scientists perceived to be "mixed" were in their infancy at this time, and anthropometrists admitted that they knew little about how to analyze their measurements.[15]

Officials ignored the contradictions between anthropometric field practice and theory and turned their attention to the practical application of the science to Indian policy. With little consensus on the reliability of anthropometry, they acknowledged that race was a social construction as much as a biological fact, and they recommended that the government "weed out" Indians who were "sociologically white, regardless of degree of blood." Indian Office staff realized that blood did not correlate directly to culture but nevertheless capitulated to anthropological theory. "It is true," the group concluded, "that degree of blood in a general way does follow in some measure the social or cultural mixture."[16] Although the OIA privileged the connection between biology and culture in determining Indian identity, it could not ignore how white supremacy constructed racial identities in Robeson County. "Since the state has set up barriers against their intermarrying with either whites or Negroes, and since they cannot by law attend any schools but those segregated for their own use, it can be seen that they have no choice in the matter but to consider themselves Indians," McNickle believed.[17] Recognizing that anthropometry alone could not define Indian identity, McNickle also reduced identity to Indians' ambivalent position within the southern racial hierarchy. The declaration that Indians had "no choice" but to claim their Indianness implied that their identity was merely a thin veneer covering their status as nonwhites, a stance that closely corresponded to the Farm Security Administration's view that Indians differed little socially or politically from any other racial group.

Although the OIA admitted that Indian identity was a social phenomenon, they did not embrace Indians' own criteria for identity. Indian leaders in Robeson County had spent the previous half century separating themselves from blacks to gain affirmation of their identity from the state and federal governments. Unlike the state of North Carolina, the OIA recognized this trend and wanted to affirm it but declined to accept it as a legitimate means of authenticating one's Indian identity. The OIA seemed oblivious to the ways that Indians demonstrated their distinct social and political organization and capitalized on their racial ambiguity to preserve those aspects of identity that sustained their community apart from white dominance. Moreover, the OIA ignored its own historic affirmation of Indian identity in Robeson County. Although the OIA could admit to the failure of anthropometry to acknowledge the social construction of race, it could not intellectually accept Indian methods of reckoning identity.

Uncertain about the role that blood should play in the perpetuation of Indian culture, the staff turned to H. Scudder Mekeel, head of the department's own Applied Anthropology Unit, which assisted tribes in writing constitutions and developing tribal governments.[18] Mekeel provided a pragmatic perspective. "It is not really possible by any method so far devised to determine degree of blood accurately," he admitted, but he thought that a combination of the genealogical and anthropometric methods promised a "reasonable" assessment "in the majority of instances." However, Mekeel warned that the potentially large number of applicants for recognition made a combination of these methods "not administratively practicable." "We shall have to accept a less accurate form of proof," he conceded, and members of the Indian Office staff determined that anthropometry, combined with testimony from applicants but without additional documentary investigation, comprised the most cost-effective method of determining the degree of "Indian blood."[19] In the end, administrative practicality shaped their decision to apply anthropometry to Robeson County's Indians.

The OIA's need for a scientifically objective standard raised issues about the appropriateness of anthropometry. Anthropologists, Collier's intellectual guides, respected anthropometry for its purported abilities to classify the human family according to racial groups. When anthropometry emerged as a field, anthropologists used it to further their project of ranking races along an evolutionary scale that situated white Americans at the top of civilization and African peoples at the bottom. With some exceptions, these views held sway in academic departments and at the Smithsonian Institution between the 1890s and the mid-twentieth century; in fact, the scientific case for the connection between race and culture encouraged lawmakers and social activists like John Collier to apply anthropology to their social-engineering efforts. Physical anthropologists defined a "race" as a people whose phenotypes conformed, with individual variations, to a standard. They observed that different races of mankind—white, yellow, brown, red, and black, as early scientists identified them—possessed distinct physical features, and they believed that measuring those features elucidated the mental capacity and cultural advancement of each racial group. These scientists sought to distinguish between the races but also to explain cultural differences between them. The most obvious explanation, one that illuminated the contemporary inequalities prevalent in their urban industrialized societies, linked one's physical traits to one's behavior. Adherents of this philosophical view argued that in a society full of technological advances and economic opportunities, the disadvantaged and dispossessed were simply biologically and physically inferior.[20]

Franz Boas of Columbia University critiqued this link between race and culture beginning in the 1890s, although Boas himself depended upon anthropometry and considered it a useful tool. Like other academics, he accepted the biology and not just the social construction of racial difference. But unlike his colleagues, Boas argued that anthropologists ought to devote their studies to historically specific cultures rather than hierarchical levels of culture. Collier reflected Boas's ideas in his creation of the OIA's Applied Anthropology Unit, but he ignored Boas's criticisms of the ability of anthropology to define racial ancestry. "Anthropological study is not a study of individuals but of local and social varieties," Boas wrote in 1899. "Individuals cannot be classified as belonging to a certain type." Collier and his advisers believed that such classification was both possible and necessary in the case of Robeson County Indians.[21] Government and other academic and museum scientists largely disregarded Boas's views in favor of an interpretation of race that also explained cultural difference.[22] The scholarship that supported racial hierarchies made stereotypes into scientific fact, and science legitimized white-supremacist agendas in the academy, in government, and in popular culture. "A social equality among the races [was] not possible because of the natural inequality between the races," according to historian of anthropology Lee Baker.[23]

Why did the OIA employ a method so supportive of social inequality, especially when they knew the method was inaccurate? Members of the OIA staff were likely naïve to the ways in which their favored method of inquiry underwrote a noxious social agenda, and they employed anthropometry because no other means seemed to provide the expert objective opinion they sought for their policy on nonreservation Indians. Collier presumed that fairness flowed from objectivity.[24] Interestingly, however, during the Indian New Deal, the OIA did not apply anthropometry equally with respect to unrecognized tribes; they only applied it to Robeson County Indians, a fact that suggests other motivations. Unlike nonreservation Indian groups in Montana, Nevada, and California that applied for recognition under the IRA in the 1930s, white supremacy subjected Robeson County's Indians to a systematic and widespread social comparison with African Americans, the only group anthropologists considered lower on the scale of racial evolution than Native Americans. Collier's sympathy for the group's position in the racial hierarchy was clear when he supported their 1932 legislation in Congress, and in 1936 he likely recognized that anthropometry was the best available way to prove scientifically that Indians were biologically as well as socially separate from blacks. Given the way that white supremacy had influenced policy makers' attitudes about Indians in the past, perhaps Collier believed that extra caution was necessary when dealing with a group that might have African American ancestry. While the OIA ostensibly cared only about the presence of "Indian blood" among tribes who applied for recognition in the 1930s, the absence of "black blood" was also a concern.

In June 1936 the OIA hired Carl C. Seltzer, a physical anthropologist who had trained under Earnest Hooton at Harvard, to conduct anthropometric tests among Robeson County's Indians and determine their quantity of "Indian blood." The Siouan Council obtained space for Seltzer, McNickle, and McMahon at the Indian Normal School, a location that signaled the acquiescence of Cherokee leaders to the tests and the centrality of the town of Pembroke to the leadership of both factions. Two days after the researchers arrived, they met with the Siouan Council at Saint Annah Church. Over 200 Indians attended the meeting and voiced support for the tests and for their recognition as Siouan Indians. The OIA representatives and several other Indians, all of them enrolled Siouans who served informally as advisers, comprised the Siouan Enrollment Commission. Seltzer conducted measurements and took two photographs of each applicant—one of the applicant's face and another of his or her profile—to provide a visual record of the physical features he measured. In 1936 the OIA examined 108 applicants. Seltzer returned to Robeson County in 1937 and examined another 101 individuals. Seltzer's work revolved around comparisons between Indians' physical characteristics and data about the Caucasian, Indian, and Negroid types that other anthropologists had compiled. In both years, Seltzer measured applicants' physical features to make a "diagnosis" of Indian ancestry, and the OIA compiled genealogies of each applicant. Interview data is only available for the 1936 applicants.[25]

Each applicant stood on a platform while Seltzer conducted a number of tests. He inspected for freckles, moles, and body hair, and he opened each subject's mouth to see their overbite and the shape of their teeth. He asked subjects to expose the skin on their inner arm, and he noted whether it was "red-brown," "brunet," "light-brown," or a variety of other shades. He measured their earlobes, the tips of their noses, the length from shoulder to hip, and the width of their chests. He felt their hair and noted its form—"straight," "low-wave," "curly," "frizzy," "wooly"—and its texture—"coarse," "medium," "fine." He scratched each one on the breastbone, looking for the color of the mark left behind. Supposedly, a reddish mark indicated mixed blood. Small wonder that so many more men participated than women; these tests to see (and touch) "race" were quite intimate. The "racial diagnosis" that Seltzer made was a summary of his findings that often seemed rather shorthanded at best or unscientific at worst. One participant had "decidedly un-Indian" hair, another's lips had "definite Negroidal suggestions," another was "an individual of strong Indian and White elements with possibly a mere trace of Negro."[26]

Other commission members handled the interviews that accompanied each applicant's anthropometric questionnaire. The OIA's experience at White Earth taught them that despite Hrdlicka's confidence in his discipline, they had difficulty relying on anthropometric tests without corroborating genealogical data. The OIA designed the interviews to concentrate on family history. Researchers hoped that an individual's ancestry included someone who they could identify as unquestionably possessing "Indian blood." To achieve this goal, they asked questions that evoked what the OIA considered to be an authentically Indian heritage: evidence of Indian languages, customs related to marriage and clan groups, and treaties between an Indian tribe and the U.S. government.[27] Although the Enrollment Commission gathered extensive genealogical data, it did not incorporate these findings into their assessments of each applicant's identity. Rather, it relied solely on Seltzer's diagnosis of an individual's racial makeup.

As the Enrollment Commission set out to determine the applicants' "Indian blood," it became clear that "blood" did not mean the same thing to Indians that it did to the OIA. As previously noted, Indians determined blood relationships by genealogy; if one's ancestors and their relatives belonged to the Indian community, then the Indian community accepted that person as an Indian, regardless of how many non-Indian ancestors one had.[28] Indians used the examinations to present their criteria for inclusion, criteria that eschewed the concept of "mixed-blood" in favor of relationships defined by family and settlement residence. An Indian also indicated political affiliation (Siouan versus Cherokee), but the more fundamental layers of kinship and settlement overshadowed political identity.

The OIA allowed the Siouan leadership to select study participants. Seltzer could only examine a limited number of applicants, and the OIA suggested that the Siouans "give preference to applicants whom they consider best qualified to pass the examinations."[29] The OIA wanted individuals who could pass its test, but the available applicant data suggests that Indians cast a broader net and selected individuals who descended from the community's "core families," particularly the descendants of James Lowry, brothers Major and John Locklear, and John Brooks. For example, 72 percent of the applicants descended from Major and John Locklear, 17 percent descended from James Lowry, 9 percent traced their ancestry to both of these families, and 1 percent had other or unidentified lineages.[30] Descendents of John Brooks were from both families because he had children with both Locklear and Lowry women. As Lumbee scholar Linda Oxendine has noted, this data reveals a "modified clan system" within the Robeson County Indian community, one that is defined strongly by matrilineal relations and incorporates but also stretches beyond settlement affiliations.[31] A survey of the 1936 and 1937 applicants reveals that many Indians claimed descent from "core families" through their mother's, rather than their father's, families. Unless family naming involved particular circumstances such as illegitimacy or adoption, however, most Indians followed American convention and used their father's surname, which honored the father's family but also obscured surviving matrilineal tendencies to OIA and other observers. Significantly, the enrollment commission did not ask most Indians about clans or matrilineal systems, although the applicants who did provide information about such systems generally said they were not aware of a formal clan arrangement among the group.[32]

This negative response stands in contrast to the overwhelming lineage patterns, however, indicating that while Indians had distinct social relations and understood them, they did not think of their society in the terms that anthropologists used. When asked to describe their reasons for claiming "Indian blood," Indians uniformly expressed themselves in terms of kinship and place. For example, one sixty-year-old respondent said, "My parents and gra[n]dparents handed it down to me. I was born among a nest of Indians, and resided there every [sic] since." A sixty-two-year-old respondent told questioners that "my grand dad[d]y and great grand daddy said that they were Indian people."[33] Indian applicants did point out ancestors who had signed treaties, spoke Indian languages, used traditional healing methods, or fought with or against Americans in various wars. One respondent remembered that "Lazy Will Locklear was a chief. He was supposed to have signed a treaty years back by which he agreed that his people would never go to war against the white people." Another applicant remembered that his grandfather "spoke some Indian language" and sang "Indian songs": "None of us understood the Indian words he used but he would tell us what they meant."[34] Indians understood these traits as clear evidence of their kinship markers and distinct identity and carefully told government officials about their past. Unlike the physical examination to "diagnose" a racial disease that Seltzer conducted—which relied on a physical sense of only the racial aspect of identity—this part of the study revealed the conversational, storytelling aspects of a wholistic identity, where markers could develop, interact, and change over time. But the OIA delegation dismissed such history as "vague references" to people who could not be "positively identified as Indians," though they did little documentary investigation to substantiate their view. The OIA proved unwilling to abandon their preconceived notions about "Indian blood" and listen to the information that Indian respondents did impart, a situation that may have encouraged Indians to withhold knowledge of their history and identity markers.[35]

The residence of the applicants displayed identification with Indian settlements and indicated their growing allegiance to the Siouan government. The Brooks Settlement, for example, comprised over half of the total number of applicants for recognition. The remaining applicants represented districts that were distant from Pembroke but had high Indian landownership and also expressed substantial support for the Siouan Council; these included Saddletree (28 percent of applicants), Burnt Swamp (21 percent), and Prospect (7 percent). Other districts that were less wealthy but still members of the Siouan movement were represented in smaller proportions, including Cherokee Chapel (2 percent), Mt. Elim (6 percent), Bethel Hill (2 percent), and areas south of Pembroke, such as Fairmont and Rowland (2 percent) (see Map 2).[36] Pembroke Township, which included the communities of Pembroke, Saint Annah, Red Banks, and Deep Branch, comprised 12 percent of the applicants for recognition. The Siouan Council reached out through their kinship and political connections to draw a wide circle of Indian communities to the OIA's examinations. Interestingly, none of the Siouan, Cherokee, or Fourth Street Power Structure leaders themselves participated in the study, but several of their siblings, in-laws, and children did.[37]

These strong kinship and settlement patterns indicate that Siouan leaders urged particular individuals from particular families to participate. Given the widespread knowledge of kin ties that exists within the Lumbee and Tuscarora communities today, one can presume that such knowledge also pervaded the community in the 1930s.[38] Indians were keenly aware of their kin networks and knew which families maintained the strongest, most readily evident cultural features of Indianness. Leaders clearly understood the basis on which the OIA evaluated their identity, but stereotypical physical features were secondary in the Siouans' selection; Seltzer photographed applicants who represented the whole spectrum of phenotypes.[39] The OIA representatives explained Seltzer's procedure to the Siouans at their meeting at Saint

Annah, and "no one questioned this procedure and in our work so far no one has refused to submit to such examination. Indeed, they are quite impressed by the anthropological technique and stand around in a kind of admiring wonder while Dr. Seltzer is at work." No doubt, Indians wondered at Seltzer's curious manner of reckoning their identity and probably admired the fact that "science" might finally catch up to their own methods, which had worked for centuries.

Siouan leaders took their knowledge of kinship and recruited particular families, including their own, whom they thought presented the strongest case for an Indian identity. The most obvious example of this is the fact that Seltzer based his 1937 study entirely within Brooks Settlement families, a group that was closely related; considered to be very traditional adherents to the reciprocity ethic, to religious and educational values, and to family influence; and formed a core constituency of the Siouan Council. Several members of the Brooks Settlement also participated in Pembroke Farms and the Red Banks Mutual Association. All of these characteristics comprised Indian identity in Robeson County, although Indians also recognized that they needed to connect their kinship patterns to the OIA's notions of "Indian blood."

Indians attempted to conform to the OIA's assumptions by declaring a percentage of Indian blood on their applications, but having never kept blood quantum records of any kind, and with the overwhelming emphasis placed on kinship rather than racial ancestry, Indian calculations were hardly precise. Most Indian applicants counted themselves and their spouses as "one-half" or "more than one-half," regardless of whether they had any non-Indian ancestry. One applicant, for example, described his calculation of blood quantum this way: "To the best of my knowledge my father . . . and my mother . . . were full blood Indians, and so considered themselves, I am only making claim to be three-quarter or more Indian, since they may have been a lesser degree of which I have no knowledge."[40] Forty-five percent of those studied in 1936 claimed to be "one-half" Indian, while 40 percent claimed "more than one-half" and only 12 percent claimed to be "full-bloods." The remaining 3 percent claimed "one-quarter" or an unknown proportion of "Indian blood." Few applicants indicated any non-Indian ancestry on their genealogy charts, which dated back five generations; but regardless of their apparent "one hundred-percent Indian" ancestry, most applicants declined to claim "full blood."[41]

Their reluctance to identify themselves as full-bloods may have resulted from a warning the OIA issued in the first few days of the examination.

"[T]here was such a unanimity of claim to one-half or more Indian blood that we took occasion . . . to point out to the [Siouan] Council secretary that such claims, when not based on reasonable grounds of belief or evidence, would prove damaging to the group as a whole, on that all claims however sound might be placed under suspicion," OIA officials reported to John Collier.[42] James Chavis, the council secretary, probably carried this message to applicants, who increasingly began to claim "one-half" for themselves and their spouses, rather than "more than one-half" or "full." The OIA was unprepared to accept Robeson County Indians' notions of kinship, genealogy, and "blood" relationships. To them, it was historically and biologically impossible for the group to unanimously claim such a high proportion of "Indian blood" because genealogy was an unacceptable standard of proof. Furthermore, the OIA explicitly stated that if Indians employed their own identity criteria, the OIA would doubt their claims and dismiss them.

The contradictory use of science to demonstrate identity left Indians confused and vulnerable to ridicule from the OIA. In commenting on one applicant's miscalculation of his "Indian blood," the commissioners wrote, "It will be noticed that this claimant could not write his name and the inconsistency [of his calculation] did not appear to impress him." Concerning another applicant's confusion, they reported, "[He] attended school only three months and presumably has small knowledge of what fractions mean."[43] As sociologist Eva Garroutte has pointed out, the OIA's manner of explaining and justifying their calculations of "Indian blood" is complicated and had an inherent social bias. The federal government explicitly created blood quantum rules to define a "mixed-blood," a legal and political category that determined when the federal government's responsibility to Indian people ended.[44] The complexity of determining one's percentage of "Indian blood"—and the irrelevance of the standard to Native peoples' own kinship and genealogical systems—ensured two things: (1) that the blood quantum criterion retained its aura of scientific objectivity and remained unintelligible to the "uneducated" and "illiterate"; and (2) that the OIA retained the prerogative to decide who was Indian and who was not, over and above Indians' own criteria.[45] When the OIA took control of Indian identity, as it did during the Indian New Deal in Robeson County, they pressured Indians into conforming to foreign notions of identity in the name of objective science. The OIA did so in order to extend services to the fewest number of the 10,000 to 12,000 Indians whom they otherwise might have recognized in Robeson County.

While the "racial diagnoses" that resulted from the tests produced the contradictions the OIA might have expected from anthropometry, the tests none-

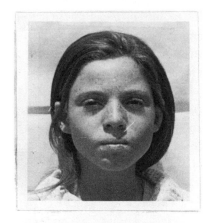

ELLA LEE BROOKS (7)

ANNA BROOKS (20)

1/2 or more Indian

Less than 1/2 Indian

FIGURE 11. Daughters of Beadan Locklear Brooks, a "borderline" Indian, and Lawson Brooks, "more than one-half Indian." Ella Lee is "one-half or more," while her sister Anna is "less than one-half Indian." (National Archives and Records Administration, Washington, D.C.)

theless accomplished their purpose in the eyes of the OIA. Of the 209 applicants, all of whom provided evidence of their Indian identity and claimed to possess one-half or more "Indian blood," Seltzer only found twenty-two applicants whom he believed passed the anthropometric test. He also identified eleven individuals as "borderline" and seven as "near borderline." A total of forty applicants, therefore, displayed features close enough to the standard Indian phenotype for Seltzer to note them as exceptions to the "less than one-half Indian" group. Of these forty, thirty-eight came from the Brooks Settlement. One might logically presume that the siblings of these "successful" applicants would also possess the same blood quantum, but Seltzer's analysis defied logic. In twelve separate cases, Seltzer identified individuals as "less than one-half Indian" while he designated their full siblings as "borderline," "near borderline," or "more than one-half Indian" (Figure 11).[46] Such unreliable results did not, however, deter the OIA from using the tests as verifiable proof of Robeson County Indians' "Indian blood."

The meaningful question, in Collier's mind, was not whether to use anthropometry as a standard of proof but whether to recognize the twenty-two Indians who had proven a sufficient quantity of "Indian blood." The Indian

Reorganization Act entitled these Indians to certain benefits, including educational assistance, employment preference in the Indian Service, and land. Members of the Siouan Council as well as applicants themselves began contacting the OIA about the status of their applications. OIA staff typically replied that they had not yet made a decision, although in January 1938, seven months after Seltzer completed his second trip to Robeson County, the OIA began pressuring Joseph Brooks to give up his recognition quest.[47] "[We cannot] see what advantage there would be in extending Departmental recognition and assistance to a handful of this group," D'Arcy McNickle told Brooks. McNickle argued that if the OIA recognized Robeson County's twenty-two Indians, the state might change its policy and refuse to support Indian schools. "They would then be in the very situation which once confronted them," McNickle speculated, "when the State classed its Indians with the negro population." The OIA also worried that recognizing twenty-two out of 200 would create "bad feeling" within the group, a statement that alluded to the factional tensions that had characterized the tribe's recognition efforts in the past. Brooks told McNickle that he could see the logic in the OIA's position, but he wanted the OIA to break the news to the Siouan Council. McNickle agreed, and a Siouan delegation visited Washington, D.C., a few months later.[48] But McNickle did not get the response he expected from the delegation. Rather than acquiesce to the test results and decline recognition, the delegation pressured McNickle and Collier to recommend that the secretary of the interior recognize the twenty-two.[49]

A conflict immediately erupted within the Indian Office. Staff members found that anthropometry did not provide objective evidence but instead raised subjective questions. One concern centered on the department's preexisting commitments to other Indians. "[W]e have not money enough or personnel enough to take care of the indubitable Indians for whom we are now responsible," wrote staff member John Herrick, implying that the Robeson County Indians were fraudulent Indians and invoking the argument that the OIA could not afford to help them. Herrick also expressed concern about factionalism, arguing that the OIA would "erect an unfortunate dividing line between the 'ins' and the 'outs.'"[50] Herrick seemed unaware that the federal government's actions had already exacerbated such divisions within the tribe. Finally, Herrick echoed McNickle's speculation that federal recognition of the twenty-two would reveal the "Negroid" traits Seltzer had applied to some of the applicants' phenotypes. "If this were to become a matter of public knowledge," Herrick wrote, "it would be just the excuse which the State is looking for to discriminate still further against the Indians." Herrick no doubt had observed the ambiguous relationship that Indians had with both whites and blacks, and his argument might have convinced an older generation of Indian leaders who were deeply invested in maintaining distance from blacks. But the Siouan Council articulated the relationship between ancestry and segregation somewhat differently. They informed John Collier later that year that "the State of North Carolina has provided certain facilities for Indians in Robeson County whereby they all participate regardless of the degree of Indian blood. These benefits are protected by citizenship clauses within the Constitution of the State of North Carolina."[51] The Siouan Council believed that "Negroid" or "Caucasian" features among the Indian community made no legal difference to southern white supremacists, however much difference they may have made to Seltzer's findings. Segregationists supported Indian schools because such schools upheld the logic of racial separation and not because Indians had "pure" Indian ancestry.

Recognition of the twenty-two also presented a problem for the OIA's application of anthropological theory to Indian policy. Staff assistant Fred Daiker, for example, wanted to hold the department to its scientific standard and base recognition "on the facts," but he also highlighted other subjective, administrative factors involved in the decision. "Are we likely to do more harm than good?" he wondered, citing Herrick and McNickle's concern about factionalism, and he asked how the decision would affect the Pembroke Farms project. Daiker mentioned a political factor as well: "Will we permit those who are recognized to form an organization and through the adoption process [bring] in those who are not otherwise eligible or recognized as half-bloods?" Such a move would result in the OIA providing services and de facto recognition to thousands of Indians, a situation his colleagues hoped to avoid. "We have a tremendous social and administrative problem to consider," Daiker concluded, a problem that the "facts" of anthropometric analysis could not solve.[52]

The Indian Office's internal discussion over whether to recognize the twenty-two Indians whom Seltzer considered "one-half or more" revealed the government's deep ambivalence about whether policy could safely employ science as a means to establish a link between race and culture. The OIA launched the anthropometric tests assuming they would present some form of conclusive evidence, but the same social and political questions about race, culture, and recognition continued to dog the staff. If they recognized Robeson County's Indians using the anthropometric tests as proof, white supremacists in North Carolina might discriminate further against the group and worsen an already bad situation. Furthermore, factional divisions might emerge as a result of the government's action. But another bureaucratic reason to deny recognition emerged when Herrick cited the department's preexisting commitments to other Indians. Like others before them, policy makers at the OIA declined to recognize Robeson County Indians because they presented an enormous administrative problem—the same rationale for the department's decision to rely upon anthropometry to determine Indian identity. Although the Indian Office considered Indians' criteria for identity unreliable, their own proposals for determining Indianness rested on flawed assumptions and subjective circumstances.

Collier let the matter drop for several months, but his instincts as a social reformer ultimately persuaded him to grant recognition to the twenty-two Robeson County Indians who passed the anthropometric tests. Collier treasured the idea that a social and scientific theory could provide a fair assessment of such a complex situation, but he also sought to fulfill aspirations to do good. In response to his staff members' opinions, Collier wrote, "These predicted consequences need not flow from the recommended action [to recognize the twenty-two]. The emotional, sentimental, earnest wishes of the Indians is something to take account of, too."[53] Although the Siouan Council undoubtedly made a powerful case for recognizing the twenty-two, Collier's own sentimentality and attachments to improving these Indians' lives under segregation trumped his staff members' administrative concerns.[54]

When the secretary of the interior approved the Indians' enrollment under the Indian Reorganization Act, the OIA notified Joseph Brooks and each of the twenty-two. The letters stated that the IRA entitled these Indians to educational assistance and Indian Service preference, but that funds for land acquisition (which the IRA had promised) were not available to individuals because such funds had already been allocated to "landless tribal groups." The letters emphasized that an individual's recognition under the IRA did not entitle him to membership in an Indian tribe or give him "tribal status." The IRA made it possible to recognize individual Indians without placing the heavy financial burden of a tribe onto the OIA, and the OIA staff made sure that the Siouan Council understood that recognition of the twenty-two did not mean recognition of the tribe as a whole nor of the Siouan Council government. Collier also reminded the recognized group that enrollment did not apply to their descendants unless they were born of a parent whom Seltzer likewise had determined to possess a blood quantum of one-half or more.[55] Although the stipulations of the IRA limited the benefits that these Indians received, recognition of the Original 22 represented a powerful political victory. To Indians, recognition legitimized their social organization and the effectiveness of tribal government.

Collier considered the Original 22 to be Indians but not a "landless tribal group," and so he did not permit them to organize as a tribe under a constitution according to the IRA's provisions. Interior Department solicitor Felix Cohen opined that Indian groups could not organize unless they lived on a reservation, meaning that the OIA had to purchase land for "landless" groups, which the secretary of the interior then proclaimed a reservation. Funds for land acquisition in 1938 went to the Mississippi Choctaw, the Shoshone in Nevada, the Quartz Valley Indian Community in California, and the St. Croix Chippewa of Wisconsin. Nothing was available for the Original 22 or the Chippewa-Cree of Montana who had been accepted as "one-half or more Indian." Legal scholar Paul Spruhan argues that Collier did not approve organization for the Chippewa-Cree and the Original 22 because he believed that recognized Indians should be members of cohesive communities and not individuals—despite the fact that the IRA defined an Indian as an individual of "one-half or more Indian blood."[56] After several years of working with Robeson County Indians, it seems unlikely that Collier did not recognize their membership in a larger community of Indian people. He may have simply equated cohesion with reservation trust land and assumed that since neither the Original 22 nor the Chippewa-Cree had such land, they did not maintain a tribal, collective existence. But this too seems like an overly simplistic explanation for Collier's decision, given his familiarity with Indian issues and with these particular situations. He may have thought that recognizing them as individuals would do no harm, but allowing them to organize under a tribal constitution would threaten the precarious resources he had to help Indians whose status was not in doubt. After all, a tribal constitution provided for enrollment and membership criteria, and Collier may have imagined the Original 22 writing a constitution that enrolled themselves and adopted many more thousands of Indians in Robeson County.

If this was indeed Collier's rationale, he understood little about the nature of Indian factionalism in Robeson County. The Original 22 did not seek to adopt the rest of Robeson County's Indians but to establish a politically autonomous group that would deliver benefits and services under the IRA to their kin in their settlement. This is what Collier's staff feared, and it was the reason for their lack of enthusiasm about recognizing the Original 22. Recognition might create an "in" group and an "out" group. But behind this fear lay an assumption that factionalism was entirely dysfunctional and therefore dangerous to social organization. Of course, political disagreements generated conflict within the community, but such conflict was not new and made sense to Robeson County Indians at the time; it emerged, in their view, from the existing decentralization and fundamental layers of identity the group possessed. Just as "blood" meant something different to the OIA and to Indians, so did "cohesion": to Collier and the OIA staff, cohesion meant political unity, a necessary condition of "tribal," collective existence; but to Robeson County Indians, it meant stability, a continuity of cultural forms and identity markers. Political unity was not necessary to maintain a collective way of life, and the community's existing divisions—by blood, name, and locale—provided a kind of cohesion they could manage.

Recognizing the Original 22 elevated the political influence of rural Indians. None of the twenty-two lived in Pembroke, nor were they close relatives of Siouan or Cherokee leaders. Unlike the previous political efforts to control Pembroke Farms and gain recognition from Congress—efforts that focused on town Indian politics—only rural Indians succeeded in gaining federal recognition. Moreover, the "progressive" values and white connections that other leaders touted as the key to Indian autonomy played no part in gaining affirmation of Indian identity from the OIA. These values might, in fact, have worked against their proponents. Instead, Indians from the Brooks Settlement (twenty of the twenty-two hailed from this community) could point to institutions such as the Longhouse and to their reliance on family and reciprocity as the factors that helped them gain federal recognition. And unlike most Indians in other settlements, the Original 22 also had the government's own criterion—blood quantum—on their side. The recognition of the Original 22 represented the first time any group of Indians in Robeson County had the official sanction of the federal *and* state governments, and these Indians used this historic opportunity to their own advantage.

Although the OIA only recognized twenty-two Indians, Seltzer's tests revealed another eighteen "borderline" cases belonging to the same families as the Original 22. From this base of forty individuals connected by kinship and settlement, a new Indian government emerged that intended to unseat the Siouan Council and deal directly with the federal government. As OIA officials debated about recognizing the Original 22 in 1938, members of the Brooks Settlement began to organize an association to advocate for themselves. Their movement stemmed from a need for economic assistance in the midst of the Great Depression, their dissatisfaction with how the Farm Security Administration apportioned the few benefits it provided, and their frustration with local white racism. Confident that their applications would pass muster with Seltzer and the government, they coordinated a family-based letter-writing campaign to the OIA asking for economic assistance as Indians. They also indicated that the FSA at Pembroke Farms was not meeting their needs.

Three generations of one family, for example, appealed to the Indian Office. Eighty-year-old Lovedy Brooks Locklear wrote, "I am half and more Indian blood. . . . [I] have worked hard all of my life and now I am disabled to help my self been defrauded mistreated. . . . [We] are under a depression we need help."[57] Her son-in-law Lawson, a leader in the Brooks Settlement Longhouse, complained that Pembroke Farms did not assist him and his nine children: "We are suffering please help me in any way you can and I will greatly appriciate [sic] it. I have ask [sic] for a job on the resettlement project but I can not get a job."[58] Pembroke Farms did not help Lawson's son Henry Brooks, either: "I went half and more Indian blood[.] [W]e indians here in Robson Co. in the State of N.C. are in a depression we can-not get a job and we are suffering."[59] The OIA responded perfunctorily, but Indians persisted with another series of letters that focused on educational benefits.[60] The OIA had examined Lovedy, Lawson, Henry, and their siblings, spouses, and children in 1936 and 1937 and found them to be one-half or more "Indian blood," but there is no evidence that they knew of Collier's ruling when they pleaded for assistance regarding the Great Depression. They simply knew they were Indians and deserved the same benefits the government gave to other Indians. They also probably perceived that the Siouan Council did not have control over Pembroke Farms and that resettlement officials and Cherokee leaders gave preference for jobs and loans to other families. Lovedy Locklear, Lawson Brooks, Henry Brooks, and other members of the community observed that the Siouan leadership had not rewarded their strong support for the Siouan Council and federal recognition.

Receiving no satisfactory response from the OIA, members of the Brooks Settlement approached the FSA. Along with other dissatisfied tenants who identified as Siouans, they circulated a petition opposing farm manager H. C. Green that articulated their dissatisfaction with their treatment at Pembroke Farms.[61] The petitioners selected two members of the Brooks Settlement—D. J. Brooks and Elisha Locklear—along with four other Siouans (none of them councilmen) to represent the group in Washington.[62] When the FSA dismissed their concerns, Brooks returned to Robeson County and, a few weeks later, organized a new council to represent their interests. They distinguished themselves from the Siouan Council by the "Indian blood" the OIA declared they had. D. J. Brooks, who had the greatest political experience with the federal government, was president of the group, his cousin Henry Brooks was vice president, his uncle Ralph (or "Pikey") Brooks was secretary, and his brother Will Brooks was treasurer. Ralph Brooks assumed the role of spokes-man, just as Joseph Brooks had done for the Siouan Council. Forty-seven in-dividuals comprised the organization that D. J. Brooks directed, which did not initially have a formal name.[63] These same teachers and farmers led the Longhouse, and only three members of their group had not applied for recog-nition in 1936 or 1937. At least 48 percent of Brooks's constituency belonged to the group Carl Seltzer had characterized as "borderline" or "one-half or more" Indian. All of the members of the Original 22 signed onto this council, except for the two who did not belong to the Brooks Settlement.[64] This new Indian government used the OIA's idea of Indian identity—blood quantum—to compensate for their disappointing treatment by the FSA, which did not appear to recognize their distinct Indian identity and their own leadership. Perhaps the Brooks Settlement intended to "play" one federal agency against another to obtain greater assistance in combating the economic subordina-tion they experienced under Jim Crow.

Elisha Locklear, great-nephew of Pikey Brooks, has shared much of the Brooks Settlement history with me. He recalled that up until the 1950s, the settlement was a closed community—"closed like a casket," he said. "In the 1920s they stopped the Trailways buses from running through there," he told me. "They'd stop them on the road, and take the people out of the bus, and beat them. They left some of them dead in Uncle John Brooks's pasture there at Brooks Landing. But things like that, . . . as far as preserving blood, it was a plus." Mr. Elisha is a Tuscarora historian and artist, and he lives in the Brooks Settlement. In this interview, he quoted a prominent Lumbee who had said that being Indian in Robeson County is a "state of mind." He disagreed strongly, arguing that this view of Indian identity "discounted any kind of blood ties." Mr. Elisha discussed his "whole blood" ancestors, and he validated the Siouan enrollment study's results as definitive on the question of who among Robeson County Indians has the most "Indian blood." This attitude seems to affirm the federal government's notion that Indian identity is synonymous with biology. But as I have reflected on my conversations with Mr. Elisha, which go back to 2001, I have begun to think about what blood can mean.[65]

Many Indians, both Lumbee and Tuscarora, discuss blood; "good blood," "bad blood," and "it's in her blood" are common phrases in social situations among community members. The idea behind those offhand remarks is that blood transmits certain qualities of behavior, power, and authority. This is nothing new: in Southeastern Indian societies, the relationship to one's mother conveyed clan membership and belonging. Of course, that relation-ship does not exist without the mother sharing literal, visceral blood with her child. Historian Melissa Meyer has argued that the deep symbolic meanings of blood are universal and that "the metaphorical connection of blood with lineage, descent and ancestry preceded its literal physiological use."[66] Societies used blood *and* kinship to establish the difference between insiders (clan members in Southeastern Indian groups) and outsiders (nonclan members). This is exactly the sense in which Lumbees and Tuscaroras discuss blood—as a way to distinguish between qualities the speaker wants in an insider and qualities one rejects or reserves for outsiders. The language of blood can conduct a kind of electrical current between generations that binds them together, even as it divides within a generation. Mr. Elisha's ancestors in the Brooks Settlement believed that even other Indians were outsiders; the only insiders were other members of that community.

Blood has personal power that everyone acknowledges, but blood has political power also. In the colonial context under which Indians in the United States have formed their identities, the personal symbolism of blood became linked to legitimate claims on land and resources. Indians themselves commonly used (and still use) the language of blood; for example, the Mississippi Choctaws used it to powerful effect during the allotment era when making claims to treaty rights. Measuring fractions of blood was intended to define cultural and biological hierarchies and deny those claims. Inequality is therefore inherent in the concept of "race," a concept that emerged long after "blood" and was very different from the meanings of kinship and connection that "blood" can imply. The separating discourse of blood, where it is divisible according to one's cultural ancestry and itself divides communities, is closer to what we mean in America by "race." In my experience as a Lumbee, this discourse takes place with outsiders, or at least in contexts where external definitions of identity hold sway. The meaning of blood, like other identity markers, is an ongoing conversation between insiders and outsiders. Even insiders don't always have the same view. Factionalism thus breeds identity formation, and identity formation does not take place without disagreements.

Some might view these disagreements—particularly the fact that Tuscarora descendents of the Original 22 have excluded Lumbees from membership in the group of Indians with "more Indian blood"—as destructive to the whole community's maintenance of their own identity markers. Indeed, such a view seems to applaud "race" and the Euro-American emphasis on race as legitimizing cultural affiliation. The woman who told Mr. Elisha that being Lumbee was a "state of mind" was probably not trying to be vague but trying to avoid identifying herself with racialized identity definitions. On the other hand, Mr. Elisha's ancestors realized that even if they rejected race, they still could not escape its destructive consequences. The OIA would have employed blood quantum anyway.[67]

Understanding that the Brooks Settlement's ability to govern itself was attached to Seltzer's findings of Indian blood, Ralph Brooks informed the OIA that his council had organized to gain benefits for their members under the Indian Reorganization Act. He inquired if a delegation from Robeson County should visit Washington. "Joseph Brooks has failed to go and represent us any longer and we Indians have organized ourselves," he wrote. "We are in a deprission [sic] here and needs help anything that you can render any help to us we will highly appriciate [sic] it."[68] Ralph Brooks received no response from the OIA, so he wrote another more specific letter a month later. "[W]e Indians have orgnized [sic] our selfs and we are not depinding [sic] on Mr. Joseph Brooks," he wrote. He asked for advice in enrolling the "borderline" cases Seltzer had identified. A third letter followed this one, which the OIA did not answer.[69]

Finally, OIA staff member Fred Daiker replied to Brooks's letters. He simply acknowledged that Joseph Brooks was no longer one of the leaders in the Siouan Council and indicated that the information "will be referred to in the future."[70] Either the OIA did not grasp the significance of the Original 22's council or they deliberately refused to recognize the group's political move. Either way, Ralph Brooks persisted: "Glad to inform you that we Indians here in Robson have orignized [sic] ourselves frome those that have a strain." Brooks separated his group of "Indians," meaning "full-blood Indians," from those who have only a "strain" of "Indian blood." "[W]e have been under opprssin [sic] long enough," he continued. "I will call on the [Indian] Office very soon for our benifits [sic] under our act[.] [G]lad to say that we Siouan Indians have reorganized out of our group." Brooks asserted that his council represented the "real Indians" recognized by the OIA and distinct from the other Siouans who were not entitled to the benefits of "our act." The Original 22's council aimed not only to receive recognition from the government but also to receive relief from the oppression of segregation.[71]

The Siouan Council learned of the Original 22's push to organize separately and attempted to thwart their efforts. "Is it possible for some other faction of these Indians to organize and deal with the Indian office?" James Chavis wrote to John Collier. The Siouan Council further indicated that "some other Indian from another tribe"—Chief Taho-wadi-heuto, or Thomas W. Shaw, of Rome, New York—was guiding the Original 22's council in this move. Shaw's home location implies that he was Mohawk, a member of the same tribe that helped the Brooks Settlement establish the Longhouse in the 1920s. If Chavis was correct, the Original 22's council might have contacted the Six Nations again to solicit advice or support for acquiring the benefits due to them under the IRA. Perhaps they attributed their success with federal recognition to institutions like the Longhouse and identification with kin group and settlement, and they sought to reinvigorate their support from other tribes. The significance of this action seemed lost on the Siouan Council, however, which worried that the tribe's communication with the OIA might become confused, as it had in the early 1930s. Chavis concluded his letter by requesting the OIA to "notify all parties who try to take separate questions with you, prior to this submission to the Council, please refer their questions to the Council so they may be handled in an orderly and systematicly [sic] manner."[72] The Siouan Council believed that the Original 22's council represented a threat to the relationship they had built with the OIA. But given the fact that the OIA refused to recognize any Indians except the Original 22, the Siouans realistically had few options in the short term to achieve recognition for the rest of Robeson County's Indians. Consequently, the council focused its energies on controlling local projects like Pembroke Farms and challenging the legal discrimination inherent in segregation.[73] In this atmosphere, the Siouans probably feared that the Original 22's council would undercut their influence within the Robeson County Indian community, and they took steps, as the Cherokee faction had done, to halt the Brooks Settlement's efforts to communicate directly with the federal government.

The organization efforts of the Brooks Settlement revealed one of the ramifications of federal recognition for Indian identity in Robeson County. The Brooks Settlement embodied the most important identity criteria shared by all Robeson County Indians—kinship and settlement, which the OIA did not recognize—but had become, based on their "Indian blood," the only Indian group the OIA officially enrolled as Indians. They then added a political layer to their kinship/settlement identity. They could not ignore, however, their scientific and legal status as "one-half or more Indian blood," and the Original 22's council ultimately based their distinctiveness on an anthropological criterion for Indian identity rather than on their own criteria. In the eyes of Indians and white government officials at that time, the OIA's sanction gave the Original 22's council considerable influence because they succeeded where other Indians had failed. The significance of recognition did not escape the Brooks Settlement families, who clearly expected their "Indian blood" to lead to benefits.

NOT SURPRISINGLY—given the OIA's interest in limiting the agency's administrative obligations—its relationship to both the Siouan and Original 22 councils grew more distant after Collier decided to recognize the twenty-two. Although his staff had objected to his action based partly on administrative concerns, Collier's decision resulted in no additional responsibilities for the OIA. Members of the Original 22 and the Siouan Council, however, continued to solicit the Indian Office for assistance. Lawrence Maynor, one of the recognized Indians who did not belong to the Brooks Settlement, failed to receive work or a loan from Pembroke Farms. He wrote to Collier in late 1939, "[T]here is some benifits [sic] in which I am entitled to in the Indian service. . . . I feel that I being ½ or more Indian I am entitled to some help from the Federal government."[74] There is no evidence that Collier replied to Maynor's request, and none of the members of the Original 22 received any assistance until 1974, when Maynor and the other surviving members sued the Department of the Interior for benefits due to them as recognized Indians. They won the lawsuit.[75]

In the meantime, Joseph Brooks and the Siouan Council pressed the OIA for educational benefits for Robeson County Indians. The OIA, convinced of the conclusiveness of Seltzer's study, was unreceptive to these solicitations. When FSA official George S. Mitchell tried to nominate Indian candidates for the OIA's educational-assistance programs in 1939, the OIA responded that the nominees did not manifest enough "Indian blood." "I had hoped that the candidates . . . would be strongly Indian in appearance," staff member J. C. McCaskill wrote, "so that we could seek anthropological confirmation of their Indian blood with some confidence in the findings. . . . As it is, an examination of the photographs attached to the applications inclines us to the opinion that your candidates are probably less than one-half Indian."[76] OIA officials had become so disenchanted with the "interminable" Robeson County question, as D'Arcy McNickle put it, that they only needed photographs to reject Indians' requests for assistance.[77] Tacitly acknowledging that science did not solve the thorny questions associated with determining Indian identity, they gave up on their own previous insistence on documentary evidence and "objective" facts. But physical characteristics remained a convenient excuse to deny recognition to tribal members.

Joseph Brooks tried to persuade the OIA to fund another round of anthropometric tests in 1939 after it had granted recognition to the Original 22. Fred Daiker worked to secure Carl Seltzer's participation in the study, but Daiker notified Brooks that the OIA had no funds available for the study and that Brooks would have to pay Seltzer by raising money from the Indian community.[78] Brooks proceeded to ask for two dollars from each Siouan member, but at least one of his constituents doubted his purpose and wrote to Collier, asking if it was legal for Brooks to collect money: "I am an Indian and would be very glad to be enrolled to the gov[ernment]. I have paid lots of money to traitors and it has been a failure." Perhaps the writer alluded to the Siouan Council's previous attempts to finance their failed recognition efforts.[79]

The OIA seized upon Brooks's idea and discussed congressional funding for a comprehensive anthropometric study of all nonreservation Indians. The OIA should not limit the survey to Robeson County Indians, staff member Joe Jennings argued, because "it would be discrimination against other groups which perhaps are far more entitled to our aid than the Robeson County Siouan group."[80] Daiker proposed taking this idea to the Senate and House Committees on Indian Affairs and allowing Congress to make a decision. However, he cautioned that the federal recognition of these Indians took power away from the states to deal with Indian people as they saw fit.[81] Assistant Commissioner William Zimmerman suggested a staff conference regarding this proposal, but Collier insisted that a conference was not immediately necessary.[82]

What might have been the source of Collier's caution? The OIA staff had considerable historical experience with Congress's efforts to fund benefits for Robeson County Indians, and Collier may simply have wanted to avoid another slew of similar federal recognition bills from other tribes claiming to be "one-half or more Indians." Another reason may have involved the way many state governments dealt with Indians and mixed-race people in the South. For example, the state of Virginia waged an identity war against its Indians, led by eugenicist Walter Plecker, which resulted in the denial of hundreds of Indians' rights to preserve their families and communities. Plecker corresponded with Collier in the early 1940s, trying to solicit his support for his campaign to eliminate "Indian" as a social and racial category.[83] While Collier's social conscience stood on the opposite end of Plecker's, he and Plecker shared anthropometry as part of the foundation of their social agendas. Anthropometric studies conceivably could encourage states like Virginia to discriminate further against their Indian citizens. The OIA's supposedly "objective" method of determining "Indian blood" only proved more and more dangerous to the rights of Native American people.

The war in Europe and the Pacific, however, was perhaps the most likely reason for Collier's reluctance to pursue the study and anything else that the Indians of Robeson County presented. In 1941 D. J. Brooks inquired again about benefits for the Original 22 under the Indian Reorganization Act. Mc-

Nickle reminded him that recognition as individual Indians did not bestow tribal status under the IRA. The Department of the Interior could theoretically purchase land for them if Congress made such funds available, but national defense precluded appropriations for land purchases.[84] Brooks inquired again in 1942, this time personally meeting with McNickle, who advised him to wait until the end of the war to renew his efforts. In the meantime, McNickle recommended that Brooks compile information about his group's landholdings, household equipment, and the condition of their homes and health.[85]

The war made Collier's relationship with Congress more tenuous, and he may have been less eager to interfere with the affairs of state government for the sake of funding programs for recognized tribes. OIA officials continued walking a tightrope when it came to upholding segregation and the state and federal governments' relationship with Robeson County Indians. They wanted both to avoid upsetting Congress and to prevent Congress from dictating how they implemented Indian policy. In 1944, for example, North Carolina senator and former governor Clyde R. Hoey became aware of Seltzer's anthropometric study of Robeson County Indians and immediately objected to the OIA's criteria for Indian identity. "I think [the report] shows a very inadequate representation [of Robeson County's Indians]," he wrote. "I have looked over the list of names and many of the best blood Indians there are not included in this list, and among this number is the postmaster of the town and many of its leading citizens." Hoey's reference to "best blood" Indians implied the town Indians whom he knew—Pembroke's postmaster at the time was Fourth Street Power Structure member D. F. Lowry, whose son applied for recognition in 1936 but was not recognized along with the Original 22. The OIA's determination of "Indian blood" clearly conflicted with white southerners' conceptions of the term, and Hoey recommended strongly that the OIA use the list of Indians the state allowed to attend Indian schools as a basis for determining identity.[86] Thinking that Hoey's concern arose from a fear that the OIA was about to grant federal recognition to Robeson County's Indians, Assistant Commissioner William Zimmerman replied that the OIA had no intention of interfering with the services being rendered by the state to Indians.[87] But Hoey was not satisfied; he wrote back, arguing that the Seltzer study classified people "improperly," and he demanded that Zimmerman discard the report.[88] Such a demand amounted to a congressman's meddling in Indian Office business.

Perhaps worried that an intrusive congressman would jeopardize the OIA's efforts to implement the IRA, Zimmerman came up with another reason to deny recognition to Robeson County's Indians. "The study made by Dr. Selt-

zer does not in fact preclude the Indians in Robeson County from having recognition," he wrote, virtually reversing the OIA's position that anthropometric tests would be used to determine every benefit for which Robeson County
Indians were eligible. Zimmerman continued, "The reason why the Indian
Service does not concern itself with these Indians . . . is that the Federal government has no treaty obligations to them."[89] The issue of "treaty obligations"
in regard to Robeson County Indians had not arisen since the Cherokee and
Siouan legislation twelve years earlier. Collier's Indian New Deal program
had found other ways to assist Indians all over the United States without
considering their treaty relationship, but efforts in Robeson County had only
resulted in greater social ambiguity and untenable policies. When confronted
with an outraged congressman, Zimmerman fell back on a pre–New Deal era
rationale for denying Robeson County Indians recognition that he believed a
southern white could accept. Zimmerman's trick worked, and Hoey dropped
his objection to the report and to anthropometry as a scientific measure of
Indian identity.

These events gave the Indian and non-Indian conceptions of "Indian
blood" a political significance that the segregated South had not appreciated.
Previously, the social and political focus was not on the presence of "Indian
blood" per se, but on the absence of "black blood." The Siouan and Cherokee
leadership had succeeded in reinforcing their own identity criteria—kinship
and settlement—while negotiating local white supremacists' priority of racial
separation. These leaders' skill at distancing themselves from blacks and embracing whites' "progressive" values had only limited success with the Indian
Office. The Original 22's council, however, accommodated the OIA's scientific agenda and achieved a long-sought victory for themselves. After this victory, success in federal recognition became associated with an insistence on
the tribe's "Indian blood" (as defined by non-Indians) and based largely on
phenotype and stereotypical "Indian" customs.

The statement by McNickle, Seltzer, and McMahon that "these people
did not have a clear understanding of the term Indian" indicates that the OIA
defined these People far differently than the People defined themselves. Identity definitions spring from history, but also from memory. In other words,
the historical process influences identity markers, and so does the historical
narrative—the way storytellers remember that process and pass it on. Both
insiders and outsiders (in this case, Robeson County Indians and the OIA,
respectively) identified themselves and one another based on knowledge of
history, even if it was very limited knowledge. The storytellers (or the historians) pass that knowledge through a filter of memory. Memory acts to make

history intelligible to contemporary audiences; it keeps the information that we need to help us understand ourselves but discards information that doesn't suit our contemporary agenda. Both the insiders and the outsiders in this story poured the past through this sieve of history and memory. Indians made their past conform to understandings that they thought assisted their circumstances under segregation, and the OIA staff made Indians conform to understandings that assisted the agency's policy objectives. In the meantime, each one's definition of the other in fact reveals a definition of self: OIA officials saw Indians as static so as to conceive of their policies as modern, while Indians saw the OIA as beneficial so as to conceive of themselves as distinct and eligible for federal recognition.

Senator Hoey's intrusion into the affairs of the Indian Office was in some ways a renewal of the historic exchange between Congress and the OIA over the recognition of Robeson County Indians. Congressmen had definite opinions about Indian identity that their segregationist attitudes and constituencies supported, while the OIA had its own notions supported by anthropological theory. As the OIA implemented its policies in cooperation with Congress and the FSA, it increasingly found scientific theory to be useless in answering the racial questions that southern Indians raised. Consequently, the only Indians directly affected were the Original 22, who themselves capitalized on their new relationship with the federal government to increase their local political influence. But caught up in a war overseas and a battle at home over Indian identity and federal recognition, the federal government was deaf to their messages. This conflict between branches of government left Indian recognition once again in the hands of Congress.

My great-uncle Theodore Maynor spent the 1930s teaching school after having earned a teaching certificate in 1928 from Cherokee Indian Normal School. He was an all-star athlete in basketball, baseball, and football and eventually became part of the first group of inductees into the school's athletic hall of fame. The Coast Guard drafted him early in World War II, and after the war he returned to college to earn a baccalaureate degree at Pembroke State College for Indians (the same institution with a different name). In 1946 Uncle Theodore joined the college Veterans' Club. That year, Lumbee photographer Elmer Hunt took a photograph of the club on the steps of Old Main for the college yearbook (Figure 12). Old Main, built in 1923, was the institution's oldest surviving building and a symbol of Indian progress and educational achievement.

Uncle Theodore had married Elizabeth Oxendine in the mid-1930s and moved from the Red Banks community to Pembroke. Elizabeth was the sister of Clifton Oxendine, the college's dean and a well-known Cherokee supporter. She got her degree in 1941, several years before her husband did.[1] When he became a Veterans' Club member, Uncle Theodore was nearly forty years old, a senior member of this group of dapper gentlemen. They might have inspired the casting and costuming for *Guys and Dolls*; their expressions and outfits announce them as good-natured men, shy adventurers, and soft-hearted rogues. Their poses are reminiscent of 1940s American culture and prosperity, so different from the motley overalls and homemade dresses of the students in Uncle Theodore's first-grade class during the Great Depres-

FIGURE 12. Veterans' Club, Pembroke State College for Indians, 1946. First row, left to right: James H. Dial, Danford Dial, Archie Oxendine, J. P. Swett, Brantley Blue, Vincent Lowry; second row, left to right: J. A. Jacobs, Grady Oxendine, Castor Locklear, Harry West Locklear, Lock B. Locklear, William Earl Oxendine, Josephus Jacobs, Simeon Cummings, Reese Bullard; third row, left to right: Henry Ford Lowry, Peter Dial, Theodore Maynor, Andrew Ransom, Warford Maynor. (Lumbee River Fund Collection, Livermore Library, University of North Carolina at Pembroke)

sion (see Figure 2). But the veterans' surnames also connect them to an older, ancient, perhaps sacred culture. Every one of them has a name that is instantly recognizable as part of the kinship community of Robeson County Indians.

My father remembers Uncle Theodore as the most politically active of his father's brothers, a "maverick who drank whiskey," a Woodmen of the World member, and a Boy Scout booster. He associated socially with members of the Fourth Street Power Structure and probably supported the Cherokee faction himself. He and Elizabeth raised their only child, Janie, to be one of the foremost Lumbee activists of the 1970s. In fact, Janie led the movement to rebuild Old Main after it burned in 1973. Indians—both Lumbees and Tuscaroras—gathered in front of the building during the fire and cried as flames consumed it. Janie's leadership was for the entire Indian community—the People—regardless of what names they adopted. Today, her tombstone simply reads "Save Old Main." She lies near her mother's people; the cemetery is known locally as the Oxendine graveyard after Janie's mother's family. Her Uncle Clifton is buried there, and another Oxendine, my great-great grandfather Henderson, also rests there. Janie's final testimony opens a door to history, to culture, and to spirituality.

Like a grave marker, a photograph is a kind of testimony from the dead to the living; as such it has a sacred quality, and today elder Robeson County Indians approach photographs with reverence. I've heard elders—people born between the 1910s and 1930s—talk for hours just about the names of the people in old photos and to whom they were kin. These present-day conversations hint of why affirming their identity as Indians was so important to these people, despite their adaptation to American culture and embrace of Jim Crow. Saying the names signifies that each individual stood up for something; Uncle Theodore and his fellow veterans stood up for a nation that had sought to incorporate them into society as citizens, though inferior citizens. They sacrificed for that nation but imagined a community for themselves as well, one that would be autonomous, one where a college could be "for Indians"—not in the segregated sense, but in the ownership sense. Perhaps they even imagined a nation that was neither "Cherokee" nor "Siouan," but "Lumbee."

World War II helped convince most Indians that they could use federal recognition to overturn their status as second-class citizens under Jim Crow. Indians believed that they needed a new name with which to appeal to the federal government. Neither Cherokee nor Siouan had brought them the relief from segregation that they sought. Their efforts to acquire recognition culminated in the 1956 Lumbee Act, a congressional remedy for their decades-long struggle to affirm their identity. But even as Robeson County Indians gained new tools to confront the disempowerment of segregation, conflicts between Congress, the Office of Indian Affairs, and the Farm Security Administration persisted. Disagreements at the federal level aggravated the tribe's internal distinctions between town and rural Indians, and class differences acquired a political dimension as town and rural Indians organized competing recognition efforts. Rural Indians, especially members of the Original 22's council, spent much of the 1940s lobbying the OIA to recognize the Robeson County Indians under a new tribal designation: "Lumbee."

Lumbee originated from the name of the river on which Indians lived and signaled a common land base that could unify this decentralized group. The name appeared to resolve some of the problems with previous appellations, especially the claims on another tribe's history that "Cherokee" implied. But a new name did not prove convincing to the OIA, and rural Indians' efforts reached an impasse. Town Indians, mostly members of the former Cherokee faction, then organized as the Lumbee Brotherhood in the early 1950s and pursued recognition through political channels in Congress rather than seek anthropological authenticity at the OIA. Their status as individual citizens and voters made this strategy possible, and the Lumbee Brotherhood promoted a Lumbee identity based on assimilationist notions of citizenship rather than the collective identity that the Original 22's council had insisted upon.

Although rural Indians laid the groundwork for federal recognition, a new policy of tribal termination at the federal level meant that town Indians, with their "progressive" attitudes and accommodation to white supremacy, ultimately secured the tribe's acknowledgment as Lumbees. Consequently, the recognition that Robeson County Indians gained in the 1950s reflected political and social divisions instead of cooperation. Rather than participate actively, those who opposed the congressional path to federal recognition simply withdrew from the discussion and sought other ways to affirm their identity. Although both factions were equally invested in the community's core layers of identity—kinship and settlement—they disagreed about how to portray their identity to outsiders. Those outsiders—politicians and bureaucrats at the state and federal levels—expected Indians to perform assimilation or perform primitivism according to what they believed would most quickly open Indians' economic resources to white control.

FOR INDIANS ALL OVER THE COUNTRY, the question of citizenship in an American nation was central to the problem of affirming an Indian identity in the twentieth century. Could an Indian, a member of a distinct political community, also be a citizen of the United States? Did an American identity undermine one's Indian identity? If Indian identity concerned whether and how a group constituted a political community, then the United States' long tradition of "civic nationalism," or a system that grants equal opportunity to everyone, seemed sufficiently broad to embrace political allegiances of all kinds.

In some ways, the 1924 Indian Citizenship Act was an example of such expansiveness. The act granted U.S. citizenship status to all Native Americans. In one sense, it tried to assimilate Indian peoples, transforming them from autonomous tribal communities into individual subjects of the United States. But the new policy could not accommodate the historical legal relationship between Indians and the federal government, which remained ambiguous in the act. While it made Indians citizens, it also did not "impair . . . the right of any Indian to tribal or other property," a necessary provision because judge-made Indian law had defined Indians as members of nations; these nations had a government-to-government relationship to the United States.[2] The Indian Citizenship Act thus failed to completely subsume Indians' tribal identification. Native peoples delicately balanced collective and individual identities through the 1940s and another national crucible—World War II. Indians consistently remade the federal government's assimilation-oriented policies into their own vehicles for identity maintenance.

Indians in Robeson County confronted similar dilemmas. They had been citizens since the founding of the United States. They voted for the Democratic Party and considered themselves citizens, basing many of their claims to recognition in the 1930s on their participation in American civic life. The 1924 Indian Citizenship Act did not apply to them directly, as they had no reservation land base or formally recognized tribal political organization. Indian groups that did come under the act had troubled relationships with the federal government, and in some ways the act was an attempt to solve those problems by ending Indians' status as tribal citizens. But Robeson County Indians sought recognition, perhaps because they did not understand the ways in which Indians with formal acknowledgment had suffered, or perhaps because they perceived the perpetrators of their civic subjugation to be local government and not the federal government. Neither they nor policy makers were likely aware of how the tactics and agendas of the local and federal governments worked so closely to subordinate Indians.

Further, World War II required many sacrifices and did not bring an immediate end to Jim Crow. After the war, many Indians renewed their questions about identity and citizenship. They had been citizens, but not equal citizens Their experience spoke strongly to a thread of American life that historian Gary Gerstle argues was coeval with "civic nationalism": "racial nationalism," where citizenship in the American nation presupposed an individual's willingness to adopt the attitudes and aspirations of European-Americans or risk exclusion, oppression, and violence. Assimilation to white standards was an expectation of full citizenship in the American nation.[3]

Individualism was also a key expectation of American belonging in the twentieth century. That philosophy lent itself to a political climate of tolerance and freedom, while it also facilitated the economic subordination of less-powerful citizens. This had been obvious under Jim Crow; citizenship for a nonwhite individual meant little more than the right to be economically exploited. Federal Indian policy also reflected this treatment of Indians and had done so since the Dawes General Allotment Act. Even Robeson County Indian citizens, who lacked a formal, recognized relationship to the federal government, felt the pressure to abandon a collective identity. Following the 1936 Siouan Enrollment Study, for example, the OIA only gave them the option to be recognized as individuals. But Indians resisted this individualistic model of political organization; they organized themselves as a community, with a representative council, a membership, and collective interests. They would not accept a solely individualized relationship to the government but believed that maintaining a collective identity best served their interests. Their agency as a group in the face of subjugation as individual citizens is outside the current paradigms of American history, which has a limited understanding of Native Americans who maintain both U.S. citizenship and tribal sovereignty. Indians, however, have insisted on the social, political, and spiritual sanctity of both the individual and the group.[4] Despite Robeson County Indians' faith in their status as citizens, they resisted the individualism inherent in liberal models of citizenship.

Indeed, Indians in Robeson County were not the only Native Americans trapped in this ambiguous political status. Like many other groups in the eastern United States, early patterns of colonization, the impact of disease, and cultural transformations also muddied their political and legal autonomy. But even in the western United States, where tribes asserted their sovereign status according to inviolable treaty rights, widely diverse traditions, political factionalism, and the varied agendas of local, state, and federal governments made Indians' status within the United States a disorienting puzzle.[5]

The true difficulty has been for historians, not for Indians. Like the veterans pictured in Figure 12, Indians themselves managed change and the conflicts presented by heterogeneous, multiple layers of identity as "Americans" and "Indians"—perhaps not effortlessly, but still with grace and aplomb. But no academic or legal paradigm exists to interpret this universal experience. Paradigms like racial naturalization apply directly to immigrants, African Americans, or other ethnic groups who have also struggled with "Americanness," but they stop short of explaining Indians' situations. The legal tools at the disposal of immigrants and other groups promoted civil rights for individuals interested primarily in inclusion. The legal tools available to Indians, however, focused on their identities as members of groups distinct from the American polity. Further, Indians faced arbitrary yet inflexible identity definitions, definitions that revolved around ideas of primitivity and ancientness that America's other nonwhite populations have largely (though not entirely) avoided.[6] These legal tools of sovereignty have led to Indians' exclusion and disempowerment.

Ignoring Indians' dual exercise of Americanness and Indianness, policy makers promoted legal alternatives to assimilation that were little more than paternalistic exercises designed to patch flawed policies. Ironically, the legislative remedies for allotment and their attendant judiciary rulings extended greater protection over Indians from local swindlers while simultaneously furthering their disfranchisement by federal officials. Policy makers and judges rationalized that powerlessness by arguing that Indians were racially backward and not fit to fully exercise citizenship.[7] Congress repeated a similar ambiguity in the 1924 Indian Citizenship Act, which made Indians subject citizens but still affirmed their tribal "rights." At the same time, the act recategorized Indians alongside other racialized ethnic groups in the United States—African Americans, Latinos, and Asians—who faced renewed discrimination in the 1920s.[8] For all of these groups, citizenship could only be enjoyed if their members accepted limited freedoms and an inferior status. According to historian Devon W. Carbado, "racial naturalization" resolved the civic and racial nationalism debates of the early twentieth century. Racial naturalization incorporated some individuals into the American political system as inferiors; in an ultimate irony of "Americanness," being a victim of racial discrimination actually facilitated one's identity as an American and one's citizenship.[9] Jim Crow was one step toward this goal, the Indian Citizenship Act was another, and the termination policy of the 1950s was a third.

Termination policy proposed to liquidate the assets of recognized tribes, extend state civil jurisdiction over reservations, and end the unique government-to-government relationship between tribal and U.S. governments. All of these measures added up to racial naturalization by incorporating Indians into states as subjugated citizens and effectively taking away their most valuable economic assets, which prevented them from elevating their status. The policy also coincided with the passage of the 1956 Lumbee Act. The struggle over Indian citizenship and identity linked the termination policy and the Lumbee Act. Congress intended to recognize Robeson County Indians but mark them as an inferior group among inferior Indians by excluding them from the benefits and services normally accorded to recognized tribes.

The ambiguities of federal policy in the twentieth century forged a different political discourse in the Robeson County Indian community, one that paved over disagreements about a tribal name and highlighted distinctions in class, political ideology, and settlement affiliation. The Lumbee Act settled the question of a tribal name for some; key to that agreement was the desire of some Indians to affirm their citizenship as equals in the larger American community. This group of largely town Indians approved of the Lumbee name and the political strategy that accompanied it, but they likely did not recognize the larger racial naturalization that was at work in the termination policy, and they did not intend to become inferior citizens by adopting the name. Other Indians, many of whom had been through the wartime experience or fought unsuccessfully for recognition in the 1930s and 1940s, displayed a different vision of reconciling racial and civic nationalism, one that would enable them to exercise autonomy. This group emphasized Indians' cultural and symbolic differences from whites. Some members went on to construct an identity as Tuscaroras, recalling a historic lineage that discarded all references to Jim Crow and the expectations of assimilation. These two approaches to recognition as Lumbee—one that performed assimilation and the other that performed primitivism—represented another method of reckoning an American identity on top of the many layers of Indian identity they had built.

While the history of Native Americans in the segregated South may seem exceptional at first glance, a closer look reveals many commonalities with Indians all over the nation and sheds new light on "Americanness" itself. The most prominent common thread for Native Americans was local, state, and federal policy makers' expectation that Indians would assimilate on non-Indian terms and make their resources—their land, their labor, the products of their labor, and their dignity—vulnerable to dispossession. Naturally, Indians resisted this expectation, but doing so fragmented the Robeson County Indian community politically.

THE WAYS IN WHICH the factionalism of the 1930s destroyed the community's attempts to achieve federal recognition had dawned on both Indians and federal officials by the 1940s. At Pembroke Farms, the government succeeded in bringing Siouans and Cherokees together to accomplish certain goals, but the Farm Security Administration's single-minded focus on political factionalism engendered greater distance between town leaders and their rural constituencies. The FSA and the OIA hoped to heal these social wounds by fostering community pride in the form of a historical and cultural pageant, produced and performed by Robeson County Indians themselves.

During the first third of the twentieth century, towns all over the United States hosted pageants as community-development activities. To paraphrase historian David Glassberg, pageant producers and town boosters believed that making history into a dramatic public ritual could bring about a "social and political transformation" that would help the community prosper. The Progressive era anchored the pageant movement; these highly symbolic portrayals of an idealized past promoted tradition as a bulwark against modernity. At the same time, Progressive forerunners of the New Deal reformers saw pageants as a useful tool to convince others that their modern proposals dovetailed with the past's most cherished values and heroic figures. In particular, Progressive educators and social workers thought that pageants could help communities ritually construct "a new communal identity and sense of citizenship anchored in the past," according to Glassberg. John Collier himself promoted pageantry when he worked in New York City prior to his involvement with Indian policy. "Pageantry is the form of art which comes nearest to expressing the new social idea," he wrote in 1913. That new idea was "freedom through cooperation." The pageant "symbolizes . . . the growing and striving community, depicted through a long course of time, gathering up into its soul the growing tradition and idealism, the strivings and hopes of its generations of men and women." For Collier, pageantry promoted social cooperation, and in depicting a community, it could regenerate that community.[10]

Collier undoubtedly saw the Robeson County Indian community as a promising place to cultivate a cooperative spirit and sense of pride. In 1940 Collier and George S. Mitchell (who had moved from the FSA's Raleigh office to Washington, D.C.) proposed employing Yankton Dakota anthropologist Ella C. Deloria to write a community pageant. Deloria belonged to a well-known and influential Dakota family; her brother Vine was an Episcopal minister and storyteller, and her nephew Vine Deloria Jr. became one of the twentieth century's foremost writers, philosophers, and activists. Ella Deloria traveled to Robeson County with her sister, Susan Mable Deloria, in 1940. By that time, she had collaborated with anthropologist Franz Boas on Dakota language texts and was writing a novel and several other works in her area of expertise.[11] The OIA and FSA hired Deloria presumably because they thought that, as a Dakota (also known as "Sioux"), she might shed some light on anthropologist John Swanton's theory of Siouan ancestry for the Robeson County Indian community. Her qualifications certainly lent academic skills to Collier's and Mitchell's goals.

Deloria's salary came from the FSA, but the agency had no funds to actually mount the pageant. Keenly aware of Indians' recent political turmoil, Mitchell thought that asking the community to raise funds and direct the activity would enhance "the somewhat obscured cultural and racial pride of this group." Mitchell and Collier told Deloria to find the things that they thought "real Indians" had: their "almost forgotten tribal lore, legends, songs, and crafts." They also charged Deloria to assist Indians "in raising their standards of living [and] improving group cooperation." Mitchell sought the approval of Congressman J. Bayard Clark, who wanted to make sure none of his Lumberton friends objected to Indians mounting such a production. Indeed, since many of the country's public celebrations searched, as Glassberg puts it, for "a picturesque Anglo-American past," a pageant for and by Indians and not just about them must have seemed controversial. But Clark approved the project, and in late July 1940, Deloria arrived in Robeson County for a five-month stay.[12]

Deloria immediately encountered Jim Crow and the puzzling effects it had on Indians' feelings of membership in the larger American nation. Initially, Deloria thought to stay in Pembroke's hotel, which a white family owned. The owners allowed her lodging, even though they did not permit local Indians to stay there. The hotel's meal plan did not suit Deloria, however, and Pembroke's town doctor and his wife, who were also white, offered her a room on the second floor of their home.[13] But a few weeks later, she changed her mind about that as well. She decided to rent a four-room cottage from an Indian family who lived about a mile from Pembroke. "There is quite a lot of nasty race prejudice, isn't there?" she asked George Mitchell. "I changed because I realized that the people stiffened a bit when I said I might live at the doctor's, as if it would alienate them from me." She told Mitchell, "I like my [new] arrangement very much."[14] Deloria showed immediate sensitivity to Robeson County Indians' position under Jim Crow, and she decided that her relationship with them would suffer if her actions did not conform to the prejudices of both whites and Indians.

To plan the pageant and solicit community support, Deloria immediately began visiting rural churches, the centers of Indian social life. Community members welcomed her to Saint Annah Church, for example, where she introduced herself and the pageant to a large crowd. But later she learned that the crowd may not have been there for the pageant after all. Someone had driven past the church and asked a group young men standing outside what the meeting was about. They replied, "We were all told to come, because there is a lady here from Washington to fix it so we don't have to go to war!"[15] At least some of the people with whom Deloria would work felt highly ambivalent about their desire to fight for the United States. Perhaps she saw this humorous misunderstanding as a window into the conflict some Indians felt about their identity as Indians, as Americans, and as an oppressed minority under Jim Crow. Or it might have just made her chuckle.

With such colorful, everyday encounters with Indian people, and by living with an Indian family, Deloria likely gained access to more authentic material than she had expected. She structured the pageant, titled "The Life-Story of a People," around the area's traditional agriculture and Indians' self-made social institutions—the schools and churches. She included episodes like the Reconstruction-era Lowry War, a subscription school, and a brush-arbor religious gathering. The pageant also consisted of dancing and singing, with scenes that dramatized Indians' pre-Columbian life. But the pageant focused more on Robeson County Indians' contemporary institutions. The play represented every religious denomination and formal social organization, including the Boy Scouts, the American Legion, and the Red Cross. The gymnasium at the Indian Normal School provided the venue for the play. The production also sustained kin ties: members of both Cherokee and Siouan groups acted in the play, and their children and grandchildren performed as well. Allen Lowry's grandchildren and great-grandchildren played the members of the Lowry gang, even though most of them were far older than the actual gang members had been. Henry Berry Lowry's surviving daughter also appeared in the show. Overall, the cast and crew included nearly 150 Indians, and they played to overflow crowds.[16]

Deloria capitalized on the general public's lack of knowledge about specific Indian cultures and rituals by adding cultural symbols and regalia that were from the Plains and not the Southeast. She probably added such symbols to resonate with the "Siouan" name, since Mitchell and Collier had charged her with finding a connection. She wrote, "Of course it is not strictly historical, since so little factual material was possible. . . . The pre-Columbian scenes are reconstructed from what little we know, and from conjecture."[17] These were the only comments she made about these scenes, which she surely developed to express Mitchell and Collier's conceptions of Indian ritual and anthropological theory. Given the importance that many people placed on such visible markers of identity, the pageant presented Indian identity as consumable and easily digestible for non-Indians. These stereotypes were a version of Indianness that non-Indians felt they understood, and their lack of authenticity played to non-Indians' preferences. Using this kind of symbolism had its own sort of authenticity in the context of Robeson County Indians, however; it is akin to the tribal name changes and attendant political disagreements, a strategy that Indians themselves employed to "play with the primitive," as historian Phil Deloria describes.[18] We don't know whether such play was conscious, but it amounted to an avenue for Indians to control, to some degree, the portrayal of their own identities.

Playing with primitivism offered some outlets for expression, while playing with their status as assimilated mixed-bloods offered others. "Some white woman from Red Springs asked to be in [the pageant]," Ella Deloria reported, "but the people feel it is their pageant . . . and they have enough blonds to play white parts. (When white men stage a show calling for Indians, they don't go out after real Indians; they make up as Indians; why can't we [make up as whites]? said one man.)" Indians may or may not have appreciated the federal government's objectives with this project, but they certainly valued the opportunity to express themselves and to control that expression. The project, and their previous years of negotiating to ameliorate segregation, empowered them to simply say "no" to the white woman who wanted to be in the pageant rather than try to accommodate her, as previous generations might have done.[19]

The play was so important to the community's leadership that the offstage committees—finance, publicity, and production—included a "who's who" of the town Indian community, including Siouan leader James Chavis and several members of the Fourth Street Power Structure. Deloria and the planning committees emphasized the "progressive" identity of Robeson County's Indians, especially their citizenship in and allegiance to the United States. Scenes depicted friendly meetings with Europeans; Indian service in the American Revolution, War of 1812, and the world wars; and Indians' focus on educational and economic advancement. In their press release for the pageant, the publicity committee wrote, "What we have attained has come not through idle waiting for possible Federal help, but through industry and sobriety and a consistent determination to survive. . . . [W]e obtained our public school system only fifty-four years ago. Yet in that short period, our people have made remarkable progress." The planning committee conveyed that their own character and community values, not the federal government's help, enabled Indians in Robeson County to "progress," to be as good as anyone else and still maintain their identity as Indians, as a People.[20] This articulation of Indian identity served town Indians well and functioned to unite Cherokee and Siouan factions around a common narrative of Robeson County Indian history that did not depend on a particular tribal name but instead on agreement about the identity markers that defined the Indian community.

The pageant's concept of culture and history centered on Indians' educational and economic self-sufficiency, ideas that resonated more with the priorities of town Indians but differed from the customs that some of Robeson

County's rural Indians emphasized. Deloria herself observed two sorts of divisions within the Indian community, which we have already witnessed: a "feud," as she called it, between Cherokees and Siouans and a split between rural and town Indians. She characterized the latter two groups as "the 85%" and "the progressives," meaning that in her estimation, rural Indians comprised 85 percent of the Indian population, while town Indians, or the "progressives," comprised the other 15 percent. Like other OIA officials, she thought of rural Indians as "illiterate" and "timid." But she also admired their insistence that this pageant would be "theirs," regardless of how socially or educationally inferior other people perceived them to be.[21]

While the pageant provided both groups with opportunities to display their Indianness to outsiders, the production also served to distance town and rural Indians from one another. The young men who attended Deloria's meeting at Saint Annah because they thought they could avoid the draft probably did not feel represented by a patriotic historical narrative. Indeed, pageants functioned in part to define the public itself; communities ostensibly agreed on their narratives, but those narratives also glossed over points of contention. In this way, a pageant's narrative could assist community cooperation while excluding members of the community.[22] Although Deloria worked with rural Indians to write the pageant, regularly visiting the rural communities around Pembroke, the process of creating the pageant itself may have paved the way for greater divisions between town and rural Indians. The very act of performance—and the preproduction wrangling over historical narratives—reproduced the tensions inherent in American citizenship in this period. The process of inclusion actually excluded, or at least marginalized, certain members of the society. Rather than marginalizing a racial "other," however, the pageant alienated a politically disfranchised segment of the Indian community.

Despite the pageant's empowering potential, production and finance concerns curtailed its impact on rural Indians. The second year of the pageant, the planning committees paid for Deloria's work entirely from profits made on the 1940 pageant. Aware of this surplus, the FSA's George Mitchell urged Deloria to perform the pageant out in the rural areas and not just in the town of Pembroke. After consulting with the planning committee, however, Deloria told Mitchell that his proposal would not work. "It is all they can do to finance this pageant and come out even," she wrote. "[T]hey don't catch the vision that more people wanting the same things will in time help the whole community. . . . It isn't enough that I work in all the people I can from that larger group. The influence of the pageant and of similar efforts doesn't reach the majority because they have no real part in it out where they are." Deloria's efforts to contact and work with rural Indians did not outweigh the town leaders' reluctance to involve them. For those leaders, the task of financing the project among a destitute community was difficult enough without having to overcome the social and geographic barriers to produce it "for the poor folks," as Mitchell wanted.[23]

But these folks weren't simply "poor"; they were politically disfranchised to a much greater extent than Indians in town. Class distinctions in the Indian community centered on political questions concerning how the tribe should represent itself to outsiders. Town Indians were always conscious of their rural Indian kin, but they tried to choose who represented their community to outsiders, and they believed that rural Indians did not adequately represent the tribe. Deloria's observation about the division between the minority town and majority rural Indians in 1941 reveals the distance between these groups. After Pembroke Farms failed to elevate everyone's economic prosperity, town and rural Indians were economically and socially farther apart than ever. Rural Indians had "no real part" in the concerns of town Indians, particularly the "leadership class" who managed and produced the pageant and who tried to control Pembroke Farms. Cherokees Martin Luther and James R. Lowry supervised raising money for the pageant, and undoubtedly their voices were the loudest in determining what they could and could not finance. In some ways, their reluctance to take the pageant to rural Indians might have reflected Cherokees' lingering efforts to exert control over the community's direction and exclude the Siouan constituency instead of Siouan leaders. Indeed, after the 1940 pageant, Mitchell, Collier, and Deloria congratulated themselves on bringing the Siouan and Cherokee leadership together. They did achieve their goals in this respect, but the accomplishment highlighted their failure to overcome the more profound division between town and rural Indians.[24]

The Pembroke Farms experience indicated that town Indians were better-equipped economically and socially to confront segregation and benefit from the system. Rural Indians, on the other hand, had fewer economic opportunities outside farming, and they marked their communities by their relationships to one another and as members of kin and settlement groups, not by their relationships to outsiders. Although town leaders valued their kin and settlement connections, they also defined themselves by their access to whites' political and economic resources. Rural Indians relied heavily on the town leaders as cultural brokers who made their plight known to agencies like the FSA. However, rural Indians still resisted the heavy-handed leadership of town Indians and preserved their own ways of seeing the world. For example, some people withheld information from Deloria when she was conducting research for the pageant. They apparently did not understand why she wanted to know certain things until they saw the finished product. Their reluctance probably stemmed from Deloria's apparent connections to town Indians with whom they did not necessarily identify or wish to help. Once they saw the pageant, however, they told Deloria that "they'd tell me or whoever was doing it all the interesting things they knew that would add to" the pageant.[25]

In the end, "The Life-Story of a People" left a mixed legacy for Robeson County's Indians, although everyone involved brought their best intentions and talents to the project. The OIA and FSA hoped that if the community understood its shared history, such cooperation would ameliorate what federal officials saw as the fundamentally destructive nature of Indian factionalism. Using their previous five years of experience at Pembroke Farms as training for cooperation, Siouan and Cherokee leaders eagerly worked together on the project. However, just as Pembroke Farms had failed the county's rural Indians, the pageant production also overlooked their articulations of Indian identity. The pageant illuminated a social and economic division within the Indian community that had been brewing for many years, but the more obvious and bitter disagreements between town leaders obscured its political importance. Although government officials, Deloria, and many Robeson County Indians were thrilled with the production, "The Life-Story of a People" had its last performance on 10 December 1941, three days after Japan attacked Pearl Harbor.[26]

Indians in Robeson County reacted to World War II with ambivalence. Some men rushed to enlist, and the military drafted others; family members at home looked upon the war with a mixture of resentment and patriotism. Joseph Brooks, for example, joined the navy in 1942 and left Robeson County Indian politics to others with whom he had cooperated and competed in the previous decade.[27] According to historian Christopher A. Oakley, at least 1,000 North Carolina Indians served in the military between the 1940s and the 1950s, and approximately forty died in service.

Indian veterans remembered surprisingly little racism. While local recruiters sometimes tried to classify Indians as "colored," soldiers typically served with white units and identified openly as Native Americans. Some fought on the front lines, unlike their African American counterparts, whom the military often relegated to menial tasks. Simeon Oxendine, son of J. C. "Sonny" Oxendine (the mayor of Pembroke and a member of the Fourth Street Power

Structure), flew with the air force's "Hell's Angels." Indian soldiers experienced treatment in the military and overseas far different from the Jim Crow society of Robeson County. Indians shared sleeping quarters, eating establishments, and ideas freely with non-Indians. When they returned home, Jim Crow incensed these men; local whites refused to serve them at lunch counters or cut their hair and informed them that they could not drink from the same water fountains as whites. Such customs seemed trivial to veterans who had risked their lives for their country.[28] Servicemen took their wartime experience and used it to resist discrimination. For example, navy veteran Luther Harbert Moore, grandson of Normal School founder W. L. Moore, served his country proudly but always remembered a childhood friend who had died in Germany "fighting for a country where he never really had an equal opportunity to acquire an education or anything else." "I felt like it was ridiculous [for] a person [who] lived in a country that treated them [as] less than what they [were] to give their life [for that country]," he said.[29] Moore's experience in World War II inspired him to find ways to provide a decent education for other Indian children so that fewer of them would have to die serving a country that did not treat them as equals.

Indians also took advantage of the military draft to seek clarification on their status as citizens. They did not doubt their legal eligibility for the draft, but their experiences with white supremacy and segregation led them to question what it meant to belong to an American nation. One Indian, C. W. Oxendine, traced these issues carefully in a letter to President Roosevelt. "We scar[ce]less have the right to citi[zen]ship," he wrote, marking the difference between legal citizenship and what historian Mae Ngai calls "substantive citizenship," or the symbolic and imagined senses of belonging to a nation.[30] Legal citizenship, for Oxendine, was scarcely enough to compensate for how the military treated Indians. He continued, "[W]hy would we be compell[ed] [to serve in the military] under such condi[tions]. I notice the[y] drauf [sic] our boys under the name of Indain [sic] until they call them to camp, and then they send them in as white." Unlike some families who emphasized their connections to whites in a white-supremacist society, Oxendine did not take pride in Indians' service with whites; he objected to drafting men whom society did not treat justly and then denying their Indian identity by listing them as "white." By rejecting association with whites, he fundamentally objected to white supremacy and the military's embrace of it.

Oxendine instead proposed that a proper society would recognize his Indian community, not as an inferior racial group but as a distinct People. "[W]e have no equal right as a nat[ion] of people," Oxendine contended. "We should be glad to kno[w] why we should not be recognized as a tribe or people." He equated discrimination under Jim Crow with the federal government's reluctance to recognize the tribe. Oxendine concluded that "under present condi[tions] we don't feel that it is justified for our boys to be drafted"; he reiterated the deep resentment some Indians had toward a government that refused to recognize their distinct status and identity.[31]

Oxendine perceived that the United States categorized individuals as racially included or excluded, making little room for Indians unless they were willing to subsume their collective identity for an individualistic one. In this formula, personal identity only intersected with national identity if Indians accepted a rank on a racial hierarchy. Oxendine also pointed to a gray area between legal and substantive citizenship when he suggested that Indians have not achieved a status as citizens if they are not included in the national body *as Indians*. Indian identity was bounded, not by individuals who could be judged as Indian by outsiders, but by collective conversations that happened over time between insiders and outsiders. Tellingly, Oxendine spoke as "we," not "I." In a sense, those identity conversations created an Indigenous nation; Oxendine privileged his membership in a nation of a People—that is, a nation bonded through kinship and place that shares a political struggle against the United States.

The White House referred the letter to the Office of Indian Affairs for comment. Staff member J. C. McCaskill replied with a standard history of Robeson County Indians' relationship with the OIA, arguing that Robeson County Indians had no treaties with the federal government and that enrollment under the Indian Reorganization Act had proven unsuccessful for all but a few. Furthermore, "Indians are subject to the draft as well as white persons, since Indians are as much citizens as white people are," the OIA wrote, citing the law that Congress passed in 1924 granting U.S. citizenship to all Native Americans. "Surely you must be mistaken in your statement that you are not recognized as a citizen of the United States," McCaskill wrote. "The fact that adequate school facilities are not provided or the cotton mill denies you the privilege of work does not mean that under the law you are not recognized as a citizen," he continued, implying that Indians should resign themselves to racial discrimination. "There is nothing we can do now to give any national recognition to such a group," McCaskill concluded, and he suggested that Oxendine speak to the management at Pembroke Farms about the economic opportunities available there.[32] Oxendine and McCaskill both clearly recognized that "racial naturalization" was at work in the 1940s. The OIA had positioned itself as the benevolent protector of Indian interests; in this instance, McCaskill proved that such federal-level "benevolence" was perfectly consistent with local racist agendas.

The simultaneous existence of Jim Crow and the wartime draft troubled Indians like Oxendine, who saw citizenship as explicitly linked to their status as an oppressed minority group. Oxendine also thought that federal recognition of his identity could end this discrimination and restore Indians' rights, but the OIA had foreclosed any possibility of helping Robeson County Indians, refusing to even help them with educational training to qualify them to work in defense industries.[33] The OIA's continuing withdrawal from the affairs of Robeson County Indians was undoubtedly a reflection of the agency's isolation from the centers of power during wartime, as well as Congress's increasing concern about the efficacy of the Indian New Deal to accomplish tribal self-sufficiency. Congress cut the Indian Office's budget repeatedly in favor of defense expenditures, and in 1942 the agency moved its offices to Chicago to make room in Washington for wartime activity. From Chicago, Collier and his staff could not maintain their coordinated efforts with other government offices—a critical part of the execution of Collier's program. In 1943 the Senate explicitly questioned Collier's vision when a report suggested that the Indian New Deal perpetuated the OIA and its guardianship instead of self-government for Indian tribes. Collier himself resigned as commissioner of Indian Affairs in 1945 after the House of Representatives threatened to cut OIA funding by two-thirds if he did not step down.[34]

In the midst of these controversies, the OIA wanted the FSA to provide economic assistance to Robeson County Indians, as McCaskill had suggested to C. W. Oxendine. The FSA, however, failed to acknowledge Indians' unique status or fundamentally alter Indians' relationships to southern society or to the federal government. This attitude led Indians to distrust the FSA and Pembroke Farms management. Furthermore, the FSA was embroiled in its own battles with Congress during the war years—battles that resulted in the closure of Pembroke Farms and resettlement programs all over the country between 1943 and 1945. Resettlement projects had been a lightning rod for FSA critics since the late 1930s, but congressional advocates for defense spending exerted even more pressure on the agency to cut its experimental programs after 1940. In 1943 the House of Representatives recommended dissolving the FSA and liquidating the resettlement projects; the House accused the agency of giving loans to borrowers who could not pay, hiring incompetent farm managers, and overestimating income from farm operations.[35]

Pembroke Farms had reached a capacity of sixty-four families by 1943. Just as it was beginning to run smoothly, the government sold the project units at a loss.[36] The FSA gave homesteader families the first opportunity to purchase their farms, and if the family did not qualify for purchase, the government offered the land to another Indian applicant. The agency then opened the remaining land and the community building they had constructed to public auction.[37] Siouan leaders, determined to preserve what economic autonomy they had gained, saw an opportunity to keep that remaining property in Indian hands. The FSA proposed to sell the vacant woodland to timber companies, who would pay a higher price than Indian farmers. "The land will go right back to the white people then," James E. Chavis protested, and the Siouan Council desired to maintain some land for Indian veterans. "You know the boys who have been drafted will not have any chance of buying a home while they are away, but if they are allowed to, fathers, mothers, and wives can buy the land for them," said Chavis.[38] Indeed, the FSA's profit motive seemed to outweigh its promotion of Indian landholding, as Manager H. C. Green avoided the Indians who offered to buy the vacant lots and referred them to the FSA Regional Office or told them that they were free to bid against any other offer.[39] In protesting the FSA's plans for the vacant woodland, Chavis asserted Indians' claims on equal economic opportunity, especially for the returning servicemen who had proven their fitness for citizenship in the United States. He recognized the discrimination inherent in the FSA's plans and sought to avoid it; their actions proved that the economic injustices for citizens under Jim Crow were not over.

In a final effort to preserve the land through grassroots means, Pembroke Farms residents formed a branch of the National Farmers' Union. No resources had been available to the Siouan Council to solve this problem, and Chavis and others hoped that pooling their resources this way, and their attachment to a national organization, would give them some leverage with which to compete with the timber companies and convince the FSA to sell to them.[40] With this goal in mind, and remembering the intent of the OIA to put Pembroke Farms land in trust for Robeson County Indians, Robeson County Indians alerted the OIA, which sent McCaskill to Robeson County to investigate.[41] But Congress bound the FSA to dispose of the land, and the FSA offered it at auction at prices up to $170 per acre before the OIA was able to intervene.[42] Indians recognized that they could do little about the woodland that the FSA sold, but they protested the sale of their community building, in which they held church services, fairs, and community meetings. The FSA did not offer to assist them, but the Indians managed to buy back the building and grounds from a local white man who had purchased it.[43]

The OIA responded to the sale of the Pembroke Farms lands with deep regret, although it had done little for Robeson County Indians' efforts to keep the land. Two weeks after the auction, three OIA officials visited Pembroke Farms and determined that "the recent sale of approximately 3,000 acres of alleged surplus lands was a mistake." "In view of our general supervision of Indian affairs I hope that in the future your administration will take no steps looking to the sale of other land . . . without first giving this Office an opportunity to consult with you. Although it should be very reluctant to assume any direct responsibility for [Pembroke Farms], it may be that the Indian Service could be helpful," OIA assistant commissioner William Zimmerman told the FSA.[44] OIA officials believed that Robeson County Indians were indeed Indians and deserved their own land base and relief from the discrimination that accompanied segregation, but they refused to risk providing that relief themselves. Instead, they wanted to hand the problem to the FSA yet still maintain some influence over the FSA's decisions. The FSA's own problems—especially its tense relationship with Congress—precluded this kind of cooperation, however, highlighting an intractable flaw in the administrative execution of the Indian New Deal. The Indian Office depended on interagency cooperation to achieve its goals, yet officials were powerless when competing congressional agendas dictated that the cooperating agency move against Indians' interests. In this political climate, OIA officials could do nothing to save a project they intended to benefit Indians.

CLOSING PEMBROKE FARMS left the Indian New Deal unfinished in Robeson County, but it also left rural Indians, who needed the project, without an economic foothold in an economy that was shifting away from agriculture and toward wage work in industry. Owning land and working it cooperatively had helped Indians preserve their kin ties and attachment to settlement communities before and during the Great Depression. But as sharecropping and landownership opportunities dwindled due to changes in farm policy and the closing of Pembroke Farms, some Indians obtained work within the new economic engine of World War II. Segregation preserved most of these jobs for whites in southeastern North Carolina; Indians who worked in wartime industries had to leave their homes and migrate to cities such as Baltimore and Detroit, where employers simply did not know their background or did not care as much as southern whites did. Indians left home reluctantly, wanting better economic opportunities but afraid of losing their connection to their community. Baltimore, in particular, became well-known among Robeson County Indians as a place to get ahead without abandoning one's distinct identity. Indians began moving there in 1944 and found work in construction and in apparel factories; gradually, a community of several thousand Robeson County Indians coalesced there. They maintained their close ties to Robeson County by returning seasonally and often sending children "back home" for relatives to raise.[45] Similar to the migration for turpentine work discussed in chapter 2, the Baltimore community demonstrated that Indians' identity as a People evolved amidst considerable shifts in relationships to kinship and place. Just as in Georgia, Indians founded their own church in Baltimore, which thrives today and belongs to the all-Indian Burnt Swamp Baptist Association in North Carolina.

While Robeson County Indians initiated their own migrations after World War II, the number of Indians living in cities nationwide doubled in the 1940s.[46] After John Collier resigned from the OIA in 1945, Congress and other OIA officials reacted to Collier's sweeping reforms by searching for ways to withdraw from Indian Affairs. In 1948 the federal government launched an informal relocation program for Native Americans that took many Indians to cities such as Baltimore, Chicago, San Francisco, and Los Angeles. These efforts intensified through the early 1950s, as Indian Commissioner Dillon S. Myer expanded funding for the program and reorganized OIA field offices to facilitate it. Relocation programs fit perfectly into Congress's agenda: as Indians left the reservation, policy makers hoped they would lose their attachments to their tribes and blend in with the American citizenry. Furthermore, states would have to begin providing services to Indians, which alleviated the burden on the federal government for Indian programs.[47]

For Indians in Robeson County, the government's relocation programs— and the general trend toward migration in the 1940s—meant that they met and interacted with Indians from other places with greater frequency and with political results. For example, members of the Brooks Settlement met Turkey Tayac, a Piscataway Indian from Maryland. Beginning in 1938, Tayac traveled to Robeson County at least four times to help the Original 22 advocate for their interests on local and national levels. Tayac married Will Brooks's daughter Martha Lee, creating a kin relationship that also furthered the cause of federal recognition. The Brooks family's relationship to Tayac served as a powerful example of how Robeson County Indians' core layer of identity—kinship—could further the group's quest to affirm its identity.[48] Tayac himself led small groups of Robeson County Indians to Baltimore and Pennsylvania after the war, helping to reignite their interest in obtaining federal recognition from the OIA.[49]

Indians believed that a legitimate and recognizably "Indian" name was critical to the achievement of federal recognition. Ralph Brooks, the spokesman for the Original 22's council, led several delegations to government agencies, members of Congress, and the National Congress of American Indians in Washington, D.C., to discuss an appropriate name and procedure for recognition. This delegation did not represent town Indians or the leadership that had previously negotiated with the OIA but instead spoke for the Original 22, the rural Indians who had the most success gaining federal recognition. But even though the pageant and the closing of Pembroke Farms had silenced rural Indians in many ways, Brooks's strategy in Washington showed that he had closely observed the government's efforts to promote unity and cooperation within the group. The name suggested was "Lumbee," after the river on which they lived; it provided a generic name that described all the Indians in the county yet still sounded authentically "Indian."[50] Brooks also informed these agencies that his group included members of both Siouan and Cherokee factions. But Brooks received little encouragement from his meetings. Congressman J. Bayard Clark promised to introduce a bill, a tactic that had been tried repeatedly and failed. The OIA consistently and flatly denied the possibility of recognition under the IRA, citing the absence of treaty agreements with Robeson County Indians. Officials at the OIA encouraged Indians to seek recognition from the North Carolina legislature under the new name. But this group of Robeson County Indian leaders did not see their interests as coinciding with those of the state. They wanted more than schools and second-class citizenship; they wanted land and an economic base with which to combat segregation and establish their autonomy as an Indian people.[51]

Brooks told North Carolina senator Clyde R. Hoey, "We feel that we are entitled to have a separate reservation and schools for our children. It is also our desire and ambition to be called a nation, with a [tribal] name of our own like all the other tribes of America."[52] This group of Robeson County rural Indians wanted Congress, the OIA, and the state of North Carolina to recognize a sovereign political relationship with the tribe rather than just an individualistic relationship that fostered citizenship in the American nation while upholding segregation and white supremacy. Recognition was a matter of fairness and equal treatment; some Robeson County Indians had been recognized as such by the OIA. Why should the federal government refuse to assist them? From the OIA's vantage point, the answer was clear: recognition of the Original 22 only entailed acknowledgment of individual Indians, and Collier had not allowed the group to organize as a "tribe" under a constitution. The status of recognized individuals differed from that of tribes, and OIA officials felt no obligation to the individuals who had been recognized as "one-half or more Indian" under the IRA. On the other hand, the Original

22 expected some sort of benefit from their recognition, perhaps believing that the OIA effectively delivered services to other tribal governments and that they deserved the same treatment. The OIA, however, was notoriously ineffective in its work on behalf of the Indian tribes for which it was responsible, and the agency had no resources to provide for recognized individuals. Like James Chavis, who had protested the sale of land by the Farm Security Administration, Brooks asserted Indians' claims to economic opportunity. But Brooks resolved the problems posed by racial naturalization with an insistence on autonomy for his People rather than a plea for their inclusion in American society.

Undeterred by these rejections, the Original 22's council began to hold large meetings at the Brooks Settlement Longhouse in the spring of 1949. In a show of militancy and concern that whites would try to disrupt their gathering, Indians stationed armed snipers in trees surrounding the meeting place. Turkey Tayac and two of his associates from Washington spoke to over 2,000 Indians about becoming members of the American Indian Organization, a new group that he and others had started to encourage Indian unity. The American Indian Organization would "give everyone a chance to work together," according to Tayac's spokesman, a Cherokee named John S. Gardner. "We don't want a reservation," Gardner said; the organization instead functioned to teach dancing, arts, and crafts and hold powwows "to thank God for giving us good land and crops."[53]

Tayac proposed a type of recognition very different from the federal government's capricious process. The recognition bestowed by the American Indian Organization emphasized political and social affiliations between Indian peoples. For the Brooks Settlement, this kind of recognition aligned with its own approach to affirming identity, and Ralph Brooks and others endorsed the plan. The group elected three men to represent them, including Lindsay Revels, who had been active in the Siouan movement of the 1930s and was first cousin to Lawrence Maynor, one of the Original 22.[54] The group adopted the name "Lumbee" at the meeting and instructed its elected representatives "to do everything in their power to make this name accepted by the Federal Government and to endeavor to have the United States give them the same benefits as are accorded to other Indians."[55] In the meantime, Ralph and Will Brooks relocated to a farm near Leonardtown, Maryland, with Turkey Tayac's help. They appealed to the OIA for assistance to help them start farming. Assistant Commissioner John Provinse informed them that the OIA had no funds to help them and suggested that they visit their local county agent or check with the Farmers' Home Administration, the successor agency to the

FSA.[56] When the Brookses relocated, Lindsay Revels took up the discussions with Washington.

While a pan-Indian approach to identity and recognition served a national political purpose, it empowered Indians on a local level as well. One Longhouse member told a reporter that the group meeting at the Longhouse was determined "to kill segregation or run the white man out of the county."[57] Recognition from other tribes meant that Indians in Robeson County did not have to feel inferior to whites or accept second-class treatment. Rural Indians easily bypassed local politicians and white supremacy to create a social institution and display an identity that appealed to other Indians and affirmed their autonomy in and ownership of their homeland.

Town Indians, whom the newspaper called "the more educated" Indians, were suspicious of Tayac's plan and distanced themselves from it and the rural Indians who led the movement. Ira Pate Lowry, professor at the Indian Normal School and D. F. Lowry's nephew, told the local newspaper that "leaders of the Indian race . . . have taken no part, generally, in the activities" in the Brooks Settlement "and residents of Pembroke have largely steered clear of the meetings." Indians at the Longhouse told at least one town resident "that he and others like him were not wanted," according to Lowry, and Lowry labeled the meetings an "agitation . . . among uneducated Indians [in] some of the rural areas."[58] "The Indians are getting along well now, and once we are on a reservation or in a club, all our opportunities and privileges will be limited," said one Indian who worked at Pembroke's Indian high school.[59] Lowry and other town Indian leaders believed that more militant groups like the one meeting at the Longhouse would undermine the gains they had made for Indian social institutions under segregation and perhaps also damage their own "opportunities and privileges" with white-supremacist politicians in the county and state. To these town Indians, citizenship went hand-in-hand with an accommodation of white supremacy. But the gathering at the Longhouse saw recognition—and the name "Lumbee"—as an explicit rejection of Jim Crow.

Seeing that he would get little support from town Indians, Revels went back to Congress. "All of our people are willing to take the name of Lumbee Indians," Revels wrote to the Senate; he also attached a list of 4,500 names of Indians they had recruited to sign on to their organization.[60] Senator Clyde R. Hoey responded positively and met with Revels and Original 22 member Lawrence Maynor in August 1950. Hoey pressed the Indian Office to support any Robeson County Indian legislation, and officials assured him they would. Hoey asked Revels and Maynor to work with Congressman Frank Ertel

Carlyle, a lawyer and Lumberton resident who represented Robeson County.[61] But Revels had difficulty getting his message heard. Hoey and Carlyle seemed slow to act on the legislation, and the OIA again refused to help them directly. Months after Revels's visit, D'Arcy McNickle sent a curt message to him: "I do not encourage you to come to Washington," McNickle wrote, "since we are in no position to help your people."[62] The "Lumbee" group, which had been energized by the desires of rural Indians for federal recognition, seemed to hit a dead end. Revels's appeals went unheard; Ralph and Will Brooks distanced themselves from the community; and in 1951 the Brooks Settlement closed the Longhouse, the social institution that had served as a physical and spiritual center for their cause.[63]

The apparent failure, however, of rural Indians' efforts to obtain recognition had little to do with their authenticity as Indians or their political strategy to obtain recognition. They approached both Congress and the OIA with a seemingly unified, democratically elected tribal representation, a documented membership, and strong anthropological evidence that they possessed "Indian blood." They also reached out to Indians from other tribes and portrayed their social and political institutions in terms that non-Indians could understand. Furthermore, they maintained and enhanced their internal identity markers. According to their previous experience under Collier's administration, these elements should have added up to a strong case for recognition, but Collier was gone and the Indian New Deal was over. Congress was effectively in charge of Indian Affairs by 1950, and its agenda revolved around termination of federal-tribal relationships and not tribal self-government.

As early as 1948, policy makers had returned to a pre–New Deal goal of assimilation for Indian policy. The Hoover Commission recommended the complete integration of Indians into modern American society and the diminishment of the OIA's intrusion into Indian life. Tribal governments and tribal sovereignty were merely a stage in Indians' "progress" toward full assimilation, according to the commission. When Dillon S. Myer became Indian commissioner in 1950, he avidly promoted federal withdrawal from Indian affairs and drew virulent criticism from both Indian and white activists. Although he resigned his post after only three years, Myer's policies encouraged Congress to pass Public Law 280, which provided for state jurisdiction over civil and criminal affairs on Indian reservations in California, Minnesota, Nebraska, Oregon, and Wisconsin. The law also allowed any other state to assume such jurisdiction by its own legislative action. Public Law 280 was one of several measures meant to end tribes' unique legal status within the United States and affirm the belief that federal trusteeship perpetuated Indian dependency and cultural "backwardness." Congressmen used words like "liberation" and "emancipation" to describe the termination policy, framing it in positive terms that drew support from "progressive" political conservatives and liberals alike.[64] As Robeson County Indians pushed for federal recognition, Congress pushed in precisely the opposite direction.

But Indians in Robeson County and elsewhere were not merely victims of termination policy. Rather, historian Kenneth Philp argues that activists turned aggressive assimilation pressure into a force for greater self-determination. Indeed, "termination" and "self-determination" were two sides of the same coin. Some of the components of termination policy had support within Indian communities; for example, everyone agreed that the Office of Indian Affairs (by then referred to as the Bureau of Indian Affairs) needed to end its paternalistic approach toward tribes. Many Indians had opposed the IRA's heavy-handed approach to tribal organization and for that reason supported a background role for the OIA in tribal affairs. In Robeson County, members of the Original 22's council would have supported termination's principle of greater autonomy. On the other hand, town Indians, like Ira Pate Lowry and D. F. Lowry, surely approved the legislation's intent to make Indians self-supporting individuals ready for inclusion in mainstream American society. Many Indian activists opposed the legislation's goal of liquidating tribal resources and the long-standing political relationship between tribes and the federal government. Robeson County Indians had little stake in that fight, however, since they had no land in trust, and IRA recognition had not incorporated them into the reservation system. But their quest for recognition in a climate of termination added another layer to the variety of Indian responses to termination policy. Philp argues that this variety "marked the beginning of a Native American movement for increased self-determination that would reverberate throughout the twentieth century."[65]

Robeson County Indians' experience of termination policy—and the ambiguous recognition it prompted—spoke especially to Indians all over the East, whose historical circumstances put them in a similarly ambiguous position relative to the federal government and American society in general. Even as termination threatened to disempower Indian tribes, the fight against it empowered Indians as citizens, both of their tribal nations and the American nation. In the termination era, American identity proved to be a double-edged sword for Native Americans all over the country, just as Robeson County Indians' embrace of segregation had been. Adapting to segregation allowed Indians to control their social organization, while it conceded whites' authority to govern race relations; similarly, adopting an American identity offered a different kind of political voice to Indians, even as it seized an instrument of their legal sovereignty.

Robeson County Indians used a congressional lobbying strategy in their battle against termination and for recognition; both Siouans and Cherokees had pursued this avenue in the 1930s. Congressional favors were critical to achieving federal recognition, and compared to their town Indian counterparts, rural Indians had little success in cultivating support from the local, state, and congressional politicians who could push recognition through. Town leaders, having openly distanced themselves from rural Indians' efforts in 1949, seized this moment of impasse to exert their influence on federal recognition. They cast the struggle in terms that their white contacts appreciated and understood. D. F. Lowry, founder of Pembroke's First Methodist Church and member of the Board of Trustees at the Indian Normal School, gathered a group of Indian ministers together, including members of the Fourth Street Power Structure, to consider the question of tribal recognition. Calling themselves the Lumbee Brotherhood, they advocated abandoning the Cherokee designation, for which some of them had fought so hard in the 1930s, in favor of the Lumbee name.[66]

"Cherokee," which in 1913 and 1933 had served white supremacy so well, no longer seemed useful to the tribe's political relationship with whites. That name no longer appealed to the group because Robeson County Indians' ancestors "had attained a much higher degree of civilization when found by the white men than had the Cherokees whose name they . . . erroneously bear," Lumbee Brotherhood leaders told a newspaper. They explained that they no longer wanted to project an image of a "traditional" Indian community. Town Indians, especially the business, educational, and religious leaders who constituted the Fourth Street Power Structure in Pembroke, had demonstrated their "progressive" credentials and assimilationist values in the previous decades. "The stated purpose of the [name]," continued the newspaper reporter, was to "restore the members of the tribe to the status of wholly free American citizens"—to liberate them, in other words, from their second-class status.[67]

On the surface, these concepts of freedom sounded like those advocated by Lindsay Revels and the rural Indians, who themselves desired an end to segregation and their marginalization from the southern economy. Lumbee, in contrast to Cherokee, represented a new set of social, economic, and political opportunities for Indian people and sidestepped the objections of the Eastern Band of Cherokees to the use of their tribal name. Since tribal members descended from several different Indian communities rather than from a single group, an original, geographically derived name had the potential to represent everyone and reflect history more accurately. Revels, in fact, involved himself visibly in the activities of the Lumbee Brotherhood, implying his support of these goals.[68] Local Indian politics in Robeson County mirrored the braiding of "termination" and "self-determination" principles on a national level.

But despite the unifying potential of the name "Lumbee," leaders remained divided. For example, with the exception of Revels, none of the men who had negotiated with Congress and the OIA in the 1940s allied with the Lumbee Brotherhood, and nor did any members of the Original 22.[69] But the omission of rural Indian leaders did not necessarily mean that rural Indians distrusted the Lumbee name or the idea of recognition; they had pursued it themselves.[70] Rather, the exclusion of prominent rural leaders likely represented a conscious decision by the Lumbee Brotherhood to restrict those who spoke for the tribe. Town leaders made no secret of their disdain for Indians they considered "uneducated" and sought to prevent such Indians from negotiating with elected officials. They had, after all, succeeded in doing so seventeen years earlier when the Siouan bill came before the Senate.

Different ideas about "Indian blood" also divided town and rural leaders. The Lumbee Brotherhood had ideas about "Indian blood" that did not match the Original 22's acceptance of the OIA's criteria. Brotherhood leaders claimed that "Indians are not a mixed race," but they nevertheless appeared to cherish the Lost Colony's possible role in tribal history and did not deny multiracial ancestry. "Let's be what we are, Lumbee Indians, meaning an English and Indian mixture," said D. F. Lowry at a public meeting, while another faction of the Brotherhood refused to admit any white ancestry in the tribe.[71] Lowry and others denied that Indians were "mixed" while simultaneously claiming white ancestry. The mixture they eschewed was that with African Americans, not European Americans; their white ancestry had been accepted and even valued by the state of North Carolina and white-supremacist politicians.

The Original 22, in contrast, had embraced the OIA's notions of blood and mixed-blood, which privileged "Indian blood" and the cultural traits that supposedly accompanied it. This concept of blood not only divided the Robeson County Indian community; it also sustained white supremacy in federal Indian policy. Yet underneath these contradictory understandings of blood, Indians generally agreed that group membership revolved around genealogical relationships and blood's symbolic ability to divide insiders from outsiders. Both groups were equally invested in the community's core layers of identity, but they disagreed on how to portray their identity to outsiders. The Lumbee

Brotherhood's conscious exclusion of rural Indians in their recognition effort, in addition to the stark differences between the two groups regarding the portrayal of their Indian ancestry, led to a division among tribal members that was not about the name "Lumbee" per se but about how their identity should be affirmed and recognition acquired.[72]

Neither approach could satisfy non-Indians' identity definitions because those definitions were based on an inherently flawed relationship between blood and culture. Segregationists saw "white blood" as an asset for the same reason OIA officials saw "white blood" as a defect: greater percentages of "white blood" signaled a proportional loss of "Indian culture." For state officials in North Carolina, assimilation had been an avowed goal of their Indian policy since the 1880s, and the more "white blood" an Indian had, the more likely he was to assimilate to "white culture" and cast his votes for the Democratic Party and white supremacy. This association between blood and culture became a very good reason to grant Robeson County Indians state recognition and to help them obtain federal recognition. The OIA, however, treated percentages of "white blood" negatively and denied recognition to Indians whom anthropometry classified as racially mixed during the Indian New Deal.

Although the era of termination policy supposedly represented a reaction against the Indian New Deal, policy makers expressed a similar belief about blood and culture. This era's impulse toward assimilation made the presence of "white blood" in the Robeson County Indian community an even more compelling reason to treat them as fully assimilated Indians and deny them recognition. Federal Indian policy was thus justified on a local level by white supremacy and in an unexpected place—among Indians that had no reservation or collective political ties to the federal government. Whether Robeson County Indians performed assimilation (by claiming "part white blood") or performed primitivism (by claiming "full Indian blood"), the ambiguous position of Indians in the American polity hounded them. They could insist neither on assimilation nor on autonomy without remaining marginalized citizens.

Indian advocates for recognition continued to shape their portrayals of their identity in terms that resonated with *both* group members and outsiders. Assimilation remained a prominent theme, as did distinctiveness. This web of blood, culture, and Indian identity manifested itself in politics when the Lumbee Brotherhood made a bid for recognition in the North Carolina state legislature between 1951 and 1953 and in Congress between 1955 and 1956. In 1951 three town members of the Lumbee Brotherhood requested that Robeson County's state legislators assist them with a recognition bill in the General Assembly.[73] D. F. Lowry then called a meeting of the Brotherhood leadership to draft the bill, and state senator Wesley C. Watts introduced it in April 1951. The bill emphasized the cultural traits that Indians shared with whites and recalled the Lost Colony connection to demonstrate how European ancestry easily transmitted European culture.

Yet the bill also reminded readers of Indians' distinctiveness in appearance, their attachment to their homeland, and their kinship patterns; it cited a selection of family names that were unique to the Indian community. The bill only stipulated that the state recognize the Robeson County Indians as Lumbees and bestowed no other privileges on tribal members. They "shall continue to be subject to all the obligations and duties of citizens under the law."[74] Such a dual emphasis on assimilation and distinctiveness fit well within the constructs of white supremacy, and the bill did not threaten Indians' status as citizen taxpayers, voters, and laborers for the racial status quo. At the same time, it articulated the identity markers that Indians had carefully preserved—kinship and place—and others they had only recently begun to appreciate, such as appearance and "Indian blood."

In the summer of 1951, the state legislature passed a resolution calling for a vote of tribal members on the name, and the Lumbee Brotherhood began using every grassroots resource at its disposal to garner support for a vote.[75] The ballot offered two choices: "remain Cherokees of Robeson County" or "become Lumbee Indians of North Carolina."[76] Faced with these choices, Indians who favored neither name had no reason to vote. The Brotherhood arranged the voting in a way that respected Indians' social institutions, settlement affiliations, and traditional leadership patterns. The group established polling places at Indian schools around the county, and volunteer poll workers belonged to the local school committee. When D. F. Lowry traveled to nearly every Indian settlement to explain the referendum and the reason for the name change, he convened the meetings at Indian schools.[77] When Indians cast their votes, they approved the Lumbee name by a margin of 2,169 to 35.[78] While this landslide seems like an overwhelming endorsement of the Lumbee Brotherhood's agenda, in reality it represents the opposition's withdrawal from the debate. This action was typical in Native American politics. In many tribes, when the group could not reach a consensus—particularly during the tribal organization efforts of the Indian New Deal—the opposing faction withdrew from the debate rather than vote against the measure.[79] State legislators openly debated the legitimacy of the referendum vote, but they ultimately accepted it. On 20 April 1953, the state finally recognized the Indians of Robeson County as Lumbees.[80]

Riding this wave of success, the Lumbee Brotherhood took their cause to Congress in 1955 and worked with Congressman F. Ertel Carlyle, whom Lindsay Revels had initially contacted about recognition in the late 1940s. Carlyle was ready to listen in the 1950s, a reflection of D. F. Lowry's influence with politicians in Congress and of the increasing tensions around civil rights issues and termination.[81] In March 1955 Carlyle introduced the Lumbee bill, which was identical to that approved by the state. The bill asked for no particular benefits or services and affirmed Indians' status as citizens and their subjection to local, state, and national laws. The House Committee on Interior and Insular Affairs held a hearing on the bill during the summer of 1955.

Carlyle, who was a junior member of Congress and did not serve on the committee, made an introductory statement at the hearing. He reminded his fellow congressmen that "there is nothing in this bill that requests one penny of appropriation of any kind," surely a strong point for a termination-oriented committee suspicious of federal expenditures on Indian programs.[82] Carlyle went on to extol the "progressive" virtues of Robeson County Indians: "They have their own schools. They are interested . . . in their churches. . . . The Indians are good farmers. They are good merchants. They are interested in civic affairs."[83] This list affirmed that Indians themselves acquiesced to segregation and the values that southern society supposedly affirmed: progress, wealth, education, and religion. Congressman Wayne Aspinall, a senior Democrat from Colorado, wondered: "What benefit do they expect to get from this? Just purely the name 'Lumbee Indian Tribe' does not appea[r] to me to give too much importance to it, unless they expect to get some recognition later on as members of some authorized tribe. . . . [S]ome of them may have some Cherokee blood in their veins. They surely would not want to get rid of their relationship to the famous tribe of Cherokees in order to become members of another tribe."[84]

D. F. Lowry was the only Indian to testify at the House hearing, and he heartily echoed Carlyle's statements about Indians' values while also addressing Aspinall's concerns.[85] He described in detail the Lost Colony connection; Indians' military service since the American Revolution; and the other tribes from which Lumbees descended, including the Cherokee, Tuscarora, and Hatteras.[86] Establishing a legitimate tribal connection helped convince Lowry's audience that the tribe possessed "Indian blood," but he also disavowed the group's persistent connection to the Cherokees and explained the problems inherent in that name for the group's ability to affirm its identity. Indians who left the state were "embarrassed" by the name, according to Lowry, because everyone knew Cherokees but no one knew Robeson County Cherokees. After these encounters, people "did not believe anything" that Robeson County Indians said about their Indian identity. These painful experiences had led Indians to seek recognition under a new, original name that evoked their Indian ancestry but did not do so in a historically specific way. "If we get the name 'Lumbee' we can go to any school in the United States and tell them we are Lumbee Indians. . . . They could look us up and find we are in the law . . . and therefore we are honest in their sight," Lowry told the committee. "That is Number One" in the rationale behind federal recognition, Lowry insisted.[87] Lowry found that Indians' own markers of identity were insufficient to explain their heritage to outsiders who depended on tribal names to mark authenticity. A new name would solve this problem and satisfy non-Indians' criteria for Indian identity.

Lowry also attempted to cast the tribe's values in light of the "progressive" notions that Carlyle outlined, a strategy that appealed to those sympathetic with both segregation and termination. In response to Aspinall's question about a reservation and future benefits, Lowry declared that any members of his tribe who favored federal trust land were men who "[have] not got any land, and [do] not want to work for anything, and [think] the Government might give [them] a little." To emphasize his point, Lowry continued: "We would leave the county before we would come under a reservation or anything like wards of the Government. We are citizens and always have been citizens. We would leave before we would come on the reservation."[88] The statement that his followers would "leave the county" was tantamount to saying that they would abandon their identity as Indians and their kinship and place connections before they would ask for benefits from the federal government. This was an extreme statement, meant to show Congress the depth of his commitment to citizenship and his political differences from his kinsmen who had sought recognition and federal benefits from the OIA in the past. A clever and experienced politician, Lowry wanted to inspire support for his cause in the committee room and did not mind rhetorically eviscerating Lumbee supporters' connection to their community's social fabric. Lowry openly appealed to whites' political agendas in order to gain his desired outcome and claim his place in history. Carlyle's political inexperience and Lowry's influence obscured the agendas and concerns of Robeson County's rural Indians.

Lowry's rhetoric succeeded, however, and the committee voted in favor of the bill without amendment.[89]

Not surprisingly, the OIA had a different opinion of the bill. "We recommend that the bill be not enacted," wrote assistant secretary of the interior Orme Lewis, and he declared that Robeson County Indians had no treaty rights, however much "Indian blood" they might have: "We are . . . unable to recommend that the Congress take any action which might ultimately result in the imposition of additional obligations on the Federal Government or in placing additional persons of Indian blood under the jurisdiction of this Department." This stance was almost identical to the ones the OIA had taken in the early 1930s regarding the Cherokee and Siouan legislation. The OIA acknowledged the Indian identity of the group but refused to rule on the question of tribal affiliation, fearful that such a ruling would encourage Congress to recognize them and create additional administrative and financial burdens for the agency. If Congress enacted the bill, Lewis wrote, "it should be amended to indicate clearly that it does not make these persons eligible for services provided through the Bureau of Indian Affairs to other Indians."[90]

Since the House had done nothing to address the OIA's concerns, the Senate Committee on Interior and Insular Affairs amended the Lumbee bill to reflect both the termination policy and congressional politicians' goals. The committee carefully drafted additional wording for the bill: "Nothing in this act shall make such Indians eligible for any services performed by the United States for Indians because of their status as Indians, and none of the statutes of the United States which affect Indians because of their status as Indians shall be applicable to the Lumbee Indians."[91] With this clause, Congress granted the Robeson County Indians federal recognition and terminated this recognition at the same time. The OIA's objections justified this wording, but Congress crafted the clause to also uphold the "progressive" ideology articulated by Representative Carlyle and D. F. Lowry. The Senate and the House of Representatives passed the "Lumbee" bill in May 1956, and President Eisenhower signed it into law on 7 June of that year, granting the Indians of Robeson County some form of official, yet limited, federal acknowledgment.[92]

The key to this success was the bill's "nothing in this act" clause, which was not only consistent with the OIA's pre–New Deal policy on Robeson County Indians but also reflected its new agenda to terminate the federal government's responsibility to tribes. On the surface, Robeson County Indians represented the kind of tribe the federal government should not assist; their spokesman characterized them as assimilated citizens who were more interested in self-sufficiency than government "handouts." Termination policy and the Lumbee bill therefore presented a solution to the historic disagreement between the OIA and Congress about Indian identity and federal recognition. The OIA depended on intellectual and administrative criteria to authenticate a tribe's Indianness, while Congress relied on political favors granted to constituents. In the past, these different approaches resulted in the failure of legislative recognition for Robeson County Indians. But in 1956, both branches of government could fulfill their agendas by acknowledging the existence of an Indian tribe without actually granting services to that tribe. The Lumbee Brotherhood provided the federal government with a historic opportunity to reach a consensus by employing a political accommodation strategy that had worked well under segregation and also worked for federal Indian policy in the termination era: appealing to "progressive" values that appeased white supremacy and secured the community's distinct identity.

Reaction to the long-sought but Pyrrhic victory of recognition was muted in some parts of Robeson County. Lowry and the Lumbee Brotherhood had excluded rural Indians from the state process several years earlier. This group apparently had no motivation to fight the federal legislation and did not immediately vocalize their dissatisfaction with the Lumbee Act to outsiders. Rather, internal opposition to the Lumbee Act took another fifteen years to coalesce and ultimately took shape in the Tuscarora organizations that became active in the 1960s and 1970s. Federal recognition based on termination principles and "progressive" values did little to assist the rural Indians who needed help the most, and some of them began actively, yet quietly, organizing another approach to nation-building and sovereignty.

They returned to their time-honored strategy of exploring contacts in other Indian communities. A New York Tuscarora activist and spiritual leader named Wallace Mad Bear Anderson visited Robeson County in 1959 to gain support for an Indian unity organization he and other Six Nations members had formed. The organization was for "treaty" Indians, and Anderson knew that Robeson County Indians had not signed treaties with the United States, but he viewed sovereignty in other ways as well. Sovereignty did not only exist for tribes who had a treaty relationship to the U.S. government; tribes who never had such a relationship could also express sovereignty through their relationships to other Indian groups and to one another. Turkey Tayac had also expressed this view, and the Brooks Settlement sealed it with Tayac's marriage to one of their daughters. Anderson's connection to Robeson County Indians came from their shared Tuscarora ancestry. Anderson wanted to reunite with the Tuscarora who had remained in the South following the eighteenth-century Tuscarora War, and he apparently found some of his kins-men in Robeson County. During his visit, he helped to design and build a Longhouse and sweat lodge with Indians near the Prospect community, about twelve miles northwest of Pembroke.[93] Ten years later, compelled by the local tensions of school desegregation and the national activities of the American Indian Movement, this Longhouse community and their supporters emerged as the Eastern Carolina Tuscarora Indian Organization and engaged in a mili-tant legal struggle for civil rights, control over Indian schools, and federal benefits for the Original 22.[94]

Over time and under intense pressure from local authorities and the Fed-eral Bureau of Investigation, Tuscaroras also divided along ideological lines, but all maintained their opposition to the Lumbee name and to the act that denied them federal assistance. The name "Tuscarora" not only reclaimed a historic and seemingly authentic tribal connection but also served as an iden-tity boundary that distinguished the group from Lumbees, a useful political strategy to accomplish Tuscarora goals in the 1970s. One of the Tuscaroras' main accomplishments of that period was winning a federal lawsuit against the Department of the Interior in *Maynor v. Morton*. The plaintiffs included Lawrence Maynor, a member of the Original 22 who negotiated with the OIA in the late 1940s. In 1971 seven surviving members of the Original 22 petitioned the secretary of the interior to establish a reservation for them as promised under the Indian Reorganization Act. The Interior Department ruled that the Lumbee Act terminated any rights that the Original 22 pos-sessed as Indians because they lived in Robeson County. Maynor and the other survivors took the federal government to court, arguing that they were not Lumbees in 1938 when the OIA had recognized them and that the Lum-bee Act did not apply to Indians whom the government had recognized prior to the passage of the act. A judge agreed with the plaintiffs and determined that Congress was unaware of the Original 22 when it passed the Lumbee Act and did not intend to deprive these recognized Indians of their rights.[95]

Maynor v. Morton was an important legal victory for all Robeson County Indians, but it had a special significance for Tuscaroras who eschewed the Lumbee designation and favored a tribal history that they believed survived scrutiny by other Indian tribes and federal Indian law. The alliance between Tuscaroras and the Original 22 was logical. Many Tuscaroras were direct de-scendants of the Original 22 and not only shared kinship but also claimed affinity with rural Indians' emphasis on their core layers of identity and their rejection of segregationist values.[96] Since the 1920s, Tuscaroras and their an-cestors in Robeson County have pursued autonomy from southern society, not through a political process of federal recognition but through ostensibly more permanent legal channels, cultural awareness at the Longhouse, and persistent connections to other recognized Indians—particularly the Six Nations in New York, with whom some of them continue to associate. As anthropologist Gerald Sider has pointed out, "people and their ways of being are the roots of sovereignty," and such ways are "a fundamental challenge to the state and to state-shaped tribal forms of governance." Tuscaroras have found a route to sovereignty that makes relationships to the government secondary in their identity.[97]

In spite of Tuscaroras' challenges to the government's control over Indian identity, the acknowledgment process still keeps Native American identity criteria in the hands of federal officials in Congress and at the OIA. Government interests keep Indian identity at least partly rooted in political processes. The factionalism that stems from such processes is a constructive response to social and economic domination by non-Indians and generates new markers of identity that continue to affirm Indian communities' survival as a socially coherent, although not always politically cohesive, people. But state and federal governments remain invisible throughout these debates and refuse to acknowledge how their own internal disagreements aggravate Indian factionalism. The federal government, in particular, prompted tribal factionalism but then repeatedly used factionalism as an excuse not to recognize Indian people. Whether and how this cycle will end is unknown, but it affects both recognized and nonrecognized tribes all over the country. The government's power to shape Native American cultures and identities will continue to intrude on the sovereign ability of tribes to determine their own identity criteria, whether the United States recognizes that sovereignty or not.[98]

ACCOMMODATING WHITE-SUPREMACIST VALUES to gain federal recognition had consequences for local Indian politics. Just as segregation contributed to class formation by empowering some Indians at the expense of others, federal recognition was also a double-edged sword for Indian social and political relations. Although the amendment emerged from the termination policy and not from D. F. Lowry himself, Lowry's portrayal of his people's commitment to assimilation and citizenship provided its own unwitting consent to the ambiguous recognition embedded in the Lumbee Act. Lowry told the House of Representatives that the bill represented the will of all of his people and in that instant gained a reputation for securing the group's federal acknowledgment. But in reality, the Lumbee Act only expressed the identity markers and community goals of a few. Lowry's statements also contributed to the disempowerment of rural Indians who had little to gain from uphold-ing white supremacy and who wanted a sovereign relationship to the U.S. government that would enhance their situation in the Jim Crow South. The Lumbee Act did nothing to further this effort because the act's proponents objected to these goals.

Although Indians' internal political disagreements had a negative impact on this process, one cannot solely blame internal factionalism for the Lum-bee Act's failure to grant a meaningful federal acknowledgment. The fact that Congress and the OIA found a way to simultaneously grant and deny federal recognition demonstrated that the concept of acknowledgment itself rested on markers of Indian identity that primarily functioned to serve non-Indians' political and social interests. Acknowledgment did not rest on identity mark-ers indigenous to Indian communities. Of course, federal policy agendas had rested on non-Indian priorities for some time; what made the Lumbee Act significant—not just to Lumbees but to other Indians as well—was the way in which it encoded the ambiguity of American citizenship in the tradition of previous Indian legislation and of American identity itself. The Lumbee Act granted a recognized but inferior status. Previously, as in the allotment era, this ambiguity was a consequence of law, but not the law's intent. Termi-nation policy brought about a new opportunity to achieve the stratification of American society—not by accident, but by willfully incorporating groups like the Lumbees as inferiors. The Indian New Deal set the stage for this opportunity; in that period, Congress and OIA policy makers intentionally crafted tribal governments and the federal recognition process to force In-dian people to articulate a single political purpose and exclude the multiple goals that tribal members of different factions often promoted. The federal government developed recognition so that officials only had to listen to one tribal voice, but the government's own divisions meanwhile forced Indians to develop many strategies to protect their own interests. Federal acknowl-edgment therefore amounted to a large-scale manipulation of Indians' social and political organization that served to enhance the power of a few Indians while silencing many and aggravating internal distinctions.

However, Americans themselves cut short elites' attempts to shape soci-ety on hierarchical lines in the 1950s. Indians, African Americans, Latinos, Asian Americans, and whites recognized the potential of the nation's "civic nationalism" to promote self-determination. Their struggles against oppres-sion affirmed their identities as American citizens; they understood the civic nationalist creed and used it to end discrimination as they knew it. The New Deal's self-determination philosophy, though flawed by John Collier's own paternalistic assumptions about Indian identity, also prepared Indians to shape their own strategies—even those that included factional disagreements—to challenge incursions on their identities. For example, in the Lumbee Act's preamble, the Lumbee Brotherhood articulated the tribe's core layers of identity, kinship, and place connections even as they performed the identity markers that matched the priorities of politicians in Congress. The previous decades of negotiating congressional legislation, New Deal projects, and Indian Reorganization Act enrollment had proven that policy makers had little understanding of the criteria tribal members used to identify one another. Instead, government officials preferred to employ ideological, administrative, and scientific justifications that conformed to their worldview and catered to their political interests. These tactics eroded Indians' legal and cultural sovereignty, but Indians had also developed other layers of identity that functioned as tools of sovereignty as well. Robeson County Indians deployed their layers of identity—social institutions, a class structure, and a tribal political organization—to accommodate these interests and simultaneously affirm the group's identity to outsiders.

Creating a Lumbee and Tuscarora Future

Despite decades of political division, Indians in Robeson County worked together to cultivate their sovereignty on 18 January 1958 at Hayes Pond, near Maxton. That night, members of the Ku Klux Klan, arguably the nation's most dangerous organization, rallied there to "put Indians in their place, to end race-mixing," according to the group's leader, James W. "Catfish" Cole. "I am for segregation," Cole announced after his followers burned crosses on the lawns of two Indian families he had accused of violating segregation's boundaries. Cole's attacks in the local media referenced Indian women's supposedly "loose morals," and he threatened an Indian woman who was dating a white man in the Robeson County town of St. Pauls.

The cross burnings had incensed Indians. Even the Robeson County sheriff tried to dissuade Cole from holding the gathering; he said that Indians had threatened to kill Cole if he spoke at the rally. But Cole secured a place for the event near Maxton, whose white residents twenty years earlier had protested the Farm Security Administration's resettlement project for Indians. Klan members arrived at their rally well armed, but 500 better-armed Indian men, plus fifty women, quickly outnumbered them.[1]

Ms. Willa Robinson, a community activist in Robeson County, grew up in Maxton. Her grandparents raised her in a house with plank floors that had such big cracks "we'd call it air-conditioned in the wintertime," she joked. Ms. Willa admired her grandmother immensely: "She always told me, 'Don't ever let anybody make you feel inferior . . . because they can't do it without your consent.'" Her family had a long history with the Klan. "She used to have to sit on the porch at night with the gun to protect my grandfather from the Ku Klux Klan because he was black," Ms. Willa told me. Her grandmother was white. "They wouldn't bother her," she said. "But they wanted him. And they'd tell her, 'Why are you always sitting on the porch? We came after Emanuel. We don't want you.' She'd tell them, 'Well, you have to come by me first.' Then one got smart and says, 'You can't kill us all.' She said, 'No, but I got two shells in this double-barrel shotgun, and at least two of them will be down when it's over.'"

With this kind of resistance to white supremacy, it's no wonder that African Americans helped Lumbees and Tuscaroras learn the setup of the Klan rally in Maxton. Ms. Willa told me that blacks who were employed with Klan members and knew a great deal about the organization's activities passed information to Indians and helped coordinate the effort.[2] The rally was well publicized, but clearly local whites knew better than to get in a fight with Indians: most of the county's Klan members stayed home, and the fifty Klan members, women, and children at the rally were part of Cole's following from South Carolina. "I really believed that [Indians] were going to kill someone [that night]," remembered Clyde Chavis, one of the Indians at Hayes Pond.[3]

Klansmen circled their cars in the center of the field and set up a small generator with a PA system and a lightbulb. As Cole began to speak, he must have feared that the sheriff's prediction would come true. Sanford Locklear, a farmer from the Prospect community, shot the lightbulb next to Cole with his rifle, and his brother-in-law Neil Lowry wrestled a Klansman's gun from his hands. A deafening roar emanated from the Indian crowd; Indians began firing shots. Ned Sampson, one of the first Indians to arrive at the site, remembered the chaos after Locklear had shot out the light—flashes from photographers' cameras, sparks from rifles and handguns. Then he saw people lying on the ground. "I didn't know if they were dead or not. When the flashes were going, I was thinking there were 40 to 50 people dead out there."

Cole took off running into the swamps. His panicked followers dropped their guns, jumped in their cars and drove in all directions, some straight into the ditches that surrounded the field. Abandoned by her husband, Cole's wife Carolyn drove her own car into a ditch; Lumbee men helped pull her out. Miraculously, no one was seriously injured. Sampson was relieved to see that the people he thought were dead "got up and started leaving." "I am still puzzled that no one got killed," said Pauline Locklear, one of the women who confronted the Klan.[4]

Along with Charlie Warriax, Simeon Oxendine—a Hell's Angels veteran, business owner, and the son of Pembroke's mayor—gathered up the Klan's banner, carried it back to Pembroke, and burned Catfish Cole in effigy. Cole himself took two days to come out of his hiding place, and the Klan has never again held a public gathering in Robeson County. I asked Ms. Willa how the black community felt after the Klan scattered, and she simply said, "We loved it. We loved it."[5] Was this a revival of the multiracial coalition organized by Henry Berry Lowry during Reconstruction? Perhaps, but Ms. Willa's own family history demonstrated that blacks surely had their own reasons for resisting the Klan; they did not simply want to help Lumbees who had, since Reconstruction, avoided helping them.

Many whites breathed a sigh of relief. Maxton's police chief had requested the FBI's presence at the rally, saying, "We do not approve of the Klan and would like to discourage its activity as much as possible." North Carolina governor Luther Hodges wanted to make sure the state knew who to blame for the violence that night. In a press release, he stated, "The responsibility for the Maxton incident rests squarely on the irresponsible and misguided men who call themselves leaders of the KKK."[6] Clearly, the authorities at the state and local level wanted no public association with the Klan's terrorist tactics; their stance seemed to uphold the civil rights of Indians and other nonwhites. But these same men did not embrace school integration. In Robeson County, as in much of the South, full integration did not occur until almost twenty years later.[7] It was one thing to denounce a group like the Klan, whose tactics were so overtly violent, but another to embrace the end of a system—a way of life and a way of knowing—that had upheld white privilege for decades.

Of course, that system had existed alongside "race-mixing." As Lumbee writer Lew Barton scoffed, "[T]he Klansmen did not realize that they were some 371 years too late. . . . [S]ome of the same Indians already had hazel eyes and auburn hair when first discovered . . . on Roanoke Island, North Carolina, in 1584."[8] Barton, and Ms. Willa's grandmother, exposed the lie in segregation: "race-mixing" had occurred for centuries and among all peoples in the South; the Klan was powerless to stop it, nor perhaps did they really want to. After all, it had not significantly diminished white power, but it was a convenient excuse to remind Indians and blacks that their place in the racial hierarchy was politically and socially immovable, regardless of how much "white blood" flowed in their veins. But on that cold night at Hayes Pond, Indians, with help from African Americans, threw that discourse on the trash heap of history.

As a Lumbee and a historian, I now plunder that trash heap to understand how a People can divide and yet remain intact. That night in 1958, the Indians of Robeson County came together; town and rural Indians, "Cherokees,"

"Siouans," "Lumbees," "Tuscaroras"—all were the same People. I first heard the story of the Klan battle when I was a young child, maybe six or seven years old. Simeon Oxendine is my cousin on my dad's side, and like most of my dad's male cousins, we called him "Uncle." Uncle Sim told me and my little brother the story at his home one night in his backyard, dim lights illuminating his face. My own memory of the story is hazy; I mostly remember the darkness, the golden light and shadows on Uncle Sim's face, and being terribly impressed by his courage and that of all my People. That was undoubtedly the impression he intended to convey and what a Lumbee child needed to know: the role of her People as a whole in securing her freedom from fear.

A People can encompass different names, bloods, residences, and ideologies; a People need not be biologically or culturally homogeneous. A People can become a nation when it exercises self-determination, when it engages its members' identities to create change in their society. For the Lumbee and Tuscarora People, politics was the engine of change, and their political engagement, both internally and externally, formed their nation. "It is our desire and ambition to be called a nation," Ralph "Pikey" Brooks told Senator Clyde Hoey in 1948. Brooks wanted others to recognize his People as an Indigenous nation, but Hoey likely had no idea what this meant. From what he knew of the "best blood" Indians in Robeson County, they already belonged to a nation—the United States—and the idea that they could form a distinct nation within a nation must have seemed impractical at best and threatening at worst. Indeed, the 1956 Lumbee Act did not succeed in affirming that nationhood status, and Brooks's challenge to Hoey still eludes the Indians in Robeson County. In this context of competing definitions of Indian identity, defining a People is so capricious that hearing stories and having conversations are sometimes the only consistent methods by which we can gain understanding. Such is the power of historical narrative; this is why I have argued that identity formation is best understood as a conversation between insiders and outsiders, something that changes and shifts over time.

But the fact that government officials did not recognize them as a nation did not prevent Indians in Robeson County from becoming a nation. Nationhood and its attendant claim of sovereignty do not depend solely on outsiders' recognition of identity; insiders' perpetual maintenance of an identity is also a critical component. Lumbee attorney Arlinda Locklear linked self-determination, nationhood, and identity for me when I interviewed her about her career. She has fought the battle for Lumbee recognition since

1983, but she was also the first Native American woman to appear before the Supreme Court; she presented oral arguments to the Court twice, and she won both times.[9] She told me that the right to nationhood comes from the People's exercise of sovereignty. "We have always been independent and self-determining communities," she said. "[Sovereignty is] not bestowed by government. . . . You really begin to understand it when you start working with non–federally recognized tribes. Because that's when you start to see that the exercise of [sovereignty] is independent of the federal government. That's where you see self-determination in its purest form."[10] Between Reconstruction and the civil rights movement, Indians practiced self-determination through affirming their identity. They strategically embraced aspects of Jim Crow that upheld perceptions of their "Indian blood," they furthered their economic autonomy, and they fostered a centralized government. Indians gained and lost in this process, and they did not achieve all of their goals. Their internal conflicts, adaptations, and petitions for assistance from outside forces represented an investment in their nationhood; they nurtured their sovereignty by trying to improve their situation. They did not always work together, but sometimes they did.

This American nation is home to other Indigenous nations that were formed around different values and strategies and under different circumstances than the American nation. If we are to understand or define the American people, we must also understand the Native peoples whose nations share the land. For Native history is linked in the most intimate ways with that of America—the land, the people, and the nation. They are linked by kinship, culture, and economy, but also by race, class, gender, and inequality. Whether the inequalities tied to citizenship in the American nation can be rectified depends largely on how we know ourselves and each other. Do we wrestle with categories of knowledge that are different from our own and assign them equal standing with our own categories? Or do we decide that some categories are more real, truthful, or scientific than others?

Obvious examples of the latter tendency populate this book, such as the misuses of modernism (like anthropometry, eugenics, or blood quantum) or the reinscription of white supremacy onto economic aid for the poor and nonwhite. Choosing that route had consequences for policy making and generated patent inequities, such as the double standards that the Office of Indian Affairs applied to tribes and the very different attitudes about Indian identity that Congress and the OIA implemented. Factionalism among Robeson County Indians stemmed directly from the hierarchies of knowledge adopted by both white-supremacist politicians and "progressive" bureaucrats. Those factions prompted the confusion over names; that confusion has character-ized the group's identity in the minds of many outsiders.

The role of the state in Native American identity formation demonstrates that Indian identity is partly derived from a political struggle against an out-side force that seems to unify the group while repressing the less influential within it. The development of the 1956 Lumbee Act showed how Indians could seem unified but in fact were not; Indians downplayed internal ten-sions and inequalities in order to mount a more-effective campaign for rec-ognition. Such a process describes nation formation in general, according to historian George Lipsitz. "The very existence of nation-states encourages cessation of internal hostilities in order to face outside foes," Lipsitz writes. "It justifies national inequalities and injustices while projecting anger and resentment against outside enemies."[11] The experiences of Robeson County Indians reflect this critique of nationalism, and those experiences helped make a People into a nation.[12] Like the American nation, the Lumbee nation has consistently struggled to achieve consent from all its members.

But factionalism was also a product of Indians' attempts to creatively com-bat outsiders' hierarchies of knowledge and place their own ways of knowing alongside them. Robeson County Indian kinship systems and relationships to place were decentralized and leadership readily contested even before the period we discuss here. Such governance may not have looked like governance to U.S. officials, but it made sense to Indians, who nevertheless also adapted their ways to the preferences of outsiders. Sometimes adaptation aggravated divisions, as it did with the Original 22; but sometimes it quelled them, as in the case of the Pembroke Farms pageant, "The Life-Story of a People." These instances involved primarily the easily fractured political layers of identity. At other times, especially the Lowry War and the Battle of Maxton, Indians unified to uphold their fundamental markers of identity as Indians, even as they expressed aspects of their southernness and Americanness.

Town and rural Indians, who had so many reasons to politically disagree in the aftermath of the Lumbee Act, found a greater reason to unify in the face of the Klan's attempts to intimidate them. No one person claimed to organize the resistance. Rather, there was a widespread feeling among Lumbee men that they ought to teach the Klan a lesson and show the world that whites could not take away their "place" in southern society; they and their people were Indians, not "Negroes," and even the Klan could not threaten their iden-tity. Furthermore, Indian men were bound to protect "their" women from Cole's insults, just as white men preached that the foundation of segregation was the protection of white women.[13] On the one hand, the routing of the Klan represented a rejection of "blackness" and an appeal to "whiteness," but much deeper manifestations of identity were working that night in 1958. Protecting their identity was no idle pastime for Indians in Robeson County. The fact that no serious injuries resulted from the incident was due partly to restraint and partly to happenstance. When pushed, Indians were willing to kill and even die to preserve their Indianness.

Yet the question of "race," and how Indians dealt with that category as a marker of identity, still lingers. It appears that Indians used race as a marker of difference strategically—to affirm their identity in the presence of white supremacists—while at other times and in private places, they discarded ideas about the racial hierarchy. Yet such actions were not consistent across the group and over time, so I am left to offer speculations and educated guesses about the relationship between race and identity.

Race is a fundamental concern for all Americans, and the contradictory ways in which the category has affected Native Americans reveal the concept's instability. The Lumbee and Tuscarora story shows that racial mixing defines identity less than what people and societies do with their multiple cultural, genetic, and political heritages. Identity is a practice that shifts over time to meet different needs, and it is constructed in layers so that a People can maintain some fundamental direction as it changes. We know that there are American identities based on race, ethnicity, gender, or class, but we seem less familiar with the notion that those categories are not, in fact, fixed concepts but have changed radically over time. The ways in which Indians in Robeson County have manipulated race, and the ways that race has been used against them, demonstrate that the concept is a social fiction that has exclusion and inequality at its core.

The Battle of Maxton also represented a positive affirmation of the fundamental layers of identity—kinship and settlement—that had persisted throughout the political turmoil of the previous decades. Indians' values of family and complementary gender roles called on men to protect their families when threatened by outsiders. The resistance tactics honored Indians' kinship with the Lowry gang's Reconstruction-era battles with white soldiers, police, politicians, and Klansmen. Henry Berry Lowry's nephews and great-nephews participated in the Klan routing as well.[14] In light of the recent passage of the Lumbee Act, the incident also had a political overtone. The Klan routing symbolized a collective yet decentralized action that helped to distinguish Lumbees from their black and white neighbors and allowed them to stand out among other Indian tribes in the national press.[15] Their action formed an identity boundary that marked Lumbees as a coherent people and also affirmed the effectiveness of their decentralized style of leadership.

The Klan rout demonstrated how the tribe preserved its internal identity markers, apart from those that non-Indians valued. Self-government is one of those markers, even when it does not mirror a nation-state. Arlinda Locklear described Robeson County Indian government as "aboriginal" in its form. "Our government had more or less been issue driven," she said, and Indian people have not recognized a single overarching leader or group of leaders who were authorized to speak on behalf of the community. In fact, Locklear argued, "non–federally recognized tribes have managed to hold onto . . . more of the aboriginal self-expression than the recognized tribes [have]. [O]nce you adapt to that recognition, your form of government becomes . . . more akin to what the outside world" views as legitimate.[16]

But despite their ability to preserve identity without outside acknowledgment, Lumbees persist in their quest for federal recognition. Since the 1970s, Lumbees have tried to redress the 1956 Lumbee Act and gain full recognition. In 1991 the Office of Indian Affairs (now the Bureau of Indian Affairs [BIA]) suggested that their efforts might be more successful if they created a constitution, a governing document to reinforce their claims on political cohesiveness.[17] "The year that our people adopted a tribal constitution was one of the most beautiful things I've ever seen," Locklear said. "And it was the purest exercise of self-determination I've ever experienced; it was just a glorious thing to watch." Locklear was one of the technical advisers during the process. She described an organic community effort whereby thirty-five Lumbee churches appointed permanent delegates to a constitutional convention that, over the course of two years, held "meetings in churches and in communities in Lumbee territory." The delegates were "working as a unit for the single goal of putting on paper the expression of the Lumbee people's desire for governance," according to Locklear. In 1994 over 9,000 Indians voted to adopt the Lumbee Constitution. Locklear described the constitution as written by a cohesive People working together for the community's future. But over the next few years, mistrust developed, and the Lumbee Regional Development Association (LRDA)—a private, nonprofit organization run by Lumbees—challenged the constitution; the group operating as the Lumbee tribal government sued the LRDA. A state judge threw out the constitution, and the Lumbees engaged in a new process to write one. Nevertheless, the new constitution is "80 to 85 percent that [old] document," Locklear said.[18]

Naturally, that constitution dictates who belongs to the group. An individual may enroll in the tribe if he or she can prove descent from someone listed as "Indian" on one or more of thirteen source documents, all of which date to around 1900. The individual also must demonstrate a continuous affiliation with the home territory of Robeson and adjoining counties. There is no specific blood quantum requirement today, nor did the source documents record blood quantum. These enrollment criteria require an applicant to demonstrate some verifiable link with the tribe, but they also allow for the flexibility inherent in genealogical systems of kinship.[19]

Every so often, tribal members have to reregister with the enrollment office in Pembroke. In 2001, intending to reregister, I walked into the office without my membership card but with my father and brother, who had their documentation. At first the enrollment officer told me she couldn't find my genealogy chart and suggested that I didn't have one, even though my father and brother had charts. We politely asked her to look again. Sure enough, a few minutes later, she emerged with my chart, her demeanor transformed from slightly hostile to very friendly. "Look at this," she said, pointing to the series of numbers and letters—a code—that were printed underneath each of my ancestor's names. She explained that the code linked each name to someone identified as Indian on the 1900 or 1910 census. There were thirty names on the chart, and every one had a code—with the exception of my grandmothers, who were Lumbee but born after 1910. The enrollment officer handed the chart to me. Smiling, she said in her classic Lumbee accent, "Honey, now that's as full-blooded as you can get."

It seems that Lumbees have fully embraced the modern, bureaucratic, regulated state and its attending notions of individualistic citizenship when a series of numbers and letters makes me a "full-blood"; a moment earlier I might have been escorted out of the office, but suddenly I was told I belonged. The enrollment process seems arbitrary, a means of confronting the BIA's categories of knowledge but replicating them at the same time. Of course, it's not surprising that I had this encounter in the tribal enrollment office. That location is ground zero for the tribal government's maintenance of identity boundaries; enrollment officers determine the legitimacy of those who identify as Lumbee to fulfill requirements set forth by the Lumbee Constitution, but they are influenced by federal government ideas about who the "real Indians" are. When I recognized the situation I was in, the enrollment process suddenly appeared strategic and systematic. A nation that is in a subordinate relationship to another larger, more powerful nation would express itself this way.

When I asked her how the Lumbee People are adjusting to this new form of self-government, Arlinda Locklear outlined the compromises inherent in pursuing federal acknowledgment.

> I think we're going through a transition period. I think federal recognition will force [the decentralized model of leadership] to change, because by virtue of being recognized, the outside world will expect to look to one person, or one set of leadership for all issues. . . . [On] a lot of reservations that have IRA constitutions, they have basically two forms of government. They've got an IRA government and they have a more traditional form that operates under the radar screen. Now that may happen [with the] Lumbee too. We may continue with our historically diffused form of leadership that's not necessarily reflected in the elected leadership of the tribal government, but nevertheless has significant internal authority. But . . . the outside world [will look to] that tribal government.

The consequences of a division between a "diffuse" style of leadership and the more centralized style written in the Lumbee Constitution disturbs Locklear. Some tribes, such as her client the Oneida Indian Nation of Wisconsin, do not face this problem. "They have an IRA constitution, but I think . . . the reason it works so well there is because the real legitimacy of their IRA government comes from the fact that the people who are in it have been their traditional leaders. It's like the traditional form of government has just taken [the IRA government] over, . . . but it's recognizable because of the individuals and the families involved. We [Lumbees] have allowed people who would not have otherwise been considered leaders in our community to take over tribal government."[20] This reality continues to alienate Lumbees and Tuscaroras, many of whom feel disconnected from tribal government and left without adequate services or representation.

Perhaps there is a way out of this bitterness, a path that has been suggested by other scholars.[21] The United States needs a workable definition of "Indian" that can be implemented in public policy and law, and Americans also need a way of knowing about Indians that is accountable to Indian people. When Congress, the Indian Office, state governments, tribes, and the academy all promote different definitions, no single definition of the term "Indian" suits everyone. A truly workable definition, however, would have to begin with understandings of identity that Native people themselves assemble, based on their histories, languages, and lands. Such a process represents the kind of self-determination Arlinda Locklear witnessed in the writing of the first Lumbee Constitution. While reservation tribes have long been part of this discussion, nonrecognized tribes need to find answers to these questions as well.

At Hayes Pond, Indians nurtured their nation and preserved their identity. That preservation activity itself constituted a political identity, and that identity did not rest with the approval of the state of North Carolina, the Office of Indian Affairs, or Congress. Indians only embraced the idea of a "tribe" with a single name and a central government when external forces demanded they conform to those identity definitions in order to affirm their Indianness. These definitions often challenged Robeson County Indians' core layers of identity and their institutional expressions. These definitions furthermore aggravated tribal divisions as Indians negotiated with non-Indians' concepts of their identity. As the Klan defeat demonstrated, affirmation of Indian identity in Robeson County did not necessarily require allegiance to a common government but rather allegiance to a common purpose. That purpose was the preservation of the People's own identity, their cultural priorities, their ways of being together, and the tradition and history they wanted to pass down to future generations. In spite of their leaders' political and historical disagreements with one another, both Lumbees and Tuscaroras had an intense desire to teach their children the value of their Indian identity and the life lessons transmitted by that identity. Federal recognition, they believed, affirmed this desire and helped support it, but the education of their children—the transmission of their birthright—continued with and without formal acknowledgment from the United States.

But without recognition, Robeson County Indians have few avenues to protect the literal bedrock of their identity: the land. Without a recognized and protected land base, they lose an important aspect of their definition as separate from other Indian people and from non-Indians. As Indian agent Fred Baker observed in 1935, Indians felt a keen sense of fear that they were losing their land; they recognized that this aspect of their identity was fragile and needed protection. Even town Indians, many of whom continued to farm and had parents who lived in rural communities and ancestors who were buried there, believed in the importance of a homeplace for their People. That homeplace had been relatively secured by Indian land ownership in the nineteenth century and by European avoidance in the eighteenth century. But in the twentieth century, federal recognition and Pembroke Farms provided a new avenue to securing their land base, an avenue that the economic disempowerment of segregation had blocked. As such, their desire to protect their identity through protecting their land bonded ideologically opposed members of the Indian community to the quest for federal recognition.

These attitudes about land are similar to those held by other Native American groups, even though Robeson County Indians do not bolster their attachment to home with treaties, with ancient stories about emergence places, or with religious rituals that pay homage to sacred sites. Although many tribes exhibit such evidence of their attachment to place and use that evidence to support land claims in U.S. courts, these markers do not wholly constitute these tribes' identification with their home places. As anthropologist Keith Basso has said of the Western Apache, for example, attachments to special places are kept alive by discussion, stories, and education, often in dialects and languages that outsiders do not understand and courts do not recognize.[22] Although contemporary Southeastern Indians appear to differ markedly from other Indian tribes, many supposed differences actually reveal similarities upon closer examination.

The history of Native Americans in the South can also find common ground with other Americans' experiences under segregation. Segregation was a widespread legal, social, economic, and political system designed to keep the races separate and the white race supreme. Historians have paid a great deal of attention to the emergence of the system in the late nineteenth century; they generally agree that the potential for a political coalition between poor white and black farmers in the 1890s raised the specter of "race-mixing" that energized white Democrats to enforce racial segregation in ways not previously tried.[23] Robeson County Indians' recognition as Croatans in 1885 was an early experiment in dividing the political coalitions that threatened white Democrats' power; in this case, Indian and black voters posed the threat. Democrats' scheme worked very well, and Native American identity became an important component to the Democrats' power in North Carolina throughout the Jim Crow era. The Mississippi Choctaws and Eastern Band of Cherokees also exchanged power with local politicians in similar ways.

While historians thoroughly analyzed the origins of segregation, they spent comparatively less time understanding the everyday workings of the system. As a result, students had only a minimal understanding of the nuances of oppression and resistance, and they perceived segregation as a dark valley between two heights of African American empowerment: Reconstruction and the civil rights movement. Gradually, this interpretation began to fade as scholars investigated black resistance, accommodation strategies, and leadership to uncover stories of persistence, hope, and abiding faith.[24] This book reveals similar themes but continues to widen historians' perspectives on segregation by discussing in detail how the system worked on a community that perpetuated an identity other than black or white.

Historians can also see Robeson County Indians' experiences in the light of some of the stories told by other southern citizens who occupied ambiguous spaces within the southern racial hierarchy—for example, Chinese, Jews, Mexicans, and mixed-race communities such as the so-called White Negroes of Mississippi.[25] Like the history of these groups, the history of how Robeson County Indians affirmed their identity points out the ways in which southern society constructed racial ancestry and class affiliation to benefit its privileged members. That history also highlights the element of choice in group membership and how individuals can creatively separate racial ancestry or class status from group identity—even against antimiscegenation laws, eugenics, and the other technologies of power that the state has deployed to prevent people from making such distinctions. Native Americans in the post-Removal South can therefore make an important impact on our historical discussion of how racial and ethnic identity is defined.

But unlike immigrant or so-called mulatto communities in the South, Lumbees' and Tuscaroras' identities incorporate a sense of place and a consciousness of their status as the continent's original sovereign nations. Their claims on a distinct identity therefore have more in common with other Indian tribes than with these racially "in-between" southern citizens. Indians' relationships to land beg questions about nationhood and sovereignty that do not apply to other southern citizens.

Our exalted names for our homeland (God's Country, the Holy Land) or our everyday names (Home-Home, or just Pembroke, Prospect, and even "on the swamp") only reveal so much about that bedrock element of Indian identity: land. The land's voice is a mere whisper, though its quietness is like that of my grandmother Lucy. When my father's family barned tobacco and tied it, grandmother Lucy set the work pace and, as my father said, "controlled you with kindness—she'd bring you iced tea and pat you on the head, but she did that to make sure you stayed on track, that you didn't hold anybody else up."[26] My family speaks of the land as our guide, our resource, our life. It is where our identity begins and ends.

Genealogy Charts

CHART 1. James Lowry Descendants

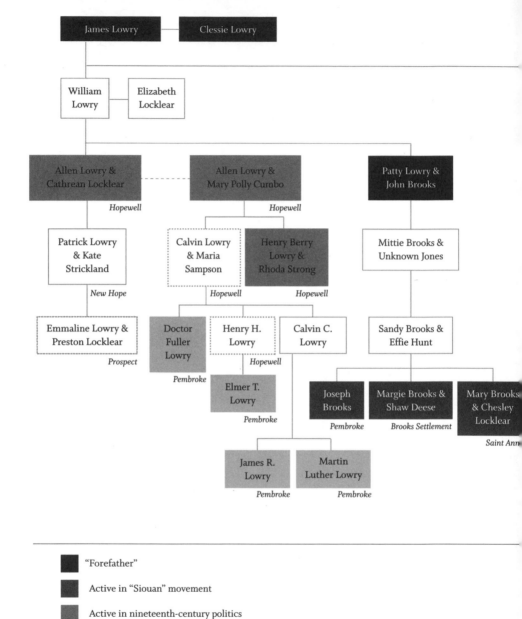

		Legend
■		"Forefather"
■		Active in "Siouan" movement
■		Active in nineteenth-century politics
■		Active in "Cherokee" movement
⬚		Nineteenth-century school/church leader
⬚		Active in Brooks Settlement Longhouse

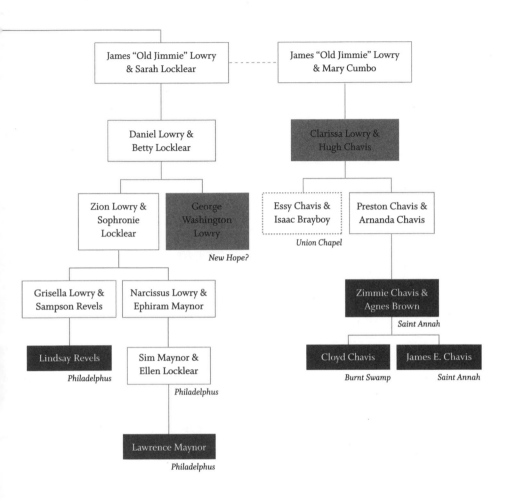

Sources: Carl C. Seltzer, "A Report on the Racial Status of Certain People in Robeson County, North Carolina," 30 June 1936 (RG 75, entry 616, box 13–15, North Carolina, National Archives and Records Administration, Washington, D.C.); James Cedric Woods, "Ethnohistory and Southeastern Non-Recognized Tribes: Connecting Families with Polities" (paper presented at the American Society for Ethnohistory Annual Meeting, 19 October 2001, Tucson, Ariz.); Lumber River Conference of the Holiness Methodist Church, *The History of the Lumbee Conference* (N.p.: Lumber River Conference of the Holiness Methodist Church, 2003); Julian T. Pierce, Cynthia Hunt-Locklear, Jack Campisi, and Wesley White, *The Lumbee Petition*, 3 vols. (Pembroke, N.C.: Lumbee River Legal Services, 1987); "Enrollment of Siouan Indians of Lumber River, North Carolina," 18 May 1935 (RG 75, entry 121, file no. 39490-1935-361 General Services, National Archives and Records Administration, Washington, D.C.); Rebecca S. Seib, *Settlement Pattern Study of the Indians of Robeson County, NC, 1735–1787* (Pembroke, N.C.: Lumbee Regional Development Association, 1983).

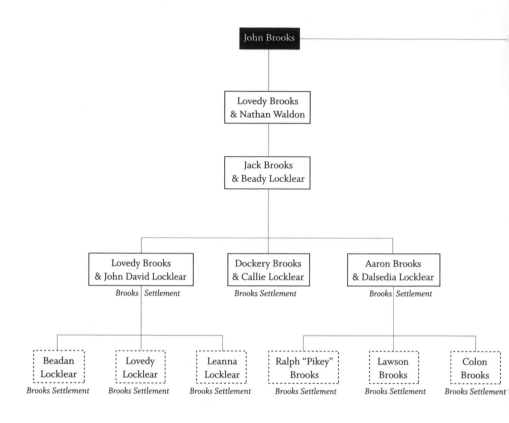

CHART 2. John Brooks Descendants

John Brooks

Lovedy Brooks
& Nathan Waldon

Jack Brooks
& Beady Locklear

Lovedy Brooks
& John David Locklear
Brooks | Settlement

Dockery Brooks
& Callie Locklear
Brooks Settlement

Aaron Brooks
& Dalsedia Locklear
Brooks | Settlement

Beadan
Locklear
Brooks Settlement

Lovedy
Locklear
Brooks Settlement

Leanna
Locklear
Brooks Settlement

Ralph "Pikey"
Brooks
Brooks Settlement

Lawson
Brooks
Brooks Settlement

Colon
Brooks
Brooks Settlement

"Forefather"

Active in "Siouan" movement

Active in nineteenth-century politics

Active in "Cherokee" movement

Nineteenth-century school/church leader

Active in Brooks Settlement Longhouse

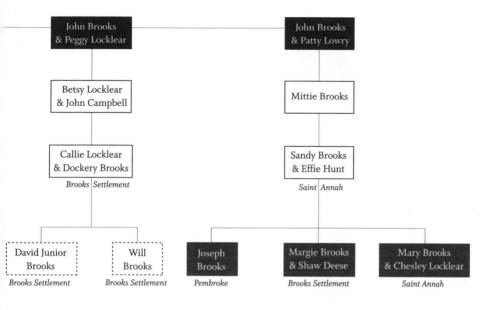

Source: Carl C. Seltzer, "A Report on the Racial Status of Certain People in Robeson County, North Carolina," 30 June 1936 (RG 75, entry 616, box 13–15, North Carolina, National Archives and Records Administration, Washington, D.C.).

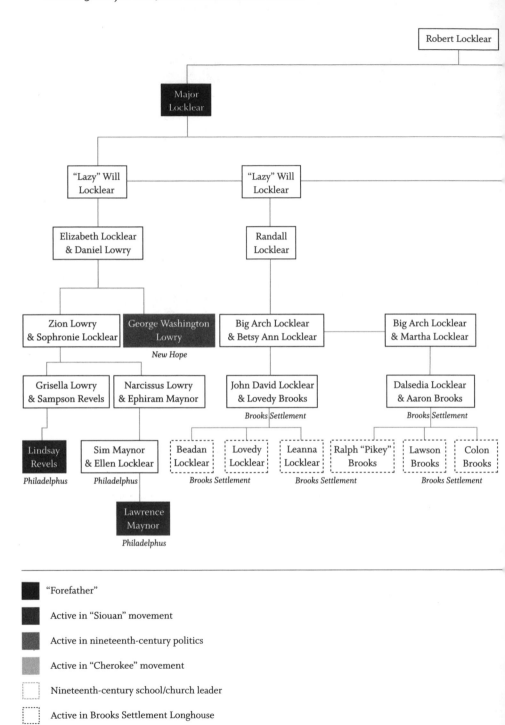

CHART 3. Major and John Locklear Descendants

Robert Locklear

Major Locklear

"Lazy" Will Locklear — "Lazy" Will Locklear

Elizabeth Locklear & Daniel Lowry

Randall Locklear

Zion Lowry & Sophronie Locklear

George Washington Lowry
New Hope

Big Arch Locklear & Betsy Ann Locklear

Big Arch Locklear & Martha Locklear

Grisella Lowry & Sampson Revels

Narcissus Lowry & Ephiram Maynor

John David Locklear & Lovedy Brooks
Brooks Settlement

Dalsedia Locklear & Aaron Brooks
Brooks Settlement

Lindsay Revels
Philadelphus

Sim Maynor & Ellen Locklear
Philadelphus

Beadan Locklear

Lovedy Locklear

Leanna Locklear
Brooks Settlement

Ralph "Pikey" Brooks
Brooks Settlement

Lawson Brooks

Colon Brooks
Brooks Settlement

Lawrence Maynor
Philadelphus

"Forefather"

Active in "Siouan" movement

Active in nineteenth-century politics

Active in "Cherokee" movement

Nineteenth-century school/church leader

Active in Brooks Settlement Longhouse

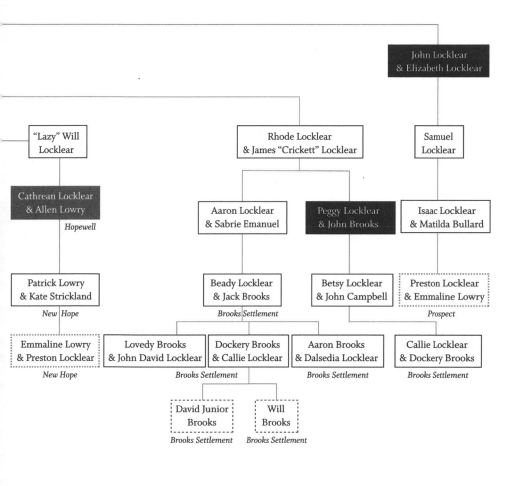

John Locklear
& Elizabeth Locklear

"Lazy" Will
Locklear

Rhode Locklear
& James "Crickett" Locklear

Samuel
Locklear

Cathrean Locklear
& Allen Lowry
Hopewell

Aaron Locklear
& Sabrie Emanuel

Peggy Locklear
& John Brooks

Isaac Locklear
& Matilda Bullard

Patrick Lowry
& Kate Strickland
New Hope

Beady Locklear
& Jack Brooks
Brooks Settlement

Betsy Locklear
& John Campbell

Preston Locklear
& Emmaline Lowry
Prospect

Emmaline Lowry
& Preston Locklear
New Hope

Lovedy Brooks
& John David Locklear

Dockery Brooks
& Callie Locklear
Brooks Settlement

Aaron Brooks
& Dalsedia Locklear
Brooks Settlement

Callie Locklear
& Dockery Brooks
Brooks Settlement

David Junior
Brooks
Brooks Settlement

Will
Brooks
Brooks Settlement

Sources: Carl C. Seltzer, "A Report on the Racial Status of Certain People in Robeson County, North Carolina," 30 June 1936 (RG 75, entry 616, box 13–15, North Carolina, National Archives and Records Administration, Washington, D.C.); Julian T. Pierce, Cynthia Hunt-Locklear, Jack Campisi, and Wesley White, *The Lumbee Petition*, 3 vols. (Pembroke, N.C.: Lumbee River Legal Services, 1987); "Enrollment of Siouan Indians of Lumber River, North Carolina," 18 May 1935 (RG 75, entry 121, file no. 39490-1935-361 General Services, National Archives and Records Administration, Washington, D.C.).

CHART 4. Charles Oxendine Descendants

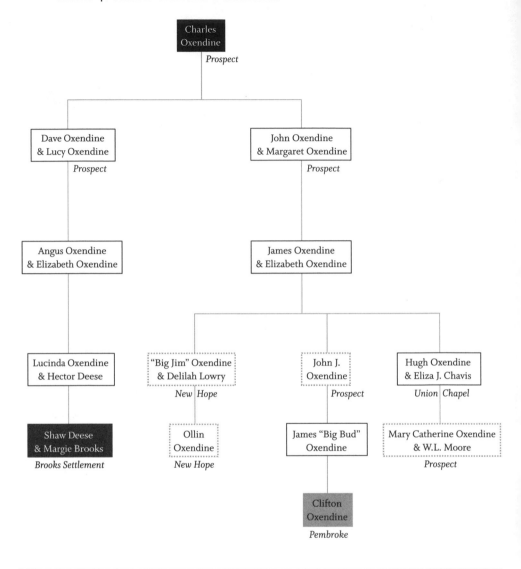

Charles Oxendine
Prospect

Dave Oxendine & Lucy Oxendine
Prospect

John Oxendine & Margaret Oxendine
Prospect

Angus Oxendine & Elizabeth Oxendine

James Oxendine & Elizabeth Oxendine

Lucinda Oxendine & Hector Deese

"Big Jim" Oxendine & Delilah Lowry
New Hope

John J. Oxendine
Prospect

Hugh Oxendine & Eliza J. Chavis
Union Chapel

Shaw Deese & Margie Brooks
Brooks Settlement

Ollin Oxendine
New Hope

James "Big Bud" Oxendine

Mary Catherine Oxendine & W.L. Moore
Prospect

Clifton Oxendine
Pembroke

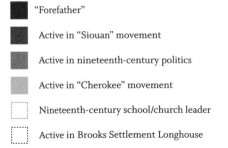

"Forefather"

Active in "Siouan" movement

Active in nineteenth-century politics

Active in "Cherokee" movement

Nineteenth-century school/church leader

Active in Brooks Settlement Longhouse

Sources: Carl C. Seltzer, "A Report on the Racial Status of Certain People in Robeson County, North Carolina," 30 June 1936 (RG 75, entry 616, box 13–15, North Carolina, National Archives and Records Administration, Washington, D.C.); Julian T. Pierce, Cynthia Hunt-Locklear, Jack Campisi, and Wesley White, *The Lumbee Petition*, 3 vols. (Pembroke, N.C.: Lumbee River Legal Services, 1987); Rebecca S. Seib, *Indians of Robeson County Land Ownership Study, 1900–1910* (Pembroke, N.C.: Lumbee Regional Development Association, n.d.).

CHART 5. Ishmael Chavis Descendants

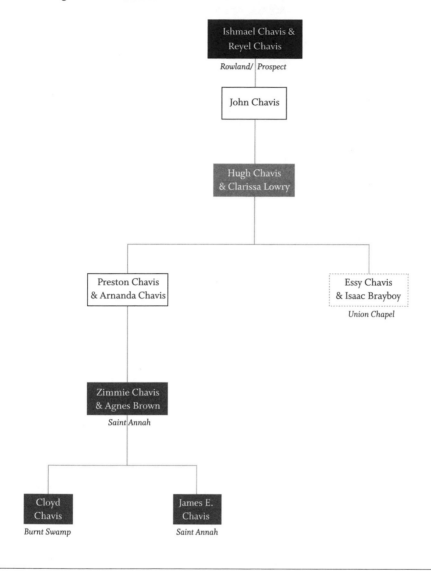

Ishmael Chavis &
Reyel Chavis

Rowland/ Prospect

John Chavis

Hugh Chavis
& Clarissa Lowry

Preston Chavis
& Arnanda Chavis

Essy Chavis
& Isaac Brayboy

Union Chapel

Zimmie Chavis
& Agnes Brown

Saint Annah

Cloyd
Chavis

Burnt Swamp

James E.
Chavis

Saint Annah

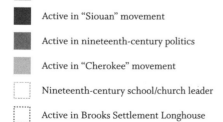

"Forefather"

Active in "Siouan" movement

Active in nineteenth-century politics

Active in "Cherokee" movement

Nineteenth-century school/church leader

Active in Brooks Settlement Longhouse

Sources: Julian T. Pierce, Cynthia Hunt-Locklear, Jack Campisi, and Wesley White, *The Lumbee Petition*, 3 vols. (Pembroke, N.C.: Lumbee River Legal Services, 1987); Rebecca S. Seib, *Settlement Pattern Study of the Indians of Robeson County, NC, 1735–1787* (Pembroke, N.C.: Lumbee Regional Development Association, 1983); Lumber River Conference of the Holiness Methodist Church, *The History of the Lumbee Conference* (N.p.: Lumber River Conference of the Holiness Methodist Church, 2003); Ed Chavis, interview with the author, Pembroke, N.C., 9 June 2004.

Notes

1. Though some Lumbees believe that Tuscaroras are marginal, and some Tuscaroras believe that the Lumbee have stolen their tribal heritage, both groups are interdependent, with their pasts, presents, and futures tightly linked by the historical process I describe here. When I feel that it will not distract the reader, I refer to "Lumbee" and "Tuscarora" when talking about contemporary Indian people; but sometimes, for the sake of simplicity, I just use "Lumbee" as a shorthand for talking about the whole group. When referring to Indian people in the past, prior to their recognition as "Lumbee," I use "Robeson County Indians" or "Indians in Robeson County"—a weak acknowledgment of their overarching existence as a people despite various tribal names. The term's weakness is largely due to the fact that the Indian community stretched beyond the Robeson County border to the adjoining counties of Hoke, Scotland, Bladen, Cumberland, and Columbus. Despite these different names and disparate locations, anthropologist Robert K. Thomas has concluded that Indians in Robeson and adjoining counties have thought of themselves as Indians since the eighteenth century. The basis for that identity was not only Indian ancestry but also a sense of "peoplehood" that they felt compelled to maintain. The origin of the Lumbee name as applied to Robeson County Indians will be discussed at length in chapter 7, but the origin of the Tuscarora name is also disputed; references to it in the documentary record are few and far between. Since "Tuscarora" only came into widespread use in the 1960s or 1970s (the decade is uncertain) and derived partly from events that are outside the scope of this book, I am not devoting the same attention to it here that I am to the name "Lumbee." However, I do occasionally use "Tuscarora" to describe Indians before the 1960s because the Tuscaroras who I have spoken to refer to their ancestors that way. Robert K. Thomas, "A Report on Research of Lumbee Origins" (unpublished typescript [1976?], North Carolina Collection, University of North Carolina at Chapel Hill), 40–42, 57–58, 60.

2. As historian Alexandra Harmon summarizes, "Too often Indians' history is written as if protagonists, authors, and readers have no reason to wonder who is Indian"; yet Indian people are burdened with defending their identity more often and more extensively than any other ethnic group in America. Alexandra Harmon, *Indians in the Making: Ethnic Relations and Indian Identities Around Puget Sound* (Berkeley: University of California Press, 1998), 3.

3. Fredrik Barth, "Introduction," in *Ethnic Groups and Boundaries: The Social Organization of Culture Difference*, ed. Fredrik Barth (London: George Allen & Unwin, 1969). For a summary of the "natural" categories on which Indian identity is based, see Russell Thornton, "Perspectives on Native American Identity," in *Studying Native America: Problems and Prospects*, ed. Russell Thornton (Madison: University of Wisconsin Press, 1998); and Joane Nagel, "American Indian Ethnic Renewal: Politics and the Resurgence of Identity," *American Sociological Review* 60 (December 1995): 947–65. Sociologists and legal historians who have questioned these categories are Angela Gonzales, "The (Re)Articulation of American Indian Identity: Maintaining Boundaries and Regulating Access to Ethnically Tied Resources," *American Indian Culture and Research Journal* 22 (1998), 199–225; Anne Merline McCulloch and David E. Wilkins, "'Constructing' Nations within States: The Quest for Federal Recognition by the Catawba and Lumbee Tribes," *American Indian Quarterly* 19 (Summer 1995): 361–87; M. Annette Jaimes, "Federal Indian Identification Policy: A Usurpation of Indigenous Sovereignty in North America," in *The State of Native*

America: Genocide, Colonization, and Resistance, ed. M. Annette Jaimes (Boston: South End Press, 1992), 123–38; C. Matthew Snipp, *American Indians: The First of This Land* (New York: Russell Sage, 1989), chap. 2; and James A. Clifton, "Alternate Identities and Cultural Frontiers," in *Being and Becoming Indian: Biographical Studies of North American Frontiers*, ed. James A. Clifton (Chicago: Dorsey Press, 1989), 11, 21–22. For treatments of American Indian history that encompass this view, see Harmon, *Indians in the Making*; Karen I. Blu, *The Lumbee Problem: The Making of an American Indian People* (New York: Cambridge University Press, 1980); Morris W. Foster, *Being Comanche: A Social History of an American Indian Community* (Tucson: University of Arizona Press, 1991); and Loretta Fowler, *Shared Symbols, Contested Meanings: Gros Ventre Culture and History, 1778–1984* (Ithaca, N.Y.: Cornell University Press, 1987). Recent work by C. S. Everett (Vanderbilt University) and Buck Woodard (College of William and Mary) concerns these trends in the sixteenth through eighteenth centuries.

4. Here I am discussing the role that blood quantum has played in scholars' discussions of Indians in the Southeast. Others have had a more nuanced view of "full-blood" and "mixed-blood" factions elsewhere in the United States. Interior Department solicitor Felix Cohen acknowledged in the 1930s that factions often had, in fact, little to do with blood quantum and more to do with social concerns. Yet scholars have typically perpetuated the language of blood in describing Indian political divisions. For a summary of the problems with defining factions according to percentages of "Indian blood," see Theda Perdue, *"Mixed Blood" Indians: Racial Construction in the Early South* (Athens: University of Georgia Press, 2003), x; and Paul C. Rosier, *Rebirth of the Blackfeet Nation, 1912–1954* (Lincoln: University of Nebraska Press, 2001), 8. For studies that attribute factionalism to outside forces, see Claudio Saunt, *A New Order of Things: Property, Power, and the Transformation of the Creek Indians, 1733–1816* (Cambridge: Cambridge University Press, 1999); Gregory Evans Dowd, *A Spirited Resistance: The North American Indian Struggle for Unity, 1745–1815* (Baltimore: Johns Hopkins Press, 1992); and J. Leitch Wright Jr., *Creeks and Seminoles: The Destruction and Regeneration of the Muscogulge People* (Omaha: University of Nebraska Press, 1986). For treatments that consider factionalism to be creative, see James Taylor Carson, *Searching for the Bright Path: The Mississippi Choctaws from Prehistory to Removal* (Lincoln: University of Nebraska Press, 1999); Gregory O'Brien, *Choctaws in a Revolutionary Age, 1750–1830* (Lincoln: University of Nebraska Press, 2002); William G. McLoughlin, *Cherokee Renascence in the New Republic* (Princeton, N.J.: Princeton University Press, 1986); Thomas Biolsi, *Organizing the Lakota: The Political Economy of the New Deal on the Pine Ridge and Rosebud Reservations* (Tucson: University of Arizona Press, 1992); and Rosier, *Rebirth of the Blackfeet Nation, 1912–1954*.

5. See Gerald Sider, *Living Indian Histories: Lumbee and Tuscarora People in North Carolina* (Chapel Hill: University of North Carolina Press, 2003); also see Blu, *The Lumbee Problem*.

6. See Robert F. Berkhofer, "The Political Context of a New Indian History," *Pacific Historical Review* 40 (August 1971): 364.

7. Personal experiences, though subject to the mistakes of memory, can provide valuable justification for historical interpretation and understanding, as oral history methods do for many historians and anthropological methods do for ethnohistorians. Simply put, these methods reveal another side of the story not told in historical documents. See Keyan

G. Tomaselli, Lauren Dyll, and Michael Francis, "'Self' and 'Other': Auto-reflexive and Indigenous Ethnography," in *Handbook of Critical and Indigenous Methodologies*, ed. Norman K. Denzin, Yvonna S. Lincoln, and Linda Tuhiwai Smith (Los Angeles: Sage, 2008), 360; William H. Chafe, Raymond Gavins, and Robert Korstad, eds., *Remembering Jim Crow: African Americans Tell about Life in the Segregated South* (New York: The New Press, 2001), xxiv–xxv; James Axtell, "Ethnohistory: An Historian's Viewpoint," *Ethnohistory* 26 (Winter 1979): 1–13; Ruth Dial Woods, "Growing Up Red: The Lumbee Experience" (Ph.D. diss., University of North Carolina at Chapel Hill, 2001), 11–12; and Philip J. Deloria, "Thinking about Self in a Family Way," *Journal of American History* 89 (June 2002), ⟨http://www .historycooperative.org/journals/jah/89.1/deloria.html⟩ (accessed 7 March 2008).

8. Benedict Anderson, *Imagined Communities: Reflections on the Origin and Spread of Nationalism* (London: Verso, 1983), 16.

INTRODUCTION

1. Daniel M. Cobb, *Native Activism in Cold War America: The Struggle for Sovereignty* (Lawrence: University Press of Kansas, 2008), 9–11.

2. Chris McKenna, conversation with the author, Durham, N.C., 18 October 2008.

3. Double consciousness, according to W. E. B. DuBois, was the "sense of always looking at one's self through the eyes of others, of measuring one's soul by the tape of a world that looks on in amused contempt and pity." W. E. B. DuBois, *The Souls of Black Folk* (Chicago: A. C. McClurg, 1907), 3.

4. D'Arcy McNickle, E. S. McMahon, and Carl C. Seltzer to John Collier, 26 January 1937, RG 75, entry 121, file no. 64190-1935-066, General Services Part 1, NARA.

5. The concept of the "tribe" itself was primarily an intellectual idea promoted by state and federal governments. Gerald Sider argues that tribal names in Robeson County are perhaps more a function of contemporaneous social conditions and a response to what is politically possible than they are historical realities or answers to questions about a legitimate Indian identity. See Gerald Sider, *Living Indian Histories: Lumbee and Tuscarora People in North Carolina* (Chapel Hill: University of North Carolina Press, 2003), 190. See also Douglas W. Boyce, "Iroquoian Tribes of the Virginia–North Carolina Coastal Plain," in *Handbook of North American Indians*, vol. 15, ed. William C. Sturtevant (Washington, D.C.: Smithsonian Institution, 1978), 283; Christian F. Feest, "North Carolina Algonquians," in *Handbook of North American Indians*, vol. 15, ed. William C. Sturtevant (Washington, D.C.: Smithsonian Institution, 1978), 277–78; and Thomas Ross, *American Indians in North Carolina* (Southern Pines, N.C.: Karo Hollow Press, 1999), 9–14, 25–35.

6. Charles M. Hudson, *The Southeastern Indians* (Knoxville: University of Tennessee Press, 1976), 185; Theda Perdue, *"Mixed Blood" Indians: Racial Construction in the Early South* (Athens: University of Georgia Press, 2003), 4, 71, 80–81, 95. For the development of the racial hierarchy, also see Edmund S. Morgan, *American Slavery, American Freedom: The Ordeal of Colonial Virginia* (New York: W. W. Norton, 1975), 316–19.

7. See Perdue, *"Mixed Blood" Indians*, 4–5, 28–29. Of course, there are exceptions to this, prominently among the slaveholding Indians of the "Five Civilized Tribes." For the academic debate this distinction has sparked, see for example Claudio Saunt, "The Native South: An Account of Recent Historiography," *Native South* 1 (2008): 45–60.

8. Julian T. Pierce, Cynthia Hunt-Locklear, Jack Campisi, and Wesley White, *The Lumbee Petition* (Pembroke, N.C.: Lumbee River Legal Services, 1987), 1:3–20, 3:1–4.

9. Scholars call this process of recombining "ethnogenesis"; a great deal of work has been done to demonstrate that ethnogenesis is the process that led to many of the Indian groups we now consider to be "tribes." See James H. Merrell to Charlie Rose, 18 October 1989, *Report together with Dissenting Views to Accompany H.R. 334*, 103rd Cong., 1st sess., 14 October 1993, H.Rpt. 290 (Washington, D.C.: Government Printing Office, 1993); Pierce, Hunt-Locklear, Campisi, and White, *The Lumbee Petition*, 1:11–14; and Sider, *Living Indian Histories*, 239–41. See also Patricia Galloway, *Choctaw Genesis, 1500–1700* (Lincoln: University of Nebraska Press, 1995), for an essential example of ethnogenesis; and James H. Merrell, *The Indians' New World: Catawbas and Their Neighbors from European Contact through the Era of Removal* (Chapel Hill: University of North Carolina Press, 1989).

10. The Lumbee and Tuscarora oral traditions about their origins can be best understood by carefully reading the various texts compiled by government officials such as Hamilton McMillan, Angus W. McLean, Charles F. Pierce, O. M. McPherson, Carl C. Seltzer, and John R. Swanton. See Hamilton McMillan, *Sir Walter Raleigh's Lost Colony: An Historical Sketch of the Attempts of Sir Walter Raleigh to Establish a Colony in Virginia, with the Traditions of an Indian Tribe in North Carolina. Indicating the Fate of the Colony of Englishmen Left on Roanoke Island in 1587* (Wilson, N.C.: Advance Press, 1888); O. M. McPherson, *Report on Condition and Tribal Rights of the Indians of Robeson and Adjoining Counties of North Carolina*, 63d Cong., 3d sess., 5 January 1915, S. Doc. 677 (Washington, D.C.: Government Printing Office, 1915); Angus W. McLean, "Historical Sketch of Indians of Robeson County," cited in McPherson, *Report on Condition and Tribal Rights*; Charles F. Pierce, *Visit among the Croatan Indians, Living in the Vicinity of Pembroke, North Carolina* (Report, in the Field at Pipestone, Minn., to the Commissioner of Indian Affairs, U.S. Indian Service, Department of the Interior, 2 March 1912), RG 75, entry 161, file no. 23202-1912-123 General Services, NARA; Carl C. Seltzer, "A Report on the Racial Status of Certain People in Robeson County, North Carolina," 30 June 1936, RG 75, entry 616, box 13–15, North Carolina, NARA; John R. Swanton, "Probable Identity of the 'Croatan' Indians," 1933, MS 4126, 3, NAA. Robert K. Thomas undertook this kind of close reading for an unpublished report he completed around 1976 for the Lumbee Regional Development Association. He discusses his methodology in Robert K. Thomas, "A Report on Research of Lumbee Origins" (unpublished typescript [1976?], North Carolina Collection, University of North Carolina at Chapel Hill), 22–24. The relative contributions of these groups are a point of much debate within the modern-day Lumbee and Tuscarora communities, but most acknowledge that their ancestry stems from some combination of all of these peoples.

11. Rebecca S. Seib, *Settlement Pattern Study of the Indians of Robeson County, N.C., 1735–1787* (Pembroke, N.C.: Lumbee Regional Development Association, 1983), 3, 8–13, 54, 62, 79; Thomas, "Report," 31; Pierce, Hunt-Locklear, Campisi, and White, *The Lumbee Petition*, 1:11–16.

12. Seib, *Settlement Pattern Study*, 22–24, 31, 140. Among these surnames are Locklear, Lowry, Chavis, and Cumbo. See also "Appendix II: Genealogical Evidence for Tuscarora Identity," 1–4, charts A–E, in Peter H. Wood, Deborah Montgomerie, and Susan Yarnell, *Tuscarora Roots: An Historical Report regarding the Relation of the Hatteras Tuscarora Tribe of*

Robeson County, North Carolina, to the Original Tuscarora Indian Tribe (Durham, N.C.: Hatteras Tuscarora Tribal Foundation, 1992).

13. Thomas, "Report," 29, 30, 38, 45, 47–49; Seib, *Settlement Pattern Study,* 117–18; Pierce, *Visit among the Croatan Indians,* 2; Cynthia Hunt, "Looking Back While Walking Forward," *Carolina Indian Voice,* 18 May 2000; James Cedric Woods, "Ethnohistory and Southeastern Non-Recognized Tribes: Connecting Families with Polities" (paper presented at the American Society for Ethnohistory Annual Meeting, 19 October 2001, Tucson, Ariz.); Seltzer, "A Report on the Racial Status of Certain People," Applicants #21, 25, 105, 61; Karen I. Blu, *The Lumbee Problem: The Making of an American Indian People* (New York: Cambridge University Press, 1980), 43–44. Some genealogists, including Paul Heinegg and Virginia DeMarce, contend that the Lumbees' ancestors were not Indian but white and black. They base this view on pre–Civil War records that labeled families with common Lumbee surnames as "mulatto," "white," "mixt," "free Negro," "other free," or "free colored." Historians have long established, however, that these labels require context, and they are not by themselves reliable indicators of ancestry. Neither Heinegg nor DeMarce attempt to define the labels or place them in context, nor do they differentiate between families identified with the Indian community in Robeson and adjoining counties and families with the same surnames who resided in other communities and sought no affiliation with the Indian community. See Paul Heinegg, *Free African Americans of Virginia, North Carolina, and South Carolina from the Colonial Period to about 1820,* ⟨http://www.freeafrican americans.com/Lemon_Lytle.htm⟩ (accessed 17 April 2009); Virginia DeMarce, "Looking at Legends—Lumbee and Melungeon: Applied Genealogy and the Origins of Tri-Racial Isolate Settlements," *National Genealogical Society Quarterly* 81 (March 1993): 24–45; Virginia DeMarce, "'Verry Slitly Mixt': Tri-Racial Isolate Families of the Upper South—A Genealogical Study," *National Genealogical Society Quarterly* 80 (March 1992): 5–35; Jack D. Forbes, "The Evolution of the Term Mulatto: A Chapter in Black-Native American Relations," *Journal of Ethnic Studies* 10 (Summer 1982): 45–66; and Winthrop D. Jordan, "American Chiaroscuro: The Status and Definition of Mulattoes in the British Colonies," *William and Mary Quarterly* 19 (April 1962): 183–200. Also see note 31 of this chapter.

14. Other families from Algonkian-speaking groups who migrated to Robeson County would have traced kinship through their father's line, so the coalescing group may have practiced both from an early time. Here I focus on matrilineal relationships because of the likely origins of the Roanoke families in matrilineal groups. The existence of a kin network in the Roanoke area is demonstrated by the Yeopim's association with the Tuscarora as a client nation and by Saponi-Tuscarora relations: Saponi families resided on the Tuscarora reservation in Bertie County after the Tuscarora War, and some Saponis and their Tutelo kin migrated to Ontario, Canada, with the Tuscaroras. These communities were matrilineal. The idea that the "core" group of Lumbee ancestors were Tuscarora may come from the fact that many of these smaller groups from the Roanoke area had kinship and adoption ties to the Tuscarora. Thomas, "Report," 35–36; Hugo Prosper Leaming, *Hidden Americans: Maroons of Virginia and the Carolinas* (New York: Garland Publishing, 1995), 42; Swanton, "Probable Identity of the 'Croatan' Indians," 3; Merrell, *The Indians' New World,* 116; Wesley White, "Tuscarora Tribe Petition for Federal Acknowledgement" (Historical Overview of the Tribes, Genealogical Filing Cabinet #2, "Tuscarora Indians," Robeson County Public Library, Lumberton, N.C.), 38–40.

15. Thomas, "Report," 48, 50; Seltzer, "A Report on the Racial Status of Certain People," Applicants #78, 44; Blu, *The Lumbee Problem*, 173–74.

16. Seib, *Settlement Pattern Study*, 17–18, 22, 33–36, 58–59, 62–63, 68–71, 81–86, 94, 98, 100–102, 125, 117–21, 136–37, 152; William McKee Evans, *To Die Game: The Story of the Lowry Band, Indian Guerillas of Reconstruction* (Baton Rouge: Louisiana State University Press, 1971), 29, 31; Sider, *Living Indian Histories*, 84.

17. Seib, *Settlement Pattern Study*, 22–24, 58, 59, 66, 68, 94, 125, 132, 139; Clarence E. Lowrey, "The Lumbee Indians of North Carolina," Public Schools of Robeson County Indian Education Resource Center, Pembroke, N.C. (1960), 28; Seltzer, "A Report on the Racial Status of Certain People," Applicant #23; Carol Smith Oxendine, conversation with the author, Pembroke, N.C., 8 October 2003. The surname "Lowry" has been spelled differently over time, appearing as "Lowrie," "Lowrey," or "Lowery." Here I have used the "Lowry" spelling throughout unless quoting a primary source.

18. These settlements, with the exception of Pembroke, are not towns; they are social and cultural centers usually with an Indian school and church and one or more "stations" (a convenience store, gas station, and small restaurant). When a Lumbee or Tuscarora refers to his home "community," he typically means the rural area around these social centers where his family's home is located. Karen I. Blu, "'Where Do You Stay At?' Home Place and Community among the Lumbee," in *Senses of Place*, ed. Steven Feld and Keith Basso (Santa Fe: School of American Research Press, 1996), 201, 205–6.

19. Waltz Maynor, conversation with the author, Pembroke, N.C., 31 July 2003.

20. Harpers Ferry was founded by Zack Brooks, the uncle of Pikey Brooks; Pikey was also a teacher at White Hill School. The community is sometimes referred to as "White Hill" because many residents attended church there also. Elisha Locklear, conversation with the author, Pembroke, N.C., 24 July 2003; Elisha Locklear, interview by author and Waltz Maynor, Pembroke, N.C., 19 January 2002, LRFC; Aunt Nudie, "The Way I Came Up," in Pembroke Senior High School literary magazine, *Lighter'd Knot* 1 (1976–77): 13, Special Collections, Mary Livermore Library, University of North Carolina at Pembroke; Colan Brooks and Rosetta Brooks, interview by Adolph Dial, Pembroke, N.C., 2 September 1969, ADT.

21. Elisha Locklear and Cecil Hunt, interview by author and Willie Lowery, Pembroke, N.C., 23 February 2004, LRFC; Ella Deloria to Franz Boas, 7 August 1940, Franz Boas Papers, American Philosophical Society, Philadelphia, Pa.; Wood, Montgomerie, and Yarnell, *Tuscarora Roots*, 109; Colan Brooks and Rosetta Brooks, interview by Adolph Dial. The distinctness of this settlement is widely recognized throughout the larger Indian community, and at least some people thought of the longhouse as "owned" by Pikey, Lawson, and the other Brookses; see Wood, Montgomerie, and Yarnell, *Tuscarora Roots*, 84; Willie A. Dial, interview by author, Pembroke, N.C., 26 April 2004. According to Elisha Locklear, the Brooks Settlement families had an even older history of relationships with other tribes. In the 1830s the Aaron and Sabrie Locklear family went to western North Carolina to investigate removing to Indian Territory with the Cherokee, where, they were told, they could get free land. Aaron and Sabrie's son, Joe, was born in Burke County, N.C., in a corral built by the army to hold Cherokees as they waited for Removal. Aaron and Sabrie brought their family back to Robeson County, however. Aaron's mother, Rhode, was a daughter of forefather Major Locklear; Aaron's sister, Peggy, married forefather John Brooks. See Elisha Locklear, interview by author and Waltz Maynor.

22. Christopher Arris Oakley, "The Reshaping of Indian Identity in Twentieth-Century North Carolina" (Ph.D. diss., University of Tennessee, Knoxville, 2002), 54; John G. Peck, "Urban Station—Migration of the Lumbee Indians" (Ph.D. diss., University of North Carolina, 1972), 67–68; quoted in Vernon Ray Thompson, "A History of the Education of the Lumbee Indians of Robeson County, North Carolina From 1885 to 1970" (Ed.D. diss., University of Miami, 1973), 24–25.

23. The same may be true if the child's mother was non-Indian, but according to the data on families provided by Seltzer, "A Report on the Racial Status of Certain People," it was much more rare for an illegitimate child to be born to a non-Indian mother and have an identification with the Indian community. Seltzer, "A Report on the Racial Status of Certain People," Applicants #7, 29, 35, 36, 44, 89, 95, 96, 107, 108. There are also some indications that men took their wives' names in the eighteenth and nineteenth centuries. For example, an Indian father and son, Cade and Jordin Chavis, moved to Robeson County from Oklahoma and may have taken the name "Chavis" from Jordin's wife's family. Seltzer, "A Report on the Racial Status of Certain People," Applicants #3, 54, 60, 7, 58. See also Seib, Settlement Pattern Study, 70–71.

24. According to oral tradition, Clarissa's grandmother, Celia Kearsey, was a Tuscarora. Seltzer, "A Report on the Racial Status of Certain People," Applicant #22.

25. Pierce, Visit among the Croatan Indians, 3. Pierce, Hunt-Locklear, Campisi, and White, The Lumbee Petition, 1:135–37, 160–61; Sophronie Locklear, interview by Bolivia Spaulding, Pembroke, N.C., 28 July 1982, PSU Oral History Project, Public Schools of Robeson County Indian Education Resource Center, Pembroke, N.C.; Dawley Maynor, interview by Darla Oxendine, Pembroke, N.C., 9 August 1982, PSU Oral History Project, Public Schools of Robeson County Indian Education Resource Center, Pembroke, N.C..

26. The literature describing Lumbees as "tri-racial isolates" goes back to the 1930s. See Brewton Berry, Almost White (New York: Macmillan, 1963); DeMarce, "Looking at Legends"; DeMarce, "'Verry Slitly Mixt'"; Guy B. Johnson, "Personality in a White-Indian-Negro Community," American Sociological Review 4 (August 1939): 516–23; J. K. Dane and B. Eugene Griessman, "The Collective Identity of Marginal Peoples: The North Carolina Experience," American Anthropologist 74 (February–April 1972): 699; William Harlen Gilbert Jr., "Memorandum Concerning the Characteristics of the Larger Mixed-Blood Racial Islands of the Eastern United States," Social Forces 24 (May 1946): 438–47; Calvin L. Beale, "An Overview of the Phenomenon of Mixed Racial Isolates in the United States," American Anthropologist 74 (February–April 1972): 706. At the heart of these arguments are two converging assumptions: one, that ancestry and cultural identity are consanguineous rather than subject to the changing contexts of human relations; and two, that white supremacy is a timeless norm rather than a social structure designed to ensure the dominance of a certain group. For a critique, see Alexandra Harmon, Indians in the Making: Ethnic Relations and Indian Identities around Puget Sound (Berkeley: University of California Press, 1998), 3.

27. See, for example, Ariela Gross, What Blood Won't Tell: A History of Race on Trial in America (Cambridge, Mass.: Harvard University Press, 2008); and Peggy Pascoe, What Comes Naturally: Miscegenation Law and the Making of Race in America (London: Oxford University Press, 2009).

28. Michelle Brattain, "Miscegenation and Competing Definitions of Race in Twen-

tieth-Century Louisiana," *Journal of Southern History* 71 (August 2005): 621–58; Peggy Pascoe, "Miscegenation Law, Court Cases, and Ideologies of 'Race' in Twentieth-Century America," *Journal of American History* (June 1996): 44–69.

29. The National Museum of the American Indian has a touring exhibition, "Indi-Visible: African and Native American Lives in the Americas," that discusses multiracial perspectives on Indian and black identities. See also articles in James F. Brooks, ed., *Confounding the Color Line: The Indian-Black Experience in North America* (Lincoln: University of Nebraska Press, 2002); and Tiya Miles and Sharon P. Holland, eds., *Crossing Waters, Crossing Worlds: The African Diaspora in Indian Country* (Durham, N.C.: Duke University Press, 2006).

30. The literature on Afro-Native identity in Oklahoma/Indian Territory is increasingly rich and complex. The most prominent examples of scholarly work include Daniel F. Littlefield's books on African-Indian relations in each of the Five Civilized Tribes; Tiya Miles, *Ties That Bind: The Story of an Afro-Cherokee Family in Slavery and Freedom* (Berkeley: University of California Press, 2005); Claudio Saunt, *Black, White, and Indian: Race and the Unmaking of an American Family* (New York: Oxford University Press, 2005); Miles and Holland, eds., *Crossing Waters, Crossing Worlds*; Brooks, *Confounding the Color Line*; Gary Zellar, *African Creeks: Estelvste and the Creek Nation* (Norman: University of Oklahoma Press, 2007); David A. Y. O. Chang, "From Indian Territory to White Man's Country: Race, Nation, and the Politics of Land Ownership in Eastern Oklahoma, 1889–1940" (Ph.D. diss., University of Wisconsin–Madison, 2002); Celia Naylor, *African Cherokees in Indian Territory: From Chattel to Citizens* (Chapel Hill: University of North Carolina Press, 2008); Circe Sturm, *Blood Politics: Race, Culture, and Identity in the Cherokee Nation of Oklahoma* (Berkeley: University of California Press, 2002).

31. Censuses taken between 1790 and 1810 did not mark race but instead recorded who in the household was "free white," "slave," or "all other free persons." Between 1820 and 1840, the adjective "colored" was added to "free persons." Not until 1850 did the term "mulatto" appear in the census. Although the terms fluctuated, none provided room to articulate an identity other than "white" or "nonwhite." If the enumerator made no mark, he assumed the individual was white—a pristine example of the extent to which the government has granted whiteness a degree of normalcy, so much so that it doesn't require notation. The census rules for racial classifications changed over time, but appearance most commonly defined them; for example, census-enumerator instructions did not specify the proof required for an individual's racial category. An enumerator may have relied on self-identification, or he may have simply classified the individual based on appearance. In other words, the enumerator may have marked someone as "mulatto" not necessarily because he had definitive knowledge of that person's ancestry but because, to the enumerator's eye, he or she looked "mulatto." Before 1870, "mulatto" was listed in the questionnaires as a color designation rather than a definitive statement of ancestry. Beginning in 1870, enumerators were told to mark those as mulatto who had "any perceptible trace of African blood." "Indian" was first allowed as a designation in 1890, and in Robeson County, the enumerator freely admitted that he could not distinguish Indians from whites based on phenotype alone and so marked most of them "white." This resulted in only 174 people listed as Indian in 1890, but the Indian school census for that year found 1,242 Indian schoolchildren. This discrepancy is evidence of the obvious differences between

Indian identity as marked by the local community and the state of North Carolina, as well as Indian identity as marked by the subjective observation of phenotype alone. For census questionnaires and enumerator instructions that list the racial information collected, see U.S. Census Bureau, "History: 1790," ⟨http://www.census.gov/history/www/index_of_questions/012292.html⟩ (accessed 17 December 2008); U.S. Census Bureau, "History: 1800," ⟨http://www.census.gov/history/www/index_of_questions/012293.html⟩ (accessed 17 December 2008); U.S. Census Bureau, "History: 1810," ⟨http://www.census.gov/history/www/index_of_questions/012294.html⟩ (accessed 17 December 2008); U.S. Census Bureau, "History: 1820," ⟨http://www.census.gov/history/www/index_of_questions/012295.html⟩ (accessed 17 December 2008); U.S. Census Bureau, "History: 1830," ⟨http://www.census.gov/history/www/index_of_questions/012296.html⟩ (accessed 17 December 2008); U.S. Census Bureau, "History: 1840," ⟨http://www.census.gov/history/www/index_of_questions/012297.html⟩ (accessed 17 December 2008); U.S. Census Bureau, "History: 1850," ⟨http://www.census.gov/history/www/index_of_questions/012298.html⟩ (accessed 17 December 2008); Minnesota Population Center, Integrated Public Use Microdata Series, "1850 Census: Instructions to Marshals and Assistant Marshals," ⟨http://usa.ipums.org/usa/voliii/inst1850.shtml⟩ (accessed 17 December 2008); Minnesota Population Center, Integrated Public Use Microdata Series, "1860 Census: Instructions to Marshals and Assistant Marshals," ⟨http://usa.ipums.org/usa/voliii/inst1860.shtml⟩ (accessed 17 December 2008); Minnesota Population Center, Integrated Public Use Microdata Series, "1870 Census: Instructions to Marshals and Assistant Marshals," ⟨http://usa.ipums.org/usa/voliii/inst1870.shtml⟩ (accessed 17 December 2008); and Minnesota Population Center, Integrated Public Use Microdata Series, "1880 Census: Instructions to Marshals and Assistant Marshals," ⟨http://usa.ipums.org/usa/voliii/inst1880.shtml⟩ (accessed 17 December 2008). Information on the 1890 census is found in Anna Bailey, "Separating Out: The Emergence of Croatan Indian Identity, 1872–1900" (Ph.D. diss., University of Washington, 2008), 104.

32. Because of the problems with racial classification in the census and the lack of racial data in the marriage records, I asked Jessica and Emily to locate common Indian surnames in the records; surnames have been fairly stable for the last 300 years. My personal knowledge of the Robeson County Indian community helped us define the criteria for our study, as I knew the surnames that characterized the Indian community and could give Jessica and Emily a list of them. I also knew that, generally speaking, Indians defined the "insiders" as those who had a typically Indian surname and had been born in Robeson or one of the adjoining counties. If Indians married people they considered to be Indians, it seemed more likely that those marriage partners would have been born in a territory that Indians considered theirs. Not a watertight set of criteria, to be sure, but we did our best to approach the data critically and with equanimity. With other time commitments as undergraduates, Jessica and Emily did not have time to examine the 1840 census.

33. "Crossblood" is novelist and literary critic Gerald Vizenor's term that describes not only people of "mixed" ancestry but also people of "mixed" social milieus, most especially rural/reservation and urban. The term acknowledges that for Indians there is no "pure" past by which our authenticity and legitimacy can be accurately measured. All Indians—indeed, all people—are "crossbloods" in that they live with and negotiate multiple identities without degenerating culturally, spiritually, socially, or physically. Lumbees are

not unique for their multiracial ancestry, even among Native Americans. The volumes of historical literature about Indians in the Southeast and Northeast, and even the "real Indians" out West, prove that Indians have loved everybody, regardless of their "race." This is the only constant in Indian history, the only thing that Indians have "always" done. But the categories of knowledge instituted by settler societies have obscured this reality in favor of a focus on purity that makes Indian people confused and angry. Contemporary Lumbee people take the pejorative association with multiracial ancestry very personally, not because we deny the truth of it, but because we know it stigmatizes us and not other ethnic groups whose ancestry is equally mixed. Gerald Vizenor, *Crossbloods: Bone Courts, Bingo, and Other Reports* (Minneapolis: University of Minnesota Press, 1990).

34. For interracial relationships in the South, see Timothy James Lockley, *Lines in the Sand: Race and Class in Lowcountry Georgia, 1750–1860* (Athens: University of Georgia Press, 2001); Victoria Bynum, *The Free State of Jones: Mississippi's Longest Civil War* (Chapel Hill: University of North Carolina Press, 2001); Brattain, "Miscegenation and Competing Definitions of Race"; Gary B. Nash, "The Hidden History of Mestizo America," *Journal of American History* 82 (December 1995): 955–56; Charles F. Robinson, *Dangerous Liaisons: Sex and Love in the Segregated South* (Fayetteville: University of Arkansas Press, 2003); Pascoe, "Miscegenation Law"; Julie Novkov, "Racial Constructions: The Legal Regulation of Miscegenation in Alabama, 1890–1934," *Law and History Review* 20 (2002), ⟨http://history cooperative.press.uiuc.edu/journals/lhr/20.2/novkov.html⟩ (accessed 6 April 2007).

35. The restrictions on voting are found in article I, section 3, paragraph 3 of the 1835 North Carolina constitution. Both Robeson County delegates voted against this resolution when it was brought before the convention, and it only passed by a narrow margin—66 to 61. North Carolina Constitutional Convention, *Journal of the Convention, Called by the Freemen of North-Carolina, to Amend the Constitution of the State, Which Assembled in the City of Raleigh, on the 4th of June, 1835, and Continued in Session Until the 11th Day of July Thereafter*, electronic edition (Raleigh, N.C.: J. Gales & Son, 1835), 98, 22.

36. Voting records from Robeson County are scarce from the antebellum period; the main evidence of Indian voting comes from evidence during and after the Civil War. Speaking to Hamilton McMillan, a white politician and newspaper editor in the 1860s, George Lowry, a grandson of "forefather" James Lowry, specifically referred to the practice of Indian voting and the end of it in a speech decrying the injustices of conscription during the Civil War. Lowry said, "The Englishmen whom we befriended always told us that if we took up the ways of the white man we would prosper and be great like the English. And so we did. . . . Yet we have come to this—enslavement! . . . [W]e fought for the liberty of the white man [in the Revolutionary War]; yet the white man whom we defended have turned upon us. They have taken away our right to vote; our right to attend school; and now our right to be free." Quoted in Lew Barton, *The Most Ironic Story in American History: An Authoritative, Documented History of the Lumbee Indians of North Carolina* (Charlotte, N.C.: Associated Printing Corporation, 1967), 50. A white Robesonian wrote to a newspaper in the 1870s: "[Indians] were allowed to vote, were required to bear arms and muster, and were more generally mixed with the whites on terms of equality. Being found useful as voters they were tolerated by the whites. [After 1835] they were generally degraded to the level of negro slaves; or, in many instances, came to be looked down upon by the slaves as beneath them." Interestingly, this writer denies any great degree of mixture between

Indians and blacks; he refers to them as "the mulattoes of Scuffletown" but proceeds to identify them this way: "[They] are undoubtedly descendents of the aborigines, probably Tuscaroras or Cherokees; many of them, direct descendents of their Indian forefathers, bear decided Indian features and characteristics. There are among them a goodly number of half-breeds crossed with the whites—rarely ever with the negroes, and they never have been . . . slaves, but always free." See *Wilmington Daily Journal*, 4 April 1872. See also U.S. Congress, *Testimony Taken by the Joint Select Committee to Inquire into the Condition of Affairs in the Late Insurrectionary States*, vol. 2, *North Carolina (Ku Klux Conspiracy)*, 42nd Cong., 2d sess. (Washington, D.C.: Government Printing Office, 1872), 283; U.S. Congress, Committee on Indian Affairs, *Hearings before the Committee on Indian Affairs on S. 3258 to Acquire a Site and Erect Buildings for a School for the Indians of Robeson County, N.C., and for Other Purposes*, 62nd Cong., 2nd sess., 14 February 1913 (Washington, D.C.: Government Printing Office, 1913), 9, 23.

37. For the role of the 1835 constitution in Lumbee racial identity, see Evans, *To Die Game*, 32–33; Blu, *The Lumbee Problem*, 46–50; Pierce, Hunt-Locklear, Campisi, and White, *The Lumbee Petition*, 1:24–25; McMillan, *Sir Walter Raleigh's Lost Colony*, 17.

38. Ernest D. Hancock, "A Sociological Study of the Tri-Racial Community of Robeson County, North Carolina" (master's thesis, University of North Carolina at Chapel Hill, 1935), 15.

39. I want to thank Forest Hazel for alerting me to the nearly 150 Indians from Robeson and surrounding counties who enlisted in the Confederate infantry. In fact, one of my ancestors, who married Henry Berry Lowry's niece, fought in the Confederacy. Hazel has extensively documented Confederate service and has found comparatively little written evidence of the large-scale conscriptions that are part of Indian oral tradition. Whether or not the conscription stories are true, there is little doubt that animosity between Brantley Harriss and the Lowrys sparked the killings that led to the Lowry War. Forest Hazel, "American Indian Service in the Confederacy from the Robeson County Area" (paper presented at Southeastern Indian Studies Conference, April 2, 2009, University of North Carolina at Pembroke, Pembroke, N.C.).

40. For more on the Lowry War, see Sider, *Living Indian Histories*, chap. 9; Evans, *To Die Game*; Adolph L. Dial and David K. Eliades, *The Only Land I Know: A History of the Lumbee Indians* (San Francisco: Indian Historian Press, 1975), chap. 3; Edward S. Magdol, "Against the Gentry: An Inquiry into a Southern Lower-Class Community and Culture, 1865–1870," *Journal of Social History* 6 (Spring 1973): 259–83; Field Notes, Mrs. Breeden, August 2, 1937, Red Springs, GBJP; U.S. Congress, *North Carolina (Ku Klux Conspiracy)*, 287; and Mary C. Norment, *The Lowrie History, as Acted in Part by Henry Berry Lowry, with Biographical Sketch of His Associates* (Lumberton, N.C.: Lumbee Pub. Co., 1909), ⟨http://digital.lib .ecu.edu/historyfiction/fullview.aspx?id=loh⟩ (accessed 7 April 2007). W. McKee Evans spoke about some of the Lowry War oral tradition at University of North Carolina at Pembroke in 2005, which was reported in Amber Rach, "Historian: Henry Berry Lowry Is Winning the War of Words," *University Newswire*, 14 December 2005, ⟨http://www.uncp .edu/news/2005/w_mckee_evans.htm⟩ (accessed 2 December 2006).

41. An account of his death is found in Dial and Eliades, *The Only Land I Know*, 81.

42. This analysis of rural southern power dynamics is inspired by Mark Schultz, *The Rural Face of White Supremacy: Beyond Jim Crow* (Urbana: University of Illinois Press,

2005), 203, chaps. 2, 4, and 5. See also Melissa Walker, "Shifting Boundaries: Race Relations in the Rural Jim Crow South," in *African American Life in the Rural South, 1900–1950*, ed. R. Douglas Hurt (Columbia: University of Missouri Press, 2003), 81–107.

43. This is the essence of Schultz's definition of the importance of personal relationships to the larger social structure. Schultz, *The Rural Face of White Supremacy*, 127.

CHAPTER 1

1. William McKee Evans, *To Die Game: The Story of the Lowry Band, Indian Guerillas of Reconstruction* (Baton Rouge: Louisiana University Press, 1971), 258–59.

2. U.S. Congress, *Testimony Taken by the Joint Select Committee to Inquire into the Condition of Affairs in the Late Insurrectionary States*, vol. 2, *North Carolina (Ku Klux Conspiracy)*, 42nd Cong., 2d sess. (Washington, D.C.: Government Printing Office, 1872), 254; Robeson County Heritage Book Committee, *Our Heritage: Robeson County, North Carolina, 1748–2002* (Waynesville, N.C.: County Heritage, 2003), 113; Robert C. Lawrence, *The State of Robeson* (New York: J. J. Little and Ives, 1939), 94–96.

3. John D. Bellamy, *Memoirs of an Octogenarian* (Charlotte, N.C.: Observer Printing House, 1942), 134; quoted in Anna Bailey, "'It Is the Center to Which We Should Cling': Indian Schools in Robeson County, North Carolina, 1900–1920," in *The History of Discrimination in U.S. Education: Marginality, Agency, and Power*, ed. Eileen H. Tamura (New York: Palgrave MacMillan, 2008), 70.

4. Democrats' tactics in Robeson County were an example of Redding's argument that white racism was not the only factor in bringing about disfranchisement. Disfranchisement in the county was also brought on by stress over Republican competition, and Democrats gained control in North Carolina not only by disfranchising blacks but also by employing the Republicans' political techniques. J. Morgan Kousser, *The Shaping of Southern Politics: Suffrage Restriction and the Establishment of the One-Party South, 1880–1910* (New Haven, Conn.: Yale University Press, 1974), 183–95; Raymond Gavins, "Fear, Hope, and Struggle: Recasting Black North Carolina in the Age of Jim Crow," in *Democracy Betrayed: The Wilmington Race Riot of 1898 and Its Legacy*, ed. David S. Cecelski and Timothy B. Tyson (Chapel Hill: University of North Carolina Press, 1998), 188–89; Kent Redding, *Making Race, Making Power: North Carolina's Road to Disfranchisement* (Urbana: University of Illinois Press, 2003).

5. Rev. W. L. Moore, an Indian from Columbus County who advocated for the legislation establishing the Croatan school system, was educated in this school. Vernon Ray Thompson, "A History of the Education of the Lumbee Indians of Robeson County, North Carolina from 1885 to 1970" (Ed.D. diss., University of Miami, 1973), 41; Maxine Locklear Amos, interview by author, Pembroke, N.C., 25 October 2001, LRFC; James Moore, interview by Waltz Maynor, Maxton, N.C., 13 July 2001, LRFC; Edward S. Magdol, "Against the Gentry: An Inquiry into a Southern Lower-Class Community and Culture, 1865–1870," *Journal of Social History* 6 (Spring 1973): 261–62.

6. Anna Bailey, "Separating Out: The Emergence of Croatan Indian Identity, 1872–1900" (Ph.D. diss., University of Washington, 2008), 74–76, 86–88.

7. Adolph L. Dial and David K. Eliades, *The Only Land I Know: A History of the Lumbee Indians* (San Francisco: Indian Historian Press, 1975), 90, 182–83.

8. Christopher Arris Oakley, "The Reshaping of Indian Identity in Twentieth-Century

North Carolina" (Ph.D. diss., University of Tennessee, Knoxville, 2002), 54–55; Karen I. Blu, *The Lumbee Problem: The Making of an American Indian People* (New York: Cambridge University Press, 1980), 63, 73.

9. Dial and Eliades, *The Only Land I Know*, 91, 184.

10. Bailey, "Separating Out," 80–81.

11. See Robert K. Thomas, "A Report on Research of Lumbee Origins" (unpublished typescript [1976?], North Carolina Collection, University of North Carolina at Chapel Hill), 2–6; Blu, *The Lumbee Problem*, 37, 40, 62–63. For more on the Lost Colony theory, see Hamilton McMillan, *Sir Walter Raleigh's Lost Colony: An Historical Sketch of the Attempts of Sir Walter Raleigh to Establish a Colony in Virginia, with the Traditions of an Indian Tribe in North Carolina. Indicating the Fate of the Colony of Englishmen Left on Roanoke Island in 1587* (Wilson, N.C.: Advance Press, 1888); Dial and Eliades, *The Only Land I Know*, 8–9; Stephen B. Weeks, "The Lost Colony of Roanoke: Its Fate and Survival," *Papers of the American Historical Association* 5 (1891), 107–46.

12. Unlike the federal government officials who argued a few years later that Robeson County Indians' level of acculturation justified denial of recognition, the state legislature apparently saw white ancestry as a reason to encourage Indians' education. Blu, *The Lumbee Problem*, 135–36; Gerald Sider, *Living Indian Histories: Lumbee and Tuscarora People in North Carolina* (Chapel Hill: University of North Carolina Press, 2003), 82, 86–90.

13. N. McInnis to A. T. Allen, 13 June 1929, Department of Public Instruction, Office of the Superintendent, General Correspondence, 1929, box 110, folder: Pembroke Normal School, North Carolina State Archives, Raleigh.

14. Maud Thomas, *Away Down Home: A History of Robeson County, North Carolina* (Lumberton, N.C.: Historic Robeson, 1982), 166.

15. Ibid., 222; H. Leon Prather Sr., "The Red Shirt Movement in North Carolina, 1898–1900," *Journal of Negro History* 62 (April 1977): 175, 178; 1898 Wilmington Race Riot Commission, "The 1898 Wilmington Race Riot Report, August 31, 2006," ⟨http://www.ah.dcr.state.nc.us/1898-wrrc/report/report.htm⟩ (accessed 5 December 2006).

16. Prather, "The Red Shirt Movement in North Carolina," 180. Scotland was carved from Robeson and Richmond Counties by the Democratic state legislature in 1899. Elected officials wanted a new county where they could be sure to win the constitutional amendment, and even though this new county was 60 percent black, the Red Shirt campaign had been so effective there that Democrats felt fully confident in victory for a black disfranchisement amendment.

17. Bailey, "It Is the Center to Which We Should Cling," 70–71.

18. W. H. Humphreys, "A Card," *Robesonian*, 26 June 1900.

19. O. R. Sampson, "A Strong Argument for the Amendment," *Robesonian*, 17 July 1900. Blacks in some places also exercised this seemingly eager accommodation to white supremacy. See John Haley, "Race, Rhetoric, and Revolution," in *Democracy Betrayed*, 212–13.

20. According to Early Bullard and Gaston Locklear, two politically active Indians from the Prospect Community, there was a time in the early twentieth century that local whites did try to prevent Indians from voting. An Indian ran for road supervisor, and to prevent his election, local whites told Indians who came to register to vote that they were not eli-

gible. See Early Bullard and Gaston Locklear, interview by Adolph Dial, Pembroke, N.C., 22 July 1969, ADT.

21. A. N. Locklear, "Another Croatan for the Amendment," *Robesonian*, 27 July 1900.

22. John R. Finger, *Cherokee Americans: The Eastern Band of Cherokees in the Twentieth Century* (Lincoln: University of Nebraska Press, 1991), 9–10, 23–24, 37, 45–46, 49–50, 110–12.

23. Katherine M. B. Osburn, "The 'Identified Full-Bloods' in Mississippi: Race and Choctaw Identity, 1898–1918" (paper presented at the Native American and Indigenous Studies Association, Athens, Ga., 10–12 April 2008). This paper has been published in revised form in *Ethnohistory* 56 (Summer 2009): 423–47.

24. Katherine M. B. Osburn, "'In a Name of Justice and Fairness': The Mississippi Choctaw Indian Federation versus the BIA, 1934," in *Beyond Red Power: American Indian Politics and Activism since 1900*, ed. Daniel M. Cobb and Loretta Fowler (Santa Fe: School for Advanced Research, 2007), 109–25.

25. For how white southerners in the late nineteenth century could rationalize the possibility of interracial unions in the Lost Colony, see Michael E. Harkin, "Performing Paradox: Narrativity and the Lost Colony of Roanoke," in *Myth and Memory: Rethinking Stories of Indigenous-European Contact*, ed. John Lutz (Vancouver: University of British Columbia Press, 2007), 103–17.

26. U.S. Senate, *Choctaw and Chickasaw Indians, Hearings before the Committee on Indian Affairs on the Choctaw and Chickasaw Indians*, 30 January 1907, S. Doc. 257, 59th Cong., 2nd sess., 19; quoted in Osburn, "The 'Identified Full-Bloods.'"

27. Ella Deloria to Franz Boas, 7 August 1940, Franz Boas Papers, American Philosophical Society, Philadelphia, Pa.; James E. Henderson, "The Croatan Indians of North Carolina," 11 December 1923, RG 75, entry 121, file no. 93807-1923-CHEROKEE SCHOOL-150), 5, NARA; Charles F. Pierce, *Visit among the Croatan Indians, Living in the Vicinity of Pembroke, North Carolina* (Report, in the Field at Pipestone, Minn., to the Commissioner of Indian Affairs, U.S. Indian Service, Department of the Interior, 2 March 1912), RG 75, entry 161, file no. 23202-1912-123 General Services, 6, NARA.

28. Bailey, "It Is the Center to Which We Should Cling," 75, 80.

29. Ernest West Morgan, "A Racial Comparison of Education in Robeson County (North Carolina)" (master's thesis, University of North Carolina at Chapel Hill, 1940), 192.

30. Ernest D. Hancock, "A Sociological Study of the Tri-Racial Community of Robeson County, North Carolina" (master's thesis, University of North Carolina at Chapel Hill, 1935), 79.

31. "Petition to the Honorable Board of Education of Robeson County, Lumberton, N.C.," n.d., Department of Public Instruction, Office of Superintendent, County files, box 20, folder: Robeson 1945–49, North Carolina State Archives, Raleigh.

32. "Petition to the Lumberton School Board and the Board of County Commissioners," n.d., Department of Public Instruction, Office of Superintendent, County files, box 20, folder: Robeson 1945–49, North Carolina State Archives, Raleigh.

33. C. L. Green to A. E. Langston, 6 December 1939, Department of Public Instruction, Office of Superintendent, County files, box 17, folder: Robeson 1933–44, North Carolina State Archives, Raleigh.

34. Sider, *Living Indian Histories*, 80–81; Julian T. Pierce, Cynthia Hunt-Locklear, Jack Campisi, and Wesley White, *The Lumbee Petition* (Pembroke, N.C.: Lumbee River Legal Services, 1987), 1:50, 53–54; Thomas, *Away Down Home*, 235–36; William S. Powell, ed., *Encyclopedia of North Carolina* (Chapel Hill: University of North Carolina Press, 2006), 10; K. Blake Tyner, *Images of America: Robeson County* (Charleston, S.C.: Arcadia, 2003), 60–61, 63–64.

35. Adam Fairclough, *Teaching Equality: Black Schools in the Age of Jim Crow* (Athens: University of Georgia Press, 2001), 4–9, 14, 21; Tyner, *Images of America*, 58.

36. Sider, *Living Indian Histories*, 51; Dial and Eliades, *The Only Land I Know*, 140; Robeson County Black Caucus, "Who's Who and What's What" in Black Robeson County (N.p., 1984), 22, Special Collections, Mary Livermore Library, University of North Carolina at Pembroke; Tyner, *Images of America*, 53, 57–59.

37. John H. Haley, *Charles N. Hunter and Race Relations in North Carolina* (Chapel Hill: University of North Carolina Press, 1981); Fairclough, *Teaching Equality*, 2–3, 5.

38. Bailey, "It Is the Center to Which We Should Cling," 86 (emphasis in original).

39. The text of the 1887 law reads: "All marriages between an Indian and a negro or between an Indian and a person of negro descent to the third generation, inclusive, shall be utterly void: Provided, This act shall only apply to the Croatan Indians." *Laws and Resolutions of the State of North Carolina, 1887* (Raleigh: Josephus Daniels, 1887), chap. 254. For the 1889 law, see *Laws and Resolutions of the State of North Carolina, 1889* (Raleigh: Josephus Daniels, 1887), chap. 60; and Bailey, "Separating Out," 89–90.

40. Sider, *Living Indian Histories*, 87–90; Peter H. Wood, Deborah Montgomerie, and Susan Yarnell, *Tuscarora Roots: An Historical Report regarding the Relation of the Hatteras Tuscarora Tribe of Robeson County, North Carolina, to the Original Tuscarora Indian Tribe* (Durham, N.C.: Hatteras Tuscarora Tribal Foundation, 1992), 83; Pierce, Hunt-Locklear, Campisi, and White, *The Lumbee Petition*, 2:43; Bailey, "Separating Out," 92–98.

41. Cedric Woods, conversation with the author, Cambridge, Mass., 21 February 2008; James E. Chavis and Gerald M. Sider, audiotaped interview with Adolph L. Dial, 20 August 1971, Pembroke, N.C., Samuel Proctor Oral History Program, Department of History, University of Florida, ⟨http://www.uflib.ufl.edu/ufdc/?b=UF00008138&v=00001⟩ (accessed 19 February 2009), 7.

42. Sider, *Living Indian Histories*, 74–80; Bailey, "It Is the Center to Which We Should Cling," 80–85.

43. Chavis and Sider interview, 7.

44. Ann Gibson Winfield, *Eugenics and Education in America: Institutionalized Racism and the Implications of History, Ideology, and Memory* (New York: Peter Lang, 2007), xvii, 5–11, 121, 131. A scholarly and thorough website on eugenics can be found at ⟨http://www.eugenicsarchive.org⟩.

45. See Winfield, *Eugenics and Education*, chap. 8.

46. Arthur H. Estabrook and Ivan E. McDougle, *Mongrel Virginians: The WIN Tribe* (Baltimore, Md.: Williams and Wilkins, 1926); AEP, ⟨http://library.albany.edu/speccoll/findaids/apap069.htm#series1⟩ (accessed 10 July 2008); Walter A. Plecker to Arthur H. Estabrook, various dates, series 1, box 1, folders 3 and 4, AEP; quote from Ivan McDougle to A. H. Estabrook, 5 July 1925, series 1, box 1, folder 4, AEP.

47. Estabrook and McDougle, *Mongrel Virginians*, 191.

48. A. F. Corbin to Arthur H. Estabrook, 8 April 1924, series 1, box 1, folder 3, AEP.

49. Arthur H. Estabrook to Ivan E. McDougle, 12 February 1924, series 1, box 1, folder 3, AEP; Min. to Arthur H. Estabrook, 15 February 1924, series 1, box 1, folder 3, AEP.

50. A. F. Corbin to Arthur H. Estabrook, 8 April 1924, series 1, box 1, folder 3, AEP.

51. Arthur H. Estabrook to A. F. Corbin, 23 June 1924, series 1, box 1, folder 3, AEP.

52. A. F. Corbin to Arthur H. Estabrook, 9 July 1924, series 1, box 1, folder 3, AEP; O. R. Sampson, "Pembroke Graded School," *Pembroke Herald*, March 1924, series 7, box 1, folder 31, AEP.

53. A. N. Locklear to Arthur H. Estabrook, 10 July 1924, series 1, box 1, folder 3, AEP.

54. Ibid.; A. F. Corbin to Arthur H. Estabrook, 8 August 1924, series 1, box 1, folder 3, AEP. The name of the society is an educated guess on my part, based on a reference to it made by Corbin in a 1926 letter to Estabrook; see A. F. Corbin to Arthur H. Estabrook, 9 March 1926, series 1, box 1, folder 5, AEP.

55. A. F. Corbin to Arthur H. Estabrook, 8 August 1924, series 1, box 1, folder 3, AEP.

56. Lonnie W. Jacobs to Arthur H. Estabrook, n.d., series 1, box 1, folder 5, AEP.

57. A. F. Corbin to Arthur H. Estabrook, 9 March 1926, and Lonnie W. Jacobs to Arthur H. Estabrook, no date, series 1, box 1, folder 5, AEP.

58. Arthur H. Estabrook to A. F. Corbin, 18 March 1926, and A. F. Corbin to Arthur H. Estabrook, 2 April 1926, series 1, box 1, folder 5, AEP.

59. David K. Eliades and Linda Ellen Oxendine, *Pembroke State University: A Centennial History* (Columbus, Ga.: Brentwood University Press, 1986), 38–39; Sider, *Living Indian Histories*, 73, 83.

60. Records of the Bureau of American Ethnology, Letters Received, box 2, folder: Indian Affairs, Bureau of, 1889–1904, NAA; Pierce, Hunt-Locklear, Campisi, and White, *The Lumbee Petition*, 1:91–97.

61. Robeson County Black Caucus, *Who's Who in Black Robeson County*, 3, 4, 13, 22.

62. See deeds to New Hope Protestant Church, 1854 and 1895, Robeson County Deed Book CC, 120, and Robeson County Deed Book XXX, 672; Reedy Branch Missionary Baptist Church, 1885, Robeson County Deed Book FFF, 139; Mount Olive Baptist Church, 1885, Robeson County Deed Book HHH, 578; Prospect Protestant Church, 1876 and 1887, Robeson County Deed Book GGG, 428, and Robeson County Deed Book III, 180; Harpers Ferry Baptist Church, 1887, Robeson County Deed Book HHH, 732; (New) Prospect Methodist Episcopal Church, 1887 and 1892, Robeson County Deed Book PPP, 95, and Robeson County Deed Book OOO, 999; St. Ana Freewill Baptist Church, 1900, Robeson County Deed Book 4D, 476; and Burnt Swamp Missionary Baptist Church, 1901, Robeson County Deed Book 4K, 535. Also see Pierce, Hunt-Locklear, Campisi, and White, *The Lumbee Petition*, 1:41, 2:65.

63. Thomas, *Away Down Home*, 113; Pembroke Senior High School literary magazine, *Lighter'd Knot* (Pembroke, N.C.: The School, 1977), 37.

64. Joseph Michael Smith and Lula Jane Smith, *The Lumbee Methodists: Getting to Know Them* (Raleigh, N.C.: Commission of Archives and History, North Carolina Methodist Conference, 1990), 62, 12–13; Lumber River Conference of the Holiness Methodist Church, *The History of the Lumbee Conference* (N.p.: Lumber River Conference of the Holiness Methodist Church, 2003), 75.

65. Magdol, "Against the Gentry," 276; Dial and Eliades, *The Only Land I Know*, 107.

66. The Oxendine family from Prospect encompassed four of the seven original trustees. The wife of Rev. W. L. Moore, Mary Catherine Oxendine, was the niece of fellow trustees John J. and James ("Big Jim") Oxendine, great-grandchildren of forefather Charles Oxendine (see Chart 4). Big Jim's son, Ollin, was also a trustee. Ollin's mother, Delilah, was a member of the Lowry family, along with several of the other wives of trustees. Delilah was the niece of Clarissa Lowry, who ten years earlier had sent George Washington Lowry to Oklahoma to research federal recognition. Clarissa's daughter Essy was the wife of trustee Isaac Brayboy. Trustee Preston Locklear, great-grandson of forefather John Locklear, was well known as the wealthiest Indian in the county at that time. His wife, Emmaline, was the granddaughter of Allen Lowry; Allen and Clarissa Lowry were first cousins, and both were the grandchildren of forefather James Lowry. Pierce, Hunt-Locklear, Campisi, and White, *The Lumbee Petition*, 1, chart 11; James Moore, interview by Waltz Maynor, Maxton, N.C., 13 July 2001, LRFC.

67. James Moore, interview by Waltz Maynor, Maxton, N.C., 13 July 2001, LRFC. Also see U.S. Bureau of the Census, *Population Schedules of the Ninth Census of the United States*, State of North Carolina, County of Robeson, Burnt Swamp Township, James and Delilly Oxendine record. Rev. Moore was the pastor of Prospect Church for its first forty-four years, from 1876 to 1920. Smith and Smith, *The Lumbee Methodists*, 30–32.

68. Karen I. Blu, "'Where Do You Stay At?' Home Place and Community among the Lumbee," in *Senses of Place*, ed. Steven Feld and Keith Basso (Santa Fe: School of American Research Press, 1996), 211–12; *History of the Lumbee Conference*, 18; Smith and Smith, *The Lumbee Methodists*, 13.

69. *History of the Lumbee Conference*, 55.

70. McMillan to S. M. Finger, 12 July 1889, quoted in ibid., 16.

71. Bauder to S. M. Finger, 29 March 1890, quoted in ibid., 16.

72. Smith and Smith, *The Lumbee Methodists*, 13.

73. Ibid., 62.

74. Ibid., 13.

75. *History of the Lumbee Conference*, 96.

76. Dial and Eliades, *The Only Land I Know*, 108.

77. Hamilton McMillan to O. M. McPherson, 2 August 1914, in O. M. McPherson, *Report on Condition and Tribal Rights of the Indians of Robeson and Adjoining Counties of North Carolina*, 63d Cong., 3d sess., 5 January 1915, S. Doc. 677 (Washington, D.C.: Government Printing Office, 1915), 242.

78. Charles F. Pierce, *Visit among the Croatan Indians, Living in the Vicinity of Pembroke, North Carolina* (Report, in the Field at Pipestone, Minn., to the Commissioner of Indian Affairs, U.S. Indian Service, Department of the Interior, 2 March 1912), RG 75, entry 161, file no. 23202-1912-123 General Services, 5, NARA.

79. Henderson, "The Croatan Indians of North Carolina," 3.

80. McMillan's daughter Cornelia related these memories to sociologist Guy Benton Johnson, who conducted fieldwork among Robeson County Indians in the 1930s. Field Notes, Cornelia McMillan, Red Springs, N.C., 5 August 1937 and 6 August 1937, GBJP. Indians generally thought of Red Springs as a racist town compared to Pembroke and Laurinburg. See Lucille Bullard and Florilla Thomas, interview by Katrina Locklear, Pembroke, N.C., 27 November 2001, LRFC.

81. Blu, *The Lumbee Problem*, 233.

82. Sherman Brooks, conversation with the author, Pembroke, N.C., July 2004; Cedric Woods, conversation with the author, Cambridge, Mass., 21 February 2008; Tina Dial, conversation with the author, Odenton, Md., 6 October 2005.

83. Blu, *The Lumbee Problem*, 180.

84. Wood, Montgomerie, and Yarnell, *Tuscarora Roots*, 82.

85. For the response to "Cro" as a racial slur, see Pierce, Hunt-Locklear, Campisi, and White, *The Lumbee Petition*, 1:51–52.

86. See A. W. McLean, "Historical Sketch of the Indians of Robeson County" and accompanying letters, in McPherson, *Report on Condition and Tribal Rights*, 120–32.

87. Field Notes, Anonymous Negro boy, Johnson Farm, 29 July 1937, GBJP; Field Notes, Blanche, n.d., GBJP; Field Notes, W. T. Parler, Red Springs, N.C., 26 July 1937, GBJP; N. M. McInnis to A. J. Maxwell, 5 June 1913, North Carolina Utilities Commission Archives Papers, North Carolina State Archives, Raleigh. Thanks to Jeff Currie for finding the McInnis letter and bringing it to my attention.

88. Memorandum to the file, from Frances Lopinsky, 25 November 1947, James E. Curry Papers, Subject file Regarding Indian Affairs, box 75, NAA.

89. Field Notes, Murphy Singleton, Red Springs, N.C., July 1937, GBJP.

90. Quoted in Wood, Montgomerie, and Yarnell, *Tuscarora Roots*, 81.

91. For other legal justice issues, see Draft Petition, 7 August 1937, GBJP; Field Notes, Mr. Skipper, Lumberton, N.C., n.d., GBJP; General Council of Siouan Indians to Secretary of the Interior, 15 July 1937, RG 75, entry 121, file no. 45499-1937-066 General Services, NARA; Henderson, "The Croatan Indians of North Carolina," 3; Wood, Montgomerie, and Yarnell, *Tuscarora Roots*, 81–82; "Indians and Negroes Get Call as Jurors," 18 August 1937, GBJP.

92. Carl C. Seltzer, "A Report on the Racial Status of Certain People in Robeson County, North Carolina," 30 June 1936, RG 75, entry 616, box 13–15, North Carolina, Applicant #22, NARA; Colan Brooks and Rosetta Brooks, interview by Adolph Dial, Pembroke, N.C., 2 September 1969, ADT.

93. Field Notes, Z. R. Chavis, Pembroke, N.C., July 1937, GBJP; Field Notes, William Erwin McConnaughey, Red Springs, N.C., July 1937, GBJP; Field Notes, Anonymous White Woman, Lumberton, N.C., n.d., GBJP; Field Notes, Murphy A. Singleton, Red Springs, N.C., n.d., GBJP.

94. Field Notes, Mrs. Stubbs and Elizabeth Stubbs, Pembroke, N.C., 30 July 1937, GBJP; Field Notes, Mr. Rogers, Lumberton, N.C., n.d., GBJP; Field Notes, Dr. M. C. Kinlaw, Pembroke, N.C., 4 August 1937, GBJP; Field Notes, Miss Clark, Red Springs, N.C., 26 July 1937, GBJP; Field Notes, Mrs. N. H. Dial, Prospect Community, N.C., 2 August 1937, GBJP; Field Notes, Mr. Chavis, Pembroke, N.C., n.d., GBJP; "Some Pertinent Problems and Questions," handwritten notes, n.d., GBJP.

95. Blu, *The Lumbee Problem*, 184–85; Malinda Maynor, producer and director, *Real Indian*, videocassette (Women Make Movies, 1996); Field Notes, Mrs. N. H. Dial, Prospect, 2 August 1937, GBJP; Anonymous, "Croatans," 25 March 1936, GBJP; Ira Pate Lowry, Untitled Presentation to Historical Research Class, 24 February 1982, PSU Oral History Project, Public Schools of Robeson County Indian Education Resource Center, Pembroke, N.C.

CHAPTER 2

1. Atelia Sampson Chavis, interview by author, and Verlain C. Emanuel, tape recording, Pembroke, N.C., 3 December 2001, LRFC; Verlain C. Emanuel, interview by author, and Atelia Sampson Chavis, tape recording, Pembroke, N.C., 3 December 2001, LRFC.

2. Brenda Dial Deese, "Ordinary People: Untucking Oral Teachings, Traditions, and Stories of Southeastern Indians" (Ph.D. diss., North Carolina State University, 2002), 136–37, 206; Jane Blanks Barnhill, "Deep Branch Church Cemetery," ⟨http://www.rootsweb .com/~ncrobeem/deep.html⟩ (accessed 2 January 2007).

3. For the multiple levels on which "race" is sensed, see Mark M. Smith, *How Race Is Made: Slavery, Segregation, and the Senses* (Chapel Hill: University of North Carolina Press, 2006).

4. Social and economic attitudes about race have been powerfully linked throughout American history but especially in the post–Civil War South, as freedmen asserted their rights to citizenship in all sectors of American life. Many elite whites responded by establishing new economic strategies intended to perpetuate their control of black people's labor. "Race" has been the reason most invoked to describe this profound inequality between blacks and whites, and for many years historians adopted southern whites' explanations of blacks' subjugated place in society: blacks were biologically inferior, primitively cultured, and fundamentally ill-suited to appreciate the benefits of citizenship. Historians have increasingly noted, however, the ways in which "race" has been a code word for "class" and/or "gender" in perpetuating inequalities in America. Scholars of the West and of American Indian history have not typically conversed with historians of the South, but common themes in the historiographic treatment of these regions abound. For example, Indians and blacks were often stereotyped similarly as "savages" or as obstacles to white progress, variously treated paternalistically or as a problem to be erased. See Frederick Jackson Turner, "The Significance of the Frontier in American History" (1893), in *History, Frontier, and Section: Three Essays by Frederick Jackson Turner* (Albuquerque: University of New Mexico Press, 1993), 59–91; and Ulrich Bonnell Phillips, "The Central Theme of Southern History," *American Historical Review* 34 (October 1928): 30–43. More recently, multiple opportunities exist to examine the exploitation of Indian and black labor and the alienation of Indian-owned and black-owned land—justified by racial stereotypes but having a much deeper motivation in white economic gain. In the South, American Indians in Robeson County are situated in both historical experiences. See Frederick E. Hoxie, *A Final Promise: The Campaign to Assimilate the Indians, 1880–1920* (Lincoln: University of Nebraska Press, 1984); Donald G. Nieman, ed., *From Slavery to Sharecropping: White Land and Black Labor in the Rural South, 1865–1900* (New York: Garland, 1994).

5. Fred A. Baker to Commissioner of Indian Affairs, 9 July 1935, in Fred A. Baker, *Report on Siouan Tribe of Indians in Robeson County, North Carolina*, RG 75, entry 121, file no. 36208-1935-310 General Services, NARA.

6. Julian T. Pierce, Cynthia Hunt-Locklear, Jack Campisi, and Wesley White, *The Lumbee Petition* (Pembroke, N.C.: Lumbee River Legal Services, 1987), 1:58, 227–30; Gerald Sider, *Living Indian Histories: Lumbee and Tuscarora People in North Carolina* (Chapel Hill: University of North Carolina Press, 2003), 31–32.

7. Pierce, Hunt-Locklear, Campisi, and White, *The Lumbee Petition*, 1:149–50; Robeson County Heritage Book Committee, *Our Heritage: Robeson County, North Carolina, 1748–*

2002 (Waynesville, N.C.: County Heritage, 2003), 101; O. M. McPherson, *Report on Condition and Tribal Rights of the Indians of Robeson and Adjoining Counties of North Carolina*, 63d Cong., 3d sess., 5 January 1915, S. Doc. 677 (Washington, D.C.: Government Printing Office, 1915), 242, Exhibit M.

8. Sider, *Living Indian Histories*, 33–35.

9. J. Morgan Kousser, "Progressivism—For Middle-Class Whites Only: North Carolina Education, 1880–1910," *Journal of Southern History* 46 (May 1980): 175, 182, 186, 190; Adam Fairclough, *Teaching Equality: Black Schools in the Age of Jim Crow* (Athens: University of Georgia Press, 2001), 10–11.

10. Fairclough, *Teaching Equality*, 12, 16; Glenda Elizabeth Gilmore, *Gender and Jim Crow: Women and the Politics of White Supremacy in North Carolina, 1896–1920* (Chapel Hill: University of North Carolina Press, 1996), 186.

11. Karen I. Blu, *The Lumbee Problem: The Making of an American Indian People* (New York: Cambridge University Press, 1980), 189.

12. For the mentality that led few Indians to think of themselves as poor, see John G. Peck, "Urban Station—Migration of the Lumbee Indians" (Ph.D. diss., University of North Carolina, 1972), 67; cited in Vernon Ray Thompson, "A History of the Education of the Lumbee Indians of Robeson County, North Carolina, from 1885 to 1970" (Ed.D. diss., University of Miami, 1973), 24. In using "middle class" here, I am appropriating a definition articulated by Richard White concerning the post–World War II middle class. In White's view, this middle class ideologically stressed "a common Americanness and a relatively homogenous set of values." This definition fits the Fourth Street Power Structure and their associates well because it does not emphasize the economic dimensions of the middle class, which are constantly in flux (and, in the Indian community, not that far removed from working-class or poor people). Rather, the definition focuses on issues of identity and how people identify themselves—in this case, with Indianness but also with Americanness and "progressive" values. Richard White, "A Commemoration and a Historical Mediation," *Journal of American History* 94 (March 2008): 1077.

13. Angelina Okuda-Jacobs, "Planting Health, Culture, and Sovereignty: Traditional Horticulture of the Lumbee Nation of North Carolina" (master's thesis, University of Wisconsin–Madison, 2000), 31; Karen I. Blu, "'Reading Back' to Find Community: Lumbee Ethnohistory," in *North American Indian Anthropology: Essays on Society and Culture*, ed. Raymond DeMallie and Alfonso Ortiz (Norman: University of Oklahoma Press, 1993), 280.

14. J. J. Blanks, "Part Two: The Croatan Indians in the Late War—Their Progress in Education and Religion," in Hamilton McMillan, *Sir Walter Raleigh's Lost Colony: An Historical Sketch of the Attempts of Sir Walter Raleigh to Establish a Colony in Virginia, with the Traditions of an Indian Tribe in North Carolina. Indicating the Fate of the Colony of Englishmen Left on Roanoke Island in 1587* (Wilson, N.C.: Advance Press, 1888), 28–35 (quote on p. 34).

15. Carroll B. Butler, *Treasures of the Longleaf Pines: Naval Stores* (Shalimar, Fla.: Tarkel Publishing, 1998), 20, 26–32; Malinda Maynor, "People and Place: Croatan Indians in Jim Crow Georgia, 1890–1920" (master's thesis, University of North Carolina at Chapel Hill, 2002); Robert B. Outland III, *Tapping the Pines: The Naval Stores Industry in the American South* (Baton Rouge: Louisiana State University Press, 2004).

16. Malinda Maynor, "People and Place: Croatan Indians in Jim Crow Georgia," *American Indian Culture and Research Journal* 21 (Spring 2005): 37–64.

17. Ruth Dial Woods, "Growing Up Red: The Lumbee Experience" (Ph.D. diss., University of North Carolina at Chapel Hill, 2001), 26; Pierce, Hunt-Locklear, Campisi, and White, *The Lumbee Petition*, 1:133–36; Fred A. Baker to Commissioner of Indian Affairs, 9 July 1935, in Baker, *Report on Siouan Tribe of Indians*, NARA; Charles F. Pierce, *Visit among the Croatan Indians, Living in the Vicinity of Pembroke, North Carolina* (Report, in the Field at Pipestone, Minn., to the Commissioner of Indian Affairs, U.S. Indian Service, Department of the Interior, 2 March 1912), RG 75, entry 161, file no. 23202-1912-123 General Services, 3, NARA; R. T. Melvin and A. M. Johnson, "Final Plans for the Pembroke Indian Resettlement Project," RG 96, entry 85, box 1, 3, region IV, Project Plans file of C. B. Faris, NARA.

18. Melvin and Johnson, "Final Plans," 3.

19. John Pearmain, "Report . . . On the Conditions of the Indians in Robeson County, North Carolina," 11 November 1935, RG 75, entry 121, file no. 64190-1935-066 part 1-A, 29, NARA.

20. Fred A. Baker to Commissioner of Indian Affairs, 9 July 1935, in Baker, *Report on Siouan Tribe of Indians*, NARA; also see Blu, *The Lumbee Problem*, 163–67; and A. M. Johnson and R. T. Melvin, "Report of Reconnaissance Survey of Pembroke Indian Community Resettlement Project Area," RG 96, entry 85, region IV, Project Plans file of C. B. Faris, box 1, 2, NARA.

21. John Pearmain, "'Reservation': Siouan Tribe of Indians of Robeson County, North Carolina" (Indian Office Handbook of Information, comp. October 1935), 42–43; Pearmain, "Report," 38; Maggie J. Oxendine, interview by author, Pembroke, N.C., 4 May 2004.

22. Pearmain, "Report," 37; Melvin and Johnson, "Final Plans," 19. These types of foreclosures due to debt were similar to those endured by Indians who were farming on allotments of reservation land under the federal government's allotment policy. An important difference between the Robeson County Indians and Indian allottees (particularly in Oklahoma) was that Indian allottees lost a vast amount of land in a generation's time, whereas Robeson County Indian loss was more gradual. Most of the land loss was due to sales of allotments or cessions of surplus reservation lands after allotment had taken place, but some foreclosures due to unpaid debt did occur. Indians in Robeson County had been private landowners since deeds were first recorded by the English Crown, and they had experienced various waves of land acquisition and loss since English settlement of the area in the 1730s. This long-term loss arguably heightened their insistence on a solution apart from futile negotiations with white creditors, who had lost economic strength themselves in the declining southern agricultural economy. Like the Kiowas in Oklahoma, however, Indians in Robeson County understood that they were losing their farms to make more land available to white farmers and white-owned companies who could profit from it. They responded to these conditions by advocating for political autonomy and self-determination, trying to turn a short-term loss into a long-term gain. Officials from the Office of Indian Affairs likely saw this connection between Robeson County Indians and reservation tribes, hence their interest in helping Indians solve an economic problem more related to the southern agricultural system than to federal Indian policy. Bonnie Lynn-Sherow, *Red Earth: Race and Agriculture in Oklahoma Territory* (Lawrence: University Press of Kansas, 2004), 126. For an important analysis of the differences between short-term

and long-term dispossession, see Emily Greenwald, *Reconfiguring the Reservation: The Nez Perces, Jicarilla Apaches, and the Dawes Act* (Albuquerque: University of New Mexico Press, 2002), 146.

23. Pearmain, "Report," 2, 17, 44, 72; Melvin and Johnson, "Final Plans," 19.

24. Okuda-Jacobs, "Planting Health, Culture, and Sovereignty," 32–33; Sider, *Living Indian Histories*, 151–53; Peter H. Wood, Deborah Montgomerie, and Susan Yarnell, *Tuscarora Roots: An Historical Report regarding the Relation of the Hatteras Tuscarora Tribe of Robeson County, North Carolina, to the Original Tuscarora Indian Tribe* (Durham, N.C.: Hatteras Tuscarora Tribal Foundation, 1992), 78; Melvin and Johnson, "Final Plans," 3; Samuel H. McCrory and Carl W. Mengel, *A Report upon the Back Swamp and Jacob Swamp Drainage District, Robeson County, North Carolina* (Washington, D.C.: Government Printing Office, 1912), 7.

25. James E. Chavis to A. A. Grorud, 22 August 1934, SIF; D. L. Locklear to A. A. Grorud, 24 August 1934, SIF.

26. Pearmain, "Reservation," 44; Fred A. Baker to Commissioner of Indian Affairs, 9 July 1935, in Baker, *Report on Siouan Tribe of Indians*, NARA.

27. Pearmain, "Report," 30, 47; Fred A. Baker to Commissioner of Indian Affairs, 9 July 1935, in Baker, *Report on Siouan Tribe of Indians*, NARA.

28. Pearmain, "Report," B, 4, 6, 7, 19, 27, 43, 48; Fred A. Baker to Commissioner of Indian Affairs, 9 July 1935, in Baker, *Report on Siouan Tribe of Indians*, NARA.

29. Theodore Saloutos, *The American Farmer and the New Deal* (Ames: Iowa State University Press, 1982), 48, 68–69, 100, 108, 151, 188–89, 255; Fred H. Drayer to George S. Mitchell, 26 April 1938, RG 96, entry 79, Correspondence Relating to Resettlement Projects, box 35, folder: 120-01-Reports (Labor Relations), NARA; A. C. Locklear to Elmer Thomas, 3 May 1941, SIF; John Wesley Oxendine to Elmer Thomas, 3 May 1941, SIF.

30. D'Arcy McNickle to Commissioner of Indian Affairs, 7 April 1936, RG 75, entry 121, file no. 45499-1937-066 General Services, NARA; Field Notes, Murphy Singleton, Red Springs, N.C., July 1937, GBJP; A. M. Johnson to Bruce Poundstone, 20 December 1935, RG 96, entry 85, region IV, Project Plans file of C. B. Faris, box 1, NARA; Pearmain, "Report," 8, 13, 14, 29, 41, 51, 53; Christopher Arris Oakley, *Keeping the Circle: American Indian Identity in Eastern North Carolina, 1885–2004* (Lincoln: University of Nebraska Press, 2005), 43.

31. Pearmain, "Report," 47, 49; Pearmain, "Reservation," 43–44.

32. Lawrence Maynor to John Collier, 1 December 1939, RG 75, entry 121, file no. 45499-1937-066 General Services, NARA. Maynor was one of the Indians recognized as having one-half or more "Indian blood" by the Department of the Interior in 1939 (see chapter 6).

33. Ella Deloria to Franz Boas, 7 August 1940, Franz Boas Papers, American Philosophical Society, Philadelphia, Pa.; J. O. Walker to George S. Mitchell, 24 March 1937, RG 96, entry 79, region IV, box 39, folder: Wolf Pit/Pembroke-913, NARA-Atlanta; Pearmain, "Reservation," 44; Fred A. Baker to Commissioner of Indian Affairs, 9 July 1935, in Baker, *Report on Siouan Tribe of Indians*, NARA; Pearmain, "Report," 29; Waltz Maynor, conversation with the author, Pembroke, N.C., 31 July 2003.

34. Blu, "Where Do You Stay At?," 208–9.

35. Purnell Swett, interview by author, Pembroke, N.C., 19 February 2004, LRFC.

36. Blu, "'Reading Back' to Find Community," 282. For the violent effects of bootlegging, see James E. Henderson, "The Croatan Indians of North Carolina," 11 December 1923, RG 75, entry 121, file no. 93807-1923-CHEROKEE SCHOOL-150, 2, NARA.

37. Joseph Earl Dabney, *Mountain Spirits: A Chronicle of Corn Whiskey from King James' Ulster Plantation to America's Appalachians and the Moonshine Life* (New York: Charles Scribner's Sons, 1974), 143–44. Rhoda Lowry, for example, the widow of Henry Berry Lowry, was put in jail for selling liquor without a license in 1897. My great-grandmother Martha was also a bootlegger. Other references in newspaper articles, court cases, and family conversations indicated the existence of female bootleggers. See *Robesonian*, 10 November 1897; see also references to Indian women selling liquor in Pembroke in the 1939 *State v. Bricey Hammonds* case. Hammonds was convicted for killing a prison guard in a drunken fray; both he and the guard had gotten drunk off of Indian women's liquor. David M. Britt to Commissioner of Indian Affairs, 23 February 1939, RG 75, entry 121, file No. 45499-1937-066 General Services, NARA. Women's role in selling and making liquor was not exceptional; historian Mary Murphy examines the phenomenon in Montana during Prohibition. Mary Murphy, "Bootlegging Mothers and Drinking Daughters: Gender and Prohibition in Butte, Montana," *American Quarterly* 46 (June 1994): 174–94.

38. Charlie Lowry, interview by Adolph Dial, 4 August 1969, ADT; Jeffrey Maynor, conversation with the author, Pembroke, N.C., 2 June 2004; Waltz Maynor, conversation with the author, Pembroke, N.C., 2 June 2004; Willie French Lowery, conversation with the author, Pembroke, N.C., 2 June 2004. See also Robeson County Heritage Book Committee, *Our Heritage*, 151; Henry A. McKinnon Jr., *Historical Sketches of Robeson County* (N.p.: Historic Robeson, Inc., 2001), 110–13; Blu, "'Reading Back' to Find Community," 286–87.

39. Elisha Locklear, interview with the author and Waltz Maynor, Pembroke, N.C., 19 January 2002, LRFC.

40. Cherokee Indian Normal School, "Catalogue, 1935–1936; Announcements for 1936–1937" (Pembroke, N.C.: June 1936), 18–19, GBJP.

41. Blu, *The Lumbee Problem*, 137–38; Woods, "Growing Up Red," 80. For attitudes espoused by African American "best men" and "best women," see Gilmore, *Gender and Jim Crow*, 3, 13–14.

42. Compare Blu, *The Lumbee Problem*, 140–42, 187–89.

43. Rev. Michael Cummings, interview with the author, Pembroke, N.C., 10 November 1996.

44. Ella Deloria to Franz Boas, 7 August 1940, Franz Boas Papers, American Philosophical Society; Ella Deloria to Ruth Bronson, 6 August 1940 (copy in personal possession of the author), NARA; Waltz Maynor, conversation with the author, Pembroke, N.C., 31 July 2003; Cherokee Indian Normal School, "Catalogue," 7; Blu, *The Lumbee Problem*, 87; Burnt Swamp Baptist Association, *The History of the Burnt Swamp Baptist Association and Its Churches* (N.p., 2002), 11–14, 32, 80–81, 94; Woods, "Growing Up Red," 33.

45. Waltz Maynor, conversation with the author, Pembroke, N.C., 31 July 2003.

46. Compare Wood, Montgomerie, and Yarnell, *Tuscarora Roots*, 88.

CHAPTER 3

1. John R. Swanton, "Probable Identity of the 'Croatan' Indians," 1933, MS 4126, 1, NAA.

2. I am inferring that Swanton met this man because Mooney died in 1918, seven years after this photograph was taken. Twenty or more years later, Swanton recalled that he met the man "a few years" before Mooney's death, and in comparison to two decades of time passing, Swanton may have remembered seven years as "a few."

3. Thanks to James Locklear's publication *Native Visions*, Pembroke's current and only Indian newspaper, for the identification of Mr. Locklear's photograph. See "Pembroke's Rich History of Print Journalism," *Native Visions* 3 (January 2008), 24.

4. For an explanation of Indians' negative reactions to the way whites used "Croatan," see Clifton Oxendine, "A Social and Economic History of the Indians of Robeson County, North Carolina" (master's thesis, George Peabody College for Teachers, 1934), 51–52. See also James E. Henderson, "The Croatan Indians of North Carolina," 11 December 1923, RG 75, entry 121, file no. 93807-1923-CHEROKEE SCHOOL-150], 1, NARA; Karen I. Blu, *The Lumbee Problem: The Making of an American Indian People* (New York: Cambridge University Press, 1980), 78.

5. Field Notes, Anonymous Negro boy, Johnson Farm, 29 July 1937, GBJP.

6. Ned Blackhawk, *Violence over the Land: Indians and Empires in the Early American West* (Cambridge, Mass.: Harvard University Press, 2006), 8.

7. Eva Marie Garroutte, *Real Indians: Identity and the Survival of Native America* (Berkeley: University of California Press, 2003), chap. 1; Alexandra Harmon, *Indians in the Making: Ethnic Relations and Indian Identities around Puget Sound* (Berkeley: University of California Press, 1998), 138–39; Blu, *The Lumbee Problem*, 36, 79.

8. House Committee on Indian Affairs, *Hearings before the Committee on Indian Affairs on S. 3258 to Acquire a Site and Erect Buildings for a School for the Indians of Robeson County, N.C., and for Other Purposes*, 62nd Cong., 2nd sess., 14 February 1913 (Washington, D.C.: Government Printing Office, 1913); A. W. McLean, "Historical Sketch of the Indians of Robeson County" and accompanying letters, in O. M. McPherson, *Report on Condition and Tribal Rights of the Indians of Robeson and Adjoining Counties of North Carolina*, 63d Cong., 3d sess., 5 January 1915, S. Doc. 677 (Washington, D.C.: Government Printing Office, 1915), 120–32.

9. House Committee on Indian Affairs, *Hearings before the Committee on Indian Affairs*, 3, 18; Julian T. Pierce, Cynthia Hunt-Locklear, Jack Campisi and Wesley White, *The Lumbee Petition* (Pembroke, N.C.: Lumbee River Legal Services, 1987), 1:54.

10. House Committee on Indian Affairs, *Hearings before the Committee on Indian Affairs*, 19.

11. Blu, *The Lumbee Problem*, 79.

12. Anna Bailey, "'It Is the Center to Which We Should Cling': Indian Schools in Robeson County, North Carolina, 1900–1920," in *The History of Discrimination in U.S. Education: Marginality, Agency, and Power*, ed. Eileen H. Tamura (New York: Palgrave MacMillan, 2008), 76; House Committee on Indian Affairs, *Hearings before the Committee on Indian Affairs*, 26.

13. John R. Finger, *Cherokee Americans: The Eastern Band of Cherokees in the Twentieth Century* (Lincoln: University of Nebraska Press, 1991), 9–11, 23–24.

14. James C. Scott, *Seeing Like a State: How Certain Schemes to Improve the Human Condition Have Failed* (New Haven, Conn.: Yale University Press, 1998).

15. Frederick E. Hoxie, *A Final Promise: The Campaign to Assimilate the Indians, 1880–*

1920 (Lincoln: University of Nebraska Press, 1984), 165; Tanis C. Thorne, *The World's Richest Indian: The Scandal over Jackson Barnett's Oil Fortune* (New York: Oxford University Press, 2003), chap. 2.

16. Historian Lawrence Kelly describes Burke as a commissioner who was unwilling to acknowledge that Indians had any rights at all, much less rights that might supercede the claims of whites. Lawrence Kelly, *The Assault on Assimilation: John Collier and the Origins of Indian Policy Reform* (Albuquerque: University of New Mexico Press, 1983), 368.

17. Bailey, "It Is the Center to Which We Should Cling," 85–86.

18. Cindy D. Padget, "The Lost Indians of the Lost Colony: A Critical Legal Study of the Lumbee Indians of North Carolina," *American Indian Law Review* 21 (Spring 1997): 404–6. See also Anne Merline McCulloch and David E. Wilkins, "'Constructing' Nations within States: The Quest for Federal Recognition by the Catawba and Lumbee Tribes," *American Indian Quarterly* 19 (Summer 1995): 361–89; Garroutte, *Real Indians*, chap. 1; Harmon, *Indians in the Making*, 138–39.

19. Gerald Sider, *Living Indian Histories: Lumbee and Tuscarora People in North Carolina* (Chapel Hill: University of North Carolina Press, 2003), 149; McPherson, *Report on Condition and Tribal Rights*, Exhibit A.

20. Policy makers' own frustration with McPherson's report, and their assessments of his recommendations, are found in Elwood P. Morey to Commissioner of Indian Affairs, n.d., JBC; D'Arcy McNickle, "Indians of Robeson County, North Carolina," 1 May 1936, 2, 8, RG 75, entry 121, file no. 45499-1937-066 General Services, NARA; Fred A. Baker to Commissioner of Indian Affairs, 9 July 1935, in Fred A. Baker, *Report on Siouan Tribe of Indians in Robeson County, North Carolina*, RG 75, entry 121, file no. 36208-1935-310 General Services, NARA.

21. Pierce, Hunt-Locklear, Campisi, and White, *The Lumbee Petition*, 1:56–60.

22. Ibid., 1:40; Charles F. Pierce, *Visit among the Croatan Indians, Living in the Vicinity of Pembroke, North Carolina* (Report, in the Field at Pipestone, Minn., to the Commissioner of Indian Affairs, U.S. Indian Service, Department of the Interior, 2 March 1912), RG 75, entry 161, file no. 23202-1912-123 General Services, NARA; McNickle, "Indians of Robeson County," 4.

23. Francis Paul Prucha, *The Great Father: The United States Government and the American Indians*, abridged ed. (Lincoln: University of Nebraska Press, 1984), 263–67, 272–73, 299–300; Hoxie, *A Final Promise*, 168, chaps. 6 and 7.

24. A. B. Locklear to A. A. Grorud, 5 October 1931, SIF; A. A. Grorud to J. W. Oxendine, 26 October 1931, SIF; Minutes of a General Meeting, 11 December 1931, SIF; Minutes of a Council and Business Committee Meeting, 16 January 1932, SIF.

25. Karen I. Blu, "'Reading Back' to Find Community: Lumbee Ethnohistory," in *North American Indian Anthropology: Essays on Society and Culture*, ed. Raymond DeMallie and Alfonso Ortiz (Norman: University of Oklahoma Press, 1993), 283.

26. Prucha, *The Great Father*, 278–79, 286–87. For a full treatment of this subject, see Vine Deloria Jr. and Clifford Lytle, *The Nations Within: The Past and Future of American Indian Sovereignty* (New York: Pantheon Books, 1984).

27. For the backgrounds of the members of the Business Committee, see Polly Crandall [pseud.], interview by author, Pembroke, N.C., 19 May 2004 (copy in personal possession of the interviewee); Business Committee of the Cherokee Indians of Robeson and Adjoin-

ing Counties, North Carolina to Cameron Morrison and Josiah W. Bailey, 29 March 1932, box 310, folder: Interior, 1932, January–March, JBC.

28. A. A. Grorud to B. G. Graham, 31 December 1931, SIF.

29. B. G. Graham, A. B. Locklear, F. L. Locklear to Senator Lynn J. Frazier, 21 January 1932, SIF; B. G. Graham, A. B. Locklear, F. L. Locklear to A. A. Grorud, 8 July 1932, SIF.

30. John Collier to Josiah W. Bailey, 26 March 1932, box 310, folder: Interior, 1932, January–March, JBC.

31. A. B. Locklear told Bailey in a letter that over 1,700 people had actually signed the petition but that he was only forwarding 600 of the names. See A. B. Locklear to Josiah W. Bailey, 2 April 1932, box 310, folder: Interior, 1932, April–June, JBC.

32. John Collier to Josiah W. Bailey, 26 March 1932, box 310, folder: Interior, 1932, January–March, JBC; Business Committee of the Cherokee Indians of Robeson and Adjoining Counties, North Carolina to Cameron Morrison and Josiah W. Bailey, 29 March 1932, box 310, folder: Interior, 1932, January–March, JBC.

33. Josiah W. Bailey to L. R. Varser, 8 April 1932, box 310, folder: Interior, 1932, April–June, JBC.

34. L. R. Varser to Josiah W. Bailey, 12 April 1932, box 310, folder: Interior, 1932, April–June, JBC.

35. Thaddeus Page to Elwood P. Morey, 13 May 1932, box 310, folder: Interior, 1932, April–June, JBC.

36. Angus W. McLean to Josiah W. Bailey, 14 May 1932, box 310, folder: Interior, 1932, April–June, JBC.

37. C. J. Rhoads to Secretary of the Interior, 24 May 1932, box 310, folder: Interior, 1933, January–March 15, JBC.

38. James Mooney, "Croatan Indians," n.d., MS 1921, NAA. The document contains the express statement: "They are not Cherokee Indians," followed by a paragraph demonstrating why. This statement leads me to believe that the document was written sometime after 1910, when it was first proposed that Robeson County Indians be designated as "Cherokees."

39. C. J. Rhoads to Secretary of the Interior, 24 May 1932, box 310, folder: Interior, 1933, January–March 15, JBC.

40. Angus W. McLean to Thaddeus Page, 22 July 1932, box 310, folder: Interior, 1932, July–December, JBC; Angus W. McLean to Josiah W. Bailey, 16 August 1932, box 310, folder: Interior, 1932, July–December, JBC.

41. A. B. Locklear to Lynn Frazier, 17 January 1933, SIF.

42. For more on the "Pocahontas Exception," see Helen C. Rountree, *Pocahontas's People: The Powhatan Indians of Virginia through Four Centuries* (Norman: University of Oklahoma Press, 1996), 221; J. Douglas Smith, *Managing White Supremacy: Race, Politics, and Citizenship in Jim Crow Virginia* (Chapel Hill: University of North Carolina Press, 2002), 87; Peggy Pascoe, *What Comes Naturally: Miscegenation Law and the Making of Race in America* (London: Oxford University Press, 2009), 148.

43. A. B. Locklear to A. A. Grorud, 29 April 1932, SIF; A. B. Locklear to A. A. Grorud, 30 April 1932, SIF; A. B. Locklear to J. W. Bailey, 30 April 1932, SIF; A. A. Grorud to A. B. Locklear, 2 May 1932, SIF.

44. A. A. Grorud to A. B. Locklear, 3 August 1932, SIF.

45. A. B. Locklear to A. A. Grorud, 2 August 1932, SIF.

46. A. B. Locklear to A. A. Grorud, 20 June 1932, SIF; A. A. Grorud to A. B. Locklear, 25 June 1932, SIF.

47. A. B. Locklear to Josiah W. Bailey, 5 July 1932, box 310, folder: Interior, 1932, July–December, JBC; Josiah W. Bailey to A. B. Locklear, 7 July 1932, box 310, folder: Interior, 1932, July–December, JBC.

48. A. B. Locklear to Josiah W. Bailey, 24 February 1933, box 310, folder: Interior, 1933, January–March 15, JBC.

49. Crandall, interview by author.

50. For Locklear's replacement by Joseph Brooks, see Joseph Brooks and B. G. Graham to Josiah W. Bailey, 13 March 1933, box 310, folder: Interior, 1933, January–March 15, JBC; Josiah W. Bailey to A. B. Locklear, 29 March 1933, box 311, folder: Interior, 1933, March 16–May, JBC; and Boss Locklear to Josiah W. Bailey, 18 April 1933, box 311, folder: Interior, 1933, March 16–May, JBC. For trip to Washington, see A. B. Locklear to A. A. Grorud, 28 February 1933, SIF.

51. Shaw Deese to Josiah W. Bailey, 7 March 1933, box 310, folder: Interior, 1933, January–March 15, JBC.

52. Colon Brooks to Josiah W. Bailey, 15 March 1933, box 310, folder: Interior, 1933, January–March 15, JBC.

53. Several scholars have demonstrated a similar reaction among other Indian tribes, including the Cherokee and Lakota. See Thomas Biolsi, *Organizing the Lakota: The Political Economy of the New Deal on the Pine Ridge and Rosebud Reservations* (Tucson: University of Arizona Press, 1992), chap. 7; and Circe Sturm, *Blood Politics: Race, Culture, and Identity in the Cherokee Nation of Oklahoma* (Berkeley: University of California Press, 2002), 48.

54. A. B. Locklear to Josiah W. Bailey, 20 March 1933, box 311, folder: Interior, 1933, March 16–May, JBC. Locklear also wrote Grorud the same letter; see A. B. Locklear to A. A. Grorud, 20 March 1933, SIF.

55. Josiah W. Bailey to A. B. Locklear, 29 March 1933, box 311, folder: Interior, 1933, March 16–May, JBC.

56. B. G. Graham and Joseph Brooks to Josiah W. Bailey, 4 April 1933, box 311, folder: Interior, 1933, March 16–May, JBC; James E. Chavis, interview by Adolph Dial, Pembroke, N.C., 19–20 August 1971, ADT.

57. Thaddeus Page to John Collier, 22 April 1933, box 311, folder: Interior, 1933, March 16–May, JBC.

58. Swanton, "Probable Identity of the 'Croatan' Indians," 1–2, 3–5; see notes and correspondence accompanying Swanton's report, MS 4126, NAA.

59. Pierce, Hunt-Locklear, Campisi, and White, *The Lumbee Petition*, 1:67, 71; copy of S. 1632, RG 75, entry 121, file no. 45499-1937-066 General Services, NARA; James E. Chavis, interview by Adolph Dial, Pembroke, N.C., 19–20 August 1971, ADT; *Robesonian*, 23 April 1934.

60. Joseph Brooks to A. A. Grorud, 23 May 1933, SIF.

61. A. A. Grorud to James Chavis, 28 July 1933, quoted in Pierce, Hunt-Locklear, Campisi, and White, *The Lumbee Petition*, 1:71.

62. Resolution of Cheraw Indians of Robeson and Adjoining Counties, 2 December 1933, box 311, folder: Interior, 1933, November 25–1934, February 5, JBC.

63. James E. Chavis, interview by Adolph Dial, Pembroke, N.C., 19–20 August 1971, ADT; U.S. Senate, *Recognition as Siouan Indians of Lumber River of Certain Indians in North Carolina*, 73rd Cong., 2d sess., 23 January 1934, S. Rpt. 204, 2; Pierce, Hunt-Locklear, Campisi, and White, *The Lumbee Petition*, 1:71.

64. U.S. Senate, *Recognition as Siouan Indians*, 2–3.

65. James E. Chavis to A. A. Grorud, 10 March 1934, SIF.

66. A. A. Grorud to B. G. Graham, 14 March 1934, SIF.

67. Clifton Oxendine to Josiah W. Bailey, 1 February 1934, box 311, folder: Interior, 1934, Feb. 6–March 13, JBC; Clifton Oxendine, interview by Carol Hunt and Jennings Bullard, Pembroke, N.C., 17 July 1982, PSU Oral History Project, Public Schools of Robeson County Indian Education Resource Center, Pembroke, N.C.

68. E. J. Britt to Josiah W. Bailey, 12 February 1934, box 311, folder: Interior, 1934, Feb. 6–March 13, JBC; Pierce, Hunt-Locklear, Campisi, and White, *The Lumbee Petition*, 1:74.

69. T. A. McNeill to Josiah W. Bailey, 12 February 1934, box 311, folder: Interior, 1934, Feb. 6–March 13, JBC.

70. O. H. Lowrey to Josiah W. Bailey, 12 February 1934, box 311, folder: Interior, 1934, Feb. 6–March 13, JBC.

71. E. B. Sampson, D. F. Lowry, J. R. Lowry, W. H. Godwin, to J. Bayard Clark, 22 February 1934, box 311, folder: Interior, 1934, Feb. 6–March 13, JBC.

72. Josiah W. Bailey to W. H. Godwin, 24 February 1934, box 311, folder: Interior, 1934, Feb. 6–March 13, JBC.

73. *Robesonian*, 23 April 1934.

74. A. A. Grorud to James E. Chavis, 28 March 1934, SIF.

75. *Robesonian*, 12 April 1934, 16 April 1934, 23 April 1934.

76. James E. Chavis to A. A. Grorud, 22 August 1934, SIF.

77. *Robesonian*, 23 April 1934.

78. Rebecca S. Seib, *Indians of Robeson County Land Ownership Study, 1900–1910* (Pembroke, N.C.: Lumbee Regional Development Association, n.d.), map 2.

79. Members of the "Fourth Street Power Structure" who took up the "Cherokee" cause were J. C. Oxendine, D. F. Lowry, and James R. Lowry; see J. H. Sampson et al. to Josiah W. Bailey, 10 February 1934, box 311, folder: Interior, 1934, Feb. 6–March 13, JBC; and E. B. Sampson, D. F. Lowry, J. R. Lowry, W. H. Godwin to J. Bayard Clark, 22 February 1934, box 311, folder: Interior, 1934, Feb. 6–March 13, JBC. Orlin H. Lowry, who wrote a letter to Bailey against the "Siouan" bill, was D. F. Lowry's first cousin and lived in the Union Chapel community; see Lumber River Conference of the Holiness Methodist Church, *The History of the Lumbee Conference* (N.p.: Lumber River Conference of the Holiness Methodist Church, 2003), 59. Clifton Oxendine may have been a cousin to J. C. Oxendine; see Seib, *Indians of Robeson County*, 218–19. L. W. Jacobs, another member of the "Fourth Street Power Structure," lived in Pembroke but was named as a "friend" of the "Siouans" by Council Secretary James E. Chavis; see James E. Chavis to Josiah W. Bailey, 10 March 1934, box 311, folder: Interior, 1934, Feb. 6–March 13, JBC. B. G. Graham, Joseph Brooks, and James E. Chavis all considered Saint Annah their home settlement, though Brooks lived closer to Pembroke; see Crandall, interview by author; Ed Chavis, interview by author, Pembroke, N.C., 9 June 2004; and Enrollment List of Siouan Indians of Lumber River, 18 May 1935, RG 75, entry 121, file no. 39490-1935-361 General Service, NARA.

The "Siouans'" heavy representation north of Pembroke is partly due to the fact that the Indian population and Indian landownership was much more dense north of Pembroke than south of Pembroke; see Seib, *Indians of Robeson County*, map 2.

80. *Robesonian*, 23 April 1934.

81. The previous two paragraphs follow closely the argument presented in Pierce, Hunt-Locklear, Campisi, and White, *The Lumbee Petition*, 1:203.

82. Blu, *The Lumbee Problem*, 137–42.

83. Compare Pierce, Hunt-Locklear, Campisi, and White, *The Lumbee Petition*, 1:203.

CHAPTER 4

1. This admittedly simplified definition of modernity is inspired most by James C. Scott, *Seeing Like a State: How Certain Schemes to Improve the Human Condition Have Failed* (New Haven, Conn.: Yale University Press, 1998). For modernity's influence on segregation, see Mark Schultz, *The Rural Face of White Supremacy: Beyond Jim Crow* (Urbana: University of Illinois Press, 2005), 68; Grace Elizabeth Hale, *Making Whiteness: The Culture of Segregation in the South* (New York: Pantheon Books, 1998); and William A. Link, *The Paradox of Southern Progressivism, 1880–1930* (Chapel Hill: University of North Carolina Press, 1992).

2. Philip J. Deloria, *Indians in Unexpected Places* (Lawrence: University Press of Kansas, 2004).

3. For the false dichotomy of modern and premodern, see Bruno LaTour, *We Have Never Been Modern*, trans. Catherine Porter (Cambridge, Mass.: Harvard University Press, 1993).

4. I am indebted to Phil Deloria's *Indians in Unexpected Places* for this language of expectation. Using "expectation" does not presume that the system of segregation or of Indian policy is normal; rather, it is simply expected and therefore a cultural construction.

5. Compare Lizabeth Cohen, *Making a New Deal: Industrial Workers in Chicago, 1919–1939* (New York: Cambridge University Press, 1990).

6. Vine Deloria Jr. and Clifford Lytle, *The Nations Within: The Past and Future of American Indian Sovereignty* (New York: Pantheon Books, 1984), 170.

7. Jack D. Forbes, "The Manipulation of Race, Caste, and Identity: Classifying Afroamericans, Native Americans, and Red-Black People," *Journal of Ethnic Studies* 17 (Winter 1990): 12; Gary B. Nash, "The Hidden History of Mestizo America," *Journal of American History* 82 (December 1995): 955–56; Michelle Brattain, "Miscegenation and Competing Definitions of Race in Twentieth-Century Louisiana," *Journal of Southern History* 71 (August 2005): 631, 644–46; Charles F. Robinson, *Dangerous Liaisons: Sex and Love in the Segregated South* (Fayetteville: University of Arkansas Press, 2003); Peggy Pascoe, "Race, Gender, and the Privileges of Property: On the Significance of Miscegenation Law in the U.S. West," in *Over the Edge: Remapping the American West*, ed. Valerie J. Matsumoto and Blake Allmendinger (Berkeley: University of California Press, 1999), 215–30; Peggy Pascoe, "Miscegenation Law, Court Cases, and Ideologies of 'Race' in Twentieth-Century America," *Journal of American History* 83 (June 1996): 44–69; Julie Novkov, "Racial Constructions: The Legal Regulation of Miscegenation in Alabama, 1890–1934," *Law and History Review* 20 (Summer 2002), ⟨http://historycooperative.press.uiuc.edu/journals/lhr/20.2/novkov.html⟩ (accessed 6 April 2007); Schultz, *The Rural Face of White Supremacy*, 68–72; Hale, *Making Whiteness*, 6–7.

8. Historian Melissa Meyer points out that most societies throughout the world have seen blood not simply as a metaphor but as a substance that conveys essential attributes. White supremacists' use of it was not new. This tendency is pervasive and "inherently human," in Meyer's view. But Meyer also points out that the fact that societies take blood literally does not mean that all of them have used it to rank peoples or determine group membership and identity. Melissa Meyer, *Thicker than Water: The Origins of Blood as Symbol and Ritual* (New York: Routledge, 2005), 16, 208. For blood as property, see Novkov, "Racial Constructions," 1–2, 13, 16; and Pascoe, "Race, Gender, and the Privileges of Property," 46. See also Cheryl Harris, "Whiteness as Property," *Harvard Law Review* 106 (1993): 1709–95; Eva Saks, "Representing Miscegenation Law," *Raritan* 8 (June 1988): 39–69; and Robinson, *Dangerous Liaisons*. For more on scientific racism, see Stephen J. Gould, *The Mismeasure of Man* (New York: Norton, 1996); and Evelynn M. Hammonds and Rebecca M. Herzig, *The Nature of Difference: Sciences of Race in the United States from Jefferson to Genomics* (Cambridge, Mass.: MIT Press, 2008).

9. The relationship between "Indian blood" and "Indian culture" evolved as the OIA implemented the 1885 Dawes General Allotment Act. See Eva Marie Garroutte, *Real Indians: Identity and the Survival of Native America* (Berkeley: University of California Press, 2003), 42; Melissa L. Meyer, "American Indian Blood Quantum Requirements: Blood Is Thicker than Family," in Matsumoto and Allmendinger, *Over the Edge*, 232–33, 239. Some have asserted that the rise of anthropologist Franz Boas's emphasis on cultural pluralism heralded the demise of this inexorable link between blood and culture; see Elezar Barkan, *The Retreat of Scientific Racism: Changing Concepts of Race in Britain and the United States between the World Wars* (Cambridge: Cambridge University Press, 1992). But legal historian Peggy Pascoe has demonstrated that the influence of Boas's views on the law and policy was not as broad as one might think; see Pascoe, "Miscegenation Law," 44–69.

10. Garroutte, *Real Indians*, 67–68.

11. Ibid., 45–46.

12. Houston A. Baker, *Modernism and the Harlem Renaissance* (Chicago: University of Chicago Press, 1987); Daylanne K. English, *Unnatural Selections: Eugenics in American Modernism and the Harlem Renaissance* (Chapel Hill: University of North Carolina Press, 2004).

13. John Collier, *From Every Zenith: A Memoir and Some Essays on Life and Thought* (Denver, Colo.: Sage Books, 1963), 1, 21, 53.

14. Ibid., 125–26; Graham D. Taylor, "Anthropologists, Reformers, and the Indian New Deal," *Prologue* 7 (Fall 1975): 154–55; Kenneth R. Philp, *John Collier's Crusade for Indian Reform, 1920–1954* (Tucson: University of Arizona Press, 1977), 3–8; David W. Daily, *Battle for the BIA: G. E. E. Lindquist and the Missionary Crusade against John Collier* (Tucson: University of Arizona Press, 2004), 10–12; Elmer R. Rusco, *A Fateful Time: The Background and Legislative History of the Indian Reorganization Act* (Reno: University of Nevada Press, 2000), 141, 160, 188–90.

15. Vine Deloria, ed., *The Indian Reorganization Act: Congresses and Bills* (Norman: University of Oklahoma Press, 2002), 20; Philp, *John Collier's Crusade for Indian Reform*, chap. 7.

16. Deloria and Lytle, *The Nations Within*, 150–51 (emphasis mine). Here I quote Deloria and Lytle's summary of section 19 of the IRA because it more precisely states the status

of unrecognized, nonreservation Indians like those in Robeson County. The definition in section 19 reads: "The term 'Indian' as used in this Act shall include all persons of Indian descent who are members of any recognized Indian tribe now under Federal jurisdiction, and all persons who are descendants of such members who were, on June 1, 1934, residing within the present boundaries of any Indian reservation, and shall further include all other persons of one-half or more Indian blood." The phrase "shall further include" implied that the act applied to nonreservation Indians who could meet the one-half-blood quantum standard. The language defining an Indian in Collier's original bill was not compressed into one section, as it was in the final act, but was dispersed over different titles. Title 1, "Indian Self-Government," defined an Indian to "include all persons of Indian descent who are members of any recognized Indian tribe, band, or nation, or are descendants of such members and were, as of February 1, 1934, actually residing within the present boundaries of any Indian reservation, and shall further include all persons of one-fourth or more Indian blood"; but it goes on to authorize the secretary of the interior or a tribe to prescribe additional membership criteria or offer membership to nonresidents. The definition in title III, "Indian Lands," defined a "member of an Indian tribe" as "any descendant of a member permanently residing within an existing Indian reservation." Collier's original bill was less precise than the final act on the role of blood quantum in determining membership but still depended on the concept. Deloria, *The Indian Reorganization Act*, 12, 17, 23.

17. Quoted in Rusco, *A Fateful Time*, 269.

18. Ibid.

19. Rusco, *A Fateful Time*, chap. 6.

20. Deloria, *The Indian Reorganization Act*, 22.

21. Deloria and Lytle, *The Nations Within*, 173; Graham D. Taylor, *The New Deal and American Indian Tribalism: The Administration of the Indian Reorganization Act, 1934–45* (Lincoln: University of Nebraska Press, 1980), 102–3.

22. Richard O. Clemmer, "The Hopi, Western Shoshone, and Southern Utes: Three Different Responses to the Indian Reorganization Act," *American Indian Culture and Research Journal* 10, no. 2 (1986): 32; Taylor, *The New Deal and American Indian Tribalism*, 37, 73–74; Rusco, *A Fateful Time*, chap. 6.

23. Paul C. Rosier, *Rebirth of the Blackfeet Nation, 1912–1954* (Lincoln: University of Nebraska Press, 2001), 6–7, chap. 3.

24. Clemmer, "The Hopi, Western Shoshone, and Southern Utes," 23–25. For more on the Hopi situation and other examples at San Carlos Apache and Yankton Sioux, see Taylor, *The New Deal and American Indian Tribalism*, 74–76, 98–101.

25. Wilcomb E. Washburn, "A Fifty-Year Perspective on the Indian Reorganization Act," *American Anthropologist* 86 (June 1984): 280–81; see also Taylor, *The New Deal and Indian Tribalism*, 29, 66–68.

26. Historians have conflated "tribe" and "reservation" to a large degree when discussing these provisions of the IRA. Deloria and Lytle, *The Nations Within*, 69–70, 141, 161–62, 164, 186–89; Rusco, *A Fateful Time*, 206, 223, 227; Taylor, *The New Deal and American Indian Tribalism*, chap. 5.

27. See Katherine M. B. Osburn, "'In a Name of Justice and Fairness': The Mississippi Choctaw Indian Federation versus the BIA, 1934," in *Beyond Red Power: American Indian*

Politics and Activism since 1900, ed. Daniel M. Cobb and Loretta Fowler (Santa Fe: School for Advanced Research, 2007), 109–25.

28. This perspective on the lack of Indian unity in response to the IRA is echoed in Thomas Biolsi, *Organizing the Lakota: The Political Economy of the New Deal on the Pine Ridge and Rosebud Reservations* (Tucson: University of Arizona Press, 1992), xx–xxi; and Taylor, *The New Deal and American Indian Tribalism*, 158.

29. As anthropologist James C. Scott observes, "Designed or planned social order is necessarily schematic; it always ignores essential features of any real, functioning social order." Scott, *Seeing Like a State*, 6.

30. Francis Paul Prucha, *The Great Father: The United States Government and the American Indians*, abridged ed. (Lincoln: University of Nebraska Press, 1984), chap. 15.

31. Margo S. Brownwell, "Note: Who Is An Indian? Searching for an Answer to the Question at the Core of Federal Indian Law," *University of Michigan Journal of Law Reform* 34 (Fall–Winter 2000–2001): 279; Garroutte, *Real Indians*, 42; Frederick E. Hoxie, *A Final Promise: The Campaign to Assimilate the Indians, 1880–1920* (Lincoln, Neb.: Bison Books, 2001), chap. 4; Circe Sturm, *Blood Politics: Race, Culture, and Identity in the Cherokee Nation of Oklahoma* (Berkeley: University of California Press, 2002), 78–79; Tanis C. Thorne, *The World's Richest Indian: The Scandal over Jackson Barnett's Oil Fortune* (New York: Oxford University Press, 2003), chap. 2; quotes on pp. 220, 48.

32. Rusco, *A Fateful Time*, 161–62.

33. Edward E. Hill, comp., *Records of the Bureau of Indian Affairs*, vol. 1 (Washington, D.C.: National Archives and Records Service General Services Administration, 1965), 5–6; Deloria and Lytle, *The Nations Within*, 61–63.

34. Joseph Brooks to John Collier, 8 January 1935, RG 75, entry 121, file no. 1651-1935-056 General Services, NARA.

35. Joseph Brooks to Josiah W. Bailey, 14 February 1935, box 312, folder: Interior, 1935, January–February, JBC.

36. Josiah W. Bailey to Joseph Brooks, 16 February 1935, box 312, folder: Interior, 1935, January–February, JBC.

37. Doctor F. Lowry to Josiah W. Bailey, 21 January 1935, box 312, folder: Interior, 1935, January–February, JBC.

38. Doctor F. Lowry to W. Carson Ryan, January 1935, GBJP.

39. Harry A. Kersey Jr., *The Florida Seminoles and the New Deal, 1933–1942* (Boca Raton: Florida Atlantic University Press, 1989); Donald L. Parman, *The Navajos and the New Deal* (New Haven, Conn.: Yale University Press, 1976); Philp, *John Collier's Crusade for Indian Reform*; Taylor, *The New Deal and American Indian Tribalism*; John C. Savagian, "The Tribal Reorganization of the Stockbridge-Munsee: Essential Conditions in the Re-Creation of a Native American Community, 1930–1942," in *American Nations: Encounters in Indian Country, 1850 to the Present*, ed. Frederick E. Hoxie, Peter C. Mancall, and James H. Merrell (New York: Routledge, 2001), 296, 300, 304.

40. The OIA pursued a similar strategy for the Stockbridge-Munsee of Wisconsin and other tribes who accepted the IRA, but purchased land was never transferred to the tribes; the U.S. government continued to hold title to it because Congress never passed a law that transferred the title. Walter V. Woehlke to Fred A. Daiker, n.d, RG 75, entry 121, file no. 45499-1937-066 General Services, NARA; Felix S. Cohen to John Collier, 8 April 1935,

RG 75, entry 121, file no. 45499-1937-066 General Services, NARA; Savagian, "The Tribal Reorganization of the Stockbridge-Munsee," 300–301.

41. Joseph Brooks to John Collier, 11 April 1935 (copy in personal possession of the author).

42. Brooks is remembered today as a smooth talker and someone whose light skin facilitated his entry into Washington circles. Ed Chavis, interview by author, Pembroke, N.C., 9 June 2004.

43. Joseph Brooks to John Collier, 29 May 1935 (copy in personal possession of the author); Joseph Brooks to John Collier, 31 May 1935, RG 75, entry 121, file no. 39490-1935-361 General Services, NARA.

44. John Collier to Joseph Brooks, 3 June 1935, quoted in Julian T. Pierce, Cynthia Hunt-Locklear, Jack Campisi, and Wesley White, *The Lumbee Petition* (Pembroke, N.C.: Lumbee River Legal Services, 1987), 2:13; "Application for Allotment of Funds under Emergency Relief Appropriation of 1935," n.d. (copy in personal possession of author).

45. William Zimmerman to Fred A. Baker, 13 June 1935, in Fred A. Baker, *Report on Siouan Tribe of Indians in Robeson County, North Carolina*, RG 75, entry 121, file no. 36208-1935-310 General Services, NARA; Fred A. Baker to John Collier, 9 July 1935, NARA.

46. John Collier to James Chavis, 24 July 1935, in Baker, *Report on Siouan Tribe of Indians*, NARA.

47. W. Carson Ryan to J. E. Sawyer, 19 February 1935, quoted in John Pearmain, "'Reservation': Siouan Tribe of Indians of Robeson County, North Carolina" (Indian Office Handbook of Information, comp. October, 1935), 40.

48. John Collier to M. R. Alexander, 1 May 1936, RG 75, entry 121, file no. 45499-1937-066 General Services, NARA.

49. W. Carson Ryan to J. E. Sawyer, 19 February 1935, quoted in Pearmain, "Reservation," 40.

50. Ibid.

51. This assessment of the half-blood provision is part of the statement of facts in *Lawrence Maynor v. Rogers C. B. Morton*, U.S. Court of Appeals, District of Columbia, argued 21 November 1974 and decided 4 April 1975 (510 F.2d 1254 1975); quoted in Gerald Sider, *Living Indian Histories: Lumbee and Tuscarora People in North Carolina* (Chapel Hill: University of North Carolina Press, 2003), 133.

52. OIA officials also asked questions about Robeson County Indians' genealogy and other cultural features, but such evidence was typically dismissed for reasons I elaborate upon in chapter 6.

53. John Collier to the Indian Office, 22 September 1936, RG 75, entry 616, box 1, folder: Memoranda and Circulars, NARA.

54. Franz Boas, architect of the cultural-pluralism theory to which Collier ostensibly adhered, ironically rejected Collier as an overly emotional proponent of Indian reform and opposed his appointment as Indian commissioner. Boas further attacked Hrdlicka's and others' attempts to link race and cultural achievement, but those views remained mainstream in the OIA as they related to the blood quantum requirement, possibly due to Hrdlicka's Smithsonian affiliation (the OIA had worked with the Smithsonian's Bureau of American Ethnology since it was founded in 1879). In other aspects of the OIA's policy

development and implementation, however, the social anthropologists of the short-lived Applied Anthropology Unit seemed to hold sway. This unit focused most of its attention on promoting the IRA among Indian tribes and on tribal reorganization in reservation communities. See Taylor, *The New Deal and American Indian Tribalism*, 155, 157; George J. Armalagos and Dennis P. Van Gerven, "A Century of Skeletal Biology and Paleopathology: Contrasts, Contradictions, and Conflicts," *American Anthropologist* 105 (March 2003): 55–56; Lawrence C. Kelly, "Anthropology and Anthropologists in the Indian New Deal," *Journal of the History of the Behavioral Sciences* 16 (Winter 1980): 7–10; Sturm, *Blood Politics*, 18; and Hoxie, *A Final Promise*, 126–27, 141.

55. Brownwell emphasizes that this contradiction was not limited to nonreservation tribes when she analyzes the OIA's jurisdiction over Indian identity. She concludes that the OIA's habit of exercising authority over tribal membership amounts to a usurping of tribal authority and is a deep and dangerous contradiction to the purpose and history of Indian policy. Nevertheless, Collier (and other officials since) consistently maintained that the fundamental relationship between the federal government and the tribes was a political one, and as such, tribes must reject members who do not have a "meaningful" political relationship with the tribe (the Indian Office, of course, determines the definition of "meaningful"). See Brownwell, "Note: Who Is An Indian?," 306–7.

56. Pearmain, "Reservation," 42 (emphasis in original).

57. D'Arcy McNickle to John Collier, 7 April 1936, RG 75, entry 121, file no. 45499-1937-066 General Services, NARA.

58. Ibid.

59. John Collier to Indian Office, 22 April 1936, RG 75, entry 121, file no. 45499-1937-066 General Services, NARA.

60. William Harlen Gilbert Jr., "Memorandum Concerning the Characteristics of the Larger Mixed-Blood Racial Islands of the Eastern United States," *Social Forces* 24 (1946): 438–47; Brewton Berry, *Almost White* (New York: MacMillan, 1963); Guy Benton Johnson, "Personality in a White-Indian-Negro Community," *American Sociological Review* 4 (August 1939): 516–23.

61. See Garroutte, *Real Indians*, 47–48, 52–53, 58–59; Sturm, *Blood Politics*, 78. The OIA's commitment to the blood quantum standard is seen in "Conference in Mr. Herrick's Office," 18 May 1936, RG 75, entry 121, file no. 45499-1937-066 General Services, and it will be discussed further in chapter 6.

62. Compare Brownwell, "Note: Who Is An Indian?," 302; Cindy D. Padget, "The Lost Indians of the Lost Colony: A Critical Legal Study of the Lumbee Indians of North Carolina," *American Indian Law Review* 21 (Spring 1997): 404–6.

CHAPTER 5

1. Stuart S. Kidd, *Farm Security Administration Photography, the Rural South, and the Dynamics of Image-Making* (Lewiston, N.Y.: Edwin Mellen Press, 2004), 22–23.

2. Margaret Jarman Hagood, *Mothers of the South: Portraiture of the White Tenant Farm Woman* (Chapel Hill: University of North Carolina Press, 1939).

3. U.S. House of Representatives, *Hearings before the Select Committee of the House Committee on Agriculture to Investigate the Activities of the Farm Security Administration, Pursuant*

to *H.Res. 119, Part 3,* 78th Cong., 1st sess., 1943, 1087–88; Edwin L. Groome to J. M. Stewart, 1 May 1936, in Fred A. Baker, *Report on Siouan Tribe of Indians in Robeson County, North Carolina,* RG 75, entry 121, file no. 36208-1935-310 General Services, NARA.

4. In 1935, when planning for Pembroke Farms began, resettlement projects were planned and funded by a separate government agency known as the Resettlement Administration (RA). The RA became part of the Farm Security Administration (FSA), which became part of the U.S. Department of Agriculture in the late 1930s. Eventually, the FSA became known as the Farmer's Home Administration in the 1940s; FSA records are housed under that title at the National Archives. Because the personnel supervising Pembroke Farms at the RA and FSA remained largely the same, and to simplify the narrative, I have referred to the agency as the Farm Security Administration throughout.

5. Sidney Baldwin, *Poverty and Politics: The Rise and Decline of the Farm Security Administration* (Chapel Hill: University of North Carolina Press, 1968), 38.

6. William Leuchtenburg, *Franklin D. Roosevelt and the New Deal, 1932–1940* (New York: Harper & Row, 1963), 332.

7. Brian Q. Cannon, "Keeping Their Instructions Straight: Implementing the Rural Resettlement Program in the West," *Agricultural History* 70 (Spring 1996): 260. Technically, Congress prohibited the FSA from purchasing any more land for resettlement projects in 1937 but did allow the agency to make loans to cooperative associations of farmers. Some additional resettlement communities, such as Pembroke Farms, were created after 1937 through this loophole. See Brian Q. Cannon, *Remaking the Agrarian Dream: New Deal Rural Resettlement in the Mountain West* (Albuquerque: University of New Mexico Press, 1996), 14.

8. Concerned Citizens of Tillery, *Remembering Tillery: A New Deal Resettlement* (Tillery, N.C.: Concerned Citizens of Tillery, 1996); Concerned Citizens of Tillery, "History House: Remembering Tillery, Our Land and Our Community," ⟨http://cct78.org/History%20 House.htm⟩ (accessed 4 December 2008).

9. Paul Nieder, "The Osage Farms Project: An Experimental New Deal Community, 1935–1943," *Gateway Heritage* 12 (Summer 1991): 50–63; Lester M. Salamon, "The Time Dimension in Policy Evaluation: The Case of the New Deal Land-Reform Experiments," *Public Policy* 27 (Spring 1979): 131–32; Donald Holley, "The Negro in the New Deal Resettlement Program," *New South* 27 (July 1972): 64; Concerned Citizens of Tillery, *Remembering Tillery*; John C. Savagian, "The Tribal Reorganization of the Stockbridge-Munsee: Essential Conditions in the Re-Creation of a Native American Community, 1930–1942," in *American Nations: Encounters in Indian Country, 1850 to the Present,* ed. Frederick E. Hoxie, Peter C. Mancall, and James H. Merrell (New York: Routledge, 2001), 302.

10. "Enrollment of Siouan Indians of Lumber River, North Carolina," 18 May 1935, RG 75, entry 121, file no. 39490-1935-361 General Services, NARA. The total Indian population is as of 1930, and is taken from John Pearmain, "Report . . . On the Conditions of the Indians in Robeson County, North Carolina," 11 November 1935, RG 75, entry 121, file no. 64190-1935-066 Part 1-A, 57, NARA.

11. Melissa L. Meyer, "American Indian Blood Quantum Requirements: Blood Is Thicker than Family," in *Over the Edge: Remapping the American West,* ed. Valerie J. Matsumoto and Blake Allmendinger (Berkeley: University of California Press, 1999), 232.

12. Rebecca S. Seib, *Indians of Robeson County Land Ownership Study, 1900–1910* (Pem-

broke, N.C.: Lumbee Regional Development Association, n.d.), 7, 15, 17; "Enrollment of Siouan Indians of Lumber River, North Carolina," 18 May 1935, RG 75, entry 121, file no. 39490-1935-361 General Services, NARA.

13. That 1943 report was not published until 1978, when it appeared in *Agricultural History*. Marion Clawson, "Resettlement Experience on Nine Selected Resettlement Projects," *Agricultural History* 52 (January 1978): 1–92. For assessments of record keeping, see p. 32.

14. James E. Chavis to A. A. Grorud, 22 August 1934, SIF.

15. Felix S. Cohen to John Collier, 8 April 1935, RG 75, entry 121, file no. 45499-1937-066 General Services, NARA; William Zimmerman to Fred A. Baker, 13 June 1935, in Baker, *Report on Siouan Tribe of Indians*, NARA. John Pearmain, "'Reservation': Siouan Tribe of Indians of Robeson County, North Carolina" (Indian Office Handbook of Information, comp. October 1935), 45.

16. John Collier to Joseph Brooks, 31 June 1935, in Baker, *Report on Siouan Tribe of Indians*, NARA. See also L. C. Gray to Homer H. B. Mask, 12 December 1935, RG 96, entry 79, folder: 200-Land Acquisition, box 36, NARA-Atlanta; and Homer H. B. Mask to R. G. Tugwell, 16 December 1935, RG 96, entry 79, folder: 200-Land Acquisition, box 36, NARA-Atlanta. This correspondence also indicates that the Resettlement Administration took control over the project from the Indian Office.

17. *Robesonian*, 29 June 1938; "RI-NC-22, Pembroke Farms, Pembroke-N.C." (map), RG 96, AD-NC-22 Pembroke Farms, box 437, NARA. For rent comparison, see Pearmain, "Report," 48. Renting to tenants while constructing the project was not unusual; see Clawson, "Resettlement Experience," 19–20.

18. Clawson, "Resettlement Experience," 16–17, 50–52; "Meeting of Homesteaders of the Pembroke Resettlement Project in Office of Mr. L. I. Hewes, Jr.," October 24, 1938, RG 96, AD-NC-22 Pembroke Farms, box 437, NARA; Letter from George S. Mitchell to W. W. Alexander, 27 November 1937, RG 96, AD-NC-22 Pembroke Farms, box 437, NARA.

19. U.S. House of Representatives, *Hearings before the Select Committee*, 1087–88; "Robeson County Indians Make Forward Strides, 'Scuffletown' Has Been Transformed," *Charlotte Observer*, 19 May 1940.

20. Ella Deloria to George S. Mitchell, 21 August 1940, NARA.

21. J. A. Sharpe Jr., "Rural Indian Resettlement Project Is Large-Scale Federal Undertaking in Pembroke Section of Robeson Co.," *Robesonian*, 29 June 1938; "Robeson County Indians Make Forward Strides"; Clawson, "Resettlement Experience," 38–40.

22. George S. Mitchell to W. W. Alexander, 27 November 1937, NARA; Irma P. Wallace to W. W. Alexander, 27 January 1939, RG 96, AD-NC-22 Pembroke Farms, box 437, NARA; Matilda Ann Wade to R. C. Williams, 21 June 1940, RG 96, AD-NC-22 Pembroke Farms, box 437, NARA; R. C. Williams to W. W. Alexander, 16 February 1939, RG 96, AD-NC-22 Pembroke Farms, box 437, NARA; U.S. House of Representatives, *Hearings before the Select Committee*, 1088; H. C. Green to John H. Workman, 2 February 1939, RG 96, entry 79, folder: 934-Education, box 39, NARA-Atlanta; Cloyd Chavis, S. M. Bell, S. S. Lowrie, and James E. Chavis to Josiah W. Bailey, 3 May 1941, RG 96, AD-NC-22 Pembroke Farms, box 437, NARA.

23. Pearmain, "Report," 27, 33, 43; William Zimmerman to Fred A. Baker, 13 June 1935, in Baker, *Report on Siouan Tribe of Indians*, NARA. For more on crop allotments, see Pete

Daniel, *Breaking the Land: The Transformation of Cotton, Tobacco, and Rice Cultures since 1880* (Urbana: University of Illinois Press, 1985).

24. "Robeson County Indians Make Forward Strides."

25. Fred A. Baker to John Collier, 9 July 1935, in Baker, *Report on Siouan Tribe of Indians*, NARA; Anonymous, "Proposed Plan, Rural Resettlement Project, Pembroke Indian Resettlement Project, Robeson County, North Carolina," n.d., RG 96, entry 85, box 1, NARA-Atlanta.

26. Clawson, "Resettlement Experience," 37–41, 43.

27. Letter from Oscar Locklear et al., "To Whom It May Concern," 22 October 1938, RG 96, AD-NC-22 Pembroke Farms, box 437, NARA.

28. R. T. Melvin and A. M. Johnson, "Final Plans for the Pembroke Indian Resettlement Project," RG 96, entry 85, Region IV, Project Plans file of C. B. Faris, box 1, 9, NARA; A. M. Johnson to Bruce Poundstone, 20 December 1935, 5, RG 96, entry 85, box 1, NARA-Atlanta; Fred A. Baker to John Collier, 9 July 1935, in Baker, *Report on Siouan Tribe of Indians*, NARA.

29. Melvin and Johnson, "Final Plans," 10.

30. Ibid., 20.

31. The phrase "almost white" did not originate with the FSA staff but is taken from sociologist Brewton Berry's book of that title. Berry argued in part that Indian communities like the one in Robeson County were victims of a biracial caste system in the South and thus sought a status of "almost white" instead of "Negro," which Berry proposed was their only other viable option. In Berry's view, no independent category of "Indian" could exist. Although FSA staff members recorded their observations nearly thirty years prior to the publication of Berry's work, I believe the similarity of the two views of a biracial system in the South merits the application of Berry's phrase to the FSA staff members' views. See Brewton Berry, *Almost White* (New York: MacMillan, 1963).

32. R. T. Melvin, "Report of Detailed Reconnaissance Survey of Pembroke Indian Resettlement Project Number—RRNC22," n.d., 2, RG 96, entry 85, box 1, NARA-Atlanta.

33. A. M. Johnson to Bruce Poundstone, 20 December 1935, 5–6, NARA-Atlanta.

34. Ibid., 4–5, NARA-Atlanta.

35. Ibid., 6, NARA-Atlanta.

36. Ibid., 5, NARA-Atlanta.

37. Melvin and Johnson, "Final Plans," 20, 6.

38. Ibid., 10.

39. A. M. Johnson to Bruce Poundstone, 20 December 1935, 5, NARA-Atlanta.

40. Edwin L. Groome to J. M. Stewart, 1 May 1936, in Baker, *Report on Siouan Tribe of Indians*, NARA.

41. Green chose Burleigh Lowry and Chesley Locklear for the committee. Both men owned large amounts of land and supported Pembroke Farms. Locklear was Brooks's brother-in-law and a Siouan councilman from Saint Annah. Saint Annah had the highest number of enrolled members and was home to some of the wealthiest Indian landowners. Burleigh Lowry was Martin Luther Lowry's brother-in-law and had sold land to the FSA for the project. George S. Mitchell to W. W. Alexander, 6 May 1937, RG 96, entry 79, box 39, folder: 911-045 Family Selection, NARA-Atlanta; J. O. Walker to George S. Mitchell, 13 May 1937, RG 96, entry 79, box 39, folder: 911-045 Family Selection, NARA-Atlanta;

George S. Mitchell to H. C. Green, 18 November 1937, RG 96, entry 79, box 34, folder: 000-General NC-22, NARA-Atlanta; H. C. Green to C. B. Faris, 27 December 1937, RG 96, entry 79, box 36, folder: 183-01 Monthly, NARA-Atlanta; "Preferred List Options for Pembroke Project," 23 November 1936, RG 96, entry 79, box 36, folder: 200-Land Acquisition, NARA-Atlanta.

42. H. C. Green to C. B. Faris, 27 December 1937, NARA-Atlanta.

43. Petition from Osker Locklear et al., 11 October 1938, RG 96, entry 79, box 39, folder: NC-22-912-035 Complaint, NARA-Atlanta.

44. Letter from Oscar Locklear et al., "To Whom It May Concern," NARA.

45. It should be noted that only heads of families enrolled; others on the list may have been children of enrollees. Four of the petitioners who were not listed as enrollees also visited Washington, D.C., to personally complain, indicating that they were fully engaged in the Siouans' political movement even if they were not enrolled themselves. It is also likely that unenrolled petitioners were followers of the Cherokee faction, but Cherokees did not keep enrollment lists.

46. Landownership statistics found in Seib, *Indians of Robeson County*, 15.

47. For more on the ways in which Pembroke Farms sustained Indian kinship patterns in Robeson County, see Ryan K. Anderson, "Lumbee Kinship, Community, and the Success of the Red Banks Mutual Association," *American Indian Quarterly* 23 (Spring 1999): 43–44.

48. Clawson, "Resettlement Experience," 34, 41–42, 62.

49. Ibid., 17.

50. George S. Mitchell to W. W. Alexander, 12 October 1938, RG 96, entry 79, box 39, folder: NC-22-912-035 Complaint, NARA-Atlanta. Meeting is documented in George S. Mitchell to J. O. Walker, 11 October 1938, RG 96, entry 79, box 39, folder: NC-22-912-035 Complaint, NARA-Atlanta.

51. Clawson, "Resettlement Experience," 44.

52. "Meeting of Homesteaders of the Pembroke Resettlement Project in Office of Mr. L. I. Hewes, Jr.," 24 October 1938, 4–9, RG 96, AD-NC-22 Pembroke Farms, box 437, NARA.

53. J. O. Walker to George S. Mitchell, 24 March 1937, RG 96, entry 79, box 39, folder: Wolf Pit/Pembroke 913, NARA-Atlanta; George S. Mitchell to W. W. Alexander, 25 March 1938, RG 96, entry 79, box 36, folder: NC-22 (300) 101 Organization, NARA-Atlanta; C. B. Baldwin and Harry L. Brown to Milo Perkins and J. O. Walker, 30 June 1938, RG 96, AD-NC-22 Pembroke Farms, box 437, NARA; "Robeson County Indians Make Forward Strides."

54. Occupancy through June '38, RG 96, entry 79, box 39, folder: NC-22-912, NARA.

55. C. B. Faris to Leo F. Stock, 14 October 1938, RG 96, entry 79, box 38, folder: 84-NC-22-780 Building Construction and Land Development, NARA-Atlanta; Maggie J. Oxendine, interview by author, Pembroke, N.C., 3 May 2004, NARA.

56. Anderson, "Lumbee Kinship," 48–49.

57. Anonymous, "Press Release, Special to the *Robesonian*, from Division of Information, Resettlement Administration," n.d., RG 96, entry 79, box 35, folder: 163-01 Articles and Press Releases, NARA-Atlanta.

58. J. O. Walker to George S. Mitchell, 24 March 1937, NARA-Atlanta; George S. Mitchell

to W. W. Alexander, 27 March 1937, RG 96, entry 79, box 39, folder: Wolf Pit/Pembroke 913, NARA-Atlanta; Edwin L. Groome to J. M. Stewart, 6 July 1936, in Baker, *Report on Siouan Tribe of Indians*, NARA; Walter E. Packard to Walter V. Woehlke, 4 November 1936, SIF; John Pearmain to Burton K. Wheeler, 27 November 1936, SIF; John Pearmain to Joseph Brooks, 27 November 1936, SIF. Pearmain's title comes from James E. Chavis to Elmer Thomas, 4 September 1945, SIF.

59. Edwin L. Groome to J. M. Stewart, 6 July 1936, in Baker, *Report on Siouan Tribe of Indians*, NARA.

60. Petition from the Citizens of Robeson County to James M. Gray, 12 May 1936, RG 96, entry 79, box 39, folder: Wolf Pit/Pembroke 913, NARA-Atlanta; Liberty Grange to James M. Gray, 3 June 1936, RG 96, entry 79, box 39, folder: Wolf Pit/Pembroke 913, NARA-Atlanta; The Mormax Club to James M. Gray, 3 June 1936, RG 96, entry 79, box 39, folder: Wolf Pit/Pembroke 913, NARA-Atlanta; Petition from John F. Bridgers et al. to W. W. Alexander, J. Bayard Clark, and Sen. Josiah Bailey, 11 February 1938, RG 96, AD-NC-22 Pembroke Farms, box 437, NARA; George S. Mitchell to W. W. Alexander, 30 April 1938, RG 96, AD-NC-22 Pembroke Farms, box 437, NARA.

61. Josiah W. Bailey to W. W. Alexander, 11 February 1938, RG 96, AD-NC-22 Pembroke Farms, box 437, NARA; J. Bayard Clark to Farm Security Administration, 15 February 1938, RG 96, AD-NC-22 Pembroke Farms, box 437, NARA.

62. George S. Mitchell to J. Bayard Clark, 28 February 1938, RG 96, AD-NC-22 Pembroke Farms, box 437, NARA.

63. J. O. Walker to George S. Mitchell, 25 April 1938, RG 96, AD-NC-22 Pembroke Farms, box 437, NARA.

64. Joseph Brooks to W. W. Alexander, 29 April 1938, RG 96, AD-NC-22 Pembroke Farms, box 437, NARA; George S. Mitchell to W. W. Alexander, 30 April 1938, RG 96, AD-NC-22 Pembroke Farms, box 437, NARA; George S. Mitchell to W. W. Alexander, 2 May 1938, RG 96, AD-NC-22 Pembroke Farms, box 437, NARA; Joseph Brooks to W. W. Alexander, 8 May 1938, RG 96, AD-NC-22 Pembroke Farms, box 437, NARA; W. W. Alexander to George S. Mitchell, 11 May 1938, RG 96, AD-NC-22 Pembroke Farms, box 437, NARA. Note from "D.Y." to C. B. Baldwin, n.d., RG 96, AD-NC-22 Pembroke Farms, box 437, NARA; George S. Mitchell to J. Bayard Clark, 16 May 1938, RG 96, AD-NC-22 Pembroke Farms, box 437, NARA; W. W. Alexander to George S. Mitchell, 20 May 1938, RG 96, AD-NC-22 Pembroke Farms, box 437, NARA; Joseph Brooks to A. A. Grorud, 8 May 1938, SIF.

65. W. W. Alexander to George S. Mitchell, 20 May 1938, RG 96, AD-NC-22 Pembroke Farms, box 437, NARA.

66. J. O. Walker to George S. Mitchell, 24 March 1937, NARA-Atlanta; "Homesteader of Pembroke, N.C." to H. D. Godfrey, n.d., RG 96, entry 79, box 39, folder: Wolf Pit/Pembroke 913, NARA-Atlanta; Cloyd Chavis, S. M. Bell, S. S. Lowrie, and James E. Chavis to Josiah W. Bailey, 3 May 1941, NARA.

67. Cloyd Chavis, S. M. Bell, S. S. Lowrie, and James E. Chavis to Josiah W. Bailey, 3 May 1941, NARA; Doctor F. Lowry to George S. Mitchell, 12 July 1938, RG 96, entry 79, box 34, folder: 84-NC-22-073 Private Individuals and Organizations, NARA-Atlanta.

68. Cloyd Chavis, S. M. Bell, S. S. Lowrie, and James E. Chavis to Josiah W. Bailey, 3 May 1941, NARA.

69. Albert Maverick Jr. to Anonymous, 19 June 1941, RG 96, AD-NC-22 Pembroke Farms, box 437, NARA.

70. C. B. Faris to Howard H. Gordon, 11 August 1941, RG 96, entry 80, box 4, folder: NC-22-913 Attitude Toward Projects, NARA-Atlanta.

CHAPTER 6

1. Carl C. Seltzer, "A Report on the Racial Status of Certain People in Robeson County, North Carolina," 30 June 1936, RG 75, entry 616, box 13–15, North Carolina, Applicants #23, 24, 43, 104, 108, 109.

2. Mrs. Stubbs and daughter Elizabeth to Guy Benton Johnson, 30 July 1937, GBJP.

3. See also Melissa L. Meyer, *The White Earth Tragedy: Ethnicity and Dispossession at a Minnesota Anishinaabe* (Lincoln: University of Nebraska Press, 1994); and Stephen Jay Gould, *The Mismeasure of Man* (New York: Norton, 1996).

4. In addition to the documents cited in chapter 4, see D'Arcy McNickle to Indian Office, 1 May 1936, RG 75, entry 121, file no. 45499-1937-066 General Services, NARA.

5. Vine Deloria Jr. and Clifford Lytle, *The Nations Within: The Past and Future of American Indian Sovereignty* (New York: Pantheon Books, 1984), chaps. 10 and 11.

6. Paul Spruhan, "Indian as Race/Indian as Political Status: Implementation of the Half-Blood Requirement under the Indian Reorganization Act, 1934–1945," *Rutgers Race and the Law Review* 8 (Fall 2006): 32, 40.

7. Spruhan, "Indian as Race/Indian as Political Status," 33–34. See also John Collier to Harold Ickes, 23 December 1935, RG 75, entry 616, box 1, folder: "Miscellaneous papers (1), Forms (2), Circulars and Memoranda," NARA. Copies of the "Application for Registration as an Indian" can be found in this file as well.

8. Spruhan, "Indian as Race/Indian as Political Status," 33–38.

9. D'Arcy McNickle to John Collier, 7 April 1936, RG 75, entry 121, file no. 45499-1937-066 General Services, NARA.

10. Joseph Brooks to John Collier, 11 April 1936, RG 75, entry 121, file no. 45499-1937-066 General Services, NARA.

11. "Conference in Mr. Herrick's Office," 18 May 1936, RG 75, entry 121, file no. 45499-1937-066 General Services, NARA.

12. Meyer, *White Earth Tragedy*, 169.

13. Ibid., 168–72.

14. Seltzer, "A Report on the Racial Status of Certain People," Exhibit A, Exhibit C.

15. David Beaulieu, "Curly Hair and Big Feet: Physical Anthropology and the Implementation of Land Allotment on the White Earth Chippewa Reservation," *American Indian Quarterly* 8 (Fall 1984): 307, 289–90; Ales Hrdlicka, *Practical Anthropometry*, 4th ed., ed. T. D. Stewart (Philadelphia: Wistar Institute of Anatomy and Biology, 1952), 37, 43–44.

16. "Conference in Mr. Herrick's Office," 18 May 1936, NARA.

17. D'Arcy McNickle, E. S. McMahon, and Carl Seltzer to John Collier, 26 January 1937, RG 75, entry 121, file no. 64190-1935-066 General Services Part 1, NARA.

18. Lawrence C. Kelly, "Anthropology and Anthropologists in the Indian New Deal," *Journal of the History of the Behavioral Sciences* 16 (Winter 1980): 10.

19. "Conference in Mr. Herrick's Office," 18 May 1936, NARA.

20. Beaulieu, "Curly Hair and Big Feet," 283, 305; Lee D. Baker, *From Savage to Negro:*

Anthropology and the Construction of Race, 1896–1954 (Berkeley: University of California Press, 1998), 35–36. Hrdlicka believed that states should use anthropometry to solve modern problems. He advocated state governments' use of anthropometry to track the physical progression or regression of their populations, a view that became instituted in the practice of eugenics. Hrdlicka, *Practical Anthropometry*, 11.

21. Franz Boas, "Some Recent Criticisms of Physical Anthropology (1899)," in *Race, Language, and Culture* (New York: MacMillan, 1940), 166, 171.

22. Baker, *From Savage to Negro*, 107; and Lee D. Baker, "Columbia University's Franz Boas: He Led the Undoing of Scientific Racism," *Journal of Blacks in Higher Education* 22 (Winter 1999): 94.

23. Baker, *From Savage to Negro*, 103, 119.

24. The Siouan Enrollment Commission expressed a hope that the effect of Seltzer's tests would be for Robeson County Indians to "feel that they have been given a fair chance." "Investigating Siouan Claims" to John Collier, 7 June 1936, RG 75, entry 121, file no. 45499-1937-066 General Services, NARA.

25. John Herrick to D'Arcy McNickle, Edward S. McMahon, and Carl C. Seltzer, 8 June 1936, RG 75, entry 121, file no. 45499-1937-066 General Services, NARA; "Investigating Siouan Claims" to John Collier, 7 June 1936, NARA; John Collier to Harold Ickes, 29 October 1938, RG 75, entry 121, file no. 45499-1937-066 General Services, NARA. See Seltzer, "A Report on the Racial Status of Certain People," for 1936 and 1937 applicants' interviews, photographs, and anthropometric questionnaires. Two of the 1936 applications are missing from NARA files, leaving data for 106, rather than 108, applicants.

26. Seltzer, "A Report on the Racial Status of Certain People," Applicants #16, 12, 86. Other details of the test procedure are taken from Meyer, *White Earth Tragedy*, 168; and Beaulieu, "Curly Hair and Big Feet," 297–98.

27. John Collier to Harold Ickes, 29 October 1938, NARA; Beaulieu, "Curly Hair and Big Feet," 300–301.

28. The White Earth Ojibwe held a similar concept of blood relationships and Indian identity, as articulated in Beaulieu, "Curly Hair and Big Feet," 288–89.

29. John Herrick to D'Arcy McNickle, Edward S. McMahon, and Carl C. Seltzer, 8 June 1936, NARA.

30. Of the 209 applicants, 35 descended from James Lowry, 151 from Major and John Locklear, 19 from both families, and 2 from other or unidentified families. Two applications are missing. "Other" or "unidentified" lineages include applicants whose genealogies did not explicitly link up with either the Major/John Locklear or James Lowry line, but that does not mean this 2 percent were not related to these lineages; it is likely that further research would reveal a genealogical linkage, but that data was not available when the studies were done. See Seltzer, "A Report on the Racial Status of Certain People," Applicants #2–108 and "Genealogical Charts of Brooks Family" file, RG 75, entry 616, box 13–15, NARA.

31. Linda Oxendine, e-mail communication with the author, 2 November 2004.

32. Although all applicants were asked for further information that would identify them as Indians, only applicant #22 specifically mentioned "clans."

33. Seltzer, "A Report on the Racial Status of Certain People," Applicants #6, 5.

34. Ibid., Applicants #19, 96. See also Applicants #4, 22, 25, 28, 30, 41, 45, 61, 68, 71, 72, 73, 78, 82, 88, 89, 91, 94, 106, 107.

35. D'Arcy McNickle, E. S. McMahon, and Carl Seltzer to John Collier, 26 January 1937, NARA.

36. Applicants identified their birthplace, their residence, and/or where they attended school on applications. Sometimes applicants identified a specific community, while other times they declared a nearby town or township. In some cases, when the designation was vague, I made a judgment based on the individual's family affiliation. The final tally was Brooks Settlement, 107; Pembroke, Deep Branch, Red Banks, 12; Fairmont, Rowland, 2; Burnt Swamp (including Philadelphus and Union Chapel), 21; Saddletree (including Lumberton and Piney Grove School), 28; Lumberton (may include Saddletree), 3; Maxton (may include Prospect), 3; Prospect, 7; Cherokee (may include Prospect), 2; Red Springs (may include Bethel Hill or Hoke County), 2; Bethel Hill, 2; Hoke County, 6; no information given, 12; and missing applications, 2. Total applicants were 209. Data from Seltzer, "A Report on the Racial Status of Certain People," Applicants #2-108; and "Genealogical Charts of Brooks Family" file.

37. See Seltzer, "A Report on the Racial Status of Certain People," Applicants #48, 104, 108, 109.

38. Julian T. Pierce, Cynthia Hunt-Locklear, Jack Campisi, and Wesley White, *The Lumbee Petition* (Pembroke, N.C.: Lumbee River Legal Services, 1987), 1:159–65.

39. See "Investigating Siouan Claims" to John Collier, 7 June 1936, NARA; and D'Arcy McNickle, E. S. McMahon, and Carl Seltzer to John Collier, 26 January 1937, NARA.

40. Seltzer, "A Report on the Racial Status of Certain People," Applicant #4.

41. Of the 183 applicants and spouses for which data is available from 1936, 22 claimed to be "full-bloods"; 74 claimed "¾," "nearly full," or "more than ½"; 82 claimed "1/2"; 3 claimed "1/4" or "1/4 or more"; 1 claimed "unknown"; and 1 did not respond. Seltzer, "A Report on the Racial Status of Certain People," Applicants #2-108. Also see D'Arcy McNickle, E. S. McMahon, and Carl Seltzer to John Collier, 26 January 1937, NARA.

42. "Investigating Siouan Claims" to John Collier, 7 June 1936, NARA.

43. Ibid.

44. Eva Marie Garroutte, *Real Indians: Identity and the Survival of Native America* (Berkeley: University of California Press, 2003), 42.

45. Compare M. Annette Jaimes, "Federal Indian Identification Policy: A Usurpation of Indigenous Sovereignty in North America," in *The State of Native America: Genocide, Colonization, and Resistance*, ed. M. Annette Jaimes (Boston, Mass.: South End Press, 1992), 123–38.

46. Seltzer, "A Report on the Racial Status of Certain People," Applicants #2-108; "Genealogical Charts of Brooks Family" file; "Genealogical Tables With Racial Diagnoses" file. Families in which full siblings did not receive the same diagnosis include the families of Leanna Locklear Brooks and Will Brooks, Emmie Locklear Jacobs and Westley Jacobs, Boss Locklear and Mary Brooks Locklear, Beadan Locklear Brooks and Lawson Brooks, Dockery Brooks and Callie Campbell Brooks, and John David Locklear and Lovedy Brooks Locklear. The OIA also did not include the families and siblings of the non–Brooks Settlement Indians Seltzer diagnosed as having "1/2 or more Indian blood."

47. John Collier to S. M. Bell, n.d., RG 75, entry 121, file no. 45499-1937-066 General Services, NARA; D. J. Brooks to William Zimmerman, 4 January 1938, RG 75, entry 121, file no. 45499-1937-066 General Services, NARA; Henry Brooks to William Zimmerman, 2 May 1938, RG 75, entry 121, file no. 45499-1937-066 General Services, NARA; Lovedy Locklear to William Zimmerman, 2 May 1938, RG 75, entry 121, file no. 45499-1937-066 General Services, NARA; Joe B. Locklear to William Zimmerman, 2 May 1938, RG 75, entry 121, file no. 45499-1937-066 General Services, NARA; Boss Locklear to William Zimmerman, 2 May 1938, RG 75, entry 121, file no. 45499-1937-066 General Services, NARA; Lawson Brooks to William Zimmerman, 1 May 1938, RG 75, entry 121, file no. 45499-1937-066 General Services, NARA; F. H. Daiker to Lovedy Locklear 31 May 1938, RG 75, entry 121, file no. 45499-1937-066 General Services, NARA; Britton Locklear to William Zimmerman, 20 January 1938, RG 75, entry 121, file no. 45499-1937-066 General Services, NARA; S. M. Bell, James E. Chavis, S. S. Lowrie, and Joseph Brooks to John Collier, 8 November 1938, RG 75, entry 121, file no. 45499-1937-066 General Services, NARA.

48. D'Arcy McNickle to John Collier, 17 February 1938, RG 75, entry 121, file no. 45499-1937-066 General Services, NARA.

49. D'Arcy McNickle to John Herrick, 2 May 1938, RG 75, entry 121, file no. 45499-1937-066 General Services, NARA.

50. John Herrick to D'Arcy McNickle, 9 May 1938, RG 75, entry 121, file no. 45499-1937-066 General Services, NARA.

51. S. M. Bell, James E. Chavis, S. S. Lowrie, and Joseph Brooks to John Collier, 8 November 1938, NARA.

52. F. H. Daiker to William Zimmerman, 3 June 1938, RG 75, entry 121, file no. 45499-1937-066 General Services, NARA. Walter V. Woehlke concurred with Daiker and Harrick and advised that the OIA not recognize the twenty-two applicants. See Walter V. Woehlke to William Zimmerman and John Collier, handwritten note, 29 June 1938, RG 75, entry 121, file no. 45499-1937-066 General Services, NARA.

53. Handwritten note on D'Arcy McNickle to John Collier, 26 October 1938, RG 75, entry 121, file no. 45499-1937-066 General Services, NARA.

54. John Collier recommended the enrollment of these Indians in John Collier to Harold Ickes, 29 October 1938, NARA.

55. William Zimmerman to Joseph Brooks, 12 December 1938, RG 75, entry 121, file no. 45499-1937-066 General Services, NARA; John Collier to Mary Lee Brooks Hammond et al., 28 January 1939, RG 75, entry 121, file no. 45499-1937-066 General Services, NARA. The twenty-two applicants also included Fannie Brooks Jacobs, Odell Brooks, Ralph Brooks Jr., Paul Brooks, Lily Jane Brooks Locklear, Rosetty Brooks Hunt, Dalseida Locklear Brooks, Henry Brooks, Lake Faddy Brooks, Ralph Brooks, Lawson Brooks, Ella Lee Brooks, Winnie Bell Locklear, Annie May Brooks Locklear, Lawrence Maynor, Lovedy Brooks Locklear, Jesse Brooks, Joe B. Locklear, and Vestia Locklear.

56. Spruhan, "Indian as Race/Indian as Political Status," 40–43.

57. Lovedy Locklear to William Zimmerman, 2 May 1938, NARA.

58. Lawson Brooks to William Zimmerman, 1 May 1938, NARA.

59. Henry Brooks to William Zimmerman, 2 May 1938, NARA.

60. Britton Locklear to Fred H. Daiker, 16 August 1938, RG 75, entry 121, file no. 45499-

1937-066 General Services, NARA; D. J. Brooks to Fred H. Daiker, 5 August 1938, RG 75, entry 121, file no. 45499-1937-066 General Services, NARA; Will Brooks to Fred H. Daiker, 15 August 1938, RG 75, entry 121, file no. 45499-1937-066 General Services, NARA.

61. Oscar Locklear et al., "To Whom It May Concern," 22 October 1938, RG 96, AD-NC-22 Pembroke Farms, box 437, NARA. The petition cited in chapter 5 was dated 11 October 1938, and Oscar Locklear was also the lead signer. Eight signers from the October 11th petition also signed the October 22nd petition, and both groups expressed the same concern, although the October 22nd petition is more detailed in its complaints. I believe both petitions represent the same effort to depose H. C. Green. Brooks Settlement members who signed these petitions included D. J. Brooks, Henry Brooks, J. C. Brooks, and Dougle Brooks. There may be others who I am not able to identify without further research.

62. "Meeting of Homesteaders of the Pembroke Resettlement Project in Office of Mr. L. I. Hewes, Jr.," 24 October 1938, RG 96, AD-NC-22 Pembroke Farms, box 437, NARA. The other men who met with the FSA were Henry Locklear, Duncan L. Locklear, A. L. Strickland, and A. L. Strickland's son, who is not named.

63. Releford [Ralph] Brooks to Bureau of Indian Affairs, 6 January 1939, RG 75, entry 121, file no. 45499-1937-066 General Services, NARA. D. J. Brooks's political experience stretched back to the 1920s, when he and his parents traveled to Washington, D.C., to appear before the "Indian Commission" to investigate "Indian rights for ourselves and the tribe." See Seltzer, "A Report on the Racial Status of Certain People," Applicant #44. He was also active in the campaign to get the Siouan bill passed in 1933 and 1934. See D. J. Brooks to J. W. Bailey, 11 March 1933, box 311, folder: Interior, 1934, Feb. 6 to March 13, JBC.

64. Twenty-three of the forty-seven members were identified as borderline or ½ or more Indian. The number may be somewhat higher than that, but some of the names are difficult to read. See Releford [Ralph] Brooks to Bureau of Indian Affairs, 6 January 1939, NARA.

65. Elisha Locklear and Cecil Hunt, interview by author and Willie Lowery, Pembroke, N.C., 23 February 2004, LRFC.

66. Meyer, "American Indian Blood Quantum Requirements," 236.

67. Compare ibid., 241. Why and how tribes and Indian people have adopted the language of blood quantum to define community membership is discussed in Kimberly Tall Bear, "DNA, Blood, and Racializing the Tribe," *Wicazo-Sa Review* (Spring 2003): 89–93.

68. Releford [Ralph] Brooks to Arch Mckle [D'Arcy McNickle], 12 January 1939, RG 75, entry 121, file no. 45499-1937-066 General Services, NARA.

69. Releford [Ralph] Brooks to John Collier, 17 February 1939, RG 75, entry 121, file no. 45499-1937-066 General Services, NARA; Releford [Ralph] Brooks to John Collier, 20 March 1939, RG 75, entry 121, file no. 45499-1937-066 General Services, NARA.

70. F. H. Daiker to Releford [Ralph] Brooks, 31 March 1939, RG 75, entry 121, file no. 45499-1937-066 General Services, NARA.

71. Releford [Ralph] Brooks to Fred Darke [Daiker], 3 April 1939, RG 75, entry 121, file no. 45499-1937-066 General Services, NARA.

72. James E. Chavis to John Collier, 3 October 1939, RG 75, entry 121, file no. 45499-1937-066 General Services, NARA.

73. For examples of Indians challenging the legal system, see Correspondence relating to State v. Bricey Hammonds, RG 75, entry 121, file no. 45499-1937-066 General Services, NARA.

74. Lawrence Maynor to John Collier, 1 December 1939, RG 75, entry 121, file no. 45499-1937-066 General Services, NARA.

75. *Lawrence Maynor v. Rogers C. B. Morton*, U.S. Court of Appeals, District of Columbia, argued 21 November 1974, decided 4 April 1975 (510 F.2d 1254 1975).

76. J. C. McCaskill to George S. Mitchell, 28 January 1939, RG 75, entry 121, file no. 10226-1943-048 Cherokee School Part 1, NARA. A group associated with the Cherokee leadership named the Indian Child Welfare Association also attempted to receive assistance from the OIA in 1944. See P. W. Danielson to Mary Livermore, 8 July 1944, RG 75, entry 121, file no. 45499-1937-066 General Services, NARA.

77. D'Arcy McNickle called the Robeson County Indian question "interminable" in D'Arcy McNickle to John Herrick, 2 May 1938, NARA.

78. Fred H. Daiker to Carl Seltzer, 2 June 1939, RG 75, entry 121, file no. 45499-1937-066 General Services, NARA; John Herrick to Joseph Brooks, 8 September 1939, RG 75, entry 121, file no. 45499-1937-066 General Services, NARA.

79. Henry Sanderson to John Collier, 13 June 1939, RG 75, entry 121, file no. 45499-1937-066 General Services, NARA.

80. Joe Jennings to William Zimmerman, 2 February 1939, RG 75, entry 121, file no. 10226-1943-046 Cherokee School Part 1, NARA.

81. F. H. Daiker to William Zimmerman, 8 February 1939, RG 75, entry 121, file no. 10226-1943-046 Cherokee School Part 1, NARA.

82. William Zimmerman to John Collier, handwritten note, n.d., RG 75, entry 121, file no. 10226-1943-046 Cherokee School Part 1, NARA; John Collier to William Zimmerman, handwritten note, 18 February (no year), RG 75, entry 121, file no. 10226-1943-046 Cherokee School Part 1, NARA.

83. Helen C. Rountree, *Pocahontas's People: The Powhatan Indians of Virginia through Four Centuries* (Norman: University of Oklahoma Press, 1990), chap. 9; RG 75, series 6 (Cherokee Indian Agency), box 45, folder: Pamunkey Indians 138, 1942–46, NARA-Atlanta.

84. D'Arcy McNickle to Ward Shepard, 31 May 1941, RG 75, entry 121, file no. 45499-1937-066 General Services, NARA.

85. John Collier to D. J. Brooks, 3 July 1942, NARA. According to legal historian and activist Vine Deloria Jr., "Had World War II not intervened in this recognition process, there is no question that thirty and perhaps as many as a hundred small, identifiable groups of Indians would have received federal status during the 1940s." See Vine Deloria Jr., "Foreword," in Frye Gaillard and Carolyn DeMerritt, *As Long as the Waters Flow: Native Americans in the South and East* (Winston-Salem, N.C.: John F. Blair, 1998), x.

86. Clyde R. Hoey to William Zimmerman, 13 January 1945, RG 75, entry 121, file no. 45499-1937-066 General Services, NARA.

87. William Zimmerman to Clyde R. Hoey, 24 January 1945, RG 75, entry 121, file no. 45499-1937-066 General Services, NARA.

88. Clyde R. Hoey to William Zimmerman, 17 February 1945, RG 75, entry 121, file no. 45499-1937-066 General Services, NARA.

89. William Zimmerman to Clyde R. Hoey, 10 March 1945, RG 75, entry 121, file no. 45499-1937-066 General Services, NARA.

CHAPTER 7

1. Mrs. Theodore Maynor to Mr. and Mrs. Guy B. Johnson, 10 December 1940, GBJP.

2. A discussion of the 1924 Indian Citizenship Act can be found in Francis Paul Prucha, *The Great Father: The United States Government and the American Indians*, abr. ed. (Lincoln: University of Nebraska Press, 1984), 273; Thomas A. Britten, *American Indians in World War I: At War and at Home* (Albuquerque: University of New Mexico Press, 1997), 176–81; Kenneth William Townsend, *World War II and the American Indian* (Albuquerque: University of New Mexico Press, 2000), chap. 5; Robert B. Porter, "The Demise of the Ongwehoweh and the Rise of the Native Americas: Redressing the Genocidal Act of Forcing American Citizenship upon Indigenous Peoples," in Robert Odawi Porter, *Sovereignty, Colonialism, and the Indigenous Nations: A Reader* (Durham, N.C.: Carolina Academic Press, 2005), 429–33.

3. The concepts of "civic nationalism" and "racial nationalism" are borrowed from Gary Gerstle, *American Crucible: Race and Nation in the Twentieth Century* (Princeton, N.J.: Princeton University Press, 2001).

4. Compare Vine Deloria Jr., "Sacred Lands and Religious Freedom," in *For This Land: Writings on Religion in America* (New York: Routledge, 1998), 203–13.

5. For an analysis of the factors leading to Indians' ambiguous status, see Vine Deloria Jr. and David E. Wilkins, *Tribes, Treaties, and Constitutional Tribulations* (Austin: University of Texas Press, 1999).

6. Classic studies of immigration examined immigrant groups in terms of static dichotomies of assimilation and preservation that were the very dichotomies that informed the policies that affected Indians so negatively in the early twentieth century. More recently, other scholars have looked at structures of American society—particularly race and class—and observed immigrants and ethnic groups being incorporated through their willing or unwilling dialogues with those structures. The distinctions between those groups and Native Americans outlined here were formulated by Frederick E. Hoxie, *A Final Promise: The Campaign to Assimilate the Indians, 1880–1920* (Lincoln, Neb.: Bison Books, 2001), 235–38; and Philip J. Deloria, *Indians in Unexpected Places* (Lawrence: University Press of Kansas, 2004), 234–37. See Oscar Handlin, *The Uprooted* (Boston: Little, Brown & Co., 1951); Rudolph Vecoli, "The Contadini in Chicago: A Critique of the Uprooted," *Journal of American History* 51 (December 1964): 404–17; John Bodnar, *The Transplanted: A History of Immigrants in Urban America* (Bloomington: Indiana University Press, 1985); Lizabeth Cohen, *Making a New Deal: Industrial Workers in Chicago, 1919–1939* (New York: Cambridge University Press, 1990); and Mae M. Ngai, "The Architecture of Race in American Immigration Law: A Reexamination of the Immigration Act of 1924," *Journal of American History* 86 (June 1999): 67–92.

7. Hoxie, *A Final Promise*, 235–38.

8. Ngai, "The Architecture of Race in American Immigration Law."

9. Devon W. Carbado, "Racial Naturalization," *American Quarterly* 57, no. 3 (2005): 633–58. This argument expands on the one offered by Hoxie in *A Final Promise*.

10. David Glassberg, *American Historical Pageantry: The Uses of Tradition in the Early Twentieth Century* (Chapel Hill: University of North Carolina Press, 1990), 4, 5, 64, 103. For Collier's involvement with pageantry and the playground movement, which heralded pageants as a form of community development, see E. A. Schwartz, "Red Atlantis Revisited: Community and Culture in the Writings of John Collier," *American Indian Quarterly* 18 (Autumn 1994): 511–12. Collier's quote is found in Lotta A. Clark, "Pageantry in America," *English Journal* 3 (March 1914): 150–51; and Glassberg, *American Historical Pageantry*, 103.

11. Philip J. Deloria, "Thinking about Self in a Family Way," *Journal of American History* 89 (June 2002), ⟨http://www.historycooperative.org/journals/jah/89.1/deloria.html⟩ (accessed 7 March 2008); Susan Gardner, "Speaking of Ella Deloria: Conversations with Joyzelle Gingway Godfrey, 1998–2000, Lower Brule Community College, South Dakota," *American Indian Quarterly* 24 (Summer 2000): 457.

12. George S. Mitchell to John Collier, 10 July 1940, RG 96, AD-NC-22 Pembroke Farms, box 437, NARA; Memorandum for Personnel, 11 July 1941 (copy in personal possession of the author), NARA; George S. Mitchell to S. A. Hammond, D. F. Lowry, Walter Smith, W. R. Maynor, C. E. Locklear, Joseph Brooks, and C. D. Brewington, 23 July 1940, RG 96, AD-NC-22 Pembroke Farms, box 437, NARA; Ella Deloria to Franz Boas, 7 August 1940, Franz Boas Papers, American Philosophical Society, Philadelphia, Pa., NARA.

13. Ella Deloria to Ruth Bronson, 6 August 1940 (copy in personal possession of author), NARA.

14. Ella Deloria to George S. Mitchell, 21 August 1940 (copy in personal possession of author), NARA.

15. Ibid.

16. Ella Deloria to George S. Mitchell, 22 October 1940, RG 96, AD-NC-22 Pembroke Farms, box 437, NARA; Ella Deloria to John Collier, 22 November 1940, RG 75, entry 121, file no. 2694-1941-047 General Services, NARA; "Outline of Pageant: 'The Life-Story of a People,'" 5 December 1940, RG 96, AD-NC-22 Pembroke Farms, box 437, NARA; "Robeson Indians Portray Early History," *Raleigh News and Observer*, 6 December 1940.

17. Ella Deloria to John Collier, 22 November 1940, NARA.

18. Philip Deloria, *Indians in Unexpected Places*, 246.

19. Ella Deloria to George S. Mitchell, 21 August 1940 (copy in personal possession of the author); Ella Deloria to George S. Mitchell, 22 October 1940, NARA.

20. Ella Deloria to C. B. Faris, 21 August 1940, RG 96, AD-NC-22 Pembroke Farms, box 437, NARA; Letter from "The Publicity Committee," n.d., RG 75, entry 121, file no. 64190-1935-066 General Services Part 1, NARA.

21. Ella Deloria to George S. Mitchell, 21 August 1940; Ella Deloria to George S. Mitchell, 22 October 1940, NARA.

22. Compare Glassberg, *American Historical Pageantry*, 22.

23. Ella Deloria to George S. Mitchell, 22 October 1940, NARA; George S. Mitchell to Ella Deloria, 26 October 1940, RG 96, AD-NC-22 Pembroke Farms, box 437, NARA; George S. Mitchell to Ella Deloria, 16 October 1941, RG 96, AD-NC-22 Pembroke Farms, box 437, NARA; George S. Mitchell to Howard H. Gordon, 16 October 1941, RG 96, AD-NC-22 Pembroke Farms, box 437, NARA; Ella Deloria to George S. Mitchell, 28 October 1941, RG 96, AD-NC-22 Pembroke Farms, box 437, NARA.

24. George S. Mitchell to Ella Deloria, 11 December 1940, RG 96, AD-NC-22 Pembroke

Farms, box 437, NARA; George S. Mitchell to John Collier, 11 December 1940, RG 96, AD-NC-22 Pembroke Farms, box 437, NARA; George S. Mitchell to John Collier, 14 January 1941, RG 96, AD-NC-22 Pembroke Farms, box 437, NARA.

25. Ella Deloria to George S. Mitchell, 28 October 1941, NARA; Ella Deloria to George S. Mitchell, 8 January 1941, RG 96, AD-NC-22 Pembroke Farms, box 437, NARA.

26. "Robeson Indians Open Pageant Tonight," *Raleigh News and Observer*, 5 December 1941.

27. Cynthia Brooks, conversation with the author, 4 May 2004, Pembroke, N.C.

28. Christopher Arris Oakley, *Keeping the Circle: American Indian Identity in Eastern North Carolina, 1885–2004* (Lincoln: University of Nebraska Press, 2005), 77–78, 95–96. See also Ruth Dial Woods, "Growing Up Red: The Lumbee Experience" (Ph.D. diss., University of North Carolina at Chapel Hill, 2001), 96–99; Adolph L. Dial and David K. Eliades, *The Only Land I Know: A History of the Lumbee Indians* (San Francisco: Indian Historian Press, 1975), 155–56.

29. Luther Harbert Moore, interview by author, Pembroke, N.C., 20 November 2003, LRFC.

30. Mae Ngai, *Impossible Subjects: Illegal Aliens and the Making of Modern America* (Princeton, N.J.: Princeton University Press, 2004), 6.

31. C. W. Oxendine to Franklin D. Roosevelt, 28 October 1941, RG 75, entry 121, file no. 45499-1937-066 General Services, NARA. See also C. W. Oxendine to J. C. McCaskill, 6 January 1942, RG 75, entry 121, file no. 10226-1943-042 Cherokee School Part 1, NARA.

32. J. C. McCaskill to C. W. Oxendine, 20 December 1941, RG 75, entry 121, file no. 45499-1937-066 General Services, NARA; J. C. McCaskill to C. W. Oxendine, 22 January 1949, RG 75, entry 121, file no. 10226-1943-042 Cherokee School Part 1, NARA.

33. Joe Jennings to D'Arcy McNickle, 8 March 1941, RG 75, entry 121, file no. 45499-1937-066 General Services, NARA.

34. Prucha, *The Great Father*, 335–37.

35. Sidney Baldwin, *Poverty and Politics: The Rise and Decline of the Farm Security Administration* (Chapel Hill: University of North Carolina Press, 1968), chap. 7, 385–89.

36. U.S. House of Representatives, *Hearings before the Select Committee of the House Committee on Agriculture to Investigate the Activities of the Farm Security Administration, Pursuant to H. Res. 119, Part 3*, 78th Cong., 1st sess., 1943, 1088. The government's average investment per farm family at Pembroke Farms was $6,428, whereas the average selling price was $4,974.

37. J. B. Slack to James E. Chavis, 22 March 1945 (copy in personal possession of the author); Auction announcement for Pembroke Farms tracts including Community Building, n.d. (likely August 1945), SIF.

38. James E. Chavis to A. A. Grorud, 4 December 1944, SIF.

39. Clifton Carter to H. C. Green, 7 February 1945, SIF; Cleatis Dial to H. C. Green, 7 February 1945, SIF; H. C. Green to Clifton Carter, 8 February 1945, SIF; Carson Locklear to H. C. Green, 8 February 1945, SIF; H. C. Green to Cleatis Dial, 10 February 1945, SIF; H. C. Green to Carson Locklear, 10 February 1945, SIF.

40. James E. Chavis to A. A. Grorud, 6 August 1945, SIF; A. A. Grorud to James E. Chavis, 10 August 1945; James E. Chavis to A. A. Grorud, 19 August 1945, SIF; A. A. Grorud to James E. Chavis, 20 August 1945, SIF.

41. A. A. Grorud to James E. Chavis, 20 August 1945, SIF; A. A. Grorud to James E. Chavis, 23 August 1945, SIF; C. Carter Chase to J. C. McCaskill, 30[?] August 1945 (copy in personal possession of author); J. C. McCaskill to Indian Office, 28 August 1945, RG 75, entry 121, file no. 45499-1937-066 General Services, NARA.

42. T. J. Crutcher to Bunyan Locklear, 10 September 1945 (copy in personal possession of the author); James E. Chavis to A. A. Grorud, 4 September 1945, SIF; James E. Chavis to Elmer Thomas, 4 September 1945, SIF.

43. J. B. Slack to Frank Hancock, 9 February 1944 (copy in personal possession of the author); T. J. Crutcher to
Bunyan Locklear, 10 September 1945 (copy in personal possession of the author); J. B. Slack to T. J. Crutcher, 12 September 1945 (copy in personal possession of the author), NARA.

44. William Zimmerman to J. Stott Noble, 25 October 1945 (copy in personal possession of the author), NARA.

45. Oakley, *Keeping the Circle*, 80–87; 93–94. See also Abraham Makofsky, "Tradition and Change in the Lumbee Indian Community of Baltimore" (Ph.D. diss., Catholic University of America, 1971).

46. Oakley, *Keeping the Circle*, 92.

47. Prucha, *The Great Father*, 344–45, 354–56; Oakley, *Keeping the Circle*, 93.

48. Billy Tayac, phone conversation with the author, 12 December 2004; "Pembroke Indians Organize to Obtain 'Special Rights,'" *Robesonian*, 22 April 1949; Gabrielle Tayac, e-mail communication with the author, 14 October 2004, 9 December 2004. See also Cecile C. Friedly to James F. Lind, 8 October 1952, RG 75, entry 121, file no. 10226-1943-042 Cherokee School Part 1, NARA. For more on Turkey Tayac's life, see "The Flickering Flame of Indianism: The Legacy of Chief Turkey Tayac," ⟨http://www.piscatawaynation.org⟩ (accessed 14 December 2004).

49. Billy Tayac, phone conversation with the author, 12 December 2004.

50. The origin of the name "Lumbee" is a subject of debate in Robeson County. The word itself first appeared in reference to the tribe in 1914, when Indian Methodists formed the Lumbee River Conference of the Holiness Methodist Church (see chapter 1), and O. M. McPherson also discussed it in his 1915 report to the Senate (see chapter 3). Local whites have traced the origin of the word to the Lumber River's ancient name, "Lumbee." Lumbee is presumed to be a word of Siouan origin. The name was used at least once in the 1920s by outside observers. Ralph Brooks referenced the "Lumbee River" several times during his meeting with NCAI, and, as stated above, the OIA and the Original 22's delegation also discussed the name "Lumber River Indians." Evidence also indicates that Turkey Tayac named the tribe "Lumbee," combining "Lumber" with the Piscataway word "bee," which means "bend." This evidence is buttressed by William H. Gilbert's suggestion to Lindsay Revels that the tribe call itself "Lumbee" (Gilbert worked closely with Tayac and traveled to Robeson County with him). Many Robeson County Indians today believe that D. F. Lowry, the moving force behind the 1956 Lumbee Act, came up with the name. I am not trying to take one particular stance or another on the origin of the name or its authenticity, but the documentation clearly indicates that the name as applied to federal recognition originated with the Original 22's efforts to reinvigorate interest in recognizing their group. D. F. Lowry even indicated this in 1973 when he stated that "a group of leaders among us

joined on support of a name *previously suggested*—Lumbee" (emphasis mine). See Lumber River Conference of the Holiness Methodist Church, *The History of the Lumbee Conference* (N.p.: Lumber River Conference of the Holiness Methodist Church, 2003), 12–13; O. M. McPherson, *Report on Condition and Tribal Rights of the Indians of Robeson and Adjoining Counties of North Carolina*, 63d Cong., 3d sess., 5 January 1915, S. Doc. 677 (Washington, D.C.: Government Printing Office, 1915), 23; House Committee on Interior and Insular Affairs, *Hearing Relating to the Lumbee Indians of North Carolina*, 84th Cong., 1st sess., 22 July 1955, 3; Memorandum for the file, from Frances Lopinsky, 25 November 1947, James E. Curry Papers, Subject file Regarding Indian Affairs, box 75, NAA; John H. Provinse to Joe Jennings, 9 July 1947, RG 75, entry 121, file no. 10226-1943-042 Cherokee School Part 1, NARA; "Pembroke Indians Organize To Obtain 'Special Rights'"; William Zimmerman to Linzy [*sic*] Revels, Alford Pevia, and Ziron [*sic*] Lowry, 4 January 1950, RG 75, entry 121, file no. 10226-1943-042 Cherokee School Part 1, NARA; Billy Tayac, phone conversation with the author, 12 December 2004; Dial and Eliades, *The Only Land I Know*, 157; D. F. Lowry, "Lumbee Indian Act of 1953: Its Origin and Rationale," *Robesonian*, 22 February 1973; Peter H. Wood, Deborah Montgomerie, and Susan Yarnell, *Tuscarora Roots: An Historical Report Regarding the Relation of the Hatteras Tuscarora Tribe of Robeson County, North Carolina, to the Original Tuscarora Indian Tribe* (Durham, N.C.: Hatteras Tuscarora Tribal Foundation, 1992), 110; Julian T. Pierce, Cynthia Hunt-Locklear, Jack Campisi, and Wesley White, *The Lumbee Petition* (Pembroke, N.C.: Lumbee River Legal Services, 1987), 1:93–94.

51. John H. Provinse to Joe Jennings, 9 July 1947, NARA; Ralph Brooks to National Congress of American Indians, 17 November 1947, James E. Curry Papers, Subject File Regarding Indian Affairs, box 75, NAA.; Prucha, *The Great Father*, 341; Memorandum for the File from Frances Lopinsky, 25 November 1947, James E. Curry Papers, NAA; Ruth M. Bronson to Ralph Brooks, n.d., James E. Curry Papers, NAA; Frances Lopinsky to Ralph Brooks, 26 November 1947, James E. Curry Papers, NAA; Ernest T. Brooks to Frances Lopinsky, 20 April 1948, James E. Curry Papers, NAA; William Zimmerman to Ralph Brooks, 26 January 1948, RG 75, entry 121, file no. 10226-1943-042 Cherokee School Part 1, NARA; D. S. Myer to Linzy [*sic*] Revels, 17 October 1950, RG 75, entry 121, file no. 10226-1943-042 Cherokee School Part 1, NARA.

52. Ralph Brooks to Clyde R. Hoey, 3 January 1948, RG 75, entry 121, file no. 10226-1943-042 Cherokee School Part 1, NARA; Ralph Brooks to William Bradley Umstead, 3 January 1948, RG 75, entry 121, file no. 10226-1943-042 Cherokee School Part 1, NARA; Ralph Brooks to J. Bayard Clark, 3 January 1948, RG 75, entry 121, file no. 10226-1943-042 Cherokee School Part 1, NARA. See also Ralph Brooks to D. E. Murphy, 3 January 1948, RG 75, entry 121, file no. 10226-1943-042 Cherokee School Part 1, NARA.

53. Billy Tayac, phone conversation with the author, 12 December 2004; "Pembroke Indians Organize to Obtain 'Special Rights.'"

54. Carl C. Seltzer, "A Report on the Racial Status of Certain People in Robeson County, North Carolina," 30 June 1936, RG 75, entry 616, box 13–15, North Carolina, Applicants #24, 43, NARA.

55. William Zimmerman to Linzy [*sic*] Revels, Alfred Pevia, and Ziron [*sic*] Lowry, 4 January 1950, NARA.

56. File memo from Erma O. Hicks, 6 January 1950, RG 75, entry 121, file no. 10226-1943-042 Cherokee School Part 1, NARA.

57. "Pembroke Indians Organize To Obtain 'Special Rights.'"

58. "Says Indians in Town of Pembroke and Educated Members of Race Have Not Taken Part in Recent Agitation," *Robesonian*, 25 April 1949.

59. "Pembroke Indians Organize To Obtain 'Special Rights.'"

60. Revels's petition was sent to the Senate Judiciary Committee and was witnessed by two members of Senator Frank Porter Graham's staff. Graham served on that committee and may have recommended that they send the petition there instead of to the Committee on Indian Affairs; see Linzy [sic] Revels and Lilly Ann Locklear to U.S. Senate Committee on the Judiciary, 27 September 1950, RG 75, entry 121, file no. 10226-1943-042 Cherokee School Part 1, NARA. See list of names in RG 75, entry 121, file no. 10226-1943-042 Cherokee School Part 1-A, NARA; see also William Zimmerman to Sarah Jane Oxendine, 3 April 1950, RG 75, entry 121, file no. 10226-1943-042 Cherokee School Part 1, NARA; and Sarah Jane Oxendine to William Zimmerman, 10 April 1950, RG 75, entry 121, file no. 10226-1943-042 Cherokee School Part 1, NARA.

61. Linesy [sic] Revels to Clyde R. Hoey, n.d., Clyde R. Hoey Collection, box 150, folder 6: Indian Affairs, 1947, 1949–50, 1954, Duke University Rare Book, Manuscript, and Special Collections Library; Clyde R. Hoey to Lindsay Revels, 12 August 1950, Clyde R. Hoey Collection, box 150, folder 6: Indian Affairs, 1947, 1949–50, 1954, Duke University Rare Book, Manuscript, and Special Collections Library.

62. D'Arcy McNickle to Linzy [sic] Revels, 27 June 1950, RG 75, entry 121, file no. 10226-1943-042 Cherokee School Part 1, NARA.

63. Elisha Locklear and Cecil Hunt, audiotaped interview with the author, 23 February 2004, Pembroke, N.C., LRFC.

64. Prucha, *The Great Father*, 344–47; Oakley, *Keeping the Circle*, 148. Interestingly, Oakley points out that liberals in Congress compared the reservation system to segregation in the South, where society prevented a particular group from participating in the benefits of American citizenship.

65. Kenneth Philp, *Termination Revisited: American Indians on the Trail to Self-Determination, 1933–1953* (Lincoln: University of Nebraska Press, 1999); quote from p. xiv.

66. Pierce, Hunt-Locklear, Campisi, and White, *The Lumbee Petition*, 1:93.

67. "Robeson Indians to Decide Name Issue," *Raleigh News and Observer*, 30 March 1951.

68. Lowry, "Lumbee Indian Act of 1953"; "Robeson Indians Will Vote on Name Proposal February 3," *Robesonian*, 8 January 1952.

69. Lumber River Conference of the Holiness Methodist Church, *The History of the Lumbee Conference*, 13; Ed Chavis, phone conversation with the author, 15 June 2004. Prominent members of the Lumbee Brotherhood, according to D. F. Lowry, were Early Bullard, Ornie Bullard, Lindsay Revels, L. W. Jacobs, Burt Locklear, Harry West Locklear, C. E. Locklear, J. A. Wilkins, Fuller Locklear, and Luther Moore. See D. F. Lowry, "Lumbee Indian Act of 1953."

70. "Indians Approve Change in Name," *Robesonian*, 2 April 1951.

71. One newspaper reporter noted that "the Siousan [sic] adherents had gone over to the 'Lumbee' proponents admitting error and there is no argument about the name." "Robeson Indians to Decide Name Issue"; "Indians Approve Change in Name."

72. It seems worth noting that these dynamics reproduced attitudes toward the name

"Cherokee" in the early 1930s (see chapter 3). With the 1932 Cherokee legislation, Indians divided not over whether the name "Cherokee" was appropriate but whether a white Democrat, Angus McLean, should represent their interests in Congress. In a sense, the division over the Lumbee name is similar, but rather than debate the issue of who would represent them, town and rural Indians debated the role that "Indian blood" should play in their outward manifestation of identity. Compare Pierce, Hunt-Locklear, Campisi, and White, *The Lumbee Petition*, 1:94.

73. The letter was written by D. F. Lowry, L. W. Jacobs, and Harry West Locklear. Lowry, "Lumbee Indian Act of 1953."

74. "'Lumbee Indians' Designated in Bill Introduced by Watts," *Robesonian*, 5 April 1951.

75. "Robeson Indians Drive toward Vote to Decide Official Name," *Robesonian*, 17 August 1951.

76. "Robeson Indians Will Vote on Name Proposal Feb. 2," *Robesonian*, 8 January 1952; "Robeson Indians Plan Vote on Name," *Raleigh News and Observer*, 10 January 1952.

77. "Robeson Indians Will Vote on Name Proposal Feb. 2"; "Series of Indian Meetings Planned," *Robesonian*, 15 January 1952; "Meeting Series Set by Indians," *Robesonian*, 21 January 1952.

78. U.S. Senate, *Relating to Lumbee Indians of North Carolina*, 84th Cong., 2nd sess., 16 May 1956, 2. See also Pierce, Hunt-Locklear, Campisi, and White, *The Lumbee Petition*, 1:94.

79. Compare Thomas Biolsi, *Organizing the Lakota: The Political Economy of the New Deal on the Pine Ridge and Rosebud Reservations* (Tucson: University of Arizona Press, 1992), chap. 3; Richard O. Clemmer, "Hopis, Western Shoshones, and Southern Utes: Three Different Responses to the Indian Reorganization Act," *American Indian Culture and Research Journal* 10, no. 2 (1986): 20. Deloria and Lytle point out that the Indian Reorganization Act was considered adopted unless a majority of Indians voted against it; this "placed the burden of action on those Indian factions that opposed the law's application." The vote for the name "Lumbee" was structured somewhat similarly. The option of Cherokee or Lumbee placed the burden of action on Indians who disapproved of both names, just as the requirement to reject the IRA placed the burden of action on Indians who opposed the IRA. In a sense, if you failed to vote against the IRA, you approved the IRA; similarly, if you failed to vote against the name "Lumbee," your inaction had the effect of approving the name. Vine Deloria Jr. and Clifford Lytle, *The Nations Within: The Past and Future of American Indian Sovereignty* (New York: Pantheon Books, 1984), 151–52, 171–72.

80. Pierce, Hunt-Locklear, Campisi, and White, *The Lumbee Petition*, 1:95; "Group Approves Name-Change for Robeson Indians," *Raleigh News and Observer*, 26 February 1953; "Robeson Legislators Clash," *Raleigh News and Observer*, 2 April 1953.

81. Carlyle signed the infamous "Southern Manifesto," which protested the Supreme Court's desegregation ruling in the 1954 *Brown v. Board of Education* case. See *Congressional Record*, 84th Cong., 2nd sess., 1956, 102, part 4.

82. House Committee on Interior and Insular Affairs, *Hearing Relating to the Lumbee Indians*, 3, 8.

83. Ibid., 3–4.

84. Ibid., 7–8.

85. According to the hearing transcript, Harry Locklear and Hayes Locklear were also present, but they made no comments. Ibid., 21.

86. Ibid., 11–13.

87. Ibid., 14.

88. Ibid., 17.

89. U.S. House of Representatives, *Relating to the Lumbee Indians of North Carolina*, 84th Cong., 2nd sess., 18 January 1956.

90. U.S. Senate, *Relating to the Lumbee Indians*, 2–3.

91. Ibid., 1.

92. Pierce, Hunt-Locklear, Campisi, and White, *The Lumbee Petition*, 1:97.

93. Penn Gray, "'Indian Nations' Sends Envoys to Tell Lumbees about Unity," *Robesonian*, 2 April 1959; Billy Tayac, phone conversation with the author, 12 December 2004; Gerald Sider, *Living Indian Histories: Lumbee and Tuscarora People in North Carolina* (Chapel Hill: University of North Carolina Press, 2003), lxi.

94. Sider, *Living Indian Histories*, lx, chap. 7. A *Robesonian* newspaper report indicates that Tuscarora political organizing began as early as 1961. See Sider, *Living Indian Histories*, 111–12.

95. *Maynor v. Morton*, 510 F. 2d 1254, D.C. Circuit Court, 1975; Cynthia Hunt, "Looking Back While Walking Forward," *Carolina Indian Voice*, 27 April 2000. The surviving members of the Original 22 were Henry Brooks, Rosetta Brooks Hunt, Annie Maw Brooks, Ella Lee Brooks, Anna Brooks, Vestia Locklear Lowery, and Lawrence Maynor.

96. Venita Jenkins, "Siouan Kin Contest Lumbee Recognition," *Fayetteville Observer*, 25 April 2004; Elisha Locklear and Cecil Hunt, audiotaped interview with the Author, Pembroke, N.C., 23 February 2004; Elisha Locklear, conversation with the author, 24 July 2003; Sider, *Living Indian Histories*, chaps. 7 and 8. See also Seltzer, "A Report on the Racial Status of Certain People," 30 June 1936, NARA.

97. Sider, *Living Indian Histories*, xxvi, l. Tuscaroras have also pursued federal recognition through the Bureau of Acknowledgement and Research process, instated in 1978 at the Bureau of Indian Affairs. See Wood, Montgomerie, and Yarnell, *Tuscarora Roots*, 116.

98. Bruce Granville Miller examines these ramifications in *Invisible Indigenes: The Politics of Nonrecognition* (Lincoln: University of Nebraska Press, 2003). Also see Sider, *Living Indian Histories*, lxvi.

CONCLUSION

1. Details of the incident vary, but this represents a typical view of the order of events. Adolph L. Dial and David K. Eliades, *The Only Land I Know: A History of the Lumbee Indians* (San Francisco: Indian Historian Press, 1975), 159–62; Julian T. Pierce, Cynthia Hunt-Locklear, Jack Campisi, and Wesley White, *The Lumbee Petition* (Pembroke, N.C.: Lumbee River Legal Services, 1987), 1:99–100; Karen I. Blu, *The Lumbee Problem: The Making of an American Indian People* (Cambridge: Cambridge University Press, 1980), 156–60; Timothy B. Tyson, *Radio Free Dixie: Robert F. Williams and the Roots of Black Power* (Chapel Hill: University of North Carolina Press, 1999), 137–40; Frye Gaillard and Carolyn DeMerritt, *As Long as the Waters Flow: Native Americans in the South and East* (Winston-Salem, N.C.: John F. Blair, 1998), 155–57; Chick Jacobs and Venita Jenkins, "Showdown at Hayes Pond— The Battle of Maxton Field," *Fayetteville Observer*, ⟨http://www.fayobserver.com/special/battle_of_maxton_field/#⟩ (accessed 22 July 2008); "An Indian Victory at Hayes Pond," *Native Visions* 3 (January 2008): 4.

2. Willa Robinson, audiotaped interview by author, Lumberton, N.C., 14 January 2004, Southern Oral History Program Collection, Southern Historical Collection, University of North Carolina at Chapel Hill.

3. Jacobs and Jenkins, "Showdown at Hayes Pond."

4. Ibid.

5. Willa Robinson, interview by author.

6. Quotes from letters on display in an exhibit about the "Battle of Maxton" are at the Native American Resource Center, University of North Carolina at Pembroke, Pembroke, N.C.

7. James Arthur Jones, as told to Malinda Maynor, "What Is Progress? Desegregating an Indian School in Robeson County, North Carolina," *Southern Cultures* 10 (Summer 2004): 87–93.

8. Lew Barton, *The Most Ironic Story in American History: An Authoritative, Documented History of the Lumbee Indians of North Carolina* (Charlotte, N.C.: Associated Printing Corporation, 1967), 97.

9. American Bar Association, "Division for Public Education: Native American Heritage Month: Arlinda Locklear," ⟨http://www.abanet.org/publiced/rblocklear.html⟩ (accessed 18 April 2009).

10. Arlinda Locklear, interview with the author, 18 April 2009, Red Springs, N.C. See also Robert B. Porter, "The Demise of the Ongwehoweh and the Rise of the Native Americas: Redressing the Genocidal Act of Forcing American Citizenship upon Indigenous Peoples," in Robert Odawi Porter, *Sovereignty, Colonialism, and the Indigenous Nations: A Reader* (Durham, N.C.: Carolina Academic Press, 2005), 432.

11. George Lipsitz, *American Studies in a Moment of Danger* (Minneapolis: University of Minnesota Press, 2001), 16.

12. This conclusion is based on a definition of nationalism that extends beyond allegiance to a common state or ideology. According to Benedict Anderson, a nation is "an imagined political community" distinguished from other nations by "the style in which they are imagined." The political processes that occurred in the Robeson County Indian community between 1872 and 1956 created such an imagined community with a distinct "Indian" style. Benedict Anderson, *Imagined Communities: Reflections on the Origin and Spread of Nationalism*, rev. ed. (London: Verso, 1983), 6.

13. Blu, *The Lumbee Problem*, 124, 158; Tyson, *Radio Free Dixie*, 138.

14. David Cecelski, "Welton Lowry: The Spirit of Henry Berry Lowry," *Raleigh News and Observer*, 10 June 2001.

15. Interestingly, Simeon Oxendine was named an honorary member of the Pawnee tribe as a result of the publicity he received. Dial and Eliades, *The Only Land I Know*, 162.

16. Arlinda Locklear, interview.

17. Gerald Sider, *Living Indian Histories: Lumbee and Tuscarora People in North Carolina* (Chapel Hill: University of North Carolina Press, 2003), lvi–lix.

18. Arlinda Locklear, interview.

19. Sider, *Living Indian Histories*, lxii; Lumbee Tribe of North Carolina, "Constitution," ⟨http://www.lumbeetribe.com/government/index.html⟩ (accessed 27 December 2004).

20. Arlinda Locklear, interview.

21. Compare Eva Marie Garroutte, *Real Indians: Identity and the Survival of Native Amer-*

ica (Berkeley: University of California Press, 2003); and Joanne Barker, Amy Den Ouden, J. Kehaulani Kauanui, Malinda Maynor Lowery, and Jean M. O'Brien, "The New Politics and Problems with U.S. Federal Recognition," Roundtable, Native American and Indigenous Studies Association, Athens, Ga., April 2008.

22. Keith Basso, "Wisdom Sits in Places: Notes on a Western Apache Landscape," in *Senses of Place*, ed. Steven Feld and Keith Basso (Santa Fe: School of American Research Press, 1996). A landmark court case in British Columbia, Canada, *Delgamuukw v. Queen*, expanded the legal evidence that tribes can use in land-claims cases to include oral history.

23. William H. Chafe, Raymond Gavins, and Robert Korstad, eds., *Remembering Jim Crow: African Americans Tell about Life in the Segregated South* (New York: The New Press, 2001), xxvi; C. Vann Woodward, *The Strange Career of Jim Crow* (New York: Oxford University Press, 1955); David S. Cecelski and Timothy B. Tyson, eds., *Democracy Betrayed: The Wilmington Race Riot of 1898 and Its Legacy* (Chapel Hill: University of North Carolina Press, 1998); Howard N. Rabinowitz, "More Than the Woodward Thesis: Assessing the Strange Career of Jim Crow," *Journal of American History* 75 (December 1988): 842–56; Joel Williamson, ed., *The Origins of Segregation* (Boston, Mass.: D. C. Heath, 1968).

24. Chafe, Gavins, and Korstad, *Remembering Jim Crow*, xxvii–xxx. See also Glenda Elizabeth Gilmore, *Gender and Jim Crow: Women and the Politics of White Supremacy in North Carolina, 1896–1920* (Chapel Hill: University of North Carolina Press, 1996); Kevin K. Gaines, *Uplifting the Race: Black Leadership, Politics, and Culture in the Twentieth Century* (Chapel Hill: University of North Carolina Press, 1996); John Dittmer, *Local People: The Struggle for Civil Rights in Mississippi* (Urbana: University of Illinois Press, 1994); Neil McMillen, *Dark Journey: Black Mississippians in the Age of Jim Crow* (Urbana: University of Illinois Press, 1989); Nell Irvin Painter, *Southern History across the Color Line* (Chapel Hill: University of North Carolina Press, 2002).

25. Victoria Bynum, *The Free State of Jones: Mississippi's Longest Civil War* (Chapel Hill: University of North Carolina Press, 2001); Neil Foley, *The White Scourge: Mexicans, Blacks, and Poor Whites in Texas Cotton Culture* (Berkeley: University of California Press, 1997); James W. Loewen, *The Mississippi Chinese: Between Black and White*, 2nd ed. (Prospect Heights, Ill.: Waveland Press, 1988); George Brown Tindall, *Natives and Newcomers: Ethnic Southerners and Southern Ethnics* (Athens: University of Georgia Press, 1995); Kent Anderson Leslie, *Woman of Color, Daughter of Privilege: Amanda America Dickson, 1849–1893* (Athens: University of Georgia Press, 1995); James McBride, *The Color of Water: A Black Man's Tribute to His White Mother* (New York: Riverhead Books, 1996).

26. Waltz Maynor, conversation with the author, Durham, N.C., 29 September 2000.

Index

Acknowledgment. *See* Recognition of Robeson County Indians

African Americans, 21, 27, 28, 31–32, 33, 34, 43, 59, 61, 62, 65, 74, 84, 125, 153, 252, 262, 278 (n. 3), 288 (n. 19). *See also* Ancestry of Robeson County Indians: tri-racial isolates; Civil Rights; Identity of Robeson County Indians: race as a marker of; Jim Crow: economic system under; Jim Crow: laws establishing; Jim Crow: racial discrimination under; Kinship of Robeson County Indians: and race; Race: mixed race; White supremacy: use of blood

Agriculture. *See* Economic activities of Robeson County Indians; Farm Security Administration; New Deal; Pembroke Farms

Alexander, W. W., 176

Allotment, federal policy of, 30, 89, 90, 126, 128, 131–32, 137, 157, 187, 205, 218–19

American Indian Defense Association, 97

American Indian Movement (AIM), 247

American Revolution, 7, 14, 224, 243

Ancestry of Robeson County Indians: Siouan (Cheraw, Keyauwee, Pedee, Saponi, Waccamaw), 5, 8, 107, 136, 221, 223; Roanoke region, 5, 26; Iroquoian (Cherokee, Tuscarora), 5, 77, 243, 285 (n. 36); Algonkian (Hatteras), 5, 243; tri-racial isolates, 12, 145, 280 (n. 13), 282 (n. 26); Croatan theory, 42, 50, 77, 100, 107. *See also* Coalescence of Robeson County Indians; Marriage practices of Robeson County Indians; Race: mixed race

Anderson, Wallace Mad Bear, 246

Anthropometry, xvii, 3, 241, 255; Office of Indian Affairs use of, 181–211 passim, 317 (n. 46), 318 (n. 55), 319 (n. 64); at White Earth Reservation, 186–87, 192; Siouan Enrollment Commission, 191–93, 196

Aspinall, Wayne, 243, 244

Assimilation, federal policy of, 26, 91, 94–95, 125–26, 128, 237, 241

Autoethnography, xvi, 19–20, 63, 64, 83, 183, 215, 254, 259, 277 (n. 7), 330 (n. 22). *See also* Oral tradition of Robeson County Indians

creator of Indian New Deal, 95, 125–32, 141–42, 145–48, 186–90, 211, 249–50; during World War II, 230, 233. *See also* New Deal; Office of Indian Affairs

Constitution of North Carolina: 1835 constitution, 14–15; 1868 constitution, 16, 22; 1875 constitution, 22

Croatan Indian Normal School. *See* Indian Normal School

Cummings, Foy and Bloss, xiii, 67, 114, 155–57, 183

Daiker, Fred, 199, 206, 208, 209

Deep Branch, xi, 55, 57, 194

Deese, Shaw, 104–5, 173

Deloria, Ella, 76, 160, 221–27

Disease, 4, 15, 186, 194

Drowning Creek. *See* Lumber River

DuBois, W. E. B., 34

Eastern Carolina Tuscarora Indian Organization, 247

Economic activities of Robeson County Indians: turpentine, 45, 64, 65–67, 156, 233; farming, 55–56, 59, 63–72, 136–37, 149, 152, 158, 160, 162, 174, 232; Bootlegging, 73–74, 298 (n. 37). *See also* Factories; Jim Crow: economic system under; Pembroke Farms

Education, for whites and blacks, 24, 31, 61. *See also* Schools of Robeson County Indians

Eisenhower, Dwight D., 245

Estabrook, Arthur H., 38–41

Eugenics, 37–41, 209, 255, 263

Factionalism: between Office of Indian Affairs and Congress, xiv-xv, 48, 92, 94, 140–41, 146, 168, 237, 246, 248–49; among other Indian tribes, 12, 218, 277 (n. 4)

Factionalism within Robeson County Indians: impact on Indian community, xiii-xiv, xviii, 63–64; Jim Crow's influence on, xiv-xv, 45–47, 49–50, 54,

59, 62, 169; Tuscarora and Lumbee, xviii, 183, 204–5, 247, 253, 276 (n. 1), 324 (n. 50); Lumbee Brotherhood and, xviii, 216, 239–43, 246, 250; rural and town, 59, 62, 78, 115, 151–52, 167–68, 180, 215–16, 220, 225–27, 234, 236, 239, 240–41, 253, 256; as strategic, 85, 86, 115–17, 250; Siouan and Cherokee, 97–98, 103, 105, 108, 110–14, 147, 152, 165, 168, 169–70, 177, 181, 191, 207, 214, 220, 223–24, 226–27, 234, 253, 301 (n. 31), 303 (n. 79); based on kinship and place, 106, 115, 117, 181; aggravated by outside forces, 147, 152, 198, 200, 215, 255–56, 261; Farm Security Administration and Office of Indian Affairs perceptions of, 151, 165, 169, 172, 201; Original 22 and, 201, 206–8, 211–12, 215–16, 234–35, 238, 240

Factories, 121–22, 162, 233

Fairmont, N.C., 43, 175, 181, 194

Faris, C. B., 178–79

Farm Security Administration (FSA), xvii, 146, 155, 170, 221, 226, 232, 251, 310 (nn. 4, 7); resettlement programs, 135–37, 151–53, 158–59, 171; photographs, 149–51. *See also* Pembroke Farms

Fayetteville, N.C., 27, 57

Federal Bureau of Investigation (FBI), 247, 253

Fletcher Plantation, 70, 173

Foreclosure. *See* Land of Robeson County Indians: land loss

Fourth Street Power Structure, 76–77, 87, 96–99, 116, 167–68, 194, 210, 214, 224, 227, 239, 295 (n. 12), 303 (n. 79)

Gardner, O. Max, 52

Gender roles of Robeson County Indians, 10–11, 51, 66, 73, 151, 157, 251, 257

Genealogy. *See* Kinship of Robeson County Indians

General Council of Siouan Indians (Siouan Council): as governing body, 95–97, 116, 138, 167, 184, 194, 204, 206,

207, 209; membership in, 134, 137, 151, 153–57, 171, 195, 313 (n. 45); negotiations with federal government, 139, 146, 158–59, 163, 170, 176–79, 186, 196, 198–200, 208, 231. *See also* Factionalism within Robeson County Indians: Siouan and Cherokee

Godwin, Hannibal, 87–88

Goins (surname), 36–37

Graham, B. G. ("Buddy"), 96, 97, 104–6, 108, 110, 114, 116

Great Depression, 30, 68, 70, 71, 119, 125, 135, 152–53, 161, 177, 202–3, 213, 232

Green, H. C., 162, 170–74, 177, 178, 203, 231

Grorud, Albert A., 69, 95–96, 102–3, 108–10, 114–15, 158–59, 164

Harlem Renaissance, 125

Harpers Ferry. *See* Brooks Settlement

Herrick, John, 198–200

Hodges, Luther, 253

Hoey, Clyde R., 210, 212, 234, 236–37, 254

Hooten, Earnest A., 186, 191

Hoover Commission, 237

Hopewell, 41, 43, 47, 76, 110, 116, 160

Hrdlicka, Ales, 141, 186–87, 192, 308 (n. 54)

Hunt, Elmer, 213

Hunter, Charles N., 34

Ickes, Harold, 106, 108, 110, 125

Identity: ways of knowing about, xi–xii, xvii, xxv–xxvi, 83, 158, 179, 218, 253, 256, 260, 276 (nn. 2, 3); as a conversation, xii, xiii, xv, 59, 83, 194, 211, 229, 254; American, xii, xviii, 215, 217–20, 223, 225, 228–29, 238–39, 249, 257, 321 (n. 6)

Identity, Indian: and factionalism, xiv, 106, 115, 117, 119, 124, 131, 133, 138, 140, 143, 146, 167, 183, 205; definition of by Office of Indian Affairs, 2, 87, 91–93, 97, 101, 106, 109, 113, 124, 133, 136, 138, 140, 144–46, 148, 169–212 passim,

240–41, 245, 249, 255; definition of by Congress, 109, 140, 212, 255; definition of by Farm Security Administration, 179, 188, 204, 312 (n. 31). *See also* Indian Reorganization Act: definition of Indian; Race; White supremacy: identity definitions under

Identity of Robeson County Indians: name as a marker of, xi, xxv, 5, 6, 9, 42, 77–78, 81, 83, 85–87, 91, 116–17, 157–58, 166, 183, 202, 256, 326 (nn. 71, 72); kinship/People as a marker of, xiii, xxv, xix, 35, 57–58, 60, 65, 77, 104, 121, 133, 135, 142, 165, 173, 179, 183–84, 192, 196, 202, 211, 224, 228, 233, 254, 261, 276 (n. 1), 317 (n. 36); race as a marker of, xviii, 4, 13, 21, 35, 40, 44, 92, 100, 127, 143, 146, 170, 187–88, 195, 204–5, 208, 257, 283 (n. 31), 284 (nn. 32, 33); tribe as a marker of, 4, 26, 43, 59, 75, 179, 261, 278 (n. 5); reciprocity as a marker of, 11, 16, 59, 64, 66, 105, 195; political organization as a marker of, 42, 78, 146, 152, 171, 179, 192, 218, 237, 250, 258; class as a marker of, 53, 57–59, 63–64, 72–75, 78, 115–16, 118, 153, 168, 171, 177, 215, 226, 248, 250, 295 (n. 12); blood as a marker of, 153, 179, 195, 202, 204–6, 224, 237, 240–42, 243, 255, 259–60, 317 (n. 41); economic autonomy as a marker of, 159, 178. *See also* Land of Robeson County Indians: significance of place

Indian Citizenship Act (1924), 95, 216–19, 229

Indian New Deal, xv, xvi, 124, 132, 137, 237, 249

Indian Normal School, 29, 39, 42, 56, 72, 76, 113, 168, 183, 213, 236, 239; Old Main, 1, 213–15; as social and political center, 2, 115, 166, 191, 223; establishment and governance, 25, 33, 35–36, 41, 44, 45–47, 74, 292 (n. 66)

Indian Removal, 4, 7, 29

Indian Reorganization Act (IRA), 126, 135;

enrollment under, xvii, 185–86, 200, 229, 250; definition of Indian, 127, 140, 144–46, 159, 183–84, 305–6 (n. 16); tribal organization under, 128–30, 138, 190, 197–201, 206–7, 209–10, 238, 242, 260, 327 (n. 79); and Robeson County Indians, 133–34, 136, 143, 154, 234, 247

Indian Territory. *See* Oklahoma

Jacobs, Lonnie W., 40, 76, 97

Jim Crow, xii, xxvi, 14, 20; Indian responses to, xvi, xviii, 12, 17, 21, 37, 118–19, 215, 224, 236, 247, 255; separate public facilities during, 1, 20, 33–34, 37, 43, 50–51, 121, 222, 228, 262; racial discrimination under, 2, 12, 27, 30, 35, 38, 40–41, 47, 49, 50–53, 70–72, 84, 93, 217, 292 (n. 80); lawsuits concerning, 12, 35–37, 38; laws establishing, 15, 25–27, 35–36, 90, 122, 207, 263, 290 (n. 39); political system under, 20–24, 27, 30–31, 35, 46, 48–49, 86, 176–77, 288 (n. 12); economic system under, 58–77, 115, 123, 137, 152–178 passim, 218, 231–32, 234, 239

Johnson, A. M., 166–68

Kinship of Robeson County Indians: organization of, xii-xiii, xv, 4, 6–9, 10, 16, 24, 27, 37, 40–57 passim, 135, 191–94, 214, 223, 232, 240, 242, 256, 259, 282 (nn. 23, 24), 292 (n. 66), 316 (n. 30); matrilineal, 6, 11, 16, 52, 66, 193, 280 (n. 14); race and, 12–13. *See also* Gender roles of Robeson County Indians; Identity of Robeson County Indians: kinship/People as a marker of; Marriage practices of Robeson County Indians

Ku Klux Klan, 16, 251–53, 256–58, 261

Labor unions, 122

Land of Robeson County Indians: significance of place, xi, xiii, xv, xix, 3, 7–8, 11, 16, 27, 35, 57, 60, 63, 66–67, 72, 193–94, 232, 242, 244, 256, 261–63, 281 (n. 18);

land ownership, 7, 9, 11, 15, 45, 55–70 passim, 131, 115, 155, 171, 232, 261; land loss, 56, 59, 68–69, 74, 90, 136, 231, 296 (n. 22)

Language of Robeson County Indians. *See* Coalescence of Robeson County Indians

Leadership of Robeson County Indians, 4, 33, 42, 45, 59–63, 75–78, 103–4, 111–12, 138, 168, 224, 226, 256–58

Leupp, Francis, 94

"Life-Story of a People, The" (pageant), 220–27, 234, 256

Locklear, Aaren Spencer, 81–82, 299 (n. 3)

Locklear, A. B., 94, 96, 102–3, 105, 108

Locklear, A. N., 29, 39

Locklear, Arlinda, 254–55, 258, 260–61

Locklear, Chesley and Mary, 67, 77, 104, 114, 153, 156–57

Locklear, Clarence E., 76

Locklear, D. L., 158, 164

Locklear, Duncan, 172

Locklear, Elisha (elder), 162, 203

Locklear, Elisha (younger), 204–5

Locklear, Janie Maynor, 214–15

Locklear, "Lazy" Will, 193

Locklear, Lovedy Brooks, 7, 181, 193

Locklear, Pauline, 252

Locklear, Preston, 45

Locklear, Sanford, 252

Lost Colony, 26, 93, 110, 240, 242–43, 289 (n. 25)

Lowrey, O. H., 113

Lowry, Allen, 15–16, 47, 76, 116, 223

Lowry, Doctor Fuller ("D. F."), 39, 87, 113, 178, 182, 210, 236; as leader of Cherokee faction and Lumbee Brotherhood, 76–77, 113, 133–35, 167, 238–40, 242, 246; negotiations with federal government, 243–45, 248

Lowry, Elmer T., 76

Lowry, George Washington, 10, 50

Lowry, Henry Berry, 15–17, 57, 58, 155, 223, 253, 257

Lowry, Henry H., 47, 72, 77

Lowry, Ira Pate, 236, 238

White Hill. *See* Brooks Settlement

White supremacy: federal support of, xv, xviii, 2, 83, 87, 91, 94, 124–25, 147–48, 165–66, 169–70, 174–76, 184, 190, 210, 229–30, 240; Indian responses to, 16–17, 27–29, 30, 34, 44, 48, 52, 62, 74, 78, 85, 92, 99, 104, 113, 116, 169, 179, 228, 241, 248, 252, 256; use of blood, 35–36, 38–40, 53–54, 88, 102, 113, 124, 169–70, 191, 211, 241, 253–54; identity definitions under, 49, 84, 101, 123, 167, 199, 210, 263; and Progressivism, 61, 75–77, 99, 118, 122–23, 145, 147–48, 169, 202, 211, 216, 221, 239, 243–46

Wilmington, N.C., 15, 28

Woehlke, Walter V., 135

Wolcott, Marion Post, 149–51

World War I, 224

World War II, xviii, 209, 213, 215, 217, 222, 227–28, 230–33

Zimmerman, William, 209–11, 232